A History of Printing
in Britain

Colin Clair has also written

Christopher Plantin *Cassell & Co Ltd*
A Kentish Garner *Bruce & Gawthorn Ltd*
Word Abiding *Bruce & Gawthorn Ltd*
Strong-Man Egyptologist *Oldbourne Press*
Kitchen and Table *Abelard-Schuman Ltd*
Of Herbs and Spices *Abelard-Schuman Ltd*
River Thames: Historic Highway *Bruce & Gawthorn Ltd*

A History of Printing in Britain

COLIN CLAIR

NEW YORK
OXFORD UNIVERSITY PRESS
1966

© *Colin Clair* 1965
First published 1965

LIBRARY OF CONGRESS CATALOG CARD NO. 66–19802

Printed in Great Britain
by Jarrold & Sons Ltd., Norwich
F.865

Preface

This book is an attempt to provide an outline history of the development of printing in Great Britain since the time of Caxton. To cram the proverbial quart into a pint pot would be less of a miracle than to provide a complete history of the subject—however desirable—in one handy volume. Nevertheless I hope that this book, even with inevitable omissions, will be a useful guide to all who are interested in the history of printing in this country. It contains little concerning the economics of the printing industry; that aspect has already been extensively and expertly covered by Miss Marjory Plant in *The English Book Trade*. Those who would like to know more about the Stationers' Company can profitably turn to the book with that title written by the late Cyprian Blagden, recognized as the outstanding authority on the history and work of that famous guild.

No bibliography has been added, since the chief sources for the facts are mentioned either in the text or in the notes. My helpers have been many, since they include most of those who have already written on one aspect or another of the subject. But particularly I would like to thank Mr Harry Carter, whose advice, always so freely given, cannot be dispensed with by anyone writing about print. To the officers and staff of the Department of Printed Books at the British Museum I likewise give thanks for their courtesy and helpfulness—attributes so customary there that one is inclined to take them for granted. My thanks must go also to Mr H. John Jarrold for his most helpful suggestions, to Mr George D. Painter and to Miss M. Pollard.

Colin Clair

Contents

Contents

Illustrations

following page 52

Acknowledgements for Illustrations

Nos. 3, 4, 5, 6, 7, 8, 9, 10, 11, 12, 13, 19, 20, 24, 25, 27, 28, 29, 30, 31, 32, 33, 34, 36, courtesy of the Trustees of the British Museum; 26, courtesy of the Bodleian Library; 39, 40, 41, courtesy of R. Hoe and Crabtree Ltd; 42, courtesy of Southern Newspapers Ltd; 43, 44, 45, 46, 47, 48, 52, courtesy of the Monotype Corporation Ltd

CHAPTER ONE

Printing Comes to England

Printing came to England comparatively late. The 42-line Bible, produced probably by Gutenberg, Fust and Schoeffer, was completed by the middle of 1455. It was not until twenty-one years later that Caxton set up his press at Westminster and became the first printer in England. During that period the new craft had spread all over Western Europe and as far east as Cracow, where the first press was functioning in 1474. There were printers at work in no fewer than seventy towns in Europe before England received its first press.

There were reasons for this. The printing press, that handmaid of the revival of learning, followed the movement of the Renaissance which from Italy spread northward into Germany and westward into France and the Netherlands, only reaching England after the rest of Europe had become attuned to the new spirit of the age. During the whole of the second half of the fifteenth century Florence was the artistic and intellectual capital of Europe, and that very period which saw the fine flowering of the Italian Renaissance was intellectually a barren period in England.

Furthermore, England, at the time of the invention of printing, was a nation of small importance both economically and politically; not until the end of the Wars of the Roses and the coming to power of the Tudors did England emerge from a position of comparative backwardness compared with her continental neighbours.

But by the time Caxton, an experienced businessman, judged it ripe to move his press from Bruges to London, the revival of learning was beginning to make itself felt in England, and there was scope, though as yet severely limited, for a printer who could count on a certain measure of patronage. That the market was as yet a small one may be best judged from the fact that in 1500—half a century after the invention of printing—there were only three master printers working in England. All three were foreigners and all were in London, for the first press to be set up in Oxford had come to an end in 1485. Scotland

and Ireland had at that time no presses. Such printed books as were needed were imported, and several printer-publishers in Europe had agents in England.

In fact, when Caxton first set up his press, he was wise enough to choose a field for his work in which he would not be harassed by foreign competition. Moreover, being a man of means, and well patronized by the Court, he was able to print what he chose and what he knew would prove to the taste of his noble patrons, and that was romance literature in the vernacular. English printing during the fifteenth century is notable, when compared with French and Italian, for an almost entire absence of classical texts; the market for works of classical scholarship was restricted, and furthermore the first English printers were unable to compete with their continental colleagues in the production of cheap and accurate texts.

For the first fifty years or more after the invention of printing the printer published and sold the books he printed. Some, like Caxton and Copland, often wrote or translated the works they decided to print. Indeed, it was not until the seventeenth century that the division between printing and publishing became clearly demarcated. On the other hand the early printers in England neither cut nor cast their own type, and until well past the middle of the sixteenth century were almost entirely dependent for their supplies on the continental printers or founders. Caxton's types were almost certainly cut, if not cast, in the Low Countries, and, to quote Carter and Ricks, 'between the death of Caxton and the appearance in 1567 of John Day's Anglo-Saxon letters it is doubtful whether any type is first found in English printing'.[1] Of type-founding in England we know very little before the time of Caslon, apart from the reference to a few aliens in the second part of the sixteenth century variously described as 'fusor typorum', or 'letter-caster for printers' in the Returns of Aliens. The earliest reference to an English founder is that to Benjamin Sympson, 1597, in the Register of the Stationers' Company.

Similarly the English printers were dependent on continental suppliers for their paper. Apart from the short-lived paper mill of John Tate at Stevenage (1495–8) no paper seems to have been manufactured in England on any substantial scale until John Spilman started his mill at Dartford in Kent about 1589. English printers ordered their supplies from factors representing the paper makers of France and Italy.

Owing to its proximity, France furnished much of the paper used by English printers, and by the first half of the seventeenth century, according to Dr Allan Stevenson, around ninety-five per cent. came from Norman mills.[2] Another district which exported great quantities of paper was Champagne, where there were a large number of mills in the vicinity of Troyes. Jean Le Bé, paper maker of Troyes, used the arms of France, found in some of Caxton's books, as a watermark, and the watermark of the parallel keys, back to back, found in Caxton's *Jason*, was used, according to Le Clert, by a paper mill of Troyes.[3]

Alfred Shorter, in his *Paper Mills and Paper Makers in England 1495–1800*, puts forward four possible reasons for the failure to establish and maintain paper making in England. First, the widespread availability of parchment, readily procurable in a land where sheep were numerous; secondly, lack of skill; thirdly, shortage of materials; and fourthly —and this last is by far the most important reason—the ability of those countries which held a good lead in paper making, especially France and Italy, to export and sell cheaply, coupled with their determination to maintain their position in the English market.

Once foreign printers realized that England, with its paucity of printers, offered a good market for their wares, they were not slow in providing them through their agents, or even, if there were a chance of profit, of supplying an English book which had gone out of print. Thus, after Caxton's death, the Antwerp printer, Gerard Leeu, quickly brought out editions of three of Caxton's works—the *History of Jason*, *Paris and Vienne* and the *Chronicles of England*. H. S. Bennett comments: 'De Worde was caught by these reprints at a moment when he was reorganizing his printing house.'[4]

This was possible because between the years 1484 and 1534 the book trade in England was completely free and unprotected and foreign printers and stationers could trade freely in this country. In 1485 a foreign dealer in books, a native of Savoy named Peter Actors, was appointed Stationer to the King by Henry VII, and we know the names of several other foreign booksellers who established themselves in London. How important the English book trade was considered by some of the best-known foreign printers and booksellers is clearly shown by Henry Plomer's articles on the importation of Low Country and French books into England, based on an examination of the Custom House returns for the Port of London at this period.[5]

Although by the latter half of the fifteenth century the accomplishments of reading and writing were no longer confined to the clergy, for educational facilities were rapidly increasing, the reading public was not yet numerous and many of the early printers in England must have found that this new craft provided them with a precarious living. For that reason many of them carried on a secondary occupation. Even the famous Plantin, while consolidating his printing business, sold leather goods, prints, and maps, whilst his wife and daughters found a lucrative side-line in the sale of gloves and mercery. So, in England, we find Richard Pynson described both as 'bokeprynter' and as 'pouch-maker'; Thomas Raynald seems to have been a physician as well as a printer;* both the Rastells were lawyers; Conrad Molyar, assistant to John Gybkyn, and a brother of the Stationers' Company, was licensed to sell ale; Garbrand Harkes, an Oxford stationer, was licensed to sell wine; and, of course, many of the early printers were also bookbinders. Caxton was probably a dealer in manuscripts, and we know that he imported printed books.

We have no detailed knowledge of what Caxton's printing press was like. The earliest printing presses were probably adaptations of the screw press used in the wine and paper making industries. There exist, it is true, some early woodcut drawings of the printing press, the earliest known being that in an edition of the *Dance of Death* printed at Lyons in 1499; but these were not made by technical draughtsmen, and as Ronald McKerrow points out, 'the evidential value of the cuts is not proportional to their number, as few of them give much detail and several go back to the same original'.[6] Basically the press consisted of a firm bed of stone, with a perfectly smooth and level face, on which the printing surface could rest, a flat piece of wood or metal known as a platen (spelt 'plattin' in some early books), which by means of a screw could be pressed down upon the paper or vellum resting on the inked type, held together in some sort of frame, and, though not perhaps at first, a travelling bed which would enable the type forme to be slid under and then withdrawn from the platen. The whole press was made of wood with the exception of the spindle, which was of iron, and the bed, which was of stone (often Purbeck). One of the great disadvantages of these very early presses was that, in order to print one side of a large sheet of paper, two separate pulls of the bar or lever which brought the platen to bear on the paper were necessary, since the platen could not cover the whole of the forme. Various minor alterations were made from time to time, but in its essentials the wooden hand press remained unchanged for some three hundred and fifty years.

---

* Heinrich Sybold of Strassburg was both physician and printer.

Although in the very early days of printing the type may have been set up directly on the forme, by Caxton's day the composing stick would almost certainly have come into use. It was made of wood, and not of light metal as nowadays. For some considerable time the composing stick held only one line of type of a given measure, and even by Moxon's time it still had little depth; that illustrated in the *Mechanick Exercises* would have held only three lines of pica.

Compared with their modern counterparts the early printers made do with a very restricted range of matrices. In England that form of textura known as 'English' or black-letter was the face most commonly used at the beginning of the sixteenth century, and it was in use right up to the eighteenth century for such things as law books and proclamations. Pynson introduced roman into England in 1509, and De Worde first employed an italic type in this country in 1524. Until the middle of the eighteenth century the English printer made use of black-letter, roman and italic, supplementing this, if he were a printer of scholarly books, with a few sizes of Greek and possibly Hebrew.

The 'case'—the receptacle for holding type—seems to have been in regular use from quite an early date, for it is shown in the earliest drawing of the interior of a printing office, that in the 1499 *Dance of Death*. From this cut it looks as though there was only one case, instead of the pair normally used together, but this is not necessarily an accurate drawing. The use of a single big case is, however, still normal practice in Germany. In France there does not seem to have been the same standardization as in England; the type of case mainly employed in France today is a single case known as the *parisienne*, and Emile Leclerc says: 'Nowadays the case known as the "parisienne" tends to replace those which were peculiar to various printing establishments, to the great benefit of the workman, who was obliged to memorize a different model whenever he joined a new firm.'*

In England, however, the pair of cases seems to have been in general use from the beginning, for early inventories of printing offices allude to 'pairs of cases'.† The upper case has always been divided into 98 equal-sized boxes. Moxon is the earliest author in England to describe the cases, and in his time the lower case was divided into 56 boxes.

---

* In his book on typography in the series of Roret encyclopedias.
† See 'Inventory of Wynkyn de Worde's House' by H. R. Plomer in *The Library*, 1915.

Smith's *Printers' Grammar* of 1755 shows 54, and the number was reduced to 53 when the long 's' was finally discarded. We do not know
the exact lay of the case in the days of Pynson and De Worde, but
taking into account the conservatism shown in the history of the
printing trade it was probably much the same as in Moxon's day.

For more than half a century, from 1476 to 1536, more than two-
thirds of the printers, booksellers and bookbinders who were working
in England were foreigners, and there is little doubt that the influx of
aliens during the fifteenth and sixteenth centuries gave a considerable
impetus to industry in this country, not only by introducing new crafts
but also by improving old ones.

The beginning of the sixteenth century saw a great deal of the
English book trade in the hands of foreigners. Apart from Caxton
almost all the early printers in England were of alien birth: Wynkyn
de Worde, John Lettou, Richard Pynson, Julian Notary, William de
Machlinia, and Richard and William Faques. And to see how numerous the foreign stationers were one has only to look through the pages
of E. Gordon Duff's *A Century of the English Book Trade*.

A. W. Pollard points out that

> many of the men who took up the new art were probably well advanced
> in life. The printer had not only to live on his resources while making his
> lengthy preparations, but to meet all sorts of expenses, and finally to pay
> a heavy bill for paper. To do this required capital, and the possession of
> capital is more often the attribute of age than of youth.[7]

It has been calculated that of 350 printers who began work before the
close of 1480 not more than ten per cent. continued in business for as
much as twenty years.

Many survived only through patronage, for without some form of
subsidy either from a wealthy person or corporation the early printers
would have found it almost impossible to sell sufficient books to make
a living. Caxton might never have completed the translation and
printing of the *Golden Legend* had not the Earl of Arundel promised
to take 'a reasonable quantyte' of the finished book and for the rest of
his life to grant him a yearly fee. Sir Hugh Brice, an Alderman of
London, offered to defray the cost of the *Mirrour of the World*, and
Caxton's other patrons included Earl Rivers and the Duke of Clarence.
Indeed, it may have been the patronage of the last-named, the favourite
brother of the Duchess of Burgundy, which induced Caxton to set up
his press in England. Wynkyn de Worde and Richard Pynson, who

had a more assured market for their books, depended less than Caxton on patronage, yet they too published a number of books with the help of influential people. De Worde, for example, printed Hilton's *Scala Perfectionis* and Fisher's *Sermon at the Funeral of Henry VII* at the command of Lady Margaret Beaufort, Countess of Richmond, so that in his colophons he was able to add the prestige appointment of printer to the King's mother. From the Privy Purse expenses of Henry VII we know that the King advanced £10 'to Richard Pynson opon a prest [loan] for massebokes to be printed'. This was on 1 November, 1503, and possibly refers to the Sarum Missal which Pynson printed in the following year.

By the beginning of the sixteenth century, with the growth of literacy, a more assured market was open to printers who were able to judge its needs. Money was to be made not from the ponderous folios of Caxton, or the learned books of Richard Pynson, but, as the more commercially astute Wynkyn de Worde soon found out, from small quarto books for schools, such as Whittinton's and Stanbridge's Latin grammars, from popular romances like *Bevis of Hampton*, or from humorous books dealing with domestic and low life, after the fashion of *The boke of mayd Emlyn*, or the book of riddles called *The Demaundes Joyous*. De Worde knew what was 'commercial', and the Subsidy Rolls show that he was a fairly rich man.

William Caxton

The craft of printing from movable types did not reach England until a quarter of a century after the first books had been printed elsewhere by this means. By that time presses had been established in nearly fifty towns of Italy and more than a score of towns in Germany.

Strangely enough, apart from Germany, England was the only country in Western Europe where the pioneer of the new art was a native of the country. Moreover, our first printer, William Caxton, was an amateur, past middle age, whose life had previously been spent almost entirely in connection with the woollen trade.

The fact that our first printer was an Englishman was purely fortuitous, for if, after thirty years' residence abroad, the mercer William Caxton had not decided to return to his native land, the honour of being the first to establish a printing press in England would have gone to a native of Cologne, Theodoric Rood, who set up a press at Oxford in 1478, two years after Caxton had begun to print at Westminster.

Of Caxton's family history we know almost nothing except that, as he tells us, he was born 'in Kente in the Weeld' and that his parents were able to send him to school—a meagre autobiography. We are doubtful when he was born, nor do we know exactly the date of his death.

No conclusive evidence has yet been found which would enable us to locate the exact spot in the Weald of Kent where Caxton was born. In those days there was no standard orthography and a name might be spelt in a number of ways. In the records of the Mercers' Company the name of a certain Thomas Cacston is almost immediately afterwards written Cawston, and other variants include Cauxton, Caston, Causton, Catston, and even Kaxsum.

The Rev. Lambert Larking tells us, from his examination of Kentish documents of the fourteenth and fifteenth centuries, that the spellings in these manuscripts all show that in the Weald the 'a' was pronounced very broad—almost like 'aw'—and that 'x' was given the value of 'ss'. 'Caxton', he writes, 'in speaking of himself would have said Causston.'[8]

Several families of the name of Caxton or Causton can be traced in various parts of Kent during the Middle Ages. A Thomas Caxton was living at Tenterden in 1420, a Hugh Caxton at Sandwich in 1453, and two more Thomas Caxtons at Lydd about the same time. In Canterbury there were several; we come across a William Caxton, mercer, who took up the freedom of that city by redemption in 1431, and a Robert Caxston or Causton, whose will was proved in the Consistory Court there. A monk named Thomas Causton was ordained at Christ Church, Canterbury, in 1455, and from the Sacrist's Rolls we find that he died there in the course of the year 1503–4. The same source tells us that brother Will. Causton was paid 9d for his first mass in 1525 or 1526.

It is clear that the name was a fairly common one in Kent at that time, and any of these Caxtons could have been related to the printer. None of these places, however, are in the Weald, and many writers have suggested the ancient manor of Caustons, near Hadlow, which is in the Weald, as the possible birthplace of the printer.

Here we are confronted with the fact that the manor of Caustons seems to have passed out of the possession of the Caxtons of Hadlow some considerable time before the birth of the printer; nevertheless they may have retained some property in the neighbourhood.

In this connection it may be pointed out that the name of William Castone occurs among the retinue of Margaret, Duchess of Clarence, when she visited the Abbey of St Albans in 1429 to be received into the fraternity, and that the duchess was the daughter of Thomas, Earl of Kent, who had lands in the parish of Hadlow, where Causton Manor was situated. This William Castone might very well be the same man whose name appears in the Kent Subsidy Roll for an unspecified date in the reign of Henry VI, and who must have been a person of some importance judging by the amount he was called upon to pay. Might not this man have been the printer's father? Additional weight is given to the Hadlow theory by the fact that

> the manor of Causton was held on the honour of Clare, the lords of which, in the fifteenth century, were that ducal and royal house by whom William Caxton was warmly patronised. Their forest of South Frith, close to Causton, descended through one of the coheiresses of Gilbert de Clare, Lord of Tonbridge, to Richard, Duke of York (father of the Duchess of Burgundy and Edward IV) whose widow possessed it at her death.[9]

If the locality of the printer's birthplace is a matter of conjecture, so, too, is the date of his birth, save that in this case one can make a fair guess, for Caxton's apprenticeship to the rich London mercer, Alderman Robert Large, is recorded in the archives of the Mercers' Company as having begun in 1438. The customary age at which a youth was then apprenticed was between fifteen and seventeen, and therefore we may be reasonably certain that William Caxton was born sometime between 1421 and 1423.

The very fact that he was apprenticed to a merchant of such repute as Robert Large (who became Lord Mayor of London in 1439-40) and thus obtained entry into the most powerful and exclusive of all the London Guilds—the Mercers' Company—presupposes his parents to have been well-to-do, and his own achievements as a servant of literature, as well as the high position to which he rose with the Merchants Adventurers, point to a sound education.

Where he was 'sette to scole' the printer does not tell us, but it may well have been at Canterbury, at the school attached to Christ Church monastery, where another William Caston was a monk; and there he may have first met his 'syngular frende' William Pratt, who was born at Canterbury, became a mercer of London and enjoyed the printer's friendship for more than thirty years.

Of Caxton's career up to the time he became a printer we know a good deal, but to relate it in detail would be outside the scope of this book. It has been well told both in the standard biography of Caxton

by William Blades and in the masterly biographical introduction to
The Prologues and Epilogues of William Caxton by W. J. B. Crotch.

In brief, then, Caxton, shortly after the death of his master, Robert
Large, in 1441, went abroad for thirty years and dwelt, as he tells us,
'in the contres of Braband and Flandres, Holland and Zeland', the
greater part of that time being spent in Bruges, then the great mart of
Western Europe (though already on the decline) and the headquarters
both of the woollen trade and the trading guild known as the Merchants Adventurers of England.

In 1453 he was in London for his reception into the livery of the
Mercers' Company, and then returned to Bruges, where he evidently
prospered in business, and in 1463 became Governor of the 'worshipful
fellowship of Merchants Adventurers', a post which he held until 1470.
It was an important post, entailing not only the supervision of the
trading community but also the administration of justice in connection
with 'their quarrels and causes whatsoever ... and to seek reformation,
to redress, appease, and compound the same'. In his capacity as Governor of the English Nation (as the resident merchants were called)
Caxton had power to summon in the King's name courts of jurisdiction and to appoint judges and mediators for the settlement of disputes.

In the year 1468 Charles the Bold, Duke of Burgundy, calculating
that an alliance with England was preferable to being swallowed up
by France, married Margaret, sister of Edward IV. The wedding was
celebrated at Bruges, to which the Merchants Adventurers had returned after a few years' residence in Utrecht because of the decree of
Charles's father, Philip the Good, banning the import of English cloth
—a decree rescinded by the ratification of a new commercial treaty
with England at the beginning of 1468.

Caxton, as Governor of the English Nation, must have taken a
prominent part in the marriage celebrations and made the acquaintance of many of those English nobles, including the future Earl
Rivers, who were to be his influential patrons in the days to come.

About the year 1470 Caxton relinquished his governorship and
apparently entered the service of the Duchess of Burgundy, for he
himself tells us that he was 'servant to her Grace' and that he received
from her 'an yearly fee and many other great and good benefits', but
we do not know in what capacity he was employed, any more than
we know the exact date at which he resigned his office with the
Merchants Adventurers, or why.

We can only speculate as to the reasons which induced Caxton to make this radical change of life at the age of about forty-eight. Certainly trade in Bruges was declining. The city was no more than a shadow of what it had been in the palmy days of the thirteenth and fourteenth centuries, when it was the entrepôt of wares from all over Europe and the Orient and the rendezvous of merchants from every known country. If the business of the Adventurers had been highly prosperous Caxton possibly would not have been obliged to 'eschewe slouthe and ydlenes' in beginning a translation of *Le Recueil des Histoires de Troyes* because he had 'no grete charge of ocupacion'.

Alternatively he may have felt that thirty years in the woollen trade was enough and welcomed a less onerous manner of life. There is another possibility, that he may have resigned his office on account of his marriage, for it is known that he had a daughter Elizabeth who was married in 1496.

Crotch states that it is not at all certain that strict celibacy was imposed upon the Merchants abroad. But we know from Wheeler[10] that by a Statute of the year 1564 any Brother of the fellowship who married 'a straunger or foreign borne woman' was 'disfranchised by reasone of such his marriage', and this statute may well have been a confirmation of an earlier one. It is not unreasonable to suppose that Caxton, after thirty years' residence abroad, may have married such a 'foreign borne woman'. If the 'Mawde Caxton' buried in the Church of St Margaret, Westminster, in 1490-1 was indeed the wife of the printer, that Maude need not necessarily have been English. Later on, Adventurers who intended to marry a foreigner could sue for Letters Patent for remission of the Statute, so that in 1590 a certain Francis Pope was readmitted to the Company of Merchants Adventurers, 'having lost his freedom by marrying a wife born beyond seas'.

In the matter of the services rendered by Caxton to the Duchess of Burgundy, we are again reduced to speculation. Blades thought it probable that, owing to his long experience in overseas trade, he acted as a kind of factor or mercantile adviser to his royal mistress, to whom in 1472 her brother, Edward IV, had granted special privileges and exemptions in connection with her own private trading in English wool. Henry Plomer, on the other hand, thought it more likely that the young duchess, who shared Caxton's love of books, and whose husband possessed what was then one of the finest libraries in Europe, offered him a post as secretary or librarian.

Whatever may have been his position, he certainly now had

greater leisure, which enabled him to indulge his hobby of translation. Among the manuscripts in the library left by Philip the Good, that famous library which rivalled in riches that of the kings of France, were no fewer than seventeen works dealing with the legend of Troy. The late duke's interest in the Trojan story is comprehensible when we remember that it was that same Philip who in 1430 had founded the order of chivalry known as the Golden Fleece.

One such volume, called *Le Recueil des Histoires de Troyes*, had been compiled from various Latin manuscripts and translated into French by Philip's chaplain, Raoul le Fèvre, who finished his task in 1464. This was the work which Caxton set himself to translate into English, having found in it 'many strange and mervayllous historyes' in which he 'had grete pleasyr and delyte'. When, in the course of an interview with the Duchess of Burgundy, he mentioned his self-appointed task, she insisted on seeing what he had done and encouraged him to finish it. When this became known, what more natural than that many others, noblemen and friends, should have wanted a copy?

Now Caxton was no professional scribe and he found the labour wearisome, his progress slow, and his eyes 'dimed with overmoche lokyng on the whit paper'. It was while he was in Cologne in the year 1471, engaged upon some business of which we now have no knowledge, that having 'good leisure' as he tells us, he finished his translation of the *Recueil*. Cologne was a city where already several printers were at work, and the first town Caxton had visited where that art was practised. He decided that he would learn something of this new craft, which would enable him to keep his promise to 'dyverce gentilmen and frendes' to let them have copies of his translation with all speed. After a brief return to Bruges he was back again in Cologne by the end of that same year and there he had his first lessons in practical printing, remaining in that city until the end of 1472.

What induced Caxton to turn printer? This was clearly his intention, for had it been merely a question of providing copies of his translation for his friends he would have had them made by a professional scribe or paid one of the printers in Cologne to do the job. It would have been expensive, but far less costly than setting up a printing press, even in partnership with another. Having exchanged the cares of office for the presumably less onerous duties of servant to the Duchess of Burgundy, what led this man of fifty suddenly to decide upon this new occupation, with all its attendant labour and financial risks, and from successful merchant to become a successful printer? It is a point on which Caxton's biographers have been silent.

Embarking on the business of master printer was no light matter. Besides the construction of presses, the making of punches and matrices, and casting of type, the prospective printer had to hire his journeymen (and often in the early days to train them as well) and to lay in stocks of paper and the materials for making ink.

It seems probable that with his long experience and sound business training Caxton at once saw the possibilities inherent in the new art, and if Louis de Bruges, Seigneur de la Gruthuyse, financed Colard Mansion, who was associated with Caxton in the first press established at Bruges, it is no less likely that the latter found similar financial support among his friends at Court.

Until comparatively recently it had been a moot point as to where Caxton learned to print. There was, it is true, one very strong piece of evidence that he did so at Cologne, for in the epilogue to the English translation of *De proprietatibus rerum*, printed by his apprentice and successor Wynkyn de Worde in 1496, the following lines occur:

> And also of your charyte call to remembraunce
> The soule of William Caxton, fyrste prynter of this boke,
> In Laten tonge at Coleyn, hymself to avaunce,
> That every well disposyd man may theron loke.

This should be authoritative, for Wynkyn de Worde had worked with Caxton from the time he first set up a press in England until his death many years later. But in 1847 an antiquary of Bruges, the Abbé C. Carton, published an article in which he concluded that Caxton learned the art of printing from Colard Mansion at Bruges. Blades adopted most of the Abbé's conclusions in his biography of Caxton, remarking that 'Caxton found the money and Mansion the requisite knowledge'.

To Blades the assertion by Wynkyn de Worde that Caxton printed a *Bartholomaeus* in Latin at Cologne was merely a careless statement.

As Caxton's stay at Cologne on the occasion of his finishing the translation of *Le Recueil* [writes Blades], was but short, the printing of this apocryphal 'Bartholomaeus' would have been at a subsequent visit, of which there is no record. No edition has yet been discovered which can, by any stretch of the imagination, be attributed to Caxton.[11]

E. Gordon Duff, however, long ago identified the Latin edition mentioned by De Worde as being one attributed to the press of the printer of a work called *Flores S. Augustini*—a press which was functioning in Cologne in 1472 and 1473. Furthermore, we now have evidence, unknown to Blades, that Caxton did return to Cologne, for Lieutenant-Colonel J. C. Birch found in the register of aliens at Cologne entries proving that Caxton arrived back in that city before 11 December, 1471, and stayed there until after Mid-summer, 1472.[12] The remaining claims on behalf of Mansion—that he was the first printer at Bruges, and was wholly or in great part responsible for six books now known to have been printed by Caxton alone—have been successfully refuted by L. A. Sheppard, who has shown that there is no evidence of the existence of a partner-ship between Colard Mansion and Caxton, that their two presses were in all probability independent one of the other and that, contrary to the conclusions of the Abbé Carton, it was from Caxton, who set up the first press in Bruges, that Colard Mansion learned his craft.[13]

No information, from official records or other sources, has yet come to light regarding Caxton's activities in 1473, but it may reasonably be assumed that his time was spent in setting up his press, purchasing type and paper and making a few trials of this newly acquired material.

None of the books printed at his first press bears any date, but since he had already finished his translation of the *Recueil* and had promised copies to his friends, that work would most probably be the first to appear, and this supposition is supported by the prologue to the *Recuyell of the Historyes of Troye*, in which he says:

> I have practysed and lerned at my grete charge and dispense to ordeyne this sayd book in prynte after the maner and forme as ye may see here, and it is not wreton with penne and ynke as other bokes ben, to thende that every man may have them attones, ffor all the bookes of this storye named the recule of the historyes of troyes thus empryntid as ye here see were begonne in oon day, and also fynysshid in oon day. . . .

Such a reference would be unlikely to occur in any but the first book to come from his press.

This book, which was probably issued either at the end of 1473 or early in 1474, is a small thick folio of 352 leaves, set in Caxton's first type, a rather rough Burgundian bastarda of a body corresponding to the English great primer. This was a type used by Caxton in four other books printed at Bruges: Jacobus de Cessolis's *The Game and*

Playe of the Chesse (translated by Caxton from Jehan de Vigny's French version); Raoul le Fèvre's *Le Recueil des Histoires de Troyes;* Pierre d'Ailly's *Meditacions sur les sept pseaulmes penitenciaulx;* and Le Fèvre's *Les Fais et Proesses de Jason.* The other book printed by Caxton while he was still at Bruges, *Les Quatre Derrenières Choses* (a French translation of a Latin religious treatise), was printed with a new fount of type, known as Type No. 2, in which type twenty-one works by Caxton are known to have been printed. This type bears a close resemblance to one used at Louvain about this time by the printer Johann Veldener, who, after printing at Cologne, moved to Louvain in 1474. So close is the resemblance that E. G. Duff thought it highly probable that Caxton obtained his material from Veldener. There is, moreover, a likelihood that Veldener was the man from whom Caxton learned to print, for some of the first type used by the German when he began to print at Louvain appears to be the same as that used for the *Bartholomaeus Anglicus* attributed to the printer of *Flores S. Augustini.*

After thirty years' residence abroad Caxton returned to England during the latter part of 1476. As to his reasons for so doing we are again obliged to speculate. Certainly trade in Bruges had declined considerably in the 1460s, and not long afterwards William Cely recorded in his diary that 'all men of substance were daily stealing away and going to Middleburg'.[14] In June, 1476, Burgundian power was sapped at Morat by the victory of the Swiss and destroyed the next year at Nancy, where Charles the Bold was slain.

In England, on the other hand, the ruthlessness and political ability of Edward IV had by now firmly established that monarch, whose despotism was faintly tempered by a regard for literature which made him welcome the new art of printing and extend his patronage to Caxton's *Tullius of Old Age.*

Whatever the reason, Caxton returned to England and settled at Westminster. He probably chose Westminster rather than the City of London on account of its proximity to the Court and his powerful patrons—for the patron was still an important figure in the literary world, and Caxton was able to number among his more influential patrons George, Earl of Warwick and Duke of Clarence (the favourite brother of the Duchess of Burgundy), the Lady Margaret, Countess of Richmond (mother of Henry VII), and Anthony Woodville, Earl Rivers (the queen's brother). And just as his 'Tully' had been produced 'under the umbre and shadowe of the noble proteccion' of

Edward IV, so his *Order of Chyvalry* was dedicated to Richard III, and his *Fayttes of Armes* was translated and printed at the desire of Henry VII.

There is perhaps an additional reason for his choice of residence, namely the likelihood that his father was then living near by, for an entry in the Abbey Burial Fees for 1478 reads:

> Itm. the day of the burying of William Caxton
> for ij torches and iiij tapirs at a lowe masse.   xx d.

This is, of course, merely conjecture. Another fact, pointed out by Crotch, is that there was then a monk at Westminster Abbey named Richard Caxston or Caston, who later became Sacrist. Crotch also gives other evidence pointing to a relationship between Richard and William Caxton.[15]

The exact date when Caxton took up his residence at Westminster is unknown, but it must have been well before the end of 1476 because an Indulgence of Pope Sixtus IV which he printed was discovered at the Public Record Office in 1928, and this is hand-dated 13 December, 1476. Moreover, the Sacrist's Rolls of Westminster Abbey show that he paid ten shillings rent for a year's tenancy of a shop, ending at Michaelmas, 1477, so that in all probability he began to work there about September, 1476.

Early writers, taking perhaps too literally the colophon 'Emprynted, in thabbey of westmester' and forgetful that the term then included all the monastic buildings and the precincts, made Caxton set up his press in one of the side-chapels of the Abbey itself. But today, thanks largely to the researches of Lawrence E. Tanner, C.V.O., the present Keeper of the Muniments, Westminster Abbey, we know with some certainty that the first printing press was set up in 'a house adjoining to or close to the Chapter House, on the left-hand side of the path leading to the south or Poets' Corner door, and that the shop was more or less associated with the production of books from that date until 1531-2'.[16]

There Caxton brought out the first dated book printed in England, *The Dictes or Sayengs of the Philosophres*, finished on 18 November, 1477. This book had been translated from the French by Caxton's friend and patron, Earl Rivers, who asked the printer to 'oversee' his translation before putting it on the press. Caxton, finding that the Earl had omitted a section by Socrates 'towchying women', added it himself, and in his prologue shows a pleasing touch of humour.

As this book is in English, we differed from all other European nations in beginning the art of printing with a book in the vernacular; unless, that is, one of the undated books, the chronological order of which has been conjecturally estimated from typographical and other evidence, had preceded it.

The *Dictes* is printed in Caxton's Type No. 2, that which he used for *Les Quatre Derrenières Choses*, and which he presumably brought with him from Bruges, unless possibly he had obtained strikes.★ This bastarda did not prove long-lived in England, for the printers who followed Caxton, many of whom were French, introduced the English textura known as 'black-letter', modelled on the Paris style, and this was adopted by other English printers, who remained faithful to it throughout the sixteenth century.

Caxton's press turned out at least thirty books within the first three years—perhaps many more, because a number of these were quite small and it is not unlikely that some others have disappeared in the course of time. But if some were but 'small storyes and pamfletes', others were fat folios, such as the first printed edition of Chaucer's *The Canterbury Tales* (372 leaves), which is undated, but was probably finished in 1478. Printed throughout in Type No. 2, it has no title-page, and the lines of the prose portions are not justified. Later, having learnt that this edition had been made from a very corrupt text, Caxton printed the whole work again, this time with woodcut illustrations.

Type No. 2 was used from 1476 until 1479, when, as it was becoming worn, the letters were filed and trimmed up, new matrices made, and the type recast. Nine books are known to have been printed in this recast type, known as Type 2★. For headlines from about 1476 onwards Caxton used a rather handsome fount of textura, which he used also for a curious advertisement relating to the *Sarum Ordinale*, the only known example of a printer's advertisement in England in the fifteenth century. It reads:

> If it plese ony man spirituel or temporel to bye any pyes of two and thre comemoracions of salisburi use, enpryntid after the forme of this present lettre whiche ben wel and truly correct, late hym come to westmonester in to the almonesrye at the reed pale and he shal have them good chepe.

★ 'Strike'—the piece of copper into which the steel punch bearing the engraved character is struck by the type-founder. After levelling and squaring-up (justification) it is called a matrix.

Underneath was an appeal in Latin, '*Supplico stet cedula*', or 'Don't tear down this advertisement'.

The term 'pye' is the French version of pica, the old Latin name for the *Ordinale*, and was probably so called because the black-letter type on white paper gave the book a magpie appearance. No separate edition of the simple *Sarum Ordinale* is known except that of Caxton, and even this exists only in two fragments in the British Museum. It was soon afterwards superseded by Clement Maydeston's *Directorium Sacerdotum*, or Priest's Guide, of which Caxton printed two editions (*c.* 1487 and 1489).

The 'Red Pale' of the advertisement is nowhere mentioned in the Abbey records, the explanation being, Tanner thinks, 'that it was a personal trade-mark hung outside the house to attract attention, and was merely attached to the house during the period of his tenancy'. For by 1480 Caxton's business had outgrown his premises, and although he continued to rent the shop by the Chapter House he took two tenements in the Almonry as well as a *camera* above the Gate of the Almonry, which stood at the eastern end of what is now Victoria Street. His move to the Almonry cannot have been later than 1479.

About 1480 Caxton's printing practice began to show signs of improvement, for in the words of Hansard 'Mr Caxton's first performances were very rude and barbarous'.[17] His earliest books have neither headline nor foliation, catchwords nor signatures, and the ends of lines are frequently uneven. Where red and black printing was called for, the red was pulled at the same time as the black by the primitive expedient of rubbing off the black ink from selected portions of type and replacing it with red ink. In fact, possibly due to his removal from the centres of activity in this new art, Caxton's technique never kept pace with that of printers on the other side of the Channel.

But under the stimulus of competition caused by the setting up in London in 1480 of a press by John Lettou, of whom we shall speak later, Caxton did introduce certain changes into his practice. Since Lettou made use of signatures, Caxton followed his example, and noticing that Lettou's smaller and neater type was much more suited to the printing of indulgences than his own, he also had a fount of small type cast, the Type No. 4, believed to have been cut in England.

He also introduced woodcuts into his books, first of all in *The*

Mirrour of the World (1481), a folio of 100 leaves printed in Type No. 2, with 34 cuts. These cuts comprise two distinct sets, one showing masters and scholars, the other consisting of diagrams so badly executed that the printer put several of them in wrong positions. In the absence of a fount sufficiently small, the explanations within the diagrams are written by hand. E. Gordon Duff first pointed out the interesting fact that in all existing copies of the book the same handwriting is found, adding, however, that it would be unsafe to conclude that it was Caxton's.[18]

A series of three treatises from the Latin came from Caxton's press in 1481: Cicero's *Of Old Age* and *Of Friendship*, and the *Declamacion of Noblesse* made by Scipio and Flaminius before the Roman Senate. The translator of *De Senectute* is unknown, and Caxton tells us that he was only able to procure a copy of the manuscript after great labour and cost. The other two pieces were translated by John Tiptoft, Earl of Worcester, an elegant Latinist and a great collector of books, but a ruthless soldier, who was captured and executed during the brief return to power of Henry VI in 1470.

Also in 1481 Caxton published *Reynart the Foxe*, a translation of the famous German classic *Reineke Fuchs*. This was the first edition in English of this celebrated satire, and Caxton tells us that he translated it himself from the 'dutche'. Although Crotch has a footnote saying that some scholars incline to take this to mean German, a comparative reading shows clearly that Caxton translated from the Dutch edition printed at Gouda by Gheraert Leeu in 1479. This traffic was two-way, for the *History of Jason* was reprinted by Leeu from Caxton's edition. Despite the fact that *Reynart the Foxe* lends itself so well to illustration there are no cuts in Caxton's edition. But before the end of the century an illustrated edition was brought out by Caxton's successor, Wynkyn de Worde.

The year 1482 saw the publication of Higden's *Polycronicon*, a folio of 450 leaves set entirely in Caxton's Type No. 4 and carefully edited by the printer, who not only revised the text throughout, but also added a continuation bringing the history down to 1460, the year of Edward IV's accession.

The version which Caxton edited and brought up to date was the English translation made from the Latin of Ralph Higden about 1387 by John Trevisa, chaplain to Lord Thomas of Berkeley. Caxton tells us that he had to change somewhat 'the rude and old englyssh' since certain words could no longer in his time be understood.

The Golden Legend, the largest book printed by Caxton, bears the date of 1483. It contains 449 leaves, and it is printed on a larger size of paper than he used for any other of his books, the full sheet measuring 22 by 15¾ inches. The book is in double columns, the headlines being in Type No. 3 and the text in Type No. 4*, a recasting of Type No. 4 (smaller than Type No. 2, but similar in design). Type No. 4* was cast on a different body from Type No. 4, giving 19 lines as against 20 lines of the latter. Possibly a larger edition than usual was run off, for it is one of the commonest of Caxton's books.

Instead of taking one existing manuscript of Jacobus de Voragine's *Legenda Aurea*, which already had been translated from the Latin into both English and French, he chose to make a completely new edition by collating manuscripts in all three tongues, with the result that he almost gave up the task, and might have done so had not the Earl of Arundel encouraged him and promised to take what Caxton terms 'a resonable quantite' of them when they were finished.

In this book Caxton made use of 17 woodcuts the full width of the page in size, as well as 50 column-width cuts of Old Testament scenes and Saints with their emblems, some of which are repeated. In addition, at the beginning is a cut of the Saints in Glory, the largest block that Caxton ever used. Hodnett tells us that these cuts were the work of two engravers.[19]

As his third illustrated book Caxton printed early in 1484 the *Fables of Aesop* in a translation of his own from the French, and enlivened it with no fewer than 186 woodcuts. As far as we know this was the first time this classic had appeared in an English dress. In this edition occurs the printer's solitary woodcut initial, a nine-line drop initial A.

Unlike the first edition, which was not illustrated, the second edition of *The Canterbury Tales* contains woodcuts which Pollard stigmatizes as 'grotesque in their accumulation of clumsiness'. They depict, for the most part, the various characters taking part in the Pilgrimage, and there is also a cut (later used by Wynkyn de Worde) showing all the pilgrims at supper seated at a large round table.

This edition of *The Canterbury Tales* is not a textual reprint of the first. The printer, with a conscientiousness that does him credit, having been told that the manuscript he used for his first edition was incorrect, went to the trouble of reprinting the work from a less corrupt version. In the Proheme to this second edition, Caxton asks his readers to 'remember the sowle of the sayd Gefferey chaucer, first auctour and maker of thys book'.

Kyng Arthur is dated 1485. This romance of Sir Thomas Malory, like the *Ordre of Chyvalry*, which was finished either that same year or a little before, was the kind of book in which Caxton delighted, and it probably needed but little persuasion from 'many noble and dyvers gentylmen' to induce him to publish it. It is a rare book and for many years only one copy was known, which led to a battle royal for its acquisition between two great collectors of the early nineteenth century, Lord Spencer and the Duke of Devonshire. Eventually this copy went to America.

Fewer books came from Caxton's press after 1485. This may be attributed partly to the fact that he was now an elderly man, and partly to the fact that certain official business connected with the King's Receipt may have taken up a good deal of his time. The *Speculum vitae Christi*, probably finished in 1486, is printed throughout in Caxton's Type No. 5—a rather handsome fount of textura, or black-letter, smaller than but very similar to Type No. 3.

This book has a series of woodcuts which are of rather better workmanship than those he had previously acquired. No copy of the first edition is known with either the beginning or the end, but judging by the second edition (*c.* 1490), which is a word-for-word reprint, differing only in some spellings, it seems likely that the first edition would have the same number of cuts, namely 25. Some of these cuts were used separately in the *Royal Book, Doctrinal of Sapyence* and in the second edition of the *Myrrour of the World*.

In 1487 Caxton made use for the first time of his well-known device, over the precise meaning of which there have been many conjectures. It is found on the verso of the last leaf of the Sarum Missal which Caxton had printed in Paris by Guillaume Maynyal. Previously Caxton had never used a printer's mark in any of his books, and must have done so on this occasion to call attention to the fact that he was the publisher, if not the printer, of this particular book.

At that time, and for some time afterwards, foreign printers, far more advanced technically than Caxton and his immediate successors, were better able to undertake the production of service books, which involved a large amount of red printing for the rubrics. At Westminster Caxton, rendered cautious perhaps by his none too successful efforts at Bruges, used red printing in only three books, all printed towards the end of his life, and as G. D. Painter points out, 'it is noteworthy that during the fifteenth century De Worde was no more able than Caxton to produce a missal of his own'.[20] The Missal printed by Maynyal is a handsome book with two woodcuts at the Canon far superior to anything that had so far been produced in England.

The Sarum Missal printed by Maynyal for Caxton bears the date 4 December, 1487. On 14 August of the following year Maynyal finished another service book which bears Caxton's device: the Sarum *Legenda*, a companion volume to the missal, a fairly complete copy of which, consisting of 351 leaves, was discovered in the library of St Mary's Church, Warwick, in 1956. The book was previously known only from twenty-nine leaves in the University Library, Cambridge, and some odd leaves in three other libraries.

This is the only book published by Caxton of which we know the published price. When Caxton's daughter Elizabeth separated from her husband, Gerard Crop, in 1496, he was awarded twenty printed *Legends* valued at 13s 4d each.[21] This Caxton *Legenda* is now in the British Museum, a faculty for its sale to the Museum having been granted by the Chancellor of the Diocese of Coventry.

In the early part of 1489 Henry VII, who had come to the throne in 1485, commanded Caxton to translate and print without delay a certain manuscript in the royal library—the *Fait d'Armes et de Chevalerie* of Christine de Pisan, a French version of Vegetius's *Epitoma Rei Militaris*.

Caxton was no sluggard. He finished the translation, as he tells us, on 9 July of the same year and had it printed by 14 July. This book, entitled *The Fayttes of Armes*, was entirely printed from a new fount of type, now known as Caxton's Type No. 6, produced for the most part from matrices formed from refurbished letters of Type Nos. 2 and 2* together with a few new letters and some sorts from other founts.

With this type he printed a number of books between 1489 and 1491, including two popular romances, *Blanchardyn and Eglantine* and *The Four Sonnes of Aymon*, both of which probably belong to the year 1489. The former was translated by Caxton from a French manuscript which he himself had long before sold to the King's mother, the Lady Margaret Beaufort, who asked him to make an English translation. To her he dedicated the printed version, begging his patroness to pardon his 'rude and comyn englyshe'.

The translation of *Les Quatre Fils Aymon* was made by Caxton at the request of John de Vere, 13th Earl of Oxford, and Caxton's 'syngular and especial lorde' sent the printer his own copy of the French version. Caxton, a prudent and business-like man, was careful to point out in the prologue to the book that it was issued at his 'great coste and charges' both in translating and in printing it, but he does not doubt 'but that hys good grace shall rewarde me in suche wise that I shal have cause to pray for his good and prosperous welfare'.

Eneydos, which most probably came from Caxton's press in 1490, was a translation he made, 'having no work in hand', from a French book called *Le Livre des Eneydes*, which itself was a romance based on Virgil's poem. It contains one of the most delightful of all the Prologues with which Caxton was fond of introducing his books to the reader; this ends with a laudatory passage praising the work of John Skelton, 'late created poete laureate in the unyversitie of oxenforde'.

Among the small devotional books which Caxton printed, one of the most interesting appeared about 1491, almost at the end of his life. This was an octavo volume of prayers called the *Fifteen O's* from the fifteen prayers each beginning with 'O'. It is the only book known of Caxton's that is ornamented with woodcut borders. Each border consists of four pieces, and eight separate sets of designs are used in the book, depicting flowers and foliage, birds and beasts. These prayers were printed, as the colophon tells us, by the command of Elizabeth of York (wife of Henry VII) and of the King's mother, Lady Margaret Beaufort, and may possibly have formed the supplement to a lost Primer. On the second page is a woodcut of Calvary forming a frontispiece, and this and the same borders were later used in the *Hours* printed by Wynkyn de Worde in 1494. Of the woodcut, Arthur Hind says: 'The designer of the *Calvary* is easily the most spirited artist engaged in book-illustration in England in the fifteenth century. He shows an individual sense of curving lines, and an incisive power of expression.'[22]

Caxton's life ended suddenly while he was still engaged in his favourite work of translation. Although the exact date of his death is unknown, it was some time in 1491, soon after he had penned the last page of his translation of the *Lyves of the Fathers*, as is attested by the colophon to Wynkyn de Worde's publication of this work, which tells us that it was 'translated oute of Frenche into Englisshe by William Caxton of Westmynstre late deed and fynyshed at the laste daye of hys lyff'.

Ames* quotes a note he found written in a copy of the *Fructus Temporum* which reads:

Of your charitee pray for the soul of Mayster Wyllyam Caxton, that in his time was a man of moche ornate and moche renommed wysdome and connyng, and decessed ful crystenly the yere of our Lord MCCCCLXXXXI.

In the Parish Accounts of St Margaret's, Westminster, is an entry:

Item. atte Buryeing of William Caxton for	
iiij torches	vij s. viij d.
Item. for the belle atte same bureyng	vj d.

Caxton, compared with some of his contemporaries abroad, was not a very good printer. Although he is known to have produced about a hundred books during his fifteen years as a printer, most of which show evidence of careful workmanship, none are more than adequate considered as examples of printing, in the technique of which Colard Mansion soon surpassed him. Updike has remarked how unfortunate it was for English typography that Caxton lived so long in the Low Countries, and modelled his printing on the work about him, rather than upon that of France or Italy.[23]

But our debt to Caxton includes more than the introduction of the printing press, which in any case would have made its appearance in this country only two years later; he was the first disseminator of good literature in the vernacular. His greatness lies in what he printed rather than how he printed.

It has been said that his books were only for the libraries of the great and rich, and that he printed nothing for the common man. Though the fact may be correct the inference is wrong. Although literacy was spreading, as shown by the increasing number of manuscripts in the vernacular produced during the fifteenth century as compared with preceding centuries, the ability to read was still confined mainly to clerical, legal and courtly circles. Moreover, without influential patrons it is unlikely that Caxton would have been able to undertake the production of so many large and costly folios.

---

* Joseph Ames (1689–1759) was the author of *Typographical Antiquities . . . an historical account of Printing in England* (1749). It was later revised and enlarged by William Herbert.

Nor did Caxton confine himself to a single class of book: his output comprised books on education, encyclopedias, classics, morality and religion, allegory, chivalry, romance, history and poetry. Had he lived but a little while longer he would have added travel to that list, for he intended to print Sir John Mandeville's *Travels;* but death overtook him before he had time to print it from the manuscript copy he obtained from the Abbey of St Albans, and it was left to his successor to bring out an edition of that work in 1499.

When Caxton began to print the English language was still in the melting-pot, for although the struggle for supremacy between Norman-French and English speech, which had begun with the Conquest, ended in the dominance of English, the English tongue itself had so many dialects that a northerner was quite incomprehensible to a southerner. When English gradually assumed a definite literary form, largely through the influence of Chaucer, Caxton, by virtue of his new craft, and in his missionary zeal for disseminating works of literature, had as much influence as any man of his time in creating a fixed form for the language. He himself translated no fewer than twenty-two of the books he published, and his own translations fill some 4,500 printed pages, mostly folio. As a translator he gave much thought to the choice of suitable renderings, and his problem, on account of the varying dialects of his day, was no easy one to solve. Though he was blamed at times for using 'curyous termes which coude not be onderstonde of comyn people', he did his best to base his work on 'the comyn termes that be dayli used'. Curt Bühler has pointed out the 'numberless words still current which made their first English appearance in the pages of Caxton's translations'.[24]

Caxton's industry was remarkable for a man past middle age, for not only did he supervise the printing and sale of the books which came from his press, but in addition he usually edited and frequently translated the works he published and to most of them he added a Prologue and Epilogue. Says Winship: 'This elderly man of the world in a year and a half, seventy-eight weeks, made ready for the printer more than 525,000 words, a daily average for that period, six days a week, of well over a thousand words.'[25]

Caxton's workmen must also have been industrious, for his editorial duties must surely have precluded him from spending much time at the press, the working of which was very laborious in those days; for when the pressman had pulled the bar to bring the platen down on the type it had to be pushed back again to its original position in order to raise the platen and release the paper. Moreover, since four separate pulls were necessary to print both sides of a sheet 22 by 16 inches (the size of paper used in the first two editions of the *Golden Legend*), the production of a large book was a slow business unless several presses and pressmen to work them were available.* What kind of press Caxton used we don't know, but it was probably similar to that shown in various devices used by Josse Bade of Paris.

With regard to the provenance of type used by Caxton we can only speculate, for we know little of the early history of type-founding in England. Carter and Ricks state that

> Caxton's types were so much like those used at the same time in Flanders and Brabant, where Jean Brito, for one, was certainly making punches and matrices, that it may be concluded that they were cut, if not cast, abroad, though we may allow that Caxton commissioned them and had a hand in the design.[26]

Whether there were any foreign workmen in England in Caxton's time making type from imported matrices we cannot tell; there is no record of any alien working as a caster in London before 1553.

For his paper, likewise, Caxton had to look abroad, for there were then no paper mills in England. The paper used for the *Epitome Margaritae eloquentiae* by Laurentius Gulielmus of Savona, a hitherto unrecorded Caxton found recently at Ripon Cathedral, bears a watermark of a scissors type, and is thought to be Italian-made, probably in Genoa. That used in the *Description of Britain* (1480) bears the mark of a unicorn and, according to Dr Allan Stevenson, came either from Normandy or Champagne.[27]

Up to the time of Caxton's death there had been only one other native printer—the still unidentified printer at St Albans. After Caxton's death there was no English master printer at work for more than twenty years. Those who followed him were mostly of French origin, and the types they used were based on the prevailing fashions of Paris and Rouen, though in many cases the types used in Rouen are found in Paris-printed books of an earlier date.

---

* Even with the improved Stanhope press of around 1800 only about 250 impressions, *on one side*, could be taken off in an hour.

CHAPTER TWO

Successors of Caxton

Wynkyn De Worde

When Caxton died his business was taken over by his chief assistant, Wynkyn de Worde, a native of Lotharingia (Lorraine), who was probably brought over to England by Caxton in 1476, for as early as 1480 there is a record of his wife having rented a house from the Abbey of Westminster. He took over Caxton's material and continued to print in the same premises at Westminster until 1500.

Whereas Caxton was something of a scholar and preferred to print books which interested him personally, Wynkyn de Worde was first of all a businessman, and was quick to see that, lacking Caxton's contacts with Court circles, he would be more successful if he were to devote his energies to producing cheap books for the many rather than costly productions for the few. Where Caxton had produced large folios of hundreds of pages, De Worde concentrated on small and saleable quarto volumes to supply the growing demand for books with a popular appeal. The ordinary citizen with a modicum of education wanted books, but was unwilling, even if he could afford it, to spend money on expensive books, for as Robert Copland's customer declares: 'A peny I trow is ynough on bokes.'[28]

During the years immediately following his master's death, Wynkyn de Worde was content, however, to finish off some of the work upon which Caxton had probably been engaged at the time of his death and to reprint some of his former editions. One or two of these books were issued without any printer's name, and the first book to bear De Worde's name as printer is the *Liber Festivalis* printed in 1493. The first book he printed following the death of Caxton is generally thought to be *Chastysing of goddes chyldern*, which is undated, but was probably printed about 1492. This folio was printed with Caxton's Type No. 6, and was the first book to be produced at Westminster with a title-page.

'At his first setting up for himself', wrote Palmer, 'his first care was to cut a new sett of puncheons, which he sunk into matrices, and cast several sorts of Printing-letter, which he afterwards us'd.'[29] There is no evidence, however, that De Worde was a punch-cutter, and most of the types he used after he left Westminster were from matrices imported from French and Low Country sources. The reprint of the so-called *Book of St Albans*, issued in 1496, was, according to Plomer,[30] printed in a type which some say he obtained from the Dutch printer Godfried van Os, and is not found in any other of De Worde's books.† He was the first printer in England to use italic, in *Complures Dialogi* (1528), a Latin translation from Lucian. This type came from the Low Countries, and is found in the books of the Antwerp printer Jan de Schryver, or Grapheus.

The few large folios which De Worde printed during the early part of his career were mainly new editions of works Caxton had printed, such as the *Golden Legend* (of which De Worde printed several editions), Chaucer's *The Canterbury Tales*, and Higden's *Polycronicon*. When Caxton printed the last-named book he had no type for the music notes and merely left a space for them to be filled in by hand. When Wynkyn de Worde reprinted the work in 1495 he got over the difficulty by using quads or reversed types, which printed as a black rectangle for the notes, the stave lines being set up from rules.†

At this point we must digress for a moment to mention a book printed in 1530 bearing the title *In this boke ar cōteynyd xx sōges*, for this book was for long attributed to Wynkyn de Worde, Colonel Isaac being the first to point out that this attribution was not justified on typographical grounds. Later, in the binding of a book at Westminster Abbey, was found the title leaf of the Medius part of this music book, and conjugate with it part of a leaf with a blank recto and a colophon on the verso. Unfortunately the binder had cut off part of the colophon, which appears to read: 'Imprynted in Londō at the signe of the black Morēs.'

The type in which the music is printed seems to have been copied from that used by the Augsburg printer Erhard Öglin, and the music printing was produced by separate impressions of the stave and the notes. So far the type has not been found in any other work, and the printer remains unidentified.[31]

In 1495 Wynkyn de Worde brought out the *Vitas Patrum* which

---

* But Duff says it was obtained from Govaert von Ghemen.
† A. Hyatt King. *Four Hundred Years of Music Printing*. 1964.

Caxton had translated in the last year of his life, and, probably in the same year, he produced one of the best-printed of all his large books —an English translation by John of Trevisa of *De proprietatibus rerum* by Bartholomaeus Anglicus. This was the book which embodied in the colophon, as already mentioned, the fact of Caxton's having worked on the undated Cologne edition. The colophon also reveals the fact that the paper (watermark an eight-point star in a circle) was made by John Tate the Younger, and the book is therefore the first to have been printed on paper made in England. Tate's mill was at Stevenage, in Hertfordshire; its life was a short one, for although the mill was still in existence at Tate's death in 1507, the manufacture of paper seems to have been abandoned after 1498.

In the year 1500, after having printed at least a hundred books at Westminster, Wynkyn de Worde moved from Caxton's old printing house and settled in Fleet Street at the sign of the Sun, probably in order to be nearer the booksellers and the new clientele for which he intended to work. In fact the turn of the century saw the departure from Westminster of both printers who were working there at the time of Caxton's death. De Worde had already moved, and Julian Notary soon followed. They must have realized that the number of customers willing to pay for works such as Caxton had printed was limited.

One of De Worde's greatest assets as a businessman was his shrewdness in judging the market; nor did he hesitate to print a book for the first time if he thought it would sell, so that out of a total of more than 700 works which he printed between 1492 and 1532, some 70 per cent. were printed for the first time. He quickly realized that a recurring profit could be made from the printing of school books; the various Latin grammars of Robert Whittinton became largely his monopoly, and were reprinted by him again and again: John Stanbridge (like Whittinton, an Informator of Magdalen College, Oxford) wrote five text-books which were printed and reprinted at least fifty times, and of these De Worde printed more than half the known editions.

Liturgies, also, he printed in large quantities—Breviaries, Hours, Hymns and Sequences, Missals and Psalters. In 1523 he published (somewhat daringly for the period) a Primer containing not only the Creed and a form of confession in English, but also 'the Pater noster in englysshe'. This was probably the earliest printing in England of the Lord's Prayer in the vernacular.

Although Wynkyn de Worde was, in the main, a popular printer of small works at modest prices, nevertheless it must be remembered that he also printed many works of literature including first editions of Froissart's and Fabyan's *Chronicles*; many of the works of John Lydgate, including his translation of Boccaccio's *The falle of Princis*; Alexander Barclay's translation of Brant's *The Shyppe of Fooles*; several of the works of Erasmus; Sir John Mandeville's *Travels*; and Thomas à Kempis's *Imitatio Christi*.

Wynkyn de Worde seems only on one occasion to have fallen foul of the ecclesiastical authorities. In 1525 he had published a Lutheran tract, *A ghoostly pamphlete . . . called the ymage of love*, by John Ryckes, translated by John Gough. In December of that year De Worde and Gough were summoned to St Paul's Cathedral by the Vicar-General to answer the charge that they had published the above-mentioned book, and after having been warned not to sell any more copies they were summoned to appear before the Vicar-General in Consistory on the third day after St Hilary to answer charges concerning suspicion of heresy. Of what happened to them on that occasion there is no existing record, but the book was later republished by Gough,* and an undated copy is in the Bodleian.

In 1499, just before he left Westminster, De Worde printed the edition of Mandeville's *Travels* which Caxton would have printed had he lived to do so. Although Pynson's undated edition of this work (of which only one copy is known) probably appeared in 1496, that of De Worde is the first illustrated edition to appear in England, and with few exceptions the woodcuts, as Malcolm Letts informs us, were taken from a German translation by Martin Velser printed in Augsburg in 1482.[32] The copy in the University Library, Cambridge, has 72 cuts, of which at least 63 are taken from Velser, with slight variations. These woodcuts, with a few others, also appear in the edition of 1568 printed by Thomas East.

Of the devotional books published by Wynkyn de Worde a number were printed for him in France, as one can tell from the type, the *criblé*† initials, and the music staves. An example is the *Manual* for York use, published in 1509, the colophon of which states:

Impressum Per Wynandū de Worde . . . pro Johanne gaschet et Jacobo feerebouc sociis.

---

* John Gough was named one of the overseers of De Worde's will.
† *Criblé*, literally 'riddled' or 'pitted', is a technical term applied to soft metal-cuts pierced all over with tiny holes, giving a speckled effect.

This book carries on the title-page a device of De Worde found only in books printed for him in France.

De Worde used at least seventeen varieties of his printer's mark, all of which embodied Caxton's device. One of the most familiar is that known as the 'sagittarius', made up of three horizontal divisions. The upper part contains the sun and stars, the central portion has Caxton's device, and the lower part contains a scroll with the words 'wynkyn de worde', accompanied by a dog on one side and the sagittarius on the other.

Wynkyn de Worde was not a particularly good printer, although he did print some fine books when the spirit moved him; but he was certainly one of the most industrious printers of his time. H. S. Bennett's useful *Handlist of Publications by Wynkyn de Worde, 1492–1535* mentions 829 editions.[33] How profitable the school books must have been to the printer is shown by the fact that he brought out 77 editions of Stanbridge's text-books and 155 of those by Whittinton.*

Although not one of the scholar-printers, De Worde was nevertheless the first to introduce letters of some of the learned languages into his books. In a grammar of Whittinton, printed in 1517, he used a few Greek words, the characters being cut in wood; in 1528, for Wakefield's *Oratio de laudibus trium linguarorum*, he printed some Greek words in movable type, as well as some Arabic and Hebrew cut in wood.

Wynkyn de Worde died either at the end of 1534 or the beginning of 1535, for his will, dated 5 June, 1534, was proved on 19 January, 1535. He was buried in the church of St Bride, near where he worked. John Byddell and James Gaver, two of his assistants, were made executors and continued to carry on printing in the same premises. Little is known of Gaver, who on 2 March, 1535, took out letters of denization, in which he is described as 'stationer from the dominion of the Emperor'.

When Pynson (see page 34) was appointed King's Printer in 1508, De Worde, presumably with official permission, described himself as printer to the King's mother, Lady Margaret Beaufort, Countess of Richmond.

John Lettou and William de Machlinia

Three years after Caxton had set up his press at Westminster a foreigner introduced the art of printing into the City of London. We

---

* A number of these were, however, farmed out to other printers.

call him Johannes or John Lettou, and the name suggests that he was a native of Lithuania. He was evidently a practised printer, though where he learned the art one will probably never know. It may have been at Rome, for the type he used when he began to print books in London is, apart from the capitals, identical with that used by a printer named Johannes Bremer, alias Bulle, who, according to Hain,* printed two books at Rome around 1478-9.

A good deal of mystery surrounds the identity of Lettou. Harold Marshall puts forward the theory that the printing attributed to Lettou was actually done by Johannes Bulle and that Lettou was the financier of a publishing venture.[34] Some have assumed that John Lettou and Johannes Bulle were one and the same person, an assumption which Conrad Haebler finds unacceptable, arguing that as we know the name and place of origin of the printer it is hardly likely that he would have used a name which not only denies completely his German origin, but also points to a very different nationality.[35]

Lettou's first work in London was to print in 1480 John Kendale's Indulgence asking for aid against the Turks, an edition of which had been recently printed by Caxton. But Lettou's small neat type was, as Duff points out, so much better suited to the printing of indulgences that its appearance probably induced Caxton to make his small Type No. 4, which he thereafter used for such work.[36]

Two other indulgences in the same year were followed by the only book printed by Lettou in 1480—*Quæstiones Antonii Andreæ super XII libros metaphysice Aristotelis*, a small folio of 106 leaves, 49 lines to the page. In the following year appeared a folio volume of 348 leaves— *Thomas Wallensis Expositiones super Psalterium*, and probably during the same year a book on ecclesiastical procedure known only from two leaves found in a binding at Corpus Christi College, Cambridge.

From the colophons we learn that these two books were printed at the charge of a certain William Wilcock, about whom we know nothing, but who was possibly a London stationer. The workmanship of Lettou was in advance of that of any printer in England at that time. He was the first in England to make use of quire signatures and to set his page in two columns.

About 1482 he was joined by another printer, William de Machlinia, a native of Mechlin (Malines) in Flanders. The two men printed in

* Ludwig Hain (1781-1836) was the compiler of *Repertorium Bibliographicum ad annum 1500.*

association five books, all of which were law books. None of them are dated, and only one, the *Tenores Novelli*, has any colophon. This gives the address as *juxta ecclesiam omnium sanctorum*, but since there were, at that time, several churches dedicated to All Hallows, the address is rather vague. The type used was a small black-letter, by no means easy to read on account of the numerous abbreviations.

With the printing of the last of these five books Lettou disappeared from printing history as mysteriously as he entered it, and Machlinia continued to print alone after moving to new premises by the Fleet Bridge. Some of his books bear the address 'in Holborn' but it is difficult to say with certainty which address was the earlier, since none of his books are dated. Two of the types which Machlinia used appear to be identical with ones also used by Jean Brito of Bruges, as can be seen by comparing Machlinia's founts 4 and 5 (referred to in Duff's *XV Century Books*) with those of Brito shown in plates qq and rr of the Type Facsimile Society's issue of 1909.

One item of historical interest printed by Machlinia is the Bull of Pope Innocent VIII granting dispensation for the marriage of Henry VII and Elizabeth of York which put an end to the hostilities between the rival houses of York and Lancaster. He also printed a *Book against the Pestilence* by Canutus, Bishop of Westeraes in Sweden, which ran into three editions, perhaps because London at that time was visited by one of its periodical outbursts of the plague. One of these editions (S.T.C. 4591) has the first known title-page in English.

Machlinia was the first of the English printers to devote himself to law books, and eleven of his thirty known publications are legal works. With Lettou he was the original publisher of Littleton's *Tenures*, almost a necessity for those beginning the study of the law, and his *Nova Statuta* was the first of a long series of volumes containing collections of statutes of various dates. He also printed a small Book of Hours, known only from various leaves now scattered among several libraries, and a Primer on vellum with eight woodcuts described by the bookseller, George Smith.[37]

One book at least Machlinia printed for a foreign dealer in English books. The *Speculum Christiani* of John Wotton was printed, so the colophon tells us, for a certain 'Henry Vrankenbergh', a partner in the firm of Henry Frankenbergh and Barnard van Stondo, merchants of printed books, who dwelt in St Mark's Alley, off St Clement's Lane.

William de Machlinia either retired or died around 1490 and his business seems to have been taken over by Richard Pynson, who used woodcut borders of Machlinia and other material, including the Lombardic initials used in Lettou's indulgences which Machlinia had retained.

Richard Pynson

Richard Pynson was a native of Normandy who probably learned his trade with Guillaume le Talleur of Rouen, whose device he later adopted, and who printed at least two of the books Pynson issued soon after he came to England. These were Littleton's *Tenures* and Statham's *Abridgement of Cases*. Pynson took over the business of Machlinia, and his first dated book was the *Doctrinale* of Alexander Grammaticus (1492). This may well have been preceded, however, by various undated books, among them an illustrated folio edition of *The Canterbury Tales*, printed in two types which appear to be of French origin.

Pynson continued to work in the parish of St Clement Dane's, just outside Temple Bar, from his arrival in this country until the end of the century, during which time he printed some 88 books. Although it was formerly thought that he came to England between the years 1486 and 1490, evidence unearthed by Henry Plomer shows that a glover named *Ric[ardu]s Pynson de parochia sancti Clementi Dacorum extra barra novi Templi, London* stood surety for a certain William Pays, alias William Symonds, in 1482. There is little doubt that this is the same man, since in one of the Plea Rolls of Henry VII examined by Plomer (who found that Pynson's name figured in six law cases brought between 1494 and 1505) he is described as both 'bokeprynter' of St Clement Dane's and as 'pouchemaker'.[38] There is nothing surprising in this, for the early printers often carried on an ancillary trade. The great Plantin himself is a case in point.

Among the books Pynson printed during this first period of his career the finest was undoubtedly the splendid Sarum Missal, printed at the expense of Cardinal John Morton and finished on 10 January, 1500. Some copies were printed on vellum, and this 'Morton Missal' remains one of the finest specimens of early printing in England. Cardinal Morton's arms appear at the beginning of the book, and a rebus or punning allusion to the begetter of this missal is incorporated into borders and initials in the form of the letters 'Mor' surmounting a tun, or barrel.

Another fine production of this period is the *falle of Princis*, a translation by Lydgate from Boccaccio (1494), which contains some charming woodcuts (borrowed from Jean Du Pré), and also has

Pynson's second printer's mark, which shows a shield bearing the initials 'R.P.' and above it a helmet on which is perched a small bird. In view of the popularity of the rebus in both architecture and printing, this is probably a finch (*pinson* in French).

In 1500 Pynson moved from St Clement Dane's into the City, setting up his new premises at the Sign of the George, next to St Dunstan's Church in Fleet Street. Considerations of safety may have prompted this move, for in that year Pynson was attacked by a mob led by one Henry Squires. It was the culmination of a series of hostile moves against him and his workmen, occasioned by a general hostility towards foreign craftsmen. Within the precincts of the City he probably felt safer.

One of the books printed by Pynson during his first year at this new address was the *Remembrance for the Traduction of the Princesse Kateryne* (1501), an eight-leaved quarto giving instructions for the reception of Katherine of Aragon and for the ceremonial of her marriage to Prince Arthur.

In 1503 Pynson printed the first English translation of the *Imitatio Christi*, and in 1504 a fine Sarum Missal, an excellent example of black and red printing, of which there is a copy on vellum in the British Museum. This is probably the book referred to in the privy purse expenses of Henry VII:

> 12 July, 1504. To Richard Pynson opon a prest for masse-bokes to be printed, £10.

In 1506 was issued Pynson's edition of the *Kalender of shepherdes*, a work which was also printed in England by Wynkyn de Worde (1508) and Julian Notary (*c.* 1518). The woodcuts in this work are of a much higher standard than is usually found in English books of this period, and comparison suggests that the blocks were those used by Antoine Vérard in his 1503 edition of the work in question.

Soon after the death of William Faques (see page 42) in 1508, Pynson succeeded him as printer to the King, an appointment which carried with it a salary of £2 a year (raised to £4 in 1515) and the right to use the title of Esquire; but most of the official printing of Pynson, such as statutes and proclamations, being ephemeral, has disappeared.

Pynson was the first printer in England to introduce roman type, which, according to A. F. Johnson, came from Paris.[39] He first used it to print a speech by the Papal Nonce, Petrus Gryphus, in 1509. The speech was intended to be delivered before Henry VII, but the death of the king prevented this. In the same year Pynson combined black-letter and roman in a folio edition of Alexander Barclay's translation of *The Shyppe of Fooles* of Sebastian Brant.

In 1516 Pynson printed the first edition of Fabyan's *Chronicles*, the forerunner of Halle and Holinshed. This edition ends with the reign of Richard III in 1485.

Pynson was the earliest systematic publisher of the Year Books, which are, says Sir William Holdsworth, 'by far the most important source of, and authority for, the medieval common law'.[40] Whereas until his appointment as King's Printer some fifty per cent. of Pynson's output had been made up of religious books, for the remainder of his career the legal side took precedence, and he printed over seventy editions of the Year Books. Between 1510 and 1528 he put out at least eight editions of Littleton's *Tenures* (first printed by Lettou and Machlinia), and in 1525 he issued that work for the first time in an octavo edition, doubtless to the relief of those who had to use it. It was in this edition that Pynson, annoyed at Robert Redman for trying to poach on what he considered his preserves, included a 'Letter to the Reader' abusing Redman in no uncertain terms and pointing out how much more correct and better printed his work was than that of Redman, 'or more properly Rudeman, for among a thousand it would be hard to find one more unskilled'.

In addition to the liturgical books which Pynson printed (including eight editions of the *Sarum Horae*) it seems probable that he had for at least eighteen years, as Dr D. E. Rhodes has shown, the profitable contract for printing the forms of admission to the Guild of St Mary at Boston, 'which bestowed certain quite extraordinary privileges on the purchasers', and were probably printed in great quantities.[41]

From 1519 to 1525 Pynson made use of a title-page border (McKerrow and Ferguson No. 7*) which seems to have been copied from a compartment attributed to Urs Graf and used by Froben at Basle. Another border used by him between 1521 and 1527 (McKerrow and Ferguson No. 11) is similar to that used at Antwerp by Michiel Hillen van Hoochstraten.

As printer to Henry VIII Pynson printed in 1521 the celebrated

---

* Numbering taken from McKerrow and Ferguson: *Title-page Borders used in England and Scotland*, 1932.

Assertio septem sacramentorum, which earned for the monarch his title of 'Defender of the Faith'.

Educational books did not form a large part of Pynson's output, but in 1519 he contracted to print for William Horman, Vice-Provost of Eton, a book entitled *Vulgaria*, a collection of aphorisms and sentences in English and Latin, which Horman had compiled for the use of his pupils. It was a quarto volume of 654 pages, bearing Pynson's device on the verso of the last leaf. Eight hundred copies were printed, with the proviso that Pynson should not reprint it within the next five years without permission. He never did, and the second edition was printed by Wynkyn de Worde in 1530.

The last book to which Pynson set his hand was John Palsgrave's *Lesclarcissement de la langue francoyse*, a large folio of over a thousand pages. Of this work Pynson printed only the first two parts, and according to the colophon the printing was finished by John Hawkins on 18 July, 1530. Pynson probably died at the beginning of 1530, for his will, dated 15 November, 1529, was proved on 18 February, 1530. Pynson's son predeceased him, and his business seems to have been taken over by Robert Redman, who had by then possibly settled his differences with his older colleague.

Pynson was worthy of his title of King's Printer, for his work was undoubtedly superior to that of his contemporaries. Although his first types were undistinguished, as soon as he had established himself he acquired new founts and ornaments, and his later books, as Duff remarks, 'bore much more resemblance to the work of a foreign than a native press'.[42] In addition to his roman, Pynson also had a fount of Greek type which he used in T. Linacre's *De emendata structura Latini sermonis* (1524). Incidentally this book contains the first reference to letter-founding in any English book.[43]

For the most part Pynson's books were better illustrated than those of his contemporaries, although he made rather a disastrous start, for the woodcuts in his 1492 edition of *The Canterbury Tales* were mostly poor copies of those used by Caxton. But as soon as he had settled down he turned to foreign sources and borrowed or copied largely from his French colleagues. Thus in 1494 his *falle of Princis* contains nine cuts from Jean Du Pré's edition of that work. For the *Kalender of shepherdes* (1506) he managed to secure the blocks used by Antoine Vérard in his curious translation into the Scottish vernacular printed at Paris in 1503. The unique copy of the Pynson edition in the British Museum is unfortunately incomplete, for it has only 47 woodcuts, whereas, according to Hodnett, a perfect copy should have about 75.

For Alexander Barclay's translation of Pierre Gringoire's *Castell of laboure* (c. 1505) a skilful engraver has copied 28 of the woodcuts from those in the Pigouchet-Vostre edition of 1499, while the 109 cuts in *The Shyppe of Fooles* are copied from the French version of Brant's work, *La Nef des folz du monde*, printed at Paris by De Marnef and Maystener in 1497. This was copying at two removes, for the illustrations of the French edition were themselves copied from the Basle edition of 1497.

Pynson printed the first English book on arithmetic in 1522. This was Cuthbert Tunstall's *De Arte Supputandi*, a quarto printed in roman type with a title-page border copied from one originally designed by Hans Holbein for Froben of Basle.

As with other early printers, it is probable that some of Pynson's work has not survived the passage of time. In the Colón Library at Seville there is a unique copy of a book printed by Pynson—Gilbert Nicolai's *Tractatus de tribus ordinibus beatissime virginis dei genetricis Mariae*. It is undated, but has Pynson's name and one of his devices. He had seven of these in all, one of which, used in *Libellus qui informatio puerorum appellatur* (c. 1500) was presumably a metal-cut, for there is a distinct bend in its lower border line (see Hind, fig. 466). This is a very elaborate device, with Pynson's initials on a shield held by two supporters and surmounted by a helm and crest, the whole enclosed in a highly decorative border.

Of considerable interest as showing details of the rates of work and pay of the early printers are various entries concerning Pynson given in the Calendar of State Papers of the reign of Henry VIII, in particular the contracts between Pynson and William Horman and Pynson and John Palsgrave, which were reproduced in full from the Record Office copies by F. J. Furnivall.[44] Palsgrave, although a Prebendary of St Paul's, did not have a very trusting nature, for after the number of copies mutually agreed upon had been printed, they were to be placed in a room in Pynson's house, 'where-off the kay schall be in the custodye off the said Master John Palsgrave or his assignes, whyche from tyme to tyme schall reckyn howe many off the hoole said somm off vii^c & fifty bokes they take owt & the same nomber expresse in wryghtynge'.

The contract stipulated that Pynson was to print 'every hoole workyng day, for the more spedyng off the saide work, a schete off

38

paper on bothe the sides, and not to cesse for none occasion (except the Kynges grace have any thynges to be prynted)'. The work in question was the *Lesclaircissement* mentioned above, a book 'very necessarye for all suche as intende to lerne to speke trewe frenche'. It appears that Palsgrave, who was a teacher of French, only allowed the book to be sold to his pupils and friends, for a certain S. Vaughan, writing to Cromwell from Antwerp asking his help in procuring a copy, says:

> I perceyve that Palsgrave hathe willed Pynson to sell none of them to any other person than to suche as he shall comaunde to have them, lest his proffit by teching the Frenche tonge myght be mynished by the sale of the same to such persons, as, besids hym, were disposed to studye the sayd tongue.

For Horman's *Vulgaria*, of which he contracted to print 800 copies, Pynson was to receive, for every whole ream of paper printed, the sum of 5s. As the *Vulgaria* contains 82 sheets, the number of reams would be 131, making a total of £32.15s.0d.—a figure which could probably be multiplied twenty-fold or more to find a modern equivalent.

Among the entries relating to Pynson in the King's Book of Payments are these:

1511, March. To Pynson, for printing of informations to the Commissioners taking musters	£10.
„ July. Pynson, printing statutes and proclamations	£6.13s.4d.
1512, July. R. Pynson, printing books of statutes for the army over sea.........................	100s.
1513, Feb. Ric. Pynson, King's Printer...........	£10.
„ June. Pynson, printing and binding 1600 books of 'statutes of war'......................	£16.13s.4d.
„ Dec. 25. Pynson, printing of the enterdityng of Scotland..................................	40s.
1514, June. Pynson, printing 100 parchment rolls of the last subsidy act, each containing four skins..	£10.
1515, March. Pynson, printing 450 skins of parchment containing the 'Acts of retendors of the statutes of Winchester'...........................	£6.13s.4d.
1515, Dec. Pynson, for printing 100 parchment skins and 125 leaves of paper of the last subsidy, and for printing the statutes....................	£18.
1517, May. Pynson, printing books concerning the subsidy	£31.13s.4d.

Pynson's business seems to have been a profitable one, for he left considerable property in Chancery Lane and Tottenham. He had only one son, also Richard, who died shortly before his father. Although the fact has not been hitherto recorded, it would appear from the Churchwardens' Accounts of St Dunstan's that he had a brother, John. Richard Pynson and William Pearson are named as Wardens for the year 1516–17, and for the year 1519–20 the two Wardens were John Gerrard and John Pynson. Pynson also supplied the church with certain service books, for an entry under 'Payments' for 1526–7 reads:

ffirst paide to pynson for ii grete bokes............   iii l, xi s. iii d.*

Julian Notary

About 1496 an edition of the *Questiones Alberti de modis significandi* was printed in London 'at St Thomas the Apostle's'. On the last leaf is a printer's mark containing three sets of initials: I. N., I. B. and I. H. The first were those of Julian Notary, a native of Brittany; the third set stood probably for Jean Huvin, a Rouen stationer who dealt in books for the English market; I. B. were for long thought to be the initials of a French printer, Jean Barbier, but are now considered to be those of John Barbour of Coventry, who called himself (it was a time when the French were producing books of a high standard) Jean Barbier, thus leading the most painstaking bibliographers into error.[45]

The partners issued a second book in 1497, a *Sarum Horae* of which only a fragment of four leaves remain, though fortunately they include the colophon, which shows that the book was printed for Wynkyn de Worde. In 1498 the printing office was moved to King Street, Westminster, and there Notary and Barbier (Huvin having left the partnership) printed a Sarum Missal, the first edition printed in England, again for Wynkyn de Worde, who probably had some interest in the press. In 1499 Barbier, or Barbour, in turn disappeared, and Notary continued to print alone, using the same device, but with the initials removed and the name Julianus Notarii inserted.

Until recently it had been assumed, by his name, that Notary was a Frenchman, but from what part of France no one knew. Fortunately C. E. Welch has discovered among the records of the Bishop of London

---

* The Vestry Minutes and Churchwardens' Accounts of the old church of St Dunstan's in the West are now in the Guildhall Library.

a volume of depositions containing a lawsuit in which Julian Notary gave evidence. From this we find that the printer was a native of Vannes, capital of the department of Morbihan, on the south coast of Brittany.[46]

One of the earliest miniature books was printed by Notary in 1500. This is a 64mo *Horae ad usum Sarum*, of which only 16 pages exist in the form of a half-sheet (i–k) now in the Public Library at Victoria, Australia. The printed page measures 1 inch by 1⅜ inches and the colophon, fortunately among these surviving pages, reads: 'Thys Emprynteth at Westminster by me Julyayn Noary [*sic*] Dwellynge in Kyng strete. Anno domini M. v C. ii die mencis Aprilis.'

The last book which Notary printed at Westminster is an edition of Chaucer's *Love and complaintes between Mars and Venus*. Then, following the example of Wynkyn de Worde, he left Westminster and installed himself in premises just outside Temple Bar, very likely the house which Pynson had only lately vacated. To this he affixed the sign of the Three Kings. Here he remained from about 1501 to 1515.

The first dated book he issued from the new premises was an edition of the *Golden Legend* printed in 1504, illustrated with woodcuts previously used by Caxton and Wynkyn de Worde, as well as five *criblé* metal engravings, all probably of French origin, and some curious initials similar to those used by André Bocard.

In 1510 Notary printed an edition of the *Sermones de tempore et sanctis*, on the title-page of which the printer tells us that they

are to be sold (where they have been printed) in London in the suburb of Temple Bar near the porch of St Clement's in the house of Julian Notary, printer and bookseller, carrying on business at the sign of the Three Kings. And they will also be found for sale in St Paul's churchyard in the same man's little shop, from which also hangs the same sign of the Three Kings.

About 1515 Notary seems to have given up his premises near Temple Bar and moved to a house in St Paul's churchyard, where he printed in 1515 *The Chronicle of England*. No dated book from his press is known between 1510 and 1515.

Like Pynson and Wynkyn de Worde, Notary printed an edition of the *Shepherd's Calendar*, a popular 'omnium gatherum' of country lore regarding weather and the seasons. Of Notary's edition there exists only one known copy, in which the date is partly destroyed, but since it was printed in St Paul's Churchyard at the Three Kings, and we know that Notary had replaced the sign of St Mark belonging to the previous occupant by 1518 with his old sign of the Three Kings, the presumed date of 1518 cannot be far out.

Notary vanishes from printing history after 1520, having printed about 48 books. Although most of his printing was concerned with liturgical books, he did, curiously enough, print two little tracts in a very different vein—one called *A merry gest and a true howe Johan Splynter made his testament*, and the other, the *Mery geste of a Sergeaunt and Frere*, neither of which are dated.

From 1507 onwards, Notary used in place of the simple merchant's mark he had hitherto employed, a more elaborate device in two sizes. The smaller had a shield bearing his mark surmounted by a helm, with a decorative border and the printer's name below. The larger block, which he sometimes used as a frontispiece, showed the smaller device fastened to a tree, surrounded by birds and flowers, and two fabulous beasts on either side of the base.

William Faques and Richard Faques

A native of Normandy, William Faques, according to Claudin, learned his trade from Jean le Bourgeois of Rouen, and though we know next to nothing of his life his books show him to have been a printer of outstanding merit. The octavo *Psalterium*, which he printed in 1504, is an excellent piece of work, printed in a well-cut black-letter, with each page enclosed in a neat chain border, and with some interesting devotional cuts which probably came from France. The first leaf bears the printer's mark, an uncommon device of two inter-laced triangles, one bearing a quotation from Psalm 37 in black letters on a white ground, and the other a piece from Proverbs 16 in white letters on a black ground. In the centre is his monogram transfixed by an arrow. At the end of the *Psalterium* the monogram is repeated on its own.

His *Statutes of An. XIX Hen. VII* shows that William Faques held the position of King's Printer—the first to do so in England. The colophon reads: 'Enprynted in London within Seynt Helens be Guil-lam Faques ye kyng Prynter.' This was near Bishopsgate Street, but he later moved to Abchurch Lane according to the colophon in two undated books: an edition of *Vulgaria Terentii* and Origen's homily *De beata Maria Magdelena*.

No more than eight books are known of William Faques's printing, and he probably died in 1508, for that was the year in which Richard Pynson was appointed King's Printer. The text 130 used by Faques was of French origin, and was used by J. Morand in 1497. Both Pynson and Wynkyn de Worde used it.

William Faques was succeeded in business by Richard Faques, who was probably either his son or some other near relative. He used the type and ornaments of his predecessor in printing, at the sign of the Maiden's Head, in St Paul's churchyard, the *Salus coporis salus anime* of Gulielmus de Saliceto. This folio volume is dated 1509. In 1511 he joined with Wynkyn de Worde in an edition of the Sarum Missal,* and also printed for Robert Wyer an undated book, *De Cursione Lunæ*.

His large device, with two unicorns and a shield, is an adaptation of that used by the Paris bookseller Thielmann Kerver. For the tree which appears on Kerver's device Faques substitutes an arrow, and as an arrow also plays an important part in the mark of William Faques, it probably has some family allusion. On the shield is the head of a woman, presumably representing the 'Maiden's Head', the sign of his business premises. Below all is a scroll with the name Richard Faques.

Later Richard Faques moved to St Paul's churchyard, at the sign of the A.B.C., from which he issued in 1523 John Skelton's *A goodly garlande or chaplet of laurell*. At this time he apparently had a shop as well as his printing house, for the colophon of this book states 'In-pryntyd by me Rycharde faukes dwellydg [*sic*] in dura rent or els in Powlis chyrche yarde at the sygne of the A.B.C.' Durham Rents was in the Strand. This book also shows a change in the spelling of his name; not only does the colophon speak of him as 'Rycharde faukes', but the anglicizing of the name is carried a step further in the accompanying printer's mark, for the 'ques' of Faques has been removed, and the letters 'kes', in type, inserted in its place. In all of the five dated books which he printed the spelling of the name undergoes a progressive change, becoming more English each time.

The latest date found in Faques's books is 1530, when he issued the *Mirrour of Our Lady*, printed at the instance of the Lady Abbess of the Monastery of Syon. In all about twenty-five books of Richard Faques are known.

The printer Michael Fawkes, who joined with Robert Copland in printing part of *A devout treatyse called the tree and XII frutes of the holy goost* (1534–5), may have been a relative of William and Richard Faques. His name occurs only in one other book—*A devoute Epystle or Treaty* . . . . by William Bonde, an undated quarto.

---

* Printed for them in Paris by Raoul Cousturier.

Robert Redman

Redman is known chiefly as a printer of law books. His first book, issued in 1523, was Sir Antony Fitzherbert's *Diversite de courtz*. In Redman's edition of the *Magna Charta*, dated 1525, his address is given as at the sign of the George in St Clement's parish—that is to say the house used first by Pynson and then by Notary. His standard of workmanship fell far below that of Pynson, and Plomer says that 'He used the types and devices of his predecessor until they were worn out. His work was slovenly and full of mistakes'.[47] Nevertheless the demand for legal works was such that the market was sufficiently lucrative to provide constant work for printers such as Pynson, Redman and John Rastell, and a handsome book was not the prime consideration for law students.

While Pynson was still alive there were frequent altercations between him and Redman, and when the latter began to issue editions of books which Pynson had come to look upon as his own property, the latter abused him roundly in various 'addresses to the reader'.

The Bibliothèque Nationale in Paris possesses the only surviving copy of the Primer printed by Redman early in 1535, of which book Butterworth writes:

> It is the first printing in English of a Primer strictly according to the 'use of Salisbury', the Latin text also being printed down the margin of each page; its English rendering is drawn from a great variety of sources; it forms a definite connecting link between the early manuscript Primers of Wycliffe's day and the printed ones ... it is the sire of a numerous progeny.[48]

Redman died in 1540, and his widow, Elizabeth Pickering, issued a few books after his death, but ceased printing when she remarried, and the printing office passed to William Middleton, who, like his predecessors at the sign of the George, printed mainly law books. Until Redman succeeded to Pynson's business in 1530 he had no printer's mark, but used three woodcuts; one of St George, one of the Trinity and one of the infant Christ. When he moved to Pynson's premises he made use of three of the deceased printer's devices.

John and William Rastell

John Rastell, together with Pynson and Redman, was one of the chief legal publishers of the beginning of the sixteenth century. The date of his birth is unknown, but he is said to have been a native of Coventry, in which city he held for some years the office of Coroner.

He was a practising lawyer and, as a compiler and translator of law books, he realized that there were great opportunities in this field for an enterprising printer qualified to undertake this highly specialized work.

About 1513 he set up a press in premises on the south side of St Paul's churchyard, where he printed an undated edition of Linacre's *Grammar*. It was probably in 1513 or 1514 that he published his *Liber Assisarum et placitorum Corone*, a concise version of the legal Year Books printed by Machlinia and Pynson. Like Pynson and Redman he made a speciality of abridgments of the Statutes, which had constantly to be kept up to date. These had hitherto been in Latin or Norman-French, and Rastell was the first to publish, in 1517, an edition in an English translation, 'as farre' he remarks 'as my symple wytt and smal lernynge wyll extende'.

His most important early work was his printing of Sir Antony Fitzherbert's *La Graunde Abbregement de le Ley*, a work in three large folio volumes (running to 798 leaves) which was sold for 40 shillings. This work, printed in a small gothic bastarda of French origin, must have called for a considerable outlay of capital. A second edition of the work was provided with an index, which undoubtedly increased its usefulness.

In 1520 John Rastell moved to 'the Mermayd at Powlys gate, next to chepe syde', a portion of which was occupied by his assistants (for it is doubtful if Rastell himself was anything more than editor and publisher) and the rest sublet to various tenants among whom were the stationers William Bonham, John Heron, Thomas Kele and John Gough. In 1525 Rastell published the *Expositiones terminorum legum anglorum*, intended, as he tells us, 'for the helpe and erudycion of them that be yong beginners whych intend to be studentys of the law'.

Up to the year 1526 John Rastell is known solely as a publisher of legal works, but in the years which followed he began to issue books of a more popular character, such as the *Twelve merry gestys of one called Edyth the lying wydow*; the *Hundred Merry Tales*; and his first illustrated book, *The pastyme of people*. This last-named work, a small folio dated 1529, is an outline history, based on Fabyan's *Chronicles*, and its chief interest today lies in the series of full-page woodcuts of kings of England from William I to Richard III.

He also printed several interludes, such as the story of Calisto and Malebea, which is quaintly entitled *A new comodye in englysh in maner of an enterlude ryght elygant and full of craft of rethoryk*. . . . Another was called *a godely interlude of Fulgens, Cenatoure of Rome. Lucres his daughter. Gayus flaminius, etc.* Yet another, entitled *a New Interlude and a mery of the Nature of the iiii Elements,* a versified cosmography printed about 1527, not only has some interesting comments relating to English navigation, showing how men could sail 'plain eastwards and come to England again', but also shows John Rastell to have been a pioneer of music printing in this country, for it contains one of the two earliest pieces of mensural music printed in England. The notes and the words to be sung are printed from type by one impression, and a reproduction is shown in A. Hyatt King's *Four Hundred Years of Music Printing.*[49]

John Rastell was Sir Thomas More's brother-in-law, having married Elizabeth More in or before 1504. At first a zealous Roman Catholic, he wrote and published in 1530 a defence of the doctrine of purgatory called *A New Boke of Purgatory,* which was answered by the reformer John Frith, who is said to have converted Rastell to his own views, for the printer later became a Protestant—a conversion which lost him many friends and ended in his imprisonment for his religious convictions. He died in confinement on 25 June, 1536, having been 'brought to extreme misery', forsaken by friends and relations.

John Rastell employed two devices, the smaller having his initials within a scroll; the larger device has in the centre the figures of a merman and mermaid rising from the water, supporting between them a shield bearing Rastell's initials. Above is a half-length figure of the Almighty, and in the upper corners are shields bearing the arms of England and the feathers of the Prince of Wales (though there was no Prince of Wales at that time).

William Rastell, eldest son of John Rastell, was born about 1508, and after studying at Oxford he followed his father's dual profession of printer-publisher and lawyer. While still studying law (he was called to the Bar in 1539) he began to print about 1529 and, although he was only active in this business until 1534, he issued more than thirty books. Unlike his father, he remained a Roman Catholic and printed several controversial books by his uncle, Sir Thomas More. His first book was probably More's *The supplycacyon of soulys,* a folio of 44 leaves printed in a bastarda of French origin.

In 1531, judging from the colophon to the *Register of the Writs,* he had his printing office in Fleet Street, in St Bride's churchyard, but no printer's mark of his is known. In that year he printed a new edition of More's *Dialogue of Heresies,* first published by his father. In 1535 he issued Fabyan's *Chronicles,* and thereby, as Arthur Reed suggests, he 'perhaps made amends for his father's rather bold and free abbreviation of the Pynson Fabyan' (namely, *The pastyme of people*).[11]

Like his father, he published several law books, including the inevitable Littleton's *Tenures*. In the preface to *Natura brevium* (1534) he inserted this advertisement:

> William Rastell to the gentylmen studentes of the law. How commodyous and profitable unto gentilmen studentes of the law be these thre bokes, Natura brevium, The old tenures, and the tenures of mayster Lyttylton, experience proveth, and the bookes them selfe declare. For lyke as a chylde goynge to scole fyrste lerneth his letters out of the a.b.c. so they that entende the study of the law do fyrste study these.

Speaking of one of William Rastell's books, A. F. Johnson says: 'One would hardly expect to find an example of a Vicentino italic in an English law book of the sixteenth century, yet oddly enough the best example of the school outside Italy and France turns up in the *Registrum brevium* by William Rastell in 1531.' According to the same authority the punches for the text, set in a calligraphic italic with swash capitals, were perhaps cut in Antwerp, where Hendrik van Middelburch was using it in 1530.[51]

In 1534 Sir Thomas More was imprisoned in the Tower of London, and in that same year William Rastell, possibly finding printing too dangerous an occupation for a Catholic printer in a country veering towards Protestantism, sold his business, probably to Thomas Gibson, a London printer, and devoted himself exclusively to the law. In 1544 he married Winifred, the daughter of Dr Clements, and on the accession of Edward VI went to Louvain, his house being seized during his absence. When Mary came to the throne he returned to England and was made a Judge of the Queen's Bench. After Mary's death he went back to Louvain, where he died in 1565.

Bther Printers of the Early Sixteenth Century

Robert Copland began his printing career as an assistant to Wynkyn de Worde. He was a man of parts: a good French scholar and translator, a printer who turned out good work for others besides himself, and an irrepressible writer of rather poor verse, which he liked to place at the beginning and ending of books. The first book to bear his imprint, the *Modus tenendi curiam Baronum* (*c*. 1514), gives his address as the sign of the Sun in Fleet Street—the address of Wynkyn de Worde. In 1515 he began to print at the Rose Garland in Fleet Stree and in that year brought out the *Boke of Justices of Peace*. The next book to bear his imprint, Alexander Barclay's *Introductory to write French*, compiled at the request of the Duke of Norfolk, did not appear until 1521.

Up to 1535 Copland seems to have printed only twelve books on his own account; some, of course, may have vanished without trace, but it appears likely that Copland printed a number of books for De Worde which appeared with the latter's imprint, and it is quite likely that he had a share in them. Many of these books contain introductory verses by Copland, and he may have been responsible for all the metrical translations in *The passyon of our lorde*, published by De Worde in 1532. Among his translations from the French are the *Life of Ipomydon*, *Kynge Appolyne of Tyre*, the *History of Helyas Knight of the Swan*, and *The Rutter of the Sea*, the first English book on navigation, translated from the French of Pierre Garcie. A book giving practical information to pilgrims is *The pylgrimage of M. Robert Langton, clerke, to saynt James in Compostell* (1522).

Copland was the author, and most likely the printer, of several humorous ballads, among them a vivid picture of the beggars and impostors of his time in *The Hye Way to the Spyttel hous;* the amusing *Complaynte of them that ben to late maryed* (published by De Worde); and the very broad humour of *Jyl of Breyntfords Testament*. Prefixed to the Wynkyn de Worde edition of Chaucer's *The Assemble of fowles* (1530) is an address in verse by 'Roberte Coplande boke-prynter' to 'new-fanglers' in four 8-line stanzas; at the end is an Envoy of three more stanzas in which he expounds on the difficulties which beset the printer when his manuscript has been

> Layde upon shelfe, in leaves all to-torne,
> With letters dymme, almost defaced clene. . . .

The last of his books was Dr Andrew Boorde's *Pryncyples of Astronomye in maner a pronosticacyon*, in which the author mentions his *Introduction of Knowledge* as 'now a pryntyng at old Robert Copland's the eldest printer of England'. Copland died, however, before completing the latter book, which was finished by his son William Copland, who printed at the Rose Garland from 1548, the presumed date of his father's death, until 1557.

Like Robert Copland, John Skot also printed a few books for Wynkyn de Worde in addition to those he printed on his own account. His press was at first in the parish of St Sepulchre, without

Newgate, and there he printed his first dated book *The Body of Policie* (1521). He later moved to St Paul's churchyard, and is also found printing in Fauster Lane, St Leonard's parish, and at George Alley Gate, in St Botolph's parish. Among the books which he printed was the celebrated ballad of *The Nut Browne Maid*.

Richard Bankes printed for a number of years at the 'longe shoppe' in the Poultry, next to St Mildred's Church, near the old Stocks market on the site of which the present Mansion House was built. We first come across him in 1523 when he issued a curious tract translated 'out of duche into englyshe' and called *A lytell newe treatyse or mater intytuled and called The ix. Drunkardes. . . .*

About 1528 Bankes brought out *The Great Rutter of the Sea*, in the printing of which he was probably associated with Robert Copland who was responsible, as we have already noted, for the translation of this work from the French. The copy he made use of was brought back from Bordeaux by an English merchant, and described the routes and ports connected with the wine trade between France and England.

Bankes also published the first book printed in England with any pretensions to be called a herbal. An anonymous quarto volume dated 1525, the book, generally known as *Bankes' Herbal*, is thought to be an abridgment of some medieval English manuscript on herbs. Its popularity was such that many editions subsequently appeared from different presses, published under a variety of titles.

Between 1539 and 1540 Bankes issued a number of works by the reformer Richard Tavener, and it was probably about this time that he printed *A compendyous olde treatyse shewynge howe that we ought to have the Scripture in Englyshe*, in which his address is given as 'in as gracious strete, besyde the cundyte' (i.e. Gracechurch Street).* Towards the end of 1540 he was in trouble with the authorities as the suspected printer of a number of broadsides directed against Thomas Cromwell, an imputation which he denied. His last publication was a *Book of Cookery* (1545), but the date of his death is not known.

Lawrence Andrewe, who came from Calais, translated several of the books printed at Antwerp by Jan van Doesborch for the English market. Andrewe began to print in London about 1527, and the work for which he is best-known is his own translation of *The vertuose*

---

* Gracious Street was a very common form in the sixteenth and seventeenth centuries (Ekwall: *Street-Names of the City of London*. Oxford, 1954.)

boke of distyllatyon by Hieronymus von Braunschweig. There are two editions, both bearing a date in April 1527, but as they vary considerably, it is likely that the later edition was published with the date unchanged.

Both of these editions are folios, as is Andrewe's reprint of Vincent de Beauvais's *Myrrour of the World* (undated but probably 1527), first issued by Caxton. Many of the original blocks were reprinted, with numerous other illustrations, in Andrewe's edition, including the Vérard block of the author presenting his book which Pynson had previously used in the 1516 edition of Fabyan's *Chronicles*.

Andrewe seems to have been associated in some way with Peter Treveris, for his device (his mark on a shield, surrounded by ornamentation) is found in some copies of the latter's *Grete Herball* of 1529. He worked in Fleet Street, at the sign of the Golden Cross.

Peter Treveris probably came, as his name suggests, from Trier in Germany.* He worked in the borough of Southwark at the sign of the 'Wodows' or savages from about 1520 until around 1533. He printed a number of grammars, his first dated book being an edition of Whittinton's *Syntaxis* issued in 1522, and it is not unlikely that he printed for De Worde many of the grammars which bear the latter's imprint.

The folio *Handy Worke of Surgery* (1525) is one of the first medical works in English to be copiously illustrated with diagrams, and Treveris's ability as a printer is well demonstrated in the 1527 edition of the *Polycronicon*, which he printed for John Reynes. The book by which Treveris is best known is probably the *Grete Herball*, of which he printed two editions, in 1526 and 1529. This was a translation of the French work known as *Le Grant Herbier* with a few borrowings from the *Ortus Sanitatis*. The woodcuts with which the *Grete Herball* is illustrated were copied (rather poorly) from the series which first appeared in the *Herbarius zu Teutsch* printed by Peter Schoeffer at Mainz in 1485.

His device (seemingly copied from that used by Hermann Baumgarten, the Cologne printer) has a shield hanging from a tree and supported by a wild man and woman carrying bows and arrows. The 'wodewose' or wild man appeared in the devices of several early printers on the Continent, including Philippe Pigouchet of Paris, and

---

* It has been suggested, not very convincingly, that the printer may have been of Cornish origin.

Michel de Toulouse. The upright borders framing the device in the *Grete Herball* are found in several books of Wynkyn de Worde, and one of them, broken off to half its length, appears as late as 1560 in an edition of *The Byrth of Mankynde*.

Robert Wyer worked at the sign of St John the Evangelist in the Bishop of Norwich's Rents at Charing Cross, where he seems to have begun printing around 1529. Most of his books were small books on popular subjects, many of them little more than tracts, and for the most part very poorly printed. But, to quote H. S. Bennett, 'that must not blind us to the enterprise and energy he showed in exploiting a hitherto little-worked market in the provision of handy, easily-read, popular guides of various kinds'.[52]

He did occasionally print more important works, such as William Marshall's *Defence of Peace* (folio, 1535) and the *Questionary of Cyrurgyens* printed for Henry Dabbe and R. Bankes. His device shows the Evangelist writing the Book of Revelation on the island of Patmos, with an eagle on his right holding an inkhorn. Below is the name Robert Wyer and a merchant's mark. One state of this device has the name wrongly spelt Wyre. Robert Wyer was one of the first English printers to specialize in cheap books for the uneducated, and he brought out a number of 'do-it-yourself' books containing recipes, particularly in the field of popular medicine, such as *The governauce of good helthe, by the moste excellent phylosopher Plutarche, the most eloquent Erasmus beynge interpretoure.*

Early Illustration of Books in England

The woodcut illustrations used in English books of the fifteenth century are almost devoid of any artistic interest, and in this respect are far inferior to contemporary work in continental Europe. The art of the wood engraver was practically unknown in England before the introduction of printing, and Duff points out that there are not probably more than half a dozen cuts now known, if indeed so many, that are of an earlier date. Indeed, it was not until about 1481 that woodcuts first appeared in an English book, the *Mirrour of the World*, Caxton's version of the *Speculum Historiale* of Vincent de Beauvais. This has two sets of cuts; one consisting of poor diagrams and the other of masters and pupils, as well as one of a woman singing while a man plays a pipe. They are of the utmost crudity. The second edition of Caxton's *The Game and Playe of the Chesse* (the first had no illustrations) has sixteen blocks which, though aping the Netherlands style, are so poorly executed that they were probably cut in Caxton's workshop by an unpractised hand.

Printers working in England at the same time as Caxton were no better equipped for illustrating their works. Lettou and Machlinia not only produced all their books without illustrations, but apparently had neither ornaments nor initials. All we know of as belonging to them is a border used in their *Hours* for Sarum use, which later came into Pynson's hands. The press of the schoolmaster of St Albans employed one or two cuts in the *Chronicles*, and even, in the case of the *Book of St Albans*, anticipated colour printing by making use of coats of arms produced by woodcuts printed with coloured inks. Most of these coats of arms are in single colours; others are in black line with one or two colours from different blocks. When Wynkyn de Worde reprinted this book in 1496 he had the coats of arms newly engraved and coloured by hand.

By and large the early book illustration in England was very poor, especially when compared with the lovely illustrations in the Books of Hours printed in France by Philippe Pigouchet or Jean Du Pré from about 1488 onwards and those of Thielman Kerver around the close of the century. In Germany, also, the standard of woodcut illustration was much higher than in England, for there the art of woodcutting had been practised long before the introduction of printing for playing cards and figures of saints, and the woodcutters had their own flourishing guild. As Pollard points out, one result of the backwardness of England in the pictorial arts at this time was that wood blocks enjoyed an unusually long life in this country before being discarded.[53]

Caxton's contemporary at Oxford, Theodoric Rood, had two series of woodcuts, though neither set was intended for the book in which it eventually appeared. One cut was intended to show Jacobus de Voragine writing the *Golden Legend*, but no copy of that work is known to have been printed at Oxford, and the figure, after all, did equally good service when used to represent William Lyndewood writing his *Opus super constituciones provinciales* (c. 1483). Others of the series appeared in the *Boke that is callid Festivall* by John Mirk (1486), but being too large for the small folio format in which that book appeared they simply had their ends lopped off.

In the matter of ornamental borders and initials, England had nothing to compare with those in use on the Continent, and Caxton's only large initial is the rustic 'A' found in the *Book of the Order of*

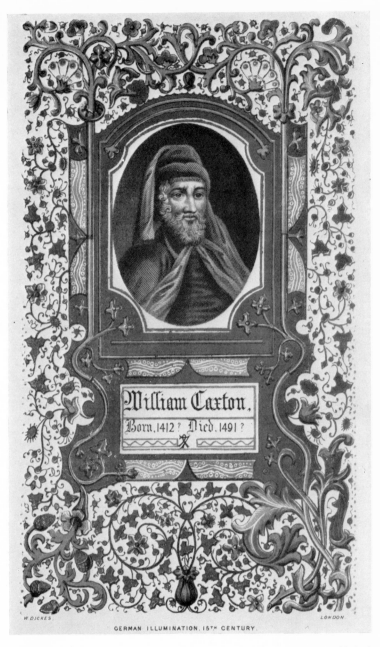

William Caxton,

Born. 1412? Died. 1491?

W. DICKES.

LONDON.

GERMAN ILLUMINATION. 15TH CENTURY.

From the chromo-lithograph frontispiece to *The History of Printing*, published by the S.P.C.K. The artist was William Dickes (1815–92), a well-known engraver and colour printer of Victorian books

If it plese ony man spirituel or temporel to bye ony
ppes of two and thre comemoraciōs of salisburi vse
enpryntid after the forme of this preset lettre whiche
ben wel and truly correct, late hym come to westmo;
nester in to the almonesrye at the reed pale and he shal
haue them good chepe .∴.

Suplico stet cedula

The first printed advertisement in England. Caxton,
before 1480

The Woodcut of the Crucifixion, frontispiece
to the *Fifteen O's and other prayers.* From the
copy in the British Museum, 1490–1

vero continere se vel incontinere se nõ est
simplicias incontinenae sed eius que est p̃
similitudinem vt et is qui arca iram eo
dem modo se habet incontinens nõ est di
cendus. Omnis enim superexcessiua pra
uitas ꝗ amencia ꝗ timiditas ꝗ intemperã
cia ꝗ crudelitas. aut immanitas est aut
morbi. Nam qui talis natura existit vt
cuncta pertimescat-eaam si sorex obstre
pueric-cimidus est timore quodam imma
mi: quidam vero muscipulã timebat prop
ter morbum ꝗ demenaũ qui natura siue
racione sunt ꝗ solum sensu viuentes. ima
nes sunt. vt quedam longe barbare nacõ
nes. Alij propter morbos. veluti mente ca
pti ꝗ insani ex morbo   Sed fieri potest
vt quis interdum aliqua istorum habeat
solum. non superetur veluti si phalaris con
cupiscat puerum comedere. ac se abstineat
vel aduersus irracionabilem coitus libi
dinem. Fieri eaam potest vt non habeat
solum. verum eaam superetur. Vt igitur
prauitas alia simpliciter dicitur-alia secundum
addicionem veluti imanis aut insana: sic
ꝗ incontinencia est-alia immanis. alia in

The Fables of Aesop. William Caxton, 1484

Chastysing of goddes chyldern, printed at Westminster
probably by Wynkyn de Worde shortly after Caxton's death

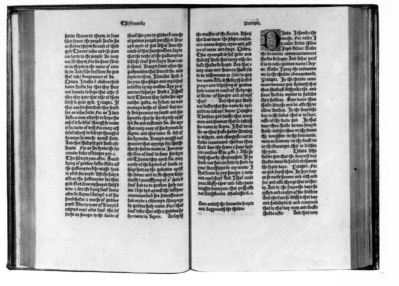

Henry Parker's *Dives and Pauper*. Richard Pynson, 1493

From John Rastell's best-known work, *The pastyme of people*, 1529. It contains 18 full-page cuts of English kings

Chaucer's *Canterbury Tales, etc.*, printed in 1526 by Richard Pynson. This was the first attempt at a collection of Chaucer's writings

The Book of St Albans. Woodcut of an angler. Wynkyn de Worde, Westminster, 1496

Salamon in his parablys sayth that a good spyryte makyth a flourynge aege; that is a fayre aege & a longe. And syth it is soo: I aske this questyon. Whiche ben the meanes & the causes that enduce a man in to a mery spyryte. Truly to my beste dyscrecōn it semeth good dysportes & honest gamys in whom a man Joyeth wythout ony repentaunce after. Thenne folowyth it þ gode dysportes & honest games ben cause of mannys fayr aege & longe life. And therfore now woll I chose of foure good dysportes & honeste gamys: that is to wyte: of huntynge: hawkynge: fysshynge: & foulynge. The beste to my symple dyscrecōn whyche is fysshynge: callyd Anglynge wyth a rodde: and a lyne

Epistola.

Petrus Gryphus:Nuncius apostolicus:Reue-
rédo patri Dño Thome Rontal Regio Secretario
Salutem plurimam.

Xegisti a me tantopere:vt oratione quam
habere instituera coram serenissimo Rege
Herico septimo:intépestiua ipsius morte
præuentam/ad te mitterem. Quod feci tardius ac
cúctatius/quá vehemétiores hortatus tui deposce-
bant.Dubitabá eni/an esset satis cógruens:vt quæ
mors vetuerat/me publice recésere:priuatim nunc
legéda exhiberem/ne ex editione nó recitati sermo
nis specié ambitionis ícurrerem. Accedebat etiam
quod cú in ea oratione cómunibus potius commo
dis & effectui iniúcti mihi muneris/quam priuatæ
vel laudi/vel iactantiæ studuissem:stilus tanq præf
sus demissusq argui posse videbatur.Cú præcipue
gratia et calor ille quem sumit oratio ex actione/ge
stu/voceq dicétis:sicut audiendo accenditur & ani
matur/sic legédo deprimaf et relíquescat:dú nullo
extrisecus actu vel sono/legentiú intétio excitatur.
Sustulisti tamen tua efflagitatione oém exhibendi
verecundiam. Cum videam me & tua auctoritate/
et meo obsequio posse excusari apud eos:qui et di-
cunt & scribút accuratius.Non habitá igif oñonem
ea simplicitate/qua incolumi Regi dicendá propo-
A.ij.

The first book printed in England entirely in roman type—
the *Oratio* of Petrus Gryphus. Richard Pynson, 1509

Boccaccio's *The fall of Princis*, translated by John Lydgate.
Richard Pynson, 1527

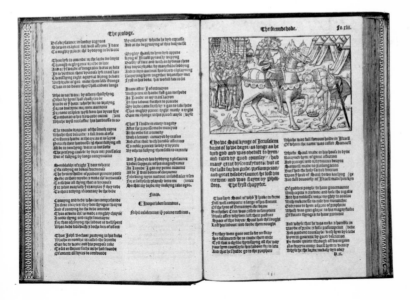

The first booke of Moyses, called in

Hebrue of the first worde of the booke * *Bereschith, and*
in Greke * *Genesis.*

ᴪ The first Chapter.

2 ¶ The earth and the deapthes. 3 Lyght. 6 ¶ The firmament or heauen.
10 ¶ The earth, and the sea. 14 ¶ The sunne, the moone, and the starres.
21 Fisshes. 24 ¶ The beastes of the earth. 26 ¶ The creation of man. 29
God geueth vnto man the power of procreation, and subdueth all
thynges vnto hym. 30 Gods prouision for lyuelode.

1 IN the beginnyng * GOD created ꝑ heauen and the earth.

2 And the earth was without fourme, and was voyde: ｆ darknes [was] vpon the face of the (a) deepe, and the (b) spirite of God moued vpon the face of the waters.

3 And God sayde, let there be light: and there was light.

4 And God sawe the lyght that it was good: and God deuided the lyght from the darknes.

5 And God called the light day, and the darknes night: "and the euenyng ｆ the mornyng were the "first day.

6 And God said: "let there be a "firmament betwene the waters, and let it make a diuision betwene waters and waters.

7 And God made the (c) firmament, and set the diuision betwene the waters which [were] vnder the firmament, and the waters that [were] * aboue (b) the firmament: and it was so.

8 And God called the firmament the heauen: and the euenyng and the mornyng were the seconde day.

9 And God sawe: "let the (c) waters vnder the heauen be gathered together into one place, and let the drye lande appeare: and it was so.

10 And God called the drye lande ꝑ earth, and the gatheryng together of waters called he the seas: and God sawe that it was good.

11 And God sayde: (f) let the earth bryng foorth

The.holie.Bible.

conteynyng the olde
Testament and the newe.

Non me pudet Euangelij Christi.
Virtus enim Dei est ad salutem
Omni credenti Rom. 1.

Facsimile of the frontispiece to *The Bishops' Bible*,
printed by Richard Jugge in 1568

View of the Caslon Foundry, from
The Universal Magazine (June 1750)

Printer's mark of Richard Jugge
engraved by Arnold Nicolai

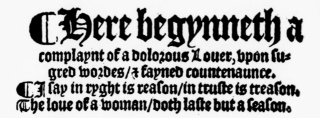

¶ Here begynneth a
complaynt of a dolorous Louer, vpon su=
gred wordes / ✝ fayned countenaunce.
¶ I say in ryght is reason / in truste is treason,
¶ The loue of a woman / doth laste but a season.

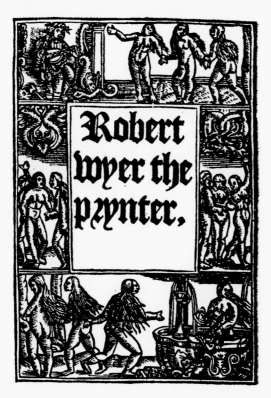

Printed by Robert Wyer about 1540 'at the sygne of saynt John Evangelyst in saynt Martyns parysshe, besyde charynge crosse, in norwytch rents'

Initials from William Cunningham's *The Cosmographicall Glasse*.
John Day, 1559

Chivalry and the *Aesop*. In the book of prayers known as the *Fifteen O's*, Caxton made use of four-piece borders of flowers, birds and beasts, in the style of, but very much inferior to, those used in France by Jean Du Pré. Indeed, it is surprising, when so many excellent foreign-printed service books were on sale in England, that English design was so crude. It was not for want of good models.

Wynkyn de Worde, when he succeeded to Caxton's business, took over a large number of his master's wood blocks and had others cut, probably in his own workshop. Few had any artistic merit. His English edition of Bartholomaeus Anglicus, *De proprietatibus rerum*, has a number of cuts which have been freely adapted in part from Jacob Bellaert's edition (Haarlem, 1485) and partly from one of the Lyons editions printed around 1482. In view of the paucity of blocks available, De Worde, in common with many other printers, used the same cuts again and again, and a single illustration was often made to serve more than once in the same book, irrespective of its subject. Both Wynkyn de Worde and Pynson had a set of narrow upright cuts of men and women with blank labels over their heads into which the name of the character could be inserted, with the result that Cayaphas on one page could be speedily transformed into Joseph on another, as in De Worde's *Nychodemus Gospell* of 1518.

Richard Pynson, on account of his close ties with the Continent, managed to borrow, for the first English edition of the *Kalendrier des Bergiers* printed in this country (the *Kalender of shepherdes*, 1506), most of the blocks used by Antoine Vérard in his 1503 edition. Many of these reappeared in Notary's edition (*c.* 1518), but the edition printed by De Worde in 1508 was illustrated largely with rather poor copies of the Vérard blocks. The unique copy of the Pynson edition in the British Museum is unfortunately imperfect, having 47 cuts out of a probable 75 for a perfect copy.

In very few books did the English woodcutters display any great originality; they were content in the main, since the question of artistic copyright would never have occurred to them, to base their cuts on those already in existence in foreign editions. In Pynson's edition of Brant's *The Shyppe of Fooles* (1509) there are 109 cuts copied from the French version, *La Nef des folz du monde*, printed at Paris in 1497 by De Marnef and Maystener. These, in turn, were copied from the original Basle woodcuts. In the *falle of Princis* (1494), Pynson managed to secure nine cuts from Jean Du Pré's edition of 1483, but

28 of the cuts in his edition of the *Castell of laboure* are very close copies of those in the Pigouchet-Vostre edition of 1499.

In the earliest woodcuts found in English books the figures are reduced to the simplest outlines, and there is a complete absence of cross-hatching, though cross-hatching is found in Germany in the frontispiece to Breydenbach's *Travels*, printed by Erhard Reuwich at Mainz in 1486. But during the first half of the sixteenth century a developing technique led the woodcutters to insert more and more lines, thus creating difficulties for the printer, since clumsy handling of the ink-balls often led to clogged-up lines and smudged impressions. In fact, by the middle of the sixteenth century the woodcut had reached a point where further refinement of line was impossible.

By the end of the century the pictorial woodcut was no longer used for serious works and survived only in chap-books and ballads turned out for the less educated classes. Although copper-plate engravings and etchings were far more expensive to make than wood blocks, they could provide far more detail, and because they were printed separately from the text on special paper they were less liable to suffer from the disabilities of the wood block. In fact, it was not until the end of the eighteenth century, when the graver was found to be capable of use on a wooden block if the surface of the block was at right angles to the grain of the wood, that wood-engraving (as distinct from wood-cutting) became once more a recognized medium for book illustration, until supplanted by the photographic half-tone block.

The Printing of Liturgical Books before the Reformation

For the printer-publisher of the fifteenth century prospective customers were embraced in a few special categories. To all intents and purposes there were no general readers, for the majority of the people were illiterate. Lawyers, doctors, schoolmasters and priests, together with those studying for these professions, were the people for whom the early printers catered, and one of the biggest markets was that of service books for the churches.

Before the religious reforms brought about in the middle of the sixteenth century there was no liturgical unity in England. Although the Roman Rite was in use throughout the land, it was modified or altered in certain respects following the accepted usage of the great cathedral churches. The five chief 'uses' were those of Salisbury (which differed least from the Roman use), York, Hereford, Bangor and Lincoln. Of lesser importance were those of Aberdeen, Abingdon, Croyland and London. Canterbury adopted the Sarum Use which lasted until 1534, and was revived during the few years of Mary's reign.

Of the several liturgical books used in pre-Reformation times the most important was the Missal, or mass-book, which contained all the recited and chanted texts of the Mass. Other service books included the Breviary, the Manual, the Processional, and for churches with choirs the Gradual or 'Grayle' and the Antiphonary. After the Norman Conquest it followed as a matter of course that the liturgy used in England should have much in common, except for certain offices for saints honoured locally, with that of the church at Rouen.

For some time after the introduction of printing into England the craft was carried on by only a small number of printers, who were quite unable to meet the demands of the church for service books, and moreover were not sufficiently advanced technically to undertake this kind of work, which needed both red and black printing. English booksellers and publishers were therefore obliged to call on the printers of the Continent for service books. There was no law at that time preventing the importation of such books.

Paris and Rouen were the main centres of the trade with England in liturgical books. Not only had the French printers greater experience in this form of printing, and far more attractive illustrations, but they could supply the books at a price with which the English printer could not compete, for both the cost of vellum and paper, as well as that of wood-engraving, was far less in France than in England.

Between the years 1492 and 1517 at least eighteen service books for English use were printed by Martin Morin of Rouen, from whose press came some of the most beautiful of the Sarum Missals. Jean Richard, a Rouen bookseller, was agent for the sale of many Rouen-printed books in England, which he seems to have visited from time to time. Rouen was indeed at that period one of the most important centres of printing in France, for it was ideally placed on the Seine either for despatching books to Paris or exporting them to England. There were, also, paper mills in many of the towns and villages of Normandy, at Fervaques, Valognes, Pont-Audemer, Maromme and other places. Duff tells us how, before setting up a press in Edinburgh, Walter Chepman sent Andrew Myllar to Rouen to learn the art of printing and to bring back material.[54]

Frère lists among the service books printed at Rouen for use in England between 1492 and 1556:

> For Salisbury use—15 Missals, 2 Breviaries, 12 Manuals, 5 Processionals, 9 Books of Hours, 17 Primers, 1 Office of the Blessed Virgin Mary, and 1 Hymnal.
> For York—4 Missals, 1 Processional, 1 Book of Hours, and 1 Hymnal.
> For Hereford—1 Missal and 1 Breviary.

The printers included Martin Morin, Pierre Olivier, Pierre Violette, Richard Hamillon, Robert and Florent Valentin, Nicolas Le Roux, and Jean Le Prest—all printers of Rouen.

Missals for Salisbury use were also printed by Michael Wenssler of Basle, Johannes Herzog of Venice, Christopher Ruremond of Antwerp and Francis Regnault, Wolfgang Hopyl, Jean Du Pré, and Berthold Rembolt of Paris.[55]

John Growte, or Groyat, a London stationer who came from Normandy, imported many service books printed in Paris by Thielman Kerver and later by his widow, Yolande Bonhomme. A Primer in English and Latin for Sarum use which he issued in 1533 bears the quaint title: *Thys prymer off salysburye use is sett owght along wythowght ony serchyng, wyth many prayers and goodly pyctures yn the kalender, yn the matyns off owr lady, yn the houres off the crosse, yn the VII psalmes, & in the dyryge, wyth the XV oos yn ynglysh & the cfessionall & Jesus psalter.*

CHAPTER THREE

From Berthelet to Barker

Thomas Berthelet

Like so many of the early printers in this country, Thomas Berthelet was of French descent, though it is usual to give his name the anglicized pronunciation of 'Bartlett'. Little is known of his early career, and the earliest work so far known to have been printed by Berthelet is a small tract by Brother Galfredus Petrus, a friar of Bayeux, called *Opus sane de deorum dearumque* . . . printed at the sign of the Roman Lucrece, near the Conduit in Fleet Street, and dated 27 September, 1524.*[56] Berthelet worked in the same premises during the whole of his active career, which lasted until about 1549.

He is said to have been apprenticed to Pynson, and Gordon Duff has sought to identify him with one Thomas Bercula who speaks of himself as the printer in some books issued by Pynson. But Pynson makes no mention of Berthelet in his will and the connection is no more than tentative, though his having worked for that printer is very possible. At any rate, on 2 February, 1529–30, Berthelet received the royal patent as King's Printer in succession to Pynson, a post he retained until Grafton's appointment in 1547. In this capacity he printed a large number of proclamations, of which many survive, though probably only a small proportion of the number he actually printed.

He was a busy printer for a quarter of a century and seems to have retired from active control of the business in 1548, when it was carried on from the same address by his nephew, Thomas Powell. W. W. Greg distinguished from thirty to forty different types used by Berthelet during his career, although some were only used occasionally and were evidently not complete founts.[57] Types used for the body-text of the works he printed number fifteen, and among

* This was the year in which he married Agnes Langwyth (London Marriage Licences, page 4). His coat of arms shows his French descent.

them some were probably Pynson's, recast. Some of his types came from Cologne and, according to Reed-Johnson, his 73 roman and 95 italic are to be found in the books of E. Cervicorn and the 109 roman in those of J. Soter. The rotunda has not been traced, but resembles Cologne models.[58]

Berthelet used at least thirteen borders, one of which, in use for a number of years, provides a trap for unwary bibliographers by having the date 1534 engraved upon it. A border first used in 1543 for the *Necessary Doctrine and Erudition for any Christen Man* may have been a metal-cut, for neither cracks nor worm-holes had appeared in it as late as 1567.

In 1531 Berthelet printed Sir Thomas Elyot's *Boke named the Governour*, a treatise on education and politics which he reprinted several times and which remained a popular book throughout the sixteenth century. He also printed other works by the same author, including the *Castel of helth* (1539) and his large *Dictionary*, which appeared in 1538.

One of the best books of his early period is Gower's *Confessio Amantis* (1532) printed in double column, 48 lines to the page, in a well-cut rotunda, with notes in bastarda and roman and running heads in roman capitals, a somewhat novel proceeding at that time, when roman was hardly ever used for display. The title-page is after a design by Geoffrey Tory.

Berthelet printed in 1540 the first complete edition of William Lily's Latin grammar—*Institutio compendiaria totius grammaticae*—which became the standard Latin grammar used by St Paul's, Eton and most of the public schools until well into the nineteenth century. This edition is said to have been produced for the young Prince Edward, for which reason it is sometimes called 'King Edward's Grammar'. The British Museum has a copy printed on vellum.

A notable work of Berthelet's was *The Institution of a Christian Man*, a treatise on various articles of religious belief, compiled by the bishops and issued under the King's authority. It was printed in both quarto and octavo form, and the former is a very handsome book with a title-page surrounded by a woodcut border of children (McKerrow 81). Latimer had tried to persuade Cromwell to have the book printed by Thomas Gibson, but without success. This is not surprising, since a book of that nature, issued under royal auspices, was undoubtedly a prerogative of the King's Printer.

In 1544, in return for £212.10s.0d. paid into the King's Treasury,

Berthelet was granted certain property in perpetuity: a house in St Bride's parish called 'Salisbury Place', several houses in Friday Street and Distaff Lane, and two dwellings in Fleet Street, all of which had been previously owned by religious houses. On the accession of Edward VI, Berthelet was replaced as King's Printer by Richard Grafton, and during the ensuing years he was less active. Many books still came from his printing house with the imprint *in aedibus Thomae Bertheleti*, but most of them were probably the work of his nephew and successor, Thomas Powell, who became a freeman of the Stationers' Company in 1556, the year following his uncle's death. The funeral of Thomas Berthelet is quaintly described by Henry Machyn in his *Diary*:

> The sam day [26 Sept. 1555] was bered master Barthelett sqwyer and prynter unto King Henry; and was bered with pennon and cote-armur and iiij dozen of skochyons and ij whytt branchys and iiij gylt candyll-stykes, and mony prestes and clarkes, and mony mornars, and all the craftes of prynters, boke-sellers and all stassyoners.[59]

Until recently it was thought that Berthelet was also bookbinder to the King, but H. M. Nixon inclines to the view that the bound books which he supplied to Henry VIII were by various unidentified binders. Later occupants of the Roman Lucrece were Henry Wykes and Ralph Newbery.

John Byddell

John Byddell, printer and bookseller, was for some time an assistant to Wynkyn de Worde, of whose will he was one of the executors. He set up as a stationer and at first had books printed for him by others, including his old master. His shop by Fleet Bridge bore the sign of Our Lady of Pity, and for some reason he called himself John Salisbury; perhaps because he was a native of that town. But after the death of De Worde he moved to that printer's premises, the Sun in Fleet Street.

In 1534 he published the first edition of William Marshall's *Primer*, which contained portions of the Bible in English; a sign that the restrictions imposed by Archbishop Arundel's 'Constitutions of Clarendon' (1408), which forbade the translation into the English tongue of any text of Holy Scripture, were coming to an end. Most of Byddell's books were of a theological nature. He printed a Sarum

Hours in 1535 and in 1539 a folio edition of Richard Taverner's Bible for Thomas Berthelet. In 1538 he issued the *Injunctions* formulated by the Bishop of Salisbury regarding the use of the Primer in church.

Among the books of a miscellaneous nature published by Byddell is the earliest botanical work of William Turner, the 'Father of English Botany'—a small quarto treatise called *Libellus de re herbaria novus* (1538). Altogether he issued some fifty or more books until his death, which probably took place in 1545, since his last dated book was published in November, 1544. He used several devices in his books, the largest of which seems to have been a copy of the device of Jean Sacon (Zacchoni), who had in turn copied his from a design in the *Historia di Milano* of Bernardino Corio (1503).

Grafton and Whitchurch: Early Printing of the English Bible

Until the art of printing had come into being the Holy Scriptures could only be made generally known by the slow process of manuscripts. Among the Biblical manuscripts in the British Museum are those of the four Gospels in what is known as the 'Wessex' version, and this is the earliest English version known, apart from interlinear glosses on Latin manuscripts, such as that which can be seen in the famous Lindisfarne Gospels. From the time of the Conquest until the fourteenth century we come across no further translations, save for some verse renderings, of any part of the Bible directly into English, probably because during that period the language of the educated classes was Norman-French.

The first translation of the Bible as a whole into English was made by the followers of John Wyclif around the years 1380–3. The main defect of the Wyclif version was that it was a translation of a translation. For a direct translation from the original Hebrew and Greek England had to wait for a further century and a half. Although before the end of the fifteenth century Bibles had been printed in German, Italian, Dutch, French, Danish, Russian, Bohemian and Spanish, England was still without a printed Bible in the tongue of the people. Caxton never printed any version of the Wyclif Bible, nor could he have done so, for in 1408 the Convocation of Oxford, presided over by Archbishop Arundel, had decreed that no man henceforward should

> by his own authority translate any text of the Scripture into English or any other tongue, by way of a book, pamphlet, or treatise; and that no man read any such book, pamphlet, or treatise, now lately composed in the time of John Wyclif or since, or hereafter to be set forth. . . .

In 1414 a further law was enacted that all persons found reading the Scriptures in the mother tongue should 'forfeit land, catel, lif, and goods from their heyres for ever'.

It was because the dissemination of the Scriptures in English was prohibited by the ecclesiastical authorities that Tyndale was obliged to take refuge in Germany to complete his translation of the New Testament, the first to be printed in the English language, which was issued by Peter Schoeffer at Worms in 1525 or 1526. Tyndale met a martyr's death in 1536 before he had translated the whole Bible, which he certainly would have done had he lived. The completion of the English Bible was due to Miles Coverdale, and this first English Bible ever to be printed was published in 1535. Even today it is not known for certain where or by whom it was printed, but from the evidence of its types most authorities consider it was printed at Cologne by Cervicorn and Soter. L. A. Sheppard, however, considers the book to have been printed by the same printers at Marburg, on the grounds that it would have been a safer place for printing the Bible in English owing to Lutheran control of that city.[60]

This Coverdale Bible was reprinted in 1537, ostensibly by James Nicolson of Southwark, a native of the Low Countries, who had a printing office in St Thomas's Hospital, but actually Nicolson only imported the sheets of the edition, which he purchased from Jacob van Meteren, the Antwerp merchant who had subsidized Coverdale's Bible.

On 4 August, 1537, Cranmer wrote to Thomas Cromwell, commending a new Bible, a copy of which he sent with his letter, and asking Cromwell to use his influence with the king to obtain

> a license that the same may be sold and redde of every person withoute danger of any acte, proclamacion or ordinaunce heretofore graunted to the contrary, untill such tyme that we the Bishops shall set forth a better translation, which I thinke will not be till a day after Domesday.

Cromwell acted swiftly and successfully. The king gave his sanction for the book to be bought and read in England. Since it had been printed abroad it could only, like Nicolson's Coverdale Bible, be sold complete in sheets to some English printer, and in this case the expense was borne by Richard Grafton (a member of the Grocers' Company) and Edward Whitchurch (member of the Haberdashers' Company) who were interested in the printing of the Bible in English, and eventually became printers and publishers, more by chance than design.

The text of this Bible was made up of the work of Tyndale and Coverdale, edited by Tyndale's disciple, John Rogers, who, in order to avoid putting the proscribed name of Tyndale on the title-page, issued the joint translation under the fictitious name of Thomas Matthew—a name suggested, perhaps, by the printer of the *Matthew Bible*, Matthew Crom of Antwerp.[61]

Now a folio Bible is an expensive book to produce, and Grafton told Cromwell that since the impression of 1,500 copies had cost him more than £500 (a sum we can multiply twenty-fold for present-day values) it was only just that he should be granted a privilege from the king forbidding any other man to reprint this Bible until he had sold all his copies, which he thought would take three years at least. To provide a market he asked Cromwell to order every curate to have one copy, and every monastery six. For, as J. F. Mozley writes: 'The publisher of scripture, particularly of a complete bible, in those days gave heavy hostages to fortune. Enemies stood on every side; the greater part of his edition may be destroyed without compensation; a speedy sale was of high importance.'[62]

Despite the fact that this translation was largely Tyndale's work, the royal licence was forthcoming and an injunction ordered the monasteries to have 'a whole bible in English to be laid fast chained in some open place either in that church or cloister'. But although Rogers had toned down a number of Tyndale's references to the Church of Rome, enough still remained to give offence in certain quarters. Cromwell therefore decided to replace the *Matthew Bible* by a new version without any polemical annotations, and Coverdale was entrusted with the revised translation. Grafton and Whitchurch were once more employed as the publishers, owing to their experience with the *Matthew Bible*, and also because both were merchants of standing who were probably better able to bear the enormous cost of financing the printing of a Bible than were Berthelet or Nicolson.

As at that date the Paris printers were better equipped technically to produce a sumptuous Bible, Cromwell decided to have the *Great Bible*, as it came to be called, printed in the French capital by François Regnault, who for some time had been printing service books for the English market. A licence was granted by the French king to Grafton and Whitchurch, allowing them to print the Bible with any printer in France and transport it to England. From May to September, 1538, all went well, but by October the English ambassador in Paris foresaw trouble, and on 17 December the Inquisitor-General for France seized the sheets that had been printed and Grafton and Coverdale hurried back to England. It was only after the French ambassador (Bonner) had made repeated efforts to have the sheets that were already printed handed over that the French authorities suggested that the type, printers and paper should be transported to England and the printing done there, but they declared that since the English Bible contained heretical matter there was no question of them returning the confiscated sheets.

Nevertheless, Grafton managed to trace some printed sheets, which had been bought by a haberdasher as waste paper, and brought four barrel-loads of them back to England; the remainder had been burnt. The hint dropped by the French authorities was taken, presses and workmen were brought from Paris, and Grafton and Whitchurch, in the words of John Foxe, 'became printers themselves (which before they never intended) and printed out the said Bible in London'.

By April, 1539, the *Great Bible*, so called because it was 'of the largest volume', suitable for placing in churches, was finished, and Cromwell, as Vicar-General, ordered that every incumbent should have a copy, the cost to be shared by the pastor and parishioners. Despite the expenses they had incurred, Grafton and Whitchurch were well rewarded, for by December, 1541, they had printed seven editions of the *Great Bible*, of which they had the sole publishing rights. The only other Cranmer Bible to appear during that time was one printed by Petit and Redman in 1540 for Berthelet, but this was poorly printed in comparison.

The second and subsequent editions of the *Great Bible* were often known as Cranmer's Bible, owing to the fact that they contain a preface by the Archbishop. But from 1542 onwards the Scripture in English was once more under a cloud. Gardiner's party was in the ascendancy, Cromwell had been executed in July, 1540, and Coverdale fled abroad for the second time. In 1543 the common folk of the land were forbidden to read the Bible in private, and it was not until the reign of Edward VI that the *Great Bible* was again reprinted. There were four further editions in folio and six in quarto, until it was finally superseded by the *Bishops' Bible* of 1568.

In the year 1560 there came from the press of Rowland Hall at Geneva a version of the English Bible produced in that city by the Marian exiles. This quarto Bible, the first English Bible to be printed in roman type, was never authorized for use in churches, the controversial notes giving offence to some of the bishops; but its importation was not forbidden, and after Archbishop Parker's death in 1575, the

Geneva version was printed in London. Although the *Bishops' Bible* of 1568 became the version used in churches, the Geneva version was the Bible read in the home, and by 1644 no fewer than 140 editions had appeared. It is sometimes called the 'Breeches Bible', from its translation of *Genesis*, iii. 7. An account of the printing of the *Bishops' Bible* is given on pages 71-2. Richard Grafton, son of Nicholas Grafton of Shrewsbury, as we have seen, entered the printing trade almost by accident, but his name, and that of Edward Whitchurch, will be for ever associated with the history of the English Bible.

After the loss of their patron, Thomas Cromwell, Grafton and his partner felt the need of some safeguard, seeing that the printing of an English Bible was hedged around with so many difficulties, and on the title-page of the *Great Bible* published in November, 1540, they announced that it was 'oversene and perused' by Cuthbert Tunstall, Bishop of Durham, and Nicholas Heath, Bishop of Rochester.

On returning to England from Paris, Whitchurch printed for a time in partnership with Grafton, who set up his press in the recently surrendered house of the Grey Friars, and in 1541 they obtained a joint exclusive privilege for printing service books; a little while later they were granted a privilege for printing Primers in Latin and English. Among the service books which they printed was the Breviary of Salisbury use, which continued to be employed in churches until the Book of Common Prayer appeared during Edward VI's short reign.

In 1545, in accordance with a ruling of Henry VIII enjoining uniformity of contents of the Primer, Grafton printed *The Primer in Englishe and Latyn, set foorth by the Kynges maiestie and his Clergie*, of which a new edition was published in 1547, the year of Edward VI's accession. This edition was in quarto, and in 1549 Grafton published an identical text in octavo, the same year in which he and Whitchurch printed the first Edwardine Book of Common Prayer, which, although it replaced the whole range of Sarum liturgies, did not affect the Primer.

Several issues of the First Prayer Book were printed in 1549, some bearing the name of Grafton and some that of Whitchurch, for in 1547 the new king had renewed their licence to print service books in English or Latin (two issues were also printed by John Oswen at Worcester). The maximum price of the book was fixed at two shillings a copy unbound and at 3s 4d a copy bound 'in paste or in boordes'. In 1550 Grafton printed *The booke of Common praier noted*, containing 'so muche of the Order of Common prayer as is to be sung in

Churches', with the exception of the Litany. This is John Merbecke's simple musical setting devised to supply a chant for the new services less ornate in character than the chant used in the Latin Sarum rites.

On the accession of Edward VI, Grafton had been appointed King's Printer in place of Berthelet, and this gave him the sole right to print all Acts and Statutes. He held the appointment only for six years, for on the King's death he foolishly printed a proclamation of the accession of Lady Jane Grey, in which he signed himself 'Printer to the Queen'. For this indiscretion he forfeited his office, which Queen Mary gave to John Cawood. After that he did no more printing. It was not the first time he had been in trouble with the authorities, for in 1541 he was committed to the Fleet for printing a 'sedicious epistle of Melanctons', and was also accused by the Privy Council of printing ballads defending the late Thomas Cromwell. In April, 1543, he and seven other printers, among them Whitchurch, were sent to prison 'for printing such books as were thought to be unlawful'. In Grafton's case it was for having printed the *Great Bible*; he could not escape the consequences of his patron's fall from favour and subsequent execution. Foxe tells us that he spent six weeks in prison and was bound in £300 neither to sell nor to print or cause to be printed any more Bibles, until the King and clergy should agree upon a translation.*

Grafton died in 1573, leaving four sons and one daughter, Joan, who married the printer Richard Tottel (see page 73). Grafton's punning device was a tree bearing grafts issuing from a tun or barrel of the kind in which books were packed for transport. On the barrel is Grafton's merchant's mark.

Whitchurch, after the death of Byddell in 1545, moved into that printer's premises, De Worde's old printing office, the Sun in Fleet Street. There he printed a number of books, including the *Paraphrases of Erasmus*. As a reformer he was in disgrace during Mary's reign and ceased to print until her death. He had been a friend of the martyr John Rogers, and on more than one occasion had stood surety for him. Needless to say there were no English Bibles or Books of Common Prayer licensed during Mary's reign.

One of the printers arrested with Grafton and Whitchurch in April, 1543, was Richard Kele, who was also sent to prison for printing unlawful books, but was released after a fortnight on the payment of

---

* In 1542 it was pronounced by Convocation that the *Great Bible* must not be read in church. A year later all private reading of the English Bible was forbidden.

a fine and the surrendering of whatever books and ballads he had bought and sold during the preceding three years. Kele printed at first in the 'long shop in the Poultry' where Richard Bankes had worked, and later moved to the Eagle in Lombard Street. According to Plomer most of the books that bear his name were printed for him by William Seres, Robert Wyer and William Copland (probably the son of Robert). He shared in an edition of Chaucer with Robert Toy and William Bonham, and issued some of John Skelton's poems, including *The Boke of Phyllip Sparowe*, *Colin Clout*, and that devastating indictment of Wolsey called *Why come ye not to Courte?* Although these were the works of a Poet Laureate they were all poorly printed with execrable woodcuts. Kele died in 1552; he had a younger brother, John Kele, who became a printer and member of the Stationers' Company. Thomas Kele, a stationer who at one time occupied the Mermaid as tenant of John Rastell, may have been their father.

Richard Jugge and John Cawood

It is convenient to deal with Jugge and Cawood together since for nearly fourteen years they were associated as royal printers. Of their lives little is known, but their work can be studied in our national libraries. The S.T.C.* has 112 entries for Cawood and 153 for Jugge, and in addition they were jointly responsible for a further 204 entries. This seems a large output, but 223 of these items were proclamations, usually a single sheet folio. The number would be larger but for the fact that many of the proclamations listed by Steele have not been found in their printed form. When we also take into account the large number of Bibles, New Testaments and Prayer Books which they printed, the number of general works which came from their presses is not very large, and cannot be compared with the generous variety of work turned out by their contemporary, John Day. Nevertheless, both were good printers and have many important books to their credit.

John Cawood (1514–72) came of an old Yorkshire family of some substance and was apprenticed to John Reynes, 'stacyoner and denysen' of London, who is best known as a bookbinder and who died in 1543 or 1544. Reynes's widow, Lucy, left a legacy to Cawood's daughter, and when in later years Cawood became a prosperous

---

* Short Title Catalogue, listing books printed in England, Scotland and Ireland, and English books printed abroad 1475–1640. The compilers were A. W. Pollard and G. R. Redgrave.

member of the Stationers' Company he had a memorial window to his former master placed in their Hall.

The first known work of Cawood according to Plomer and others is *The Decree for tythes to be payed in London*, 1546. They probably omitted to study the colophon, which reads: 'Imprynted at London in Powles Churchyarde by John Cawood, Printer to the Quenes Maiestye.' In 1546 Henry VIII was still on the throne, and Cawood was not appointed Royal Printer by Queen Mary until 1553. Actually this small octavo is a reprint of a decree first published in 1546, in folio, by Thomas Berthelet.

In 1553, then, Cawood replaced Richard Grafton as Royal Printer, the latter having forfeited the post by printing the proclamation declaring Jane, wife of Guilford Dudley, to be Queen of England. For his official salary of £6.13s.4d. per annum, Cawood was directed to print all 'statute books, acts, proclamations, injunctions, and other volumes and things, under what name or title soever' in English, with the profit appertaining. He was also granted the reversion of Reyner Wolfe's patent, authorized in 1547, for printing Latin, Greek and Hebrew books, for which he was to receive an additional 16s.8d. per annum 'and all other profits and advantages thereto belonging'. He never enjoyed this reversion, for he died a year before Wolfe, and in any case Wolfe's patents were renewed when Elizabeth I came to the throne.

The first Proclamation printed by Cawood was that 'against seditious rumours', 28 July, 1553 (S.T.C. 7848. Steele 425). Upon his appointment as Queen's Printer, Cawood was licensed to 'take workmen of the art or mistery of printing to work at his appointment', and was given a writ of aid, addressed to mayors, sheriffs, bailiffs, constables and other officers, enabling him to take up, during one year, 'as many prynters, composytours and founders as well householders as prentyces and jornymen as others' for his work, and also 'paper, ynke, presses and matrices', which he was to pay for immediately at a reasonable rate. (At that time the Master of the Mint was furnished with a similar licence to impress workers and given a like writ of aid.)

Although he printed 'Protestant books under Edward VI, Catholic books under Mary, and again Protestant books under Elizabeth', Cawood seems to have been a Catholic, for when Queen Mary refounded the Guild of Jesus and in July, 1556, granted the fraternity the use of the chapel called the Crowdes, under the Choir and east end of Old St Paul's, Cawood was appointed one of the wardens.

In 1553 Cawood seems to have acquired a certain amount of printing material from Steven Mierdman (see page 79), who on the accession of Mary had been obliged to leave England and finally settled at Emden. In that year a number of books printed by Cawood contain initials formerly used by the Netherlands printer. John Harpsfield's *Concio quaedam admodum elegans....* (1553), a small octavo of 27 leaves, published by Cawood, contains a number of initial letters found in Mierdman's books. In fact the book bears so many marks of Mierdman's work that it might even have been printed by him before he left England. Mierdman's initials also appear in at least four other books published by Cawood during 1553.

In 1555 appeared a book called *A supplicacyon to the quenes maiestie*, with the colophon 'Impryntid at London by John Cawoode Prynter tho [sic] the quenes Mayestie wyth here most gracyns [sic] lycence'. As Ames remarked, 'it cannot rationally be supposed to be his, being such a stinging satyr on the clergy and obliquely on the queen herself'.[63] Isaac* says it was printed abroad by the printer of S.T.C. 24246, *A treatise of Cohabitacyon of the faithfull with the unfaithfull*. The false imprint did not deceive Miles Huggard, who in his *Displaying of the Protestants*, 1566, wrote: 'Your fine fetches in putting the names of maister Cawode, the quenes printer, and others (who with harte detesteth your doynges) to your beggarly libelles as to bee imprinter thereof, every man nowe espieth.'

In 1555 Cawood printed the *Homelies* of Edmund Bonner, Bishop of London, in which thirteen pictorial initials are used which for long were attributed to an artist named Anton Silvius, whose name was born of a blunder, long perpetuated, by J. M. Papillon. In fact they were the work of an Antwerp engraver named Arnold Nicolai who in the course of a long career worked for a number of Antwerp printers, including Christopher Plantin. One or two of the initials, comprising an alphabet which Charles Sayle says 'in some ways takes the first place in all English typography' were previously used by Berthelet in certain of his proclamations, and they were so popular that some of them were still being used as late as 1642.[64]

Upon the incorporation of the Stationers' Company in May, 1557, Cawood was one of the Wardens (Henry Cooke being the other), and he became Master in 1561, 1562 and 1566. During his

---

* Frank Isaac, author of two important works on printing types: *English and Scottish Printing Types 1501–35, 1508–41*. 1930; and *English and Scottish Printing Types 1535–58, 1552–58*. 1932.

lifetime Cawood was a great benefactor to the Company, though unfortunately his gifts, including the 'ii new glasse wyndowes in their hall, the one for John Reynes, his master, and the other for hymselfe' perished in the Great Fire.

As Queen's Printer to Mary, Cawood was responsible for printing the proclamations and acts published during her reign, but on the accession of Elizabeth I, the proclamation of 17 November, 1558, to that effect was printed by Richard Jugge (S.T.C. 7886. Steele 493), who subsequently printed several others and was termed in a letter from the Privy Council dated 20 December, 1558, 'the Quenes Majesties Prynter'. On 25 January, 1559, Cawood's name was conjoined with Jugge's in the printing of *An Acte whereby certayne offences be made Treason* (Steele 499), and from that time they continued jointly to print the State papers, a royal patent being issued granting

> for life in survivorship . . . to Richard Jugge and John Cawood, the queen's servants, of the office of printers of all statute books, libels of acts of Parliament, proclamations, injunctions, and service books and other volumes printed by authority of Parliament, in English, or English and another tongue mixed (except Latin grammars). . . .

Jugge was made the senior and his name always appears first on their joint publications.

Richard Jugge is thought to have been born at Waterbeach, in Cambridgeshire. He was educated at Eton and King's College, Cambridge, to whose library he bequeathed many books. On 4 October, 1541, he was admitted a freeman of the Stationers' Company, and his first business address was the sign of the Bible near the north door of St Paul's. According to some writers he began printing about 1545, but it is more likely that for the first half-dozen years of his career he was a bookseller, the books bearing his imprint having been printed for him by others, principally by Steven Mierdman, the prolific printer of Reformation books. For Jugge, as Timperley informs us, 'was zealous for the success of that great work' (i.e. the Reformation). Even the early New Testaments attributed to Jugge are really specimens of Antwerp printing.[65]

It is not until 1551, after he had received royal licence as 'citizen and stationer of London' to print the New Testament in English, that we come across the type of book generally associated with Jugge the printer, and exemplified in his quarto New Testaments and folio Bibles, printed in large black-letter and enlivened with large and frequently handsome pictorial initials which he was apt to use some-what indiscriminately. That the earlier books have colophons with his name as printer may mean little more than an attempt to circum-vent the law against the importation of foreign books.

It was on 15 January, 1551, that Jugge was granted a licence (Pat. 4 Ed. VI. m. 11) to print the New Testament in English, 'this privilege being granted', the licence runs, 'because printing by strangers has led to errors of translation as well as in the words and orthography, is to last eight years, during which no other subject may print the New Testament in English'.

Although undated, the earliest of Jugge's illustrated quarto editions of Tyndale's version of the New Testament (Fry No. 29) was presum-ably printed in 1552. On the verso of the title-page in some copies is printed 'The copy of the byll assigned by the Kynges honorable counsell for the Auctorisinge of this Testamente' dated Greenwich, 10 June, 1552. The price was fixed at not more than 'twenty and two pens for every boke in papers and unbounde'.

This Testament was a credit to the printer, handsomely printed and illustrated with 86 competently executed woodcuts, probably of Flemish origin. The woodcuts of the four Evangelists are those which had appeared in the Coverdale Bible of 1535. Jugge published many editions of the New Testament, and his octavo edition of 1553 was probably the last to be published during the reign of Edward VI, for although during that king's short reign some forty editions of the Bible and New Testament were published in English, Mary's reign saw only one—the New Testament of 1557, and that was translated by an exile, William Whittingham, and printed by Conrad Badius at Geneva.

Shortly after the accession of Elizabeth I, the Act of Uniformity, passed on 28 April, 1559, authorized once more the use of the Second Prayer Book of Edward VI, which, with certain slight alterations—notably the abrogation of the rubric of 1552 regulating the vestments of the clergy—became the official prayer book in use throughout the Queen's reign.

Between 1559 and 1571 Jugge and Cawood jointly printed thirteen editions of the Book of Common Prayer, and after Cawood's death in 1572 Jugge printed a further six editions on his own account. The folio Prayer Book of 1564 is a rich repository of Jugge's decorated initials, for this edition contains no fewer than 398—65 more than in Grafton's folio Prayer Book of 1552.

The highlight of Jugge's career as a printer was his printing of the so-called *Bishops' Bible*. The *Geneva Bible*, printed in that city by Rowland Hall in 1560,* became so popular in England that it threatened to oust the *Great Bible* sponsored by Thomas Cromwell. However, Convocation could not accept what we might term this 'left-wing' Bible, with its Calvinistic annotations, as an authorized version licensed by the Queen. Political considerations, apart from other motives, made it plainly impossible. Consequently Matthew Parker, Archbishop of Canterbury since 1558, planned a revision of the *Great Bible*, and appointed a panel of translators from among the bishops 'to peruse and collate', as Strype says, 'each the book or books allotted to him'.[66]

As senior Queen's Printer, Richard Jugge was entrusted with the printing of the new Bible, which was finished in the autumn of 1568, and on 5 October a bound copy was presented to the Queen. In a letter to the principal Secretary, Sir William Cecil, Parker wrote:

> The Printer hath honestlie done his diligence, yf your honor wold obtaeine of the Queens highnes, that the edicion might be Licensed and only comended in publike reading in Churches, to draae to one uniformitie, yt weare no greate cost to the most parishes and a Relief to him for his great charges susteined . . . Sir, I pray your honor be a means that Jug only may have the preferment of this edicion, for yf any other shuld Lurche him to steale from him thes copies [i.e. 'copyrights'] he weare a great Loser in this first doing. And Sir without doubt he hath well deserved to be preferred. A man wold not thinke that he had devoured so much payne as he hath susteined.[67]

As long as he lived Parker kept the *Geneva Bible* from being printed in England and secured the monopoly of the new Bible for its printer, Richard Jugge.

The first edition of the *Bishops' Bible* was a handsome folio, illustrated with engravings, woodcuts and maps to the total of 143. On the first title is a half-length engraved portrait of Elizabeth which, though it bears no signature, is generally attributed to Franciscus Hogenberg, one of the many foreign craftsmen in the employ of Archbishop Parker. The illustrations are copies of the wood engravings originally drawn by Virgil Solis for the folio Lutheran Bible published at Frankfurt in 1560 by David Zöpfel, Johann Rasch and Sigmund Feyerabend. The blocks seem to have been borrowed for this first edition of the

---

* This Bible was translated by Whittingham, with the assistance of Anthony Gilbey, Thomas Sampson and other English exiles in Geneva.

Bishops' Bible, for they do not appear in subsequent editions. The second folio edition, of 1572, to compensate for this lack of illustration, makes a profuse display of decorated initials, of which there are no fewer than 114. One, at least, was not happily chosen, for when this handsome initial, beginning the Epistle to the Hebrews, was found to represent Leda and the Swan, such incongruity was severely censured.

The *Bishops' Bible* displaced Cromwell's *Great Bible*, no edition of which was printed after 1569, but it was an unsatisfactory translation and held its place until the coming of the Authorized Version of 1611 solely because it was the only version recognized by Convocation, which in 1571 ordered that 'every archbishop and bishop should have at his house a copy of the Holy Bible of the largest volume as lately printed in London, and that it should be placed in the hall or large dining-room, that it might be useful to servants or to strangers'. Jugge was no doubt thankful for this high episcopal sanction which enabled him to recoup himself for the great expenses he had incurred in printing what was 'in typography and illustration perhaps the most sumptuous in the long series of folio English Bibles'.[68]

As Christopher Barker remarked ten years later: 'The whole Bible together requireth so great a sum of money to be employed in the printing thereof, as Mr Jugge kept the Realme twelve yere withoute before he durste adventure to print one impression.' But there was another reason for this delay, apart from the expense (which Grafton had already noted) of printing a Bible. It is true that the Queen's Printers produced no Bible between 1560, when Cawood printed a quarto edition of the *Great Bible*, and the publication of the *Bishops' Bible* in 1568, but the reason is this: on 8 January, 1561, a licence for seven years was granted to John Bodley (father of Sir Thomas) to print the very popular Genevan version of the Bible, provided it was done under episcopal supervision. Although the licence was later recommended for an extension, Bodley never made use of it, possibly because, having been associated in Geneva with Whittingham and the others responsible for this version, he found the supervisory conditions unacceptable.

Jugge could not, therefore, print this version, and as Richard Harrison had produced a quarto volume of the *Great Bible* in 1562, there was little Jugge could do in the way of Bible printing until the copy for the *Bishops' Bible* was ready.

Although Jugge's work, in his later years, was almost exclusively confined to the printing of Bibles, Prayer Books, Homilies, Injunctions, Proclamations, and all the official work that fell to the lot of a royal printer, he issued one celebrated medical work, *The birth of mankynde, otherwyse named the womans booke*, by the physician Thomas Raynalde. This was the first book on obstetrics in English, and was first printed in 1540 by Thomas Raynald, thus arousing conjecture as to whether printer and physician were one and the same man. Jugge issued two editions of this work, which contains small copper engravings, in 1565.

Cawood died in 1572, and his second son, Gabriel, was a stationer who was admitted to the Livery of the Stationers' Company in 1578, and twice became Master. The books he published, which included John Lily's *Euphues. The Anatomy of Wit* . . . , seem to have all been printed for him.

At Cawood's death the royal patent remained with Jugge, as the survivor. Alone, and in advancing years, he found that the official work he had to do by virtue of his patent was more than he could cope with, and the rate of printing of Bibles grew so unsatisfactory that pressure was put on Jugge to share his Bible privilege with others. In 1575, after an acrimonious discussion with the members of the Stationers' Company, of which he was Master at the time, Jugge was officially instructed by the Queen's High Commissioners to limit himself to printing the Bible in quarto and the Testament in 16mo. All other Bibles and Testaments were 'to be at the liberty of the printinge of the rest of the Stationers'. Jugge had now no patron to speak on his behalf, for Archbishop Parker had died just three weeks before this injunction was issued. Richard Jugge himself died two years later; his son John was a member of the Stationers' Company and his daughter Katherine married another printer, Richard Watkins, who took over some of his father-in-law's material.

Richard Tottel

The earliest of the 'class' monopolies was that for law books, and of all the monopolies this was possibly the least obnoxious, for such work was highly specialized and unsuited to the average printer. Richard Tottel, who obtained from Philip and Mary a patent to print for seven years all 'duly authorized books on common law' is said to have obtained his privilege 'at the suit of the judges'. This privilege was allowed and confirmed by the Stationers' Company soon after its incorporation, and at the expiration of the seven years Tottel received from Queen Elizabeth a life grant to 'imprint all manner of books concerning the common law of this realm'.

All manner of difficulties beset the printer of law books, for not only were most of the legal works at this period written in Norman-French, but the manuscript was quite likely to prove bad copy—ill-written, with many corrections and interlinings and full of legal contractions, so that legal help was frequently necessary before a fair copy could be handed to the compositor.

In the preface to his edition of *The Great Charter* (1556) Tottel speaks of the many problems facing the law-publisher, and says 'For the exact truth thereof, my copies I might wel folow as thei were, but I could not myself correct them as they ought to be. Therfore in some workes where I could, with my entreatie or cost, procure learneder helpe, ye have them not smally amended.'

Tottel worked for forty years in Fleet Street at the sign of the Hand and Star, between the two gates of the Temple. Although law books were his chief publications, he was a lettered man, and the few volumes that he printed apart from his law books were of literary merit. One which proved especially popular was his *Miscellany,** of which he printed seven editions between 1557 and 1574, and which preserves all the original verse of the Earl of Surrey and of Sir Thomas Wyatt known to be extant. A book which went through three editions in the printer's lifetime (1562, 1576, 1591) was Gerard Legh's *Accedens of Armory*, printed throughout in italic, and containing many illustrations of coats of arms. Tottel also printed More's *Dialogue of Comfort* (1553), Lydgate's *fall of Princis* (1554), Stephen Hawe's *Pastime of Pleasure* (1555), and Tusser's *A hundreth good poyntes of Husbandrie* (1557). In 1562 he printed *Romeus and Juliet*, a boring poem by Arthur Broke which was nevertheless in plot (taken from Bandello via François de Belleforest) the main source of Shakespeare's play of that name.

Among Tottel's more ephemeral publications was a 40-page quarto recording the ceremonies and pageants occasioned by the coronation of Queen Elizabeth, which took place on 14 January, 1559. By 23 January Tottel had two separate editions on sale (S.T.C. 7590, 7591) to satisfy the public interest while the event was still topical.

In 1573 Richard Tottel sought to set up a paper mill, undertaking

---

* Its correct title is *Songes and Sonettes, written by the ryght honorable Lorde Henry Haward late Earle of Surrey, and other.*

to establish such a mill in England if the Government would give him land for the purpose and grant him the sole privilege for thirty years of making paper. Nothing ever came of it, however.

Tottel was an original member of the Stationers' Company, and became Master in 1578 and 1584. He married a sister of Richard Grafton and this probably led to his printing editions of Grafton's *Chronicles* as well as gaining possession of that printer's best woodcut borders. Towards the end of his life he retired to Wiston, in Pembrokeshire, where he died in 1593.

John Day

One of the most industrious and enterprising, as well as one of the best printers of the sixteenth century, was John Day, born in the now-vanished town of Dunwich, Suffolk, in 1522. As a youth he was apprenticed to Thomas Raynald (or Reynolds), and about 1546 we find him in partnership with William Seres, likewise at the outset of his career. Their books were at first issued from Snow Hill, near St Sepulchre's Church, and they seem to have had in addition a small shop in Cheapside; but whether Day did very much printing during the early part of his career is open to question. The words 'imprinted by' in a colophon were often, in the fifteenth century, merely a synonym for 'sold by', and many of the Day and Seres publications issued between the years 1546 and 1549, in which year Day moved to Aldersgate, have all the appearance of books printed in the Low Countries. Some, from internal evidence, seem either to have been printed by Steven Mierdman, a printer from Antwerp who worked for various booksellers or from type supplied by him. The folio Bible issued by Day and Seres in 1549 was most probably the work of the Flemish printer, twenty-three of whose initial letters are found therein; also the various types used on the title-page are all of Low Country origin. None of these early books with Day's imprint bears any sign of the typographical skill displayed by that printer from 1556 onwards.

During the reign of Queen Mary, according to an entry in Machyn's Diary, Day was imprisoned in the Tower 'for pryntyng of noythy bokes', but how long he spent there is not known. Some say he sought refuge abroad, together with his fellow-printers Hugh Singleton, Edward Whitchurch and Thomas Gibson, but there is no convincing evidence to support this view.[68] In 1556 he was admitted to the Livery of the Stationers' Company.

The accession of Elizabeth found him established as an important printer and his work from this time onwards shows such marked improvement that it strengthens the belief that he was little more than a bookseller at the outset of his career. He was fortunate in securing the patronage of Archbishop Parker, with whose help and encouragement he cut several founts. He was, indeed, the first English printer of whom we can say with certainty that he was his own letter-founder.

Under Parker's direction Day had cut the first Anglo-Saxon fount (rather less than a great primer in body) about 1566, and it was first used in 1567 for a Saxon homily by Abbot Ælfric entitled *A Testimonie of Antiquitie*, which Parker edited. The type was apparently lent by Parker to another of his favourite printers, Richard Jugge, for it appears in the undated *A Defence of priestes mariages*, which was probably printed about 1567.

The publication of *A Testimonie of Antiquitie* was a carefully calculated move by Archbishop Parker. By going back to Ælfric's Saxon Homily, in the editing of which he probably received considerable help from his chaplain, John Jocelyn, a sound Anglo-Saxon scholar, he was able to show, in the words of Foxe, that 'the religion presently taught and professed in the Church at thys present is no new reformation of thinges lately begonne, which were not before, but rather a reduction of the Church to the Pristine state of old conformitie which once it had'.

Day used this fount again in several books printed between 1567 and 1574. Reed-Johnson says: 'The accuracy and regularity with which this fount was cut and cast is highly creditable to Day's excellence as a founder', and Astle remarks: 'Day's Saxon types far excel in neatness and beauty any which have since been made.'[69]

Carter and Ricks, in their foreword to Mores's *Dissertation*, doubt the assertion contained in the anonymous preface to Asser's *Ælfredi regis res gestae* that Day himself cut the Anglo-Saxon types in that book, and think it likely that the roman letters were of Flemish origin and the runes mixed with them were made in London by one of Day's foreign journeymen.

The same authorities also point out that[70] 'in his typography and even more in his Anglo-Saxon printing Day must have been seconded by John Foxe, who lived with him in 1564 and worked one day a week in his house for a longer time'. Foxe, who had worked as a corrector for Oporinus, was well acquainted with the best printers on the Continent.

Another work of Parker's, *De Antiquitate Ecclesiae Britannicae*, set in a Granjon italic, is said to have been printed by Day at a private press in Lambeth Palace, and to have been the first privately printed book issued in England.

Day also had a fount of Greek with which he printed in 1578 the *Christianae pietatis prima institutio* of Alexander Nowell, the Dean of St Paul's. This is a very handsome type copied from the famous French *grecs du roi*. Day was also one of the first English printers to cut roman and italic letters on uniform bodies.

Day's printing, after the accession of Elizabeth, was on a far more ambitious scale than hitherto, and this was no doubt in part due to the fact that he had been allowed to take a number of skilled refugee workmen into his employ. In 1563 he brought out the first edition of *Acts and Monuments of these latter and perilous days . . .* , better known as Foxe's *Book of Martyrs*. This enormous folio volume of some two thousand pages printed in double column, was illustrated with more than fifty woodcuts which, though often crude, were vigorous and calculated to appeal to the unlearned reader. The book was reprinted in 1570, and at the opening of this edition the author added a Latin poem to the effect that 'although the Monuments are a heavy charge on you, you need not doubt, Day, that the looked-for gain will repay you for everything'. In this Foxe was right, for the book met with such approval (on the part of the Protestants) that three editions were sold out during Day's lifetime. Day's epitaph in Little Bradley church, Suffolk, mentions this work, in the following words:

> He set a Foxe to write how martyrs run
> By death to life. Foxe ventured pains and health
> To give them light: Daye spent in print his wealth,
> But God with gain restored his wealth again,
> And gave to him as he gave to the poor.

Another book printed by Day which had great popularity was *A Book of Christian Prayers* (1569), often called 'Queen Elizabeth's Prayer Book', and modelled on a French book of Hours. It was reprinted in 1853 by the Chiswick Press with the original cuts copied by Mary Byfield. It cannot compare in delicacy with the work of Tory, on which it was largely based, but Updike's condemnation of it as a 'rough, tasteless black-letter volume' seems a little harsh.[71]

The famous Dr John Dee wrote an elaborate work in four volumes called *The British Complement of the Perfect Art of Navigation*. Of this work only the first volume was ever printed, and came from the press of John Day in 1577 with the title of *General and Rare Memorials Pertayning to the Perfect Arte of Navigation*. The allegorical title-page has as its centre-piece a ship within which the Queen is seated.

One of the first books to call attention to John Day for the excellence of his workmanship was *The Cosmographicall Glasse*, by the Norwich physician William Cunningham (1559). 'As a piece of printing', writes Updike, 'nothing better had hitherto appeared in England.'[72] The text is set in a handsome italic, probably cut by François Guyot, and used also by Nicholas Hill and Richard Tottel. The book contains diagrams and maps, a portrait of the author, and a plan of Norwich as well as a number of large woodcut pictorial initials (63 × 63 mm.), one of which is signed I.B., possibly John Bettes, while others bear the monogram of an I within a C. These were almost certainly cut by Jean Croissant, a French woodcutter who worked for Thielman Kerver in Paris, and whom A. J. Delen identifies with the Hans Cressone who worked for Plantin.[73]

Day printed the first English translation of Euclid's *Elements of Geometry* in 1570—a folio with text set in roman and italic, while the folding table which accompanies the book provides as it were a specimen sheet of Day's various founts. In the same year Day printed the most famous of Roger Ascham's books, *The Scholemaster*,* intended by Ascham, who was tutor to the Princess Elizabeth, to teach children 'to understand, write and speak in Latin tong'. The book also contains a moving description of Lady Jane Grey. This quarto volume is set mainly in textura, but with English verse quotations in roman and Latin in italic. Some of the large pictorial initials are very similar to those used by Richard Jugge.

John Day held some very lucrative privileges, and in 1577 he and and his son Richard were granted a patent for life with survivorship to print the Psalms in Metre, the A.B.C. with the little Catechism and the Catechism in Latin and English, a monopoly procured through the good offices of the Earl of Leicester. These were some of the best paying copies in the trade, and later became the subject of numerous complaints from the poorer members of the Stationers' Company (see pages 100–1).

Day's music printing was not confined to the metrical Psalms, but included secular music, for in 1571 he printed Thomas Whythorne's *Songes for three, fower, and five voyces*. But the songs did not sell as fast

---

* The title entered in the Register was *The Schoolmaster of Windsor*.

as their author would have wished, which he attributed first to the fact that Day 'had heretofore printed music which was very false printed',[74] and secondly to lack of advertisement. In all Day had five founts of music type, used mainly for printing the metrical psalters. Richard Day succeeded to his father's patent in 1584 and John Wolfe became one of his assigns.

Day lived at Aldersgate from 1549 onwards, and many of his books bear the imprint 'Over Aldersgate'. There is a passage in Stowe's *Survey* which states: 'John Daye, stationer, a late famous printer of many good bookes, in our time dwelled in this gate, and built much upon the wall of the citie, towards the parish church of St Anne.' But Day's building work did not survive the rebuilding of the gate in 1617. In 1572 Day tried to acquire a small shop by the north-west door of St Paul's, a proceeding which roused the jealousy of his commercial rivals, who obtained from the Corporation of London an injunction preventing him from so doing; but Parker came to the rescue, and Day got his shop.

After an active career of almost forty years, John Day died on 23 July, 1584, at Walden in Essex and was buried in the parish church of Bradley Parva, Suffolk. He was twice married, and is said to have had thirteen children by each of his wives. His son Richard followed his father's profession and another son, John, became a Fellow of Oriel College, Oxford, and Vicar of Great Thurlow.

Steven Mierdman

Contemporary with Day and Jugge was Steven Mierdman, who printed in Antwerp, London and Emden, and was among the most important Netherlands printers of Reformation books. Born about 1510 at Hooge Mierde, a village of the Netherlands close to the Belgian frontier, he became a freeman of the city of Antwerp in November, 1543. There he printed from 1543, in which year he married Elizabeth, sister of the printer Mattheus Crom, until some time after 1546, when, to escape proceedings for having printed heretical books, he and his wife came to England. In the Return of Aliens for 1549 he is mentioned as living in the parish of St Mary-at-Hill, Billingsgate Ward.

In July, 1550, Mierdman, who had already taken out letters of denization, was granted a royal licence for five years 'to print various books hitherto unprinted' and to 'employ printers, English and foreign'.[75] While he was in England he printed a number of books in Latin,

English, French, Italian and Dutch, the majority being Reformation tracts, many of them by members of the Dutch Reformed Church, such as the *Brevis et dilucida de Sacramentis Ecclesiae Christi tractatio* . . . . (1552) by Joannes à Lasco, and Martin Mikroen's *Een claer bewijs* (1552). In French he printed *Le Temporiseur* of Wolfgang Musculus (1550), and in Italian the *Cathechismo*, translated from Latin into the Tuscan tongue by Michelagnolo Florio (1553?).

In English he printed *The market or fayre of Usurers*, by William Harrys (1550) and the first part of William Turner's *A new Herball* (1551). This last-named, and several other of Mierdman's books, were to be sold by John Gybkyn, a foreign stationer who had a shop in St Paul's churchyard. On the accession of Queen Mary Mierdman had to uproot himself once again and eventually settled at Emden.[76]

But that is not the whole of the story, for the number of books which bear the imprint of Steven Mierdman on title-page or colophon are but a small part of the extremely large output of this printer, who worked for a number of stationers and printed many books bearing fictitious names and addresses. For Gwalter Lynne, the Dutch bookseller who had premises on Summers Key, Billingsgate, and a shop in St Paul's churchyard, he printed ten or more books between 1548 and 1550, mostly Reformation tracts. This is not surprising, seeing that they both came from Antwerp as refugees from religious persecution, were members of the Dutch church at Austin Friars, and lived in the same ward. Internal evidence shows that Mierdman was most probably the printer of the edition of Sir Thomas More's *Utopia* published by Abraham Veale in 1551, and at least one book of Robert Crowley must have come from Mierdman's press—the 1549 *Psalter of David*.

Van Ortroy, in his book on Belgian printers who worked abroad, writes of Mierdman: '*Nous ne parvenons pas à expliquer la solution de continuité que présente sa carrière de 1546 à 1549.*'[77] The solution may well be that he was printing books for the English market, and if we hear no mention of his name it is for a good reason: in 1546 the Emperor Charles V made an edict (instigated, Joye thinks, by Gardiner) forbidding the printing of any English books at Antwerp, which was why Mierdman had to print with false names and addresses, whilst others, sent over to England in sheets, had the colophon of an English printer in London added to them later. The New Testament of 1548 (Fry No. 20), which has a colophon 'Rychard Jugge, London, 1548' set in type which differs from the rest of the book, was most probably imported from Antwerp by Jugge and printed by Mierdman. The medallion head of Christ on the title-page is surely from the same block as that on the title-page of Mierdman's Dutch New Testament of 1545, in which book are also to be found most of the illustrations used three years later in this Testament bearing Jugge's imprint. Many of the blocks and initials are those taken over from Crom by his son-in-law when he succeeded to the business.

The booke of Marchauntes (1547), which has the colophon 'Imprinted in Lodon & ar to be sold by Richard Jugge, at the North doore of Pouls' is another book which, from internal evidence, seems to have come from Mierdman's press. With regard to the many English books printed in Antwerp by Mierdman with fictitious names and addresses, these are outside the scope of a book dealing with the history of printing in Britain. But a personal investigation of the work of Steven Mierdman by myself (for books in English) and by H. F. Wijnman (for those in Dutch printed at Emden) raises many questions, among them being a general one as to how many printers who figure in the S.T.C. and elsewhere printed for a much shorter time than colophons or imprints suggest, or perhaps never printed at all. It certainly bears out the warning made many years ago by E. Gordon Duff that 'colophons . . . are not to be implicitly trusted'.[78]

Reyner Wolfe

Scattered over Europe at this period were a number of printers named Wolfe, and it is probable that Reyner, or Reginald, Wolfe was related to one or more of them. His first known printings are in a Continental roman and italic identical with the type used by Johann Wolf at Frankfurt. He seems to have come to England about 1530 and obtained letters of denization in 1533, being described as a native of Gelderland. The earliest mention of him appears to be in a letter from Thomas Tebold to the Earl of Wiltshire dated 4 April, 1530, in which he is named as a bookseller of St Paul's churchyard.

His shop bore the sign of the Brazen Serpent, which led Sir Sidney Lee to conjecture that he might have learnt to print from Conrad Néobar, whose device it was. The device was, however, a fairly common one. More to the point would have been the fact that Néobar was King's Printer in Greek to Francis I of France, and that Wolfe was the first printer in England to possess a large stock of Greek type and later held a patent for printing in Greek.

Wolfe's first known printings are of 1542, and began with several of the writings of John Leland the antiquary, with whom he was acquainted. Bagford states that Leland died at Wolfe's house, in St Michael's parish. On the verso of the last leaf of Leland's *Genethliacon* is Wolfe's charming printer's mark, showing children knocking down apples from a well-laden tree, with the motto *Charitas*.

The *Homilies* of Saint John Chrysostom (1543) in Latin and in Greek, is notable for some very fine pictorial initial letters, which A. W. Pollard considered to be of Italian origin, or possibly cut by Italians living in England.[79] Wolfe was the first printer in England to possess a complete fount of Greek type, and this seems to have been of Basle origin.

In 1543 Wolfe printed an early treatise on arithmetic, *The grounde of artes*, by Robert Record, which, though of no particular merit as a piece of printing, is of importance to the history of education. He also printed an edition of another famous school-book, Lily's *Latin Grammar*.

Wolfe was admitted, by special favour, a freeman of the Stationers' Company in 1536, and upon the incorporation of that Company his name is found seventh on the list; he was elected Master in 1560, 1564, 1567 and 1572. In April, 1547, he was granted by Edward VI a patent for life as

> king's typographer and bookseller in Latin, Greek and Hebrew; and licence not only to print all Latin, Greek and Hebrew books, but also grammars of Greek or Latin, although mixed with English, and also charts and maps useful or necessary to the king and his countries in those tongues.

A learned man, and a friend of Cromwell and Cranmer, Wolfe, as a promoter of the Reformation, is little heard of during the short reign of Mary, but his patents were renewed by Queen Elizabeth and he became one of the select group of printers who were favoured with the patronage of Archbishop Parker, whose edition of Bishop Jewel's *Apologia* he printed in 1562. Matthew Paris's *Historia Major*, likewise edited by Parker, he printed in a folio edition in 1571, a book ornamented with an engraved title-page and with several fine pictorial initials.

Wolfe died in 1573, before he had had time to print the material, collected during a quarter of a century, for what was to have been a *Universal Cosmogony*. This, left unarranged at his death, later formed the basis of the work known as Holinshed's *Chronicles*. In his will Wolfe left to his widow, Joan, the house he had built on the site of the old charnel house in St Paul's churchyard, which he had purchased from the King at the dissolution of the monasteries. Stowe tells us that in 1549 he paid for the removal of more than a thousand cartloads of bones from the charnel house. One of the houses he had let to the stationer Luke Harrison.

In addition to the device already mentioned Wolfe had another, which showed a brazen serpent entwined around a Tau cross within a hoop held on either side by a wolf. He probably had a carved street sign to hang outside his shop, for a brazen serpent is part of the goods bequeathed by Wolfe's widow to her son Robert. Joan Wolfe died soon after her husband and was buried by his side in the church of St Faith, in the crypt of Old St Paul's. In her will she expressly states that

> Raphell Hollingshed shall have and enjoye all such benefit, proffit, and commoditie as was promised unto him by my late husbande Reginald Wolfe, for or concerning the translating and prynting of a certain crownacle which my said husband before his decease did prepare and intend to have prynted.[80]

Henry Bynneman

Bynneman's career as a printer lasted from 1566, when he became free of the Stationers, until 1583. He had been apprenticed to Richard Harrison in 1560, but that printer died about January, 1563, and Bynneman served the remainder of his apprenticeship with Reynold Wolfe. 'He printed good literature and he printed it well' is Plomer's justified comment, and probably for that reason he became one of that select group of printers, which included Jugge and Day, to whom Archbishop Parker extended his patronage. According to Hansard it was Parker who allowed him to have a shop at the north-west door of St Paul's, at the sign of the Three Wells, which was leased to him in 1574 by Richard Smith, a draper.[81]

The first book with which Bynneman was associated seems to have been Crowley's *Apologie, or Defence of Predestination*, issued from the 'Blacke Boy' in Paternoster Row. Bynneman possibly had a share in the copy, for some examples bear Denham's name, and from typographical evidence we may assume that the book was actually printed by Denham, with whom Bynneman later worked in partnership.

In 1567 Bynneman was working for a time at the sign of the

Mermaid in Paternoster Row, but in the same year he transferred his printing office and the sign to Knightrider Street, where he remained until 1580. He then moved to Thames Street, near Baynard's Castle, where he stayed until his death. The Three Wells in St Paul's church-yard was probably his retail shop.

One of his first important books was the second volume of William Painter's *Palace of Pleasure* (1567), a collection of stories translated from the Latin, Greek, French, and Italian, and a mine from which many of the Elizabethan dramatists, including Shakespeare, drew their plots. The book was printed by Bynneman for the stationer Nicholas England, the first volume having been printed the year before by Henry Denham.

In 1568 he printed *Jacob and Esau*, an early comedy or interlude, which was entered to Henry Sutton in 1557. But if Sutton ever printed it, the edition has not survived and Bynneman's is the first known. It was later reprinted by W. C. Hazlitt in his edition of Dodsley's *Old Plays*.

A number of books printed by Bynneman are presumably lost to us. The *Songes and Sonnettes* by Thomas Bryce were entered in 1567, and Bynneman must have printed it, for 75 copies were noted in the inventory found in the P.R.O. and published by Mark Eccles.[82] But no copy is now known. Nor is any copy of *The Fearfull Fancies of the Florentine Cooper* known earlier than the 1599 edition, although it was entered to Bynneman in 1567. These are but two of the books of Bynneman which have not survived the passage of time.

For Matthew Parker Bynneman printed in 1574 a fine folio edition of Thomas Walsingham's *Historia Brevis Thornae*. Walsingham, a fif-teenth century historian, was a native of Norfolk and a Benedictine monk of St Albans, who was appointed historiographer royal about 1440. A curious book of 1575 was *The Mariners boke, containing godly and necessary orders and prayers, to be observed in every ship . . .*, by Thomas Mors.

Through the good offices of Leicester and Hatton, Bynneman ob-tained a privilege to print 'all Dictionaries in all tongues, all Chronicles and histories whatsoever'. It was the only privilege Bynneman could obtain, and not a particularly valuable one, since it demanded a large capital to exercise it without the promise of rich returns. Unfortun-ately for him all the most profitable patents had been taken up by others. But the privilege enabled Bynneman to print that very famous book known as Holinshed's *Chronicles*, which came out in 1577. A second and enlarged edition appeared in 1587, sponsored jointly by John Harrison, George Bishop, Ralph Newbery, Henry Denham and Thomas Woodcock, Denham being the printer. Holinshed died in 1580 and this second edition, the one which Shakespeare probably used, was revised and augmented by Raphael Holinshed, William Harrison and others.

In association with the publisher Ralph Newbery, Bynneman brought out in 1584 Thomas Cooper's Latin-English dictionary, a folio volume which, as a piece of printing, is quite equal to anything produced by his contemporaries. But Bynneman died before he could make any further use of his dictionary privilege, and others, such as Morelius's Greek-Latin-English dictionary and the *Nomenclator* of Hadrianus Junius, were published after his death, the former by assignation to his principal creditor, a certain Richard Hutton, and the latter by Newbery with Denham as printer.

Bynneman had three presses, and as the inventory of his property shows, he had a varied stock of type, including Greek and Hebrew, for after Wolfe's death Bynneman had acquired much of his material. But he never lived to print the New Testament in Greek which he had entered in the Register, nor the Homer in Greek and Latin which he hoped to bring out; nor did he print the Hebrew lexicon of Reuchlin.

Bynneman was the first printer in England to use a script type of the kind known as *civilité* or 'secretary'. This appears in the colophon of the 1576 edition of A. Guarna's *Bellum grammaticale*, and according to A. F. Johnson is a genuine English script type.[83]

Bynneman died on 15 April, 1583, and left a son, Christopher, who was apprenticed to the printer Thomas Dawson and was made free of the Stationers in 1615.

Henry Denham

As a printer Henry Denham has been somewhat neglected, yet there is little doubt that he was one of the outstanding printers of the sixteenth century; if proof were needed one has only to examine his *Monument of Matrones*. He was apprenticed to Richard Tottel and took up the freedom of the Stationers' Company on 30 August, 1560. In 1564 he set up his own printing house in White Cross Street, Cripplegate, but in the following year he moved to Paternoster Row, at the sign of the Star, where he remained for many years.

The first copy entered by Denham was a sermon by the Rev.

Thomas Cole (1564). In that year he printed for both Lucas Harrison and John Charlewood, and during the ensuing years he printed for many of the well-known London booksellers—Humphrey Toy, William Norton, Thomas Chard, Thomas Hacket—and in 1566 he printed that very famous collection of stories, William Painter's *Palace of Pleasure*, for his old master, Richard Tottel, and William Jones, who shared the edition.

His printing office was well supplied with good type in all sizes, from nonpareil to great primer, and he had a fine range of initial letters, ornaments and borders. Denham was particularly fond of arranging his titles with a lace border formed of printers' flowers and showed much ingenuity in their arrangement. Despite De Vinne's assertion that 'decorative borders of flowers are flagrant examples of the debasement of typography'[84]—and certainly they can be atrociously bad—in Denham's hands they assumed delicate filigree patterns through skilful handling and crisp press-work. In the case of *An Almanack . . . in forme of a Booke of Memorie* (1571) the flowered border is executed in red and black. Among the initials used by Denham were some of the very handsome ones cut by Arnold Nicolai and used by Cawood as well as a number of copies of that attractive alphabet. Other initials were very similar to sets used by Day, Jugge and Wolfe, which looks rather as if they were supplied from a common source— a woodcutter who worked for the printers of London as Arnold Nicolai did for the printers of Antwerp. Of one of the smaller sets of initials Charles Sayle wrote: 'It is quite unlike any other work in England and, further, is not used anywhere abroad.' This is the set of initials figuring cherubs, many of which can be seen in *An Answer to the two first and principall Treatises. . . .* (1584).[85]

In 1563 a bill was passed by Parliament allowing the Bible to be translated into Welsh for use in the churches of Wales, and the first part to be printed after the passing of the Act was the New Testament, translated by W. Salesbury and R. Davies, and printed in 1567 by Denham, who was granted a patent for printing the New Testament in Welsh. It was printed for Humphrey Toy and dedicated to Queen Elizabeth by William Salesbury, the translator, who was the author of another book printed by Denham for Humphrey Toy—*A playne and familiar Introduction, teaching how to pronounce the letters in the Brytishe tongue, now commonly called Welshe* (1567).

Among the best-known books to come from Denham's press were Thomas Tusser's *Five hundred pointes of good Husbandrie*, which he printed as the assignee of William Seres (1580); Gesner's *The newe Jewell of Health* (1576); Reynold Scot's *A perfite platforme of a Hoppe Garden* (the first book to be published in England entirely on the subject of hop-growing—1574); a quarto edition of Castiglione's *The Courtier* (1577) and John Baret's *An Alvearie* (1573 and 1580). The first edition of this last-named book was a dictionary in English, French and Latin, to which, for the 1580 edition, Greek definitions were added. In that year also, Denham brought out another pedagogic book—a curious volume by William Bullokar called *Bullokars booke at large for the amendment of orthographie for English speech.*

When Henry Bynneman died in 1583 he appointed Henry Denham and Ralph Newbery to be his executors. Shortly after this it is thought that Denham started the Eliot's Court Printing House, run by a syndicate of printers, three of whom—Ninian Newton, Arnold Hatfield, and Edmund Bollifant—had been apprenticed to Denham. Shortly afterwards Bollifant went into partnership with John Jackson.

Denham was an industrious printer and in 1583 was returned as having four presses; in 1586-7 and 1588-9 he served as Junior Warden of the Stationers' Company, but he never became Master. About 1585 he removed his sign of the Star to Aldersgate Street, where in 1587 he printed an edition of Holinshed's *Chronicles*, the edition being shared by himself, John Harrison the eldest, George Bishop, Ralph Newbery and Thomas Woodcock.

Denham took as his device a star surrounded by the motto *Os homini sublime dedit*, and as an assign of William Seres he occasionally made use of a cut of the Bear and Ragged Staff within the Garter, which had been used by Seres. Ames says of him that 'he was an exceeding neat printer, and the first who used the semicolon with propriety'. The propriety did not, apparently, extend to his language, for on 6 April, 1584, he was fined 20s (later remitted) 'for using undecent speaches to the elder Warden'.[86]

Eliot's Court Press

After Bynneman's death most of his ornaments, borders and pictorial initials came into the possession of a syndicate of four men: Edmund Bollifant, Arnold Hatfield, John Jackson and Ninian Newton. Bollifant, Hatfield and Newton were stationers and printers, and had served their apprenticeship with Henry Denham, one of Bynneman's assigns. Jackson was a member of the Grocers' Company; he does not seem ever to have been a printer, and probably provided the capital for the partnership, which set up as printers to the trade in Eliot's Court, Little Old Bailey.

The formation of this syndicate, of whose business arrangements we are unfortunately ignorant, seems to have been welcomed by the more important booksellers and for more than a decade stationers such as George Bishop, Ralph Newbery, Francis Coldocke, John and Bonham Norton, employed the Eliot's Court Press, which took as its device the mark of a caduceus (McKerrow 293). The first book to come from this press was Edmund Bunny's edition of Robert Parsons's *Booke of Christian Exercise*, which was published in 1584 (S.T.C. 19355) with the imprint 'N. Newton and A. Hatfield for J. Wight'. Curiously enough, as Henry Plomer points out, although the syndicate held stock and printing material in common, their names never appear all together in the imprint to any book they issued.[87] Jackson's name usually appears in conjunction with that of Edmund Bollifant, and in 1585 this pair put their names to an edition of *Aesop's fables in true ortography, with grammer notz*, to which was added the *short sentencez of the wyz Cato* (both widely used in schools) translated from the Latin by William Bullokar, one of the first Englishmen to propose a system of simplified spelling (see page 87). In the following year Jackson and Bollifant brought out his *Bref Grammar*.* In that same year they produced an octavo edition of *Cicero* in nine volumes, while Newton and Hatfield were busy with editions of *Horace* and Caesar's *Commentaries*. Plomer notes that the Eliot's Court Press was responsible for printing most of the Latin Bible published by the assigns of Christopher Barker in 1592–3.

Newton's name does not appear after 1586, Jackson's is not found after 1596, and Bollifant died in 1602, his place being taken by Melchisidec Bradwood, who was responsible for printing the Savile *Chrysostom* (see page 134). Bradwood took down to Eton from Eliot's Court all the material he needed and workmen to help him, having received from the Stationers' Company special permission to employ six apprentices to help him. But Bradwood's name appears nowhere in this eight-volume work, the whole credit for which was taken by John Norton, who together with John Bill supplied many books to Eton College.

In 1606 the *Theatrum Orbis Terrarum* by the famous geographer Abraham Ortelius, was brought out in an English edition, *The Theatre*

---

* The only known copy, lacking the title-page, is in the Bodleian.

of the Whole World, with the name of John Norton, King's Printer, on title-page and colophon. The caduceus device, together with the initials, point to the Eliot's Court Press as the actual printers.

Thomas Vautrollier

Among the many craftsmen who, persecuted for their religious opinions, fled from France and Flanders during the sixteenth century and sought refuge in England, was a Frenchman from Troyes in Champagne named Thomas Vautrollier, a Huguenot by conviction, who was granted letters of denization on 9 March, 1562. From that time onwards his name occurs regularly in the Returns of Aliens under such variant spellings as Vantrolly, Woultrulier, van Troveler, Vantroviller, etc.

Admitted a Brother of the Stationers' Company on 2 October, 1674, he began his career as bookbinder and bookseller. In 1567, maybe earlier, Vautrollier, in association with another Huguenot bookseller, Jean Desserans, acted as London agent for the Antwerp printer-publisher, Christopher Plantin. Towards the end of 1568 this partnership was dissolved, possibly because Vautrollier had by that time set up as a printer on his own account. The preface to his first book, the writing-book called *A Booke containing divers sortes of hands*, by Jean de Beau Chesne and John Baildon, is dated January, 1569. This book, dedicated to the Earl of Arundel, is, as far as is known, the earliest writing-book to have been published in England. The British Museum copy is dated 1571, but one copy is known, possibly unique, with the date 1570. Vautrollier followed this with a similar kind of book, *A newe booke of copies, containing divers sortes of sundry hands*, in 1574. Licence for this work is recorded in Arber (Vol. 1, p. 443) but only one copy, in the Bodleian Library, Oxford, is known.

From 1570 until 1587 Vautrollier worked as a printer in London, with two brief interludes in Edinburgh, and during that time he built up a substantial business. With his wife Jacqueline, *née* Du Thuit, he lived in Blackfriars, in a house with a garden situated in or close to Carter Lane, and he was registered in the ward of Farringdon Within.

Rather surprisingly, since he was a foreigner, Vautrollier managed to secure some valuable privileges and patents from the Crown, mainly in Latin books, which included such important copies as the New Testament of Théodore de Bèze, Augustin Marlorat's *Divinæ scripturæ thesaurus*, Pierre de la Ramée's *Dialectica*, and works of Ovid and Cicero. He also secured a patent for printing and publishing the *Phrases linguae latinae* of Aldus Manutius, and since this would normally have fallen within the province of Thomas Marsh, a well-known member of the Stationers' Company who had a patent covering Latin school-books, there was probably some arrangement between them.

Such privileges, which could be freely bought and sold, were valuable rights, and it is not surprising that there should have been a certain resentment on the part of the less fortunate printers. The unprivileged ones protested against these monopolies, and this opposition led to the commissioners' report to the Privy Council in 1583, whereby it was recommended that 'Marshe and Vautrollier, which have the sole printing of sundry school-books . . . may be treated with to choose . . . some sorts and leave the rest at liberty'.[88]

One of Vautrollier's most lucrative ventures was with the French tutors compiled by the Huguenot Claude de Sainliens (Claudius Holyband; Claudius a Sancto Vinculo), of which the most successful was *The French Littleton*, so called to show that it was as essential to the student of French as the original 'Littleton' had been for students of law. It went into many editions from 1576 onwards and was several times reprinted by Vautrollier's successor, Richard Field. Another popular school-book from Vautrollier's press was Francis Clement's *The Petite Schole*, to which were appended examples of secretary and roman hands.

The French Littleton brought Vautrollier into conflict with the bookseller Abraham Veale, who seems to have claimed a property in it. The dispute was submitted to arbitration of the Court of the Stationers' Company, which decided that Veale should be given 100 copies from each 1,250 printed during his lifetime, for which the bookseller was to provide the paper.[89]

More than once Vautrollier was fined for printing books without a licence: in 1578 for the unlicensed printing of Luther's *Special and chosen Sermons*, and in the following year for a similar omission with regard to Robert Travers's *Exposition made upon the cxi Psalm*.

In 1579 Vautrollier printed the first edition of Sir Thomas North's translation of Amyot's rendering of Plutarch's *Lives of the noble Grecians and Romanes*. This large folio of 1,175 pages was published jointly by the printer and the bookseller John Wight, whose shop was in St Paul's churchyard at the sign of the Rose. Each 'life' is headed by a medallion portrait enclosed in a frame of geometrical pattern, and the book hardly deserves Updike's stricture that it was a very tasteless performance.[90] A. W. Pollard thought it 'one of the handsomest of Elizabethan books'.[91]

Certainly Vautrollier was not in the habit of producing large and handsome folios, for the bulk of his work was in octavo editions notable for the beauty of their type and the high standard of the press-work. His roman and italic were well-designed founts, the roman being in the main the work of the French punch-cutter Pierre Hautin, and probably supplied by his nephew, Jerome Hautin, 'lettercaster for printers' who was working in London at that time. The best of Vautrollier's italic types were by another Frenchman, Robert Granjon, while some of the roman, both text and titling, can safely be attributed to Claude Garamond.

Vautrollier also printed music part-books, his first venture in this line being an edition in 1570 of the songs of Orlando de Lassus, the famous Flemish composer. He was later commissioned by Thomas Tallis and William Byrd, who held the privilege for the publication of music (apart from metrical psalters), to print for them their *Cantiones* in six parts (1575). There is no record as to the provenance of his music-types, but some of them are thought to have come from Johann Petreius of Nuremberg.

A work with which Vautrollier was particularly associated was Calvin's *Institutes*, of which he printed both a Latin edition and an English version by Thomas Norton, either on his own account or for other booksellers, such as William Norton and Humphrey Toy. The frequency with which the *Institutes* were printed shows how popular this work was at the time, and how lucrative to the printer. The great Latin edition of 1576 was edited by Vautrollier himself with the assistance of Edmund Bunney, the incumbent of Bolton Percy in Yorkshire, who was also responsible for the Latin *Compendium* published in the same year as the complete work. At least part of this edition was published jointly with the bookseller George Bishop, who commissioned several books from Vautrollier's press.

The first unabridged English translation of the *Institutes* printed by Vautrollier in 1578 was made by a Thomas Norton, who can almost certainly be identified with the part-author of *Gorboduc*. Then in 1583 there came from Vautrollier's press the Latin *Epitome* of the *Institutes* made by the preacher William de Lawne, whose son Gideon became apothecary to James I.

Somewhere about the year 1577 Vautrollier seems to have entered into a working arrangement with the Edinburgh publisher

Henry Charteris, for he published in London two editions of George Buchanan's *Baptistes sive Calumnia* (1577 and 1578), a play which Charteris published in Edinburgh in 1578, and in 1577 they shared the publication of John Rutherford's *Commentariorum De Arte Disserendi*. The printer in both cases was Vautrollier.

This was Vautrollier's first trade connection with Scotland, but in July, 1580, at the instance of the General Assembly of the Church of Scotland, he was invited to set up a press in Edinburgh, for although Alexander Arbuthnot was working in that city his slowness in providing Bibles seems to have annoyed the Assembly, which felt that a more active man was needed.

Vautrollier had already, it seems, an agent in the Scottish capital for the sale of books, for on 6 April, 1580, the Town Council of Edinburgh demanded payment of customs duties on all books he had brought into the kingdom, 'under the payne of wairding', i.e. imprisonment. In April, 1582, his servant, John Cowper, was hauled before the magistrates for retailing books and binding them within the burgh, since neither he nor his master were freemen of Edinburgh.[92] However, Vautrollier had friends at Court who secured his exemption from the customary dues. In 1583 he at last set up his press in Edinburgh and there printed eight books before returning to England (see page 125).

Although he went to Edinburgh on the recommendation of the General Assembly of the Church of Scotland, no edition of the Book of Common Order (the authorized manual for public worship in the Church of Scotland from 1556 until 1644) came from his Edinburgh press, the two editions of 1587 (Cowan 17 & 18) being printed in London after his return.

One of the last books which Vautrollier put to press was a Greek New Testament, based on that issued by Henry Estienne in 1576. The printer was taken ill on his return from Scotland, and the work of the firm was superintended with considerable ability—as it had been during Vautrollier's absences from London—by his wife Jacqueline and his apprentice Richard Field, who had been with him since 1579. Vautrollier died in July, 1587, and his will shows that he had four sons living—Simeon, Manasses, Thomas, and James.

To Manasses he left the printing press he brought back from Scotland, 'furnished with all her appurtenances that is to saye with fower Chassis and three Ffrisketts, two timpanes and a Copper plate'. Among the residue of the goods divided between his wife and the other sons were the remaining 'presses, leters caracters of cast mettell, and matrices'.

Little is known of the subsequent career of Thomas Vautrollier II, who was apprenticed to John Legat (afterwards University Printer at Cambridge) and took up his freedom of the Stationers' Company on 7 May, 1604. The only book known which bears his name is *Alberici Gentilis . . . Regales Disputationes Tres*, dated 1605, which bears the imprint *Londini, apud Thomam Vautrollierum*. Manasses is known to have worked in Cambridge from 1592 to 1594 as a privileged stationer of the University, and as late as 1633 his name occurs as a bookbinder in Edinburgh.

Vautrollier's sons were probably too young at the time of their father's death to be able to carry on the business which passed into the very capable hands of his apprentice, Richard Field, who married Thomas Vautrollier's widow, Jacqueline. Vautrollier's device (which Field also used) was an anchor held by a hand issuing from clouds, with branches of laurel and the motto *Anchora Spei*, the whole enclosed within an oval frame.

Thomas East

Part-singing was a favourite pastime among the English in the sixteenth and seventeenth centuries, and the average educated Elizabethan liked nothing better than to join in a madrigal. The music for each voice was printed separately and the part-books were laid on the table for all who would to join in.

One of the best-known music printers of the Elizabethan period was Thomas East, yet he had been printing for twenty years before he struck out in that line. In a working career of some forty-two years, East, a Buckinghamshire man, printed at five addresses. He became free of the Stationers' Company on 6 December, 1565, but there is no record of his apprenticeship. As a printer his name first occurs as having printed for Francis Coldocke a translation by Peter Beverley of Ariosto's *History of Ariodanto and Jeneura*, which, though undated, may be ascribed to the year 1566. It was entered at Stationers' Hall to Henry Wekes, or Wykes, in 1565–6, though he himself does not seem to have had anything to do with the printing of it.

For a time East printed in association with Henry Middleton, a partnership which continued until 1572, during which time they printed a number of medical and theological works, and also lighter and more ephemeral matter, such as a pamphlet or broadside (no copy exists) of *A lamentable confession of margaret Dorington . . . whoe was executed in the pallace at Westmynster for murderinge Alice Foxe.* Catnach was not the first to realize the lucrative possibilities of murderers' 'confessions'.

One of the most popular books of the sixteenth century, the *Travels of Sir John Maundeville*, with its stories of things 'right rare and strange', was printed by East in a quarto edition in 1568, and in the same year he issued another popular work—the courtesy book of Hugh Rhodes, called the *Book of Nurture*. In the field of medical books he was represented by a folio edition of Joannes de Vigo's *Workes of Chirurgerye* (1571) and Andrew Borde's *Breviary of Health* (1575). In 1581 he printed, for Gabriel Cawood, Lily's *Euphues* in quarto, and in the following year a folio edition of *Bartholomaeus Anglicus*—the edition which came to be known as 'Batman on Bartholomew', as distinct from the editions previously published by Wynkyn de Worde and Berthelet.

East twice printed an edition of *The Shepherds Calendar*; the first in 1581 for John Harrison the younger, the second in 1586, for the same bookseller. Both were reprints of the edition printed by Hugh Singleton in 1579, and the same woodcuts of the seasons appear in all three editions.

As appears from an examination of the list of his printings, until 1587 almost every category of literature was represented, and in the main he worked for the well-known booksellers such as John Wight, Lucas Harrison, William Norton, John Harrison the Younger, Francis Coldocke and others.

Then in 1588 he began to print music and became the first regular English music printer and publisher. It came about in this way: in 1575 William Byrd, the organist of the Chapel Royal, was granted conjointly with Thomas Tallis, the sole right to print and sell, or allow to be printed and sold, all musical works in England. The patent appears at the end of Tallis and Byrd's *Cantiones*, printed by Vautrollier in 1575.

For some reason no other work is known to have been printed under this joint patent until after Tallis's death in 1585, when John Wolfe, the chief insurgent against the patent system, brought out Cosyn's *Psalmes*, which would seem to have been covered by Byrd's patent. Byrd, as the survivor, still held on to his patent, and at the end of 1587 assigned the privilege to Thomas East. The music type, which had been imported from Johann Petreius of Nuremberg, and which had not been used since 1575, but which was apparently the composer's property, was transferred to East's premises, and on 6 November, 1587, the Register of the Stationers' Company records the entry by East of 'a set of part-books by William Burd'. This was probably the *Psalmes, Sonets and songs of sadnes and pietie*, by William Byrd which East printed in 1588, and which were 'to be sold at the dwelling-house of the said T. East, by Paules wharfe'. It is interesting to note that some of the delightful 'cherub' initials used by Denham (see page 86) are found in this work. In 1589 Byrd's *Songs of Sundrie Natures* and the first book of his *Cantiones Sacrae* were published by East at the sign of the Black Horse in Aldersgate Street.

In 1594 East no longer styles himself as Byrd's assign, and after the composer's patent expired in 1595, for the next three years East and Peter Short were printing music, presumably by licence from the Stationers' Company. In 1598 a fresh patent was granted to Byrd's pupil, Thomas Morley, who assigned licences to East, Short, and a publisher named William Barley. The last few years of the sixteenth century and the beginning of the seventeenth saw the publication of most of the masterpieces of the English madrigalists, such as *The Triumphes of Oriana*, by Thomas Morley, Morley's *First Booke of Balletts to Five Voices*, and the first set of John Wilbye's *Madrigals*, all printed by Thomas East, as well as compositions by John Dowland and Thomas Weelkes.

The exact date of East's death is not known, but it was prior to June, 1609, that the copyrights of some of his books were transferred to Thomas Snodham, *alias* East 'with the consent of Mistress East'. The adoption of the alias by Snodham was, suggests Plomer,[93] a trade advertisement to show that he was the successor to the business. The copyright of the music books was transferred in 1610 to the bookseller John Browne, and in 1611 copies were entered again in the names of Matthew Lownes, John Browne and Thomas Snodham. Altogether, from the time he began printing and publishing music in 1588 until the time of his death, hardly a year went by without several volumes of sacred or secular music coming from the press of Thomas East, of whose origins we know nothing. In his books he spells his name East, Est, and Este. Fuller-Maitland suggested, from the frequency with which the printer's name appears as Este, and the fact that he was chosen to introduce in England the great collection of Italian madrigals entitled *Musica Transalpina*, that he may have been of Italian extraction.[94]

Christopher Barker

An outstanding figure in the printing trade towards the end of the sixteenth century was Christopher Barker, a shrewd business man who managed to acquire the most lucrative of all patents—for a man with sufficient capital to exercise it—namely the Bible patent. Born around 1529, Christopher Barker was a wealthy member of the Drapers' Company with powerful friends at Court, for he was closely connected with the Walsingham family. He is thought to have been the grand-nephew of Sir Christopher Barker, a former Garter King of Arms, which would explain his wealth, since the various properties of Sir Christopher ultimately passed into the possession of his nephew, Edward Barker, thought to have been the printer's father.

Christopher Barker became interested in the printing trade and is first heard of as a publisher in 1569, when he entered as his copy *Serten prayers of my Lady Tyrwhitt* (printed for him by H. Middleton in 1574) and *Serten prayers of master Bullion*. The former is a collection of devotional pieces, a copy of which, superbly bound, is said to have been frequently carried by Queen Elizabeth. The title is printed within a border of printers' flowers, and the book has Barker's punning device of a man barking timber, with the couplet

A Barker if ye will
In name, but not in skill.

In 1575 Middleton printed for him two editions of George Gascoyne's *The glasse of governement* (S.T.C. 11643 and 11643a) in which Barker's address is given as the sign of the Grasshopper, in St Paul's churchyard.

In 1576 he is found at the sign of the Tiger's Head, also in St Paul's churchyard. This device, which he adopted as his printer's mark, was the crest of the Walsingham family; the Walsingham coat of arms is found in many of his books and border pieces, and many of his earlier books were dedicated to members of the Walsingham family. In that same year Barker started on his career as a Bible printer, having obtained a privilege to print the Geneva version of the Bible (already printed abroad) in England, since John Bodley had never made use of his privilege (page 72).

As we have already seen, only three weeks after the death of Archbishop Parker the printers pressed their demands to be allowed to share Jugge's patent, and it was decided, much to Jugge's annoyance, that apart from the Bible in quarto and the New Testament in 16mo, other sizes were left free to other printers, providing they could obtain a licence.

The Geneva version was outside the scope of Jugge's patent, which had been for the *Bishops' Bible*, and several of the leading stationers, anxious that the newcomer should not spoil their market, hurriedly brought out a folio edition of the *Bishops' Bible*, each of them taking a portion of this new edition, which appeared in 1575. Barker brought out two folio editions of the *Geneva Bible* in 1576 and in 1577 another folio as well as an edition in octavo. His Bible was excellently printed and it followed the original edition of Rowland Hall in being printed throughout in roman type instead of the black-letter favoured by English printers of Bibles. The two editions of 1576 resemble each other paginatim but not always lineatim, and one edition has what the other lacks—an illustration of the Vision of Ezekiel, from the same block as those of the English and French editions of 1560. There was an edition of the Psalms in Metre published the same year in folio to match these editions of 1576, having at the end a thoroughly Calvinistic confession of faith. On the last page of Revelation in the 1576 Bible appears Walsingham's crest with the Italian motto *Tigre Reo Animale del Adam Vecchio. Figliuolo Merce L'Evangelio Fatto N'Esta Agnello.*

Barker had shown his shrewdness in obtaining the privilege for the *Geneva Bible*, for the Bishops' version was never popular, either with laity or clergy, and the attempt to popularize it for family reading by issuing a quarto version in 1569 was a failure. On the other hand, between 1576 and 1600, Christopher Barker and his assigns and deputies had brought out more than fifty editions of the Genevan version.

Although in August, 1577, Christopher Barker had been one of the stationers who signed the petition against privileges,[95] on 28 September of that same year he purchased from the diplomat Sir Thomas Wilkes, Clerk of the Privy Council, an extensive patent which included the Old and New Testament in English, with or without notes, of any translation. This was a purely commercial transac-action between two private individuals, but as no monopolies were supposed to be granted in restraint of trade, by a legal fiction the patent specified that it was granted in consideration of the skill shown by the said Christopher Barker in the art and mystery of printing. The full patent (*Patent Roll, 19 Eliz. Part 8*) granted to Barker the office of royal printer of all statues, books, bills, acts of parliament, proclamations, injunctions, Bibles, and New Testaments, in the English tongue of any translation, with or without notes, whether previously in print or to be printed at the Queen's command. Also of all service books to be used in churches, and all other volumes ordered to be printed by the Queen or Parliament. Thus Barker was given a complete monopoly of printing English Bibles of every kind. This was the beginning of the subsequent Bible Patents.

Privileges and Patents

During the fifteenth century in England the number of printers was too small to arouse any fears of undue competition; but once the number increased each one was understandably afraid that his labour and outlay on a particular work might be nullified by the duplication of his book by another printer, for there was then no law of copyright. The first step towards ensuring that a printer should reap the reward of his labours without unfair competition was the conferring by royal grant of a privilege which gave the printer the sole right to print and sell a certain book, or class of books, for a specified number of years. This was clearly most important in the case of books which entailed considerable expense, such as law books, which were by their nature voluminous and had to be supervised and corrected by experts in legal matters.

Henry VIII granted a number of such royal privileges. The first edition of Sir Thomas Elyot's Latin-English dictionary (1538), a folio of some 450 pages set in double column, bears a notice to the effect that its printer, Thomas Berthelet, was granted the royal privilege for six years of having the sole right in all books that he should be the first to print, and, states the royal patron 'we will and command you that . . . none of you presume to print any of the said books . . . as ye intend to eschew our displeasure'. To such books the printer, as a warning to possible pirates, affixed the words *cum privilegio regali*. In 1538 appeared the King's proclamation against 'naughty printed books', and in it printers were instructed that to the words *cum privilegio regali* they must henceforward add *ad imprimendum solum*.

As the demand for books increased, and the number of printers also, it became impossible to apply for a royal privilege for everything that was printed, and copyright in a particular work in this sense of privilege became the affair of the Stationers' Company. After a book had been duly licensed by the authorities the title was entered, in return for a small fee, in the Register of the Company, and this was recognized as giving a right to the title or 'copy' of any lawful book to the first stationer to enter it, and he alone had the right to print and/or publish it. Such 'copies' could, however, be transferred, assigned, sold or bequeathed.

The most enterprising publishers and printers saw the financial advantages of securing a privilege, not for a single copy, but for a whole class of books, and during the reign of Queen Elizabeth in particular there were granted a series of monopolies which, towards the end of the sixteenth century, were to cause an upheaval that seriously threatened the unity of the Stationers' Company.

Thus Richard Tottel, who had been granted by Edward VI the sole privilege to print law books for seven years, had the royal patent renewed by Elizabeth for life. He was a rich man, with three presses, but often allowed two of his presses to remain idle and could not be compelled to print a law book against his will; and the view of many of the Stationers' Company was that he 'selleth the same bookes at excessive prices'. John Day secured the privilege for printing the A.B.C. and Catechisms; Jugge that for Bibles and Testaments; William Seres for 'all Psalters, all manner of Prymers englishe or latten . . . and all manner of prayer bokes, with the revercion of the same to his sonne'; James Roberts and R. Watkins for Almanacs; Thomas Marsh for Latin grammars; and Tallis and Byrd for music printing. Private individuals who had no connection with printing at all could, if they paid sufficient, be sure of obtaining a royal patent, so that we find Queen Elizabeth granting a patent as 'Her Majesty's printer of the English' to Sir Thomas Wilkes and one as 'Her Majesty's printer of the Latin' to a certain Francis Flower, who farmed it out to Vautrollier and other assigns for £100 a year.

All these were very valuable properties, since the classes of books enumerated were those for which there was the greatest sale. Plays, however, do not seem to have been considered a sufficiently valuable property to induce anyone to apply for a patent for them. This change-over from short-term privileges to a system of life monopolies is attributed by E. Wyndham Hulme to an Italian jurist named Acontius, who settled in England and advocated it in 1559.[96] 'It strengthened the hand of the Crown', writes Siebert, 'by making it possible to withdraw a printing patent.'[97] It was also a source of revenue to the Crown, and only the wealthy could afford to apply for one. Monopolies had their legitimate uses, but unfortunately Queen Elizabeth and the early Stuarts merely looked upon them as an excellent way of raising money or of rewarding their favourites at no expense to themselves.

Agitation against these monopolies in the printing trade grew steadily during the latter half of the sixteenth century, and in 1577 some of the Stationers drew up a 'Complaint of diverse of their hynderance by grauntes of Privelidges' (Lansdowne MS. 48), in which it was stated that 'the privilidges latelie granted by her Majestie . . . hath and will be the overthrowe of the Printers and Stacioners within this Cittie, being in number 175'.[98]

The chief leader of the insurgents was John Wolfe, a former apprentice of John Day. He began to print whatever he pleased, regardless of other men's rights in their 'copy', and when remonstrated with, and 'friendly persuaded to live in order and not print other men's privileged copies', he replied that 'he would print all their bokes if he lacked work' and added that 'it was lawfull for all men to print all lawfull bookes, what commandement soever her Majestie gave to the contrary'.[99] John Wolfe was an extremely able man, as his subsequent career shows, and we would respect his stand against monopolies more had he not allowed himself to be bought off by being given a share in Day's patent, which he had previously infringed. On 1 July, 1583, Wolfe, who had been a freeman of the Fishmongers' Company, was translated to the Stationers' Company on payment of a fee of 3s.4d.

In December, 1582, Christopher Barker, then Upper Warden of the Stationers' Company, drew up for Lord Burghley a detailed report of the existing privileges, after the grievances among the underprivileged printers had been so strongly manifested that a Royal Commission was set up to investigate the matter. In his report Barker, being now in possession of the most fruitful monopoly, set himself out to show that nobody really made money out of the patent system. He declared that he himself had given hostages to fortune in the great sum he had paid to Master Wilkes (though he does not say how much that was), and yet, he complained,

> myne owne office of her Majesties Printer of the English tongue gyven to Master Wilkes is abridged of the cheefest comodities belonging to the office, as shall hereafter appear in the Patentes of Master Seres and Master Day . . . In the priviledge or private licence graunted to Master Day are among other thinges the Psalmes in meeter, with notes to sing them in the Churches, which being a parcell of the Church service, properly belongeth to me.[100]

With regard to the Book of Common Prayer, which was also included in Barker's patent, the situation was complicated by the fact that he held it only for the Prayer Book printed as a whole. The privilege of printing certain parts of it separately—the Psalms, Collects, Litany and Primer (made up of the Catechism together with a few psalms)—belonged to Seres, while the 'Psalmes in meeter' with musical notation, was Day's monopoly.

Bynneman's patent for dictionaries, chronicles and histories, placed him, according to Barker, 'in more Daunger to be undone then likely to gayne' (which was possibly true); Tottel's benefit from law books, he intimated, was waning; Thomas Marsh's privilege for Latin textbooks might have been profitable, he wrote, but for Marsh's being 'the unfittest man in England' to exercise it; and as for Flower's patent for 'the Grammar and accidens for the instruction of youth', he declared that the five printers to whom it had been farmed out had been heard to say they would gladly pay to be rid of it.

From all this one might imagine that Barker was in favour of abolishing the monopoly system. Far from it; he knew well enough on which side his bread was buttered. He would, of course, if it were 'beneficiall to the common wealth' for privileges to be dissolved 'yeeld myne opinion so', but he professes to have the interests of the journeyman in mind, who would be 'utterlie undone' if these privileges were done away with.

The rebellion against the privileged printers had no great effect. A certain number of privileged books were surrendered to the Company of Stationers by the patentees, ostensibly for the benefit of the Company's poor, but as one might expect, they were far from being the most valuable copies.

A monopoly which probably caused more resentment than any other on the part of the Stationers' Company was that granted to the poet George Wither by King James I in 1623.[101] Not only did this give him a monopoly for 51 years of his *Hymns and Songs of the Church*, but the grant also required all stationers to insert the work in every copy of the Psalms in Metre, the rights in which had previously been granted to the Company. Furthermore, Wither was given the right to search for and to seize any copies of the Psalms in Metre sold without the inclusion of his hymns.

There was enough rivalry in business within the Company without this unfair competition from an outsider, and the Stationers refused to bind up Wither's Hymns with the Psalter. They petitioned Parliament in 1624, and that part of the poet's grant which required the compulsory insertion of his work in the psalter was recalled. Wither thereupon attacked the Company in a tract called *Scholars' Purgatory* —an attack which, although it was naturally far from impartial, contained many palpable hits, as when he asserted that the Stationers' Company

> by the laws and orders of their corporation can and do settle upon the particular members thereof a perpetual interest in such books as are registered by them at their Hall in their several names; and are secured in taking benefit of these books, better than any author can be by the King's grant, notwithstanding their first copies were purloined from the true owner or imprinted without his leave.

To return to the career of Christopher Barker—his business continued to thrive, and from 1588 onwards he conducted it mainly through his deputies, George Bishop and Ralph Newbery. On the disgrace of Wilkes in 1589, Barker managed to obtain a renewal of his exclusive patent with reversion for life to his son Robert. Father and son lived in London at Bacon House, in Noble Street, Aldersgate, at that time full of handsome houses belonging to the nobility. Christopher Barker also had a house at Datchet, to which he retired after 1588, and there he died on 29 November, 1599. No one could say of him that he had not exercised his patent in a fitting manner, for not only did he and his deputies supply the country with about seventy editions of the Scriptures between 1575 and 1599, but they were accurate and well printed. He was succeeded in the post of royal printer by his son Robert. The site of the first Queen's Printing House, established by Christopher Barker in 1577, was at Northumberland House, in Aldersgate Street, once the residence of that Percy known as 'Hotspur'.

Peter Short

Peter Short may be considered the last of the more famous printers of the sixteenth century, for his active career extended from 1590 to his death in 1603. Although he printed many books for his own account he was also a trade printer, working for William Ponsonby and other well-known London stationers. For John Harrison the Younger he printed in 1598 an edition of Shakespeare's *Lucrece* (the first edition had been printed in 1594 by Richard Field for the same publisher), and for Andrew Wise, in the same year, he printed *Henry IV, Part I*, in a quarto which bore no author's name.

Short took over Denham's business and material after the latter's death, and completed the edition of Foxe's *Book of Martyrs* begun by Denham (1596–7). He was an active printer, for some 130 books of his are listed in the S.T.C. Perhaps his most famous publication was Dr William Gilbert's *De Magnete* (1600) which has been called 'the first major original contribution to science that was published in England', a work which influenced men like Galileo, Kepler and Newton. This book contains the device of the brazen serpent on a Tau cross printed from the identical block used by Reyner Wolfe fifty years before in his edition of Cranmer's *Defence of the . . . doctrine of the Sacrament* (1550). From his widow it passed to Henry Bynneman, thence to Denham, and so to Peter Short. Humphrey Lownes, having married Short's widow, in turn used it, and as late as 1636 we find it in the possession of Miles Flesher. Short also used Denham's device of the Star, which was also the sign of his premises on Bread-street Hill.

Among other books printed by Peter Short were Thomas Blunde-ville's *Art of Riding* (1597); an edition of the *Imitation of Christ*, translated by Thomas Rogers (1596); and a complete edition of the *Works of Josephus* (1602), a large folio of 812 pages, the publication of which was shared by George Bishop, Simon Waterson, Peter Short and Thomas Adams. Short also printed music under licence and in 1597 printed Dowland's *First booke of songes* and Morley's *Plaine and easie introduction to practicall musicke*, the former making use on its title-page of the elaborate compartment first used by John Day for *The Cosmographicall Glasse* in 1559 (MacKerrow & Ferguson 99).

Peter Short was admitted a freeman of the Stationers' Company by redemption on 1 March, 1588–9, and died in 1603. His widow Emma married Humphrey Lownes, an event which gave rise to the following pungent entry in the Register of the Company:

> 1603. Hump[h]rey Lowndes married Short's widdowe.
> holds ye printing house though uncapable.

CHAPTER FOUR

The Regulation of Printing in the Early Days

For some years after the introduction of the craft of printing into England the output of the few printers working in this country was far from sufficient to meet the demand for books of the more educated, nor was the choice of books available sufficiently wide. 'Except for service books', writes Curt Bühler, 'Caxton produced little that would have interested a studious cleric, and nothing at all that would have appealed to the Humanist. The Renaissance had as yet hardly touched England.'[102] Whoever wanted the classics had to procure them from abroad if they could, for no English printer could supply him, though much was being done to popularize good literature in the vernacular. But as late as 1540 no Greek book had appeared from the press of an English printer.

Therefore, when an act was passed in the first year of Richard III to regulate and restrict the conditions under which aliens carried on trade in England, it was clearly stated

> Provided alwayes that this acte, or any parcel therof, nor none other acte made or to be made in the sayd parlyament, shal not extend or be in prejudice, disturbauns, damage or impedyment to any artifycer or marchaunt straunger, of what nacyon or countrey he be or shal be or for bryngynge into this realme, or sellyng by retayle or otherwyse, anye bookes written or prynted, or for the inhabityng within this sayde realme for the same intent, or anye scrivener, allumynour, redar or prynter of suche bookes, whiche he hath or shall have to sell by waye of marchaundyse, or for theyr dwellynge within this sayde realme for the exercyse of the sayd occupacyons. This acte or any parte therof notwithstandynge.[103]

As a result of this act numerous foreign stationers and printers had their agents in London and the English trade became for them a very lucrative one. On 5 December, 1485, a foreign stationer named Peter Actors, who had for some time been visiting the principal fairs with his partner Joannes de Aquisgrano to supply books, was appointed Stationer to King Henry VII. His patent is thus summarized:

> Grant for life to Peter Actoris, born in Savoy, of the office of Stationer to the King; also license to import, so often as he likes, from parts beyond the sea, books printed and not printed into the port of the city of London, and other ports and places within the kingdom of England, and to dispose of the same by sale or otherwise without paying customs etc. thereon and without rendering any accompt thereof.

A lucrative grant indeed. Actors is last heard of about 1501, and he was succeeded by William Faques (see page 42) who, since he was a printer, had the official title altered to that of Printer to the King.

The chief centre of the book trade was at that time and for many years afterwards St Paul's churchyard, and the Missal for Sarum use printed at Paris in 1504 by Jean Du Pré for the English market, bears an inscription *Venales apud bibliopolas in cimyterio sancti Pauli London invenientur*. Not only were service books (as we have shown elsewhere) printed for the English market by foreign printers; shortly after Caxton's death the Antwerp printer Geeraert Leeu, sensing a rich opportunity, quickly printed editions of three of Caxton's works—the *History of Jason, Paris and Vienne* and *The Chronicles of England*—while Wynkyn de Worde was busy setting up his new printing house in Fleet Street. As Duff remarks, 'the foreign printers awoke to the fact that England, with so few printers of her own, was a very desirable country to exploit'.[104] It has been estimated that until about 1535 some two-thirds of those connected with the book trade were aliens, and it was not long before the Government's encouragement of the foreign printers and booksellers led to bitter feeling against all aliens. Even an established London printer like Richard Pynson suffered from the hostility felt against alien workmen, and his appeal to the Court of Star Chamber in 1500 against Harry Squire, Cordwainer, and others for a murderous attack against himself and his servants is given in *Select Cases . . . in the Star Chamber* published by the Selden Society in 1903.

Whereas in 1500 there were only five printers in London, by 1523 there were thirty-three or more printers and booksellers, and the English market was becoming less dependent on books from abroad. The free trade which had previously existed came to an end in the reign of Henry VIII, and several acts were passed which severely limited the activities of foreign craftsmen. In 1523 was promulgated an act 'Concerning the Taking of Apprentices by Straungers', by the terms of which apprentices were to be of English birth, and not more than two foreign journeymen were allowed to be employed in one printing house. Every alien was placed under the supervision of the warden of his craft, that is to say of the as yet unincorporated Stationers' Company. 'It seems already to have been the custom of the trade', writes Duff, 'that no freeman of the Stationers should take any foreigner as an apprentice, so that this act did away with foreign apprentices altogether and as a consequence prevented them, with one or two rare exceptions, from ever becoming members of the Stationers' Company.'[105]

In 1529 'undenizened aliens'—that is, those who had not obtained naturalization or taken out letters of denization enabling them to live and trade on a footing with the native Englishman—were forbidden to set up shop and 'occupy any handy craft'. In 1534 came the Act 'for prynters and bynders of bokes' which repealed the clause in the Act of 1484 allowing the free importation of books. Henceforward, dealing in foreign-bound books was forbidden (to protect the native binders), and no one was permitted to buy books of any foreigner unless he was a denizen of the kingdom. This clause was aimed at preventing aliens from coming into the country with books, possibly of a seditious nature, to sell up and down the country at fairs, as they had done hitherto.

Not only were steps taken to safeguard the interests of the native stationers, but such was the flood of controversial books being published from about 1525 onwards that a stream of proclamations came from the press of the King's Printer, threatening dire penalties against the sellers of seditious books. During the time of Caxton and his contemporaries, when printing was concerned mainly with the dissemination of literature, little attention was paid to the new craft by the authorities, but when the printed book began to deal with religious and political controversy, the Government began to act and a relentless war was carried on against all books and tracts labelled as heretical or seditious. Under the Tudors the authority of the Crown to control the press was almost unlimited, and although the royal proclamations may have been in many cases illegal from the point of view of common law, they were nevertheless enforced as law.

A printer could be prosecuted for 'unseemly words' or 'evil opinions' and in January, 1541, the printers Richard Grafton and Richard Bankes were charged with printing 'invectives', and the former was also charged with having in his possession a 'sedicious epistle in the englishe tongue writen by Melancton' and was committed to prison.

Henry VIII's proclamation of 1538 against 'naughty printed books', in addition to forbidding the importation of English books from abroad except under royal licence, forbade also the printing of any book in the English language 'unless upon examination made by some of his Grace's Privy Council, or other such as his Highness shall appoint, they shall have licence to do so'. Various proclamations followed in much the same strain, insisting upon the licensing of any matter to be printed or distributed in the English tongue.

The Stationers' Company

On 4 May, 1557, the Stationers' Company was granted its royal charter—an event of great importance in the history of English printing. The Company had its origin in a medieval guild, formed in 1403, which grouped together the ancient fraternities of the Scriveners, Limners, Bookbinders and Stationers. Application for a royal charter was made in 1542, but it was not until fifteen years later that the application was granted, and by this time the scriveners had been almost entirely superseded by the printers.

While the Stationers saw in the charter a means of protecting their craft from unregulated competition, the Crown saw in it the means of controlling the increasingly powerful printing press from which came so many seditious and heretical books; for despite a steady flow of Government proclamations, forbidden books continued to arrive in the country, whilst many were surreptitiously printed in England itself, often with a false foreign imprint.

By the Charter of 1557 no one was allowed to print unless he belonged to the Company or held a licence under royal letters patent. This had the effect of restricting printing to London, for the only outside body empowered to print by royal licence was the University of Cambridge, and there printing had lapsed since 1522. The University of Oxford had no legal warrant for printing until 1586, when an ordinance of Star Chamber allowed one press; and although printing had earlier been practised at a few provincial towns, most of these presses no longer functioned, so that the monopoly granted to the Stationers' Company did not, in fact, mean the closing down of any provincial presses.

The government of the Company was vested in a Master and two Wardens, elected annually, and the Assistants, consisting of from eight to twelve senior members. The Master and Wardens were, by the terms of the Charter, empowered 'to make search whenever it shall please them, in any place, shop, house, chamber, or building of any printer or bookseller' and seize any books printed contrary to any act, statute or proclamation. The first Master of the newly incorporated Company was Thomas Dockwray, by profession a notary and, as might be expected, an ardent Catholic. He did not enjoy his appointment for long, for he died on 23 June, 1559.

But although the Company was now in a position to supervise printing in London, it could do little to stop the importation of books and tracts from the pens of the Reformers on the Continent which continued to find their way into England in considerable numbers, sometimes with the connivance of the port 'searchers', who were not above committing 'sondrye frawdes and deceytes' in the exercise of their offices. So abhorrent had this influx of Reformation tracts become in the eyes of Queen Mary, that in June, 1558, a few months before her death, she issued a further proclamation, which decreed that any person

> found to have any of the said wicked and seditious books, or, finding them, do not forthwith burn the same, without showing or reading the same to any other person, shall in that case be reputed and taken for a rebell, and shall without delay be executed for that offence according to the order of Marshall lawe.

By the time Queen Elizabeth came to the throne foreign competition in the printing trade had been virtually eliminated. A further order restricting aliens had been promulgated by the Mayor and Commonalty of London in 1555, whereby no citizen was allowed to employ a foreigner except in certain trades, which did not include printing and bookselling. This elimination of foreign competition, although welcomed by the English printers, was a hindrance to technical improvement, with the result that for the next century and more the quality of English printing was poor in comparison with that of France, Holland, Switzerland and Italy. In effect all printing and bookselling in England was controlled by the hundred-odd men who made up the Stationers' Company at the time of its incorporation.

The internal organization of the Stationers' Company was in most respects similar to that prevailing in the City of London Livery Companies in general. The governing body of a Livery Company is known as 'The Court' or 'Court of Assistants', and the Charter of the Stationers' Company was the first in which the 'Court of Assistants' appears officially as part of the constitution. The non-governing body consisted of the liverymen and the freemen or yeomen, and as vacancies occurred in the Court it became the practice to co-opt members of the livery. The steps of advancement were Apprentice, Yeoman, Liveryman, Assistant, Warden, Master.

Membership of the Stationers' Company was by servitude, patrimony, redemption or translation. The length of service of an apprentice before he was made free of the Company was not less than seven years, and in any case he could not become a freeman before the age of twenty-four. The son of a Stationer could be admitted by patrimony provided his father was a freeman of the Company at the time of his birth. Freedom by purchase was the only way in which aliens could be admitted to membership, and even so, very few were admitted. Reyner Wolfe was specially admitted a freeman of the Company, possibly owing to the recommendation of Anne Boleyn, but it was made a condition of his acceptance that he should take none but English apprentices. For those who were already free of the City in another Company it was possible to become a Stationer by translation from the other Company if permission was obtained from both parties.[106]

The earliest public enactment to mention the Stationers' Company by name was the *Injunctions* of Queen Elizabeth, published in 1559, the 51st clause of which dealt with the licensing of books and pamphlets, 'because', the enactment ran, 'there is a great abuse in the printers of bookes, which for covetousnes chefely regarde not what they print, so they may have gayne'. Once again the principal concern of the Crown is to ensure that no printed matter 'should be eyther hereticall, seditious, or unseemely for Christian eares'. Any new books were to be licensed, prior to printing, either by the Queen herself in writing, or by six of her Privy Council, or by one of the following: the Archbishops of Canterbury and York, the Bishop of London, and the Chancellors of both Universities.

One of the provisions of this regulation was that the names of the licensers should be placed at the end of every work, but few printed books of this period show them. Either the provision was not strictly enforced or the names were merely endorsed on the manuscript.

These *Injunctions* formed the basis of subsequent licensing, and were issued by the Crown under its authority as head of the Church. Siebert says that 'the queen, as guardian of the religion of her people, assumed like her father that the authority to control the press was implicit in the powers of the sovereign'.[107]

More stringent penalties for printing contrary to these regulations were laid down by an Order of the Privy Council dated 29 June, 1566. Offenders were to be debarred for life from printing, to go to prison for three months, and be fined ten pounds.

Elizabethan regulation of the printing and publishing trades culminated in the famous Star Chamber decree of 1586,[108] the provisions of which determined the course of the English book trade for the next half-century. Among its various clauses it stipulated that

> no printer of bookes, nor any other person or persons whatever, shall sett up, keepe, or mayntein, any presse or presses, or any other instrument or instruments for imprinting of bookes, ballades, chartes, pourtraictures, or any other thing or things whatsoever, but onelye in the cittie of London, or the suburbs thereof (except one presse in the universitie of Cambridge, and one other presse in the universitie of Oxforde, and no more) and that no person shall hereafter erect, sett up, or maynteyne in any secrett or obscure corner, or place, any suche presse.

The Stationers' Company was given authority to inspect all printing offices and to seize any presses or material which infringed the decree. These were to be broken up or defaced. Hardly had the decree been promulgated than the Wardens of the Company raided the premises of Roger Ward, who had already been in trouble for printing 10,000 copies of the A.B.C., the privilege for which belonged to John Day,* with the forged imprint of the latter. In October, 1586, the Wardens seized three presses belonging to Ward, together with 'divers other parcells of pryntinge stuffe'. Four years later they made another descent upon Ward, and found that he was printing with a clandestine press which he kept in a tailor's premises near his house, 'and did hide his letters in a hen house near St Sepulchre's Churche, expressely against the Decrees of Star Chamber'. All this material was duly destroyed, but Ward continued to defy the authorities, and only six months later at Hammersmith another press belonging to him was impounded and broken, and the types defaced.

Despite the rigours of the Star Chamber decrees, the authorities were quite unable to stop the flow of prohibited books, and the Puritans, no less than the Roman Catholics, were a thorn in the flesh of Elizabeth and her ministers. The more extreme Puritans, unable openly to attack the episcopacy embodied in the uncompromising Whitgift, made use of secret and illegal presses, the best-known of

---

* In the case of Richard Day (John Day's son) versus T. Dunn, R. Robinson and others (1585) it was stated that the defendants had printed and disposed of 10,000 copies of the A.B.C. and Catechism in eight months.

which is that of the printer Robert Waldegrave, who was responsible for the frequently scurrilous pamphlets which were issued under the pseudonym of 'Martin Marprelate'. Waldegrave, who was twice put in prison for printing Puritan works, moved his press from place to place, but in the end the chase grew too hot, and to escape further imprisonment Waldegrave fled overseas to La Rochelle, and thence, in 1590, to Edinburgh, where he was appointed King's Printer to King James VI. When James succeeded to the English throne, Waldegrave returned to London, where he died in 1604. The Marprelate press was, after the flight of Waldegrave, carried on by others. Another of the illegal presses was the Jesuit press with which Robert Parsons and Edmund Campion were connected, and which operated first at Greenstreet House, East Ham, and later at Stonor Park.

'For the avoyding of the excessive number of printers within this realme', the decree of 1586 limited the number of apprentices a master printer might have. A Master, or Upper Warden, of the Company was allowed three; an Under Warden and Liverymen, two; the yeomanry, one. The Queen's Printer, however, was permitted to have six. The printers at Oxford and Cambridge were allowed no more than one apprentice at a time, but were given permission to 'have and use the help of any journeyman, being freemen of the city of London, without contradiction'.

In 1587 a regulation of the Stationers' Company limited the size of an edition, for the protection of the journeyman, and it was ordered 'that no formes of letters be kept standing to the prejudice of workmen'. Editions were, for the general run of printing, to be of from 1,250 to 1,500; an exception was made for grammars, prayer books and catechisms, of which there might be three or four impressions a year, each of from 2,500 to 3,000. Calendars, almanacs and prognostications, for which there was always a great demand, were exempted from this ruling, and the official work of the Queen's Printer was not limited. In practice, however, the provisions of this order seem to have been largely disregarded, for in 1635 they were replaced by new regulations which gave more consideration to special cases and allowed a greater measure of freedom.

With regard to the entry of copies, it was stipulated that, should a work go out of print, the owner of the copy must either reprint it within six months of a warning to do so, or surrender it to the Company so that it could be reprinted for the benefit of journeymen lacking work.

CHAPTER FIVE

Printing outside London

Early Provincial Printing

Apart from in the university cities of Oxford and Cambridge there was no great call for printing in the provincial towns of Britain during the fifteenth and the first half of the sixteenth century. When the Charter incorporating the Stationers' Company was granted by Philip and Mary in May, 1557, its provisions virtually restricted printing to London and the two Universities; but at the time this made little difference, for what printing there had been elsewhere had already ceased, and the monopoly granted to the Stationers' Company did not result in the closing of any provincial presses. The literate population was so small in most provincial towns at that time that, apart from service books for the churches, there was little scope for a printer.

Up to 1557 printing had been introduced into ten towns outside London; these were Oxford, St Albans, York, Cambridge, Tavistock, Abingdon, Ipswich, Worcester, Canterbury and Norwich.

The first book printed at Oxford gave rise to an erroneous belief that English printing had originated in that city, for it was dated MCCCCLXVIII, and the omission of an 'X' by the printer (for it is now generally accepted that the date of printing was 1478) led to the publication in 1664 of a book which invented a tale of one Frederick Corsellis having been privily taken from Haarlem to Oxford to introduce into England the art of printing.[109]

The wrongly dated book was *Exposicio Sancti Ieronimi Apostolorum* (actually by Rufinus, bishop of Aquileia), which bore no printer's name. It was followed in 1479 by *Tractatus fratris Egidii de peccato originali* and *Textus Ethicorum Aristotelis*. All three books were set in a distinctive type used by Gerhard ten Roem at Cologne. The colophon of the Ægidius, in red, is the earliest example in England of printing in colour.

In 1481 appeared the commentary of Alexander of Hales upon

Aristotle's *De Anima*, which has the earliest woodcut border known in England. In this book the printer's name is given as Theodoric Rood of Cologne, whose previous history has not been traced. About 1483 he went into partnership with an Oxford stationer named Thomas Hunte, and the eleven books known to have been produced by the press between 1481 and 1486 make use of some new founts of type, all of which resemble types used at Cologne. It is just possible, considering the change of type when Rood produced his signed work, that the first three books issued from Oxford were not printed by Rood, though this is very unlikely.

The last book to be issued from this press is the *Liber Festivalis* of John Mirk, 1486, which was signed by Hunte alone, Rood having apparently left England in 1485.

There was no further printing from Oxford until a second press was established in 1517 by John Scolar, part of whose material seems to have come from Wynkyn de Worde. This second Oxford press is, says Madan, 'peculiar for its short and almost unrecorded work, and for the entire absence of Theology among its products, whereas in the first press Theology and Classics were about evenly balanced'.[110] Scolar produced only a few books in 1517 and 1518. In 1519 one book was issued by Charles Kyrfoth, printed with Scolar's types, after which the press ceased, and there was a gap of nearly sixty years in Oxford printing until Joseph Barnes became the first University printer in 1585.

The second English provincial press was set up at St Albans, where eight books were printed by a printer of whom we know next to nothing, but who was referred to by Wynkyn de Worde as 'sometyme scole master of Saynt Albons'. He used three bastarda types and one text, all very like Caxton's types. The first book issued by the schoolmaster-printer was an edition of *Super Eleganciis Tullianis* by Augustinus Datus, undated, with a colophon which merely says *Apud Sanctum Albanum*. It was probably printed in 1479 or 1480.

The first dated book from this press was the *Rhetorica Nova* of Laurentius de Saona (which Caxton was printing about the same time). The colophon states: *Impressum fuit hoc presens opus Rethorice facultatis apud villa sancti Albani. Anno domini M.CCCC.Lxxx.* This was followed by four other scholastic works, printed presumably for the Abbey school, and finally two works of more general interest, the *Chronicles of England* and treatises on hawking, hunting and coat armour, known collectively as the *Book of St Albans*. The second treatise ends 'Explicit Dam Julyan Barnes in her boke of Huntyng', and this has led to all three treatises being ascribed to a certain Dame Juliana Berners, supposedly the daughter of Sir James Berners (beheaded in 1388), and Prioress of the Nunnery of Sopwell, a dependency of St Albans. Most of the two hawking and hunting treatises seems to derive from Twici's *L'Art de Vénerie*, and the *Livre de Chasse* of Gaston, Comte de Foix, known as Gaston Phoebus. This was translated into English under the title *The Master of Game* by Edward III's grandson, Edward the second Duke of York.

The treatise on coat armour has the distinction of containing the first specimen of colour work in English printing,* for the heraldic shields at the end are coloured. Burch says:

> Considering the rude nature of the appliances then in use, the press work is fairly well done, and the register maintained between the different colours is usually good. Red, blue, and brown were used, in addition to the common black, the yellow that appears on some of the shields being most likely added by hand. The same tints were also used in printing the initials throughout the book.[111]

The *Book of St Albans* is dated 1486, and was, as far as we know, the last book to be printed at St Albans until 1534, when John Herford worked there for about five years.

Owing to the great similarity between the types used by the schoolmaster of St Albans and those used by Caxton it has at various times been suggested that there was a close connection between the two presses, and A. W. Pollard says of the St Albans printer that 'he appears to have borrowed some type from Caxton, so that it was presumably with the latter's goodwill that he reprinted his version of the *Chronicles of England*, adding thereto an appendix entitled *Fructus Temporum*.'[112] This, however, seems to be an error, since the text is a different version, later reprinted by De Worde.

Speculation, indeed, surrounds the mysterious printer of St Albans. Whether or not it has any significance, it is interesting to note that his device—a double cross and orb with the arms of St Albans—strikingly resembles the devices of the early Italian printers. The orb and cross device was also used by Italians working in other countries, for example de Portonariis and Giunta at Lyons.

---

* Apart from the colophon in the Oxford book mentioned above.

The first connection between York and the art of printing seems to date from 1493, when a well-known stationer named Frederick Egmont commissioned Joannes Hertzog of Venice to print a Breviary for York use. In 1497 a Dutchman named Frederick Freez (probably Vries), became a freeman of the city, where he traded as bookbinder and stationer. He may also have been a printer, for in a lawsuit of 1510–11 he is described as a 'buke-prynter'; but nothing of his is known. His brother Gerard, who took the name of Wandsforth, was also a York stationer for whom Pierre Violette of Rouen printed in 1507 an edition of the *Expositio Hymnorum et Sequentiarum*, the first book with a York imprint.

The first books known to have been printed in York, six in all, were the work of two printers—Hugo Goes and Ursyn Mylner. The first-named may have been connected with the famous Antwerp printer Mathias van der Goes, but there is no evidence for this other than the similarity of name. The only book of his now known is an edition of the York *Directorium*, which he printed in the Steengate in 1509. The type appears to have been one formerly used by Wynkyn de Worde. He is said also to have printed a *Donatus Minor cum Remigio* and an *Accidence*, according to a York barrister, Christopher Hildyard, who described them in 1664. They were then bound up with a copy of a grammar printed by Wynkyn de Worde in 1506, but whether they still exist is unknown.

The other York printer was Ursyn Mylner, who about 1513 printed two service books *in cimiterio ministerii Sancti Petri*; one was the *Festum visitationis B.M.V.*, and the other a supplement to the Sanctorale of the Breviary. He later moved to Blake Street, in St Helen's parish, and became a freeman of the city. In December, 1516, Mylner issued an edition of Whittinton's *Editio de concinitate grammatices et constructione*, a small quarto of 24 leaves, having at the end Ursyn's device of a shield hanging on a tree, supported by an ass and a bear (the latter an allusion to his name Ursyn); on the shield are a sun and a windmill (the latter referring to his name of Mylner). The title-page has a woodcut of a schoolmaster and pupils, which had been used in several grammars by Wynkyn de Worde. He in turn seems to have had it from Govaert van Ghemen, who used it in a grammar printed at Gouda in 1486.

After 1516 nothing further is heard of Mylner, and from that time until 1533 practically all the York book trade was in the hands of a French stationer named John Gachet, whose name is first mentioned in the colophon of a *Manual* for York use printed by Wynkyn de Worde *pro Johanne gaschet et Jacobo ferrebouc sociis*; at least the colophon says *Impressum per Wynandum de Worde*, but the type, the music staves and the *criblé* initials all point to the book's French origin, and as Duff points out, the Wynkyn de Worde device on the title-page is only found in books printed for him in France. Jacques Ferrebouc was a Paris stationer, but Gachet settled in York and in 1516 and 1517 issued other service books for York use, printed for him by Pierre Olivier of Rouen. He then left York and is next heard of in Hereford, where he issued, in May, 1517, a Rouen-printed *Ortus Vocabulorum*. A William Gachet, stationer of York some years later, was probably his son.

In 1525 a translation by John Walton of Boethius, *De Consolatione Philosophiae*, was printed at Tavistock under the title *The boke of comfort*, by a monk of the exempt monastery called Thomas Rychard. It was, according to the colophon, produced at the request of Robert Langdon, a Cornish gentleman whose arms appear at the end of the book. The only other Tavistock book known is the Statutes of the Stannary, or *Charter Perteyninge to All the Tynners within the County of Devonshire*, printed in 1534. This quarto of 26 leaves contains a wood-cut of God the Father used also in the Boethius. Exeter College, Oxford, possesses the only known copy of this work.

The early press at Abingdon is represented by a single book—a Breviary printed for the Benedictines of St Mary's Monastery by John Scolar in 1528. He must have been the Oxford printer of 1517–18. The only copy known (lacking two of the full complement of 358 leaves) is in the library of Emmanuel College, Cambridge.

Canterbury's first printer was John Mychell, who, after printing at least two books in London at 'the long shop in the Poultry', migrated to Canterbury about 1549 and there printed a number of books, of which the first was an edition of the Psalms, which also survives as a unique copy. His last book, published in 1556, was Cardinal Pole's *Articles to be enquyred in the ordinary visitacion of the Dioces of Cantorbury*. He printed one book by Lancelot Ridley, cousin to the martyred bishop, called *An Exposityon in Englyshe upon the Epistyll of Saynt Paule to the Phillipias . . .*, an undated book, probably of 1550, printed by Mychell 'in Saynt Paules Paryshe'.

The earliest printing at Ipswich provides us with some puzzling

PHILOBIBLON

RICHARDI DVNELMENSIS

sive

DE AMORE LIBRORVM, ET INSTI-
TVTIONE BIBLIOTHECÆ,
tractatus pulcherrimus.

Ex collatione cum varijs manuscriptis editio jam secunda;

cui

Accessit appendix de manuscriptis Oxoniensibus.

Omnia hæc,
Opera & studio T. I. Novi Coll. in alma Academia
Oxoniensi Socij.

B. P. N.
Non quæro quod mihi vtile est, sed quod multis.

Oxoniæ,
Excudebat *Iosephus Barnesius.* 1599.

Richard de Bury's *Philobiblon* was first printed at Cologne in 1473. The first edition
in England was printed at Oxford by Joseph Barnes in 1599, and edited by Thomas
James, Bodley's first librarian

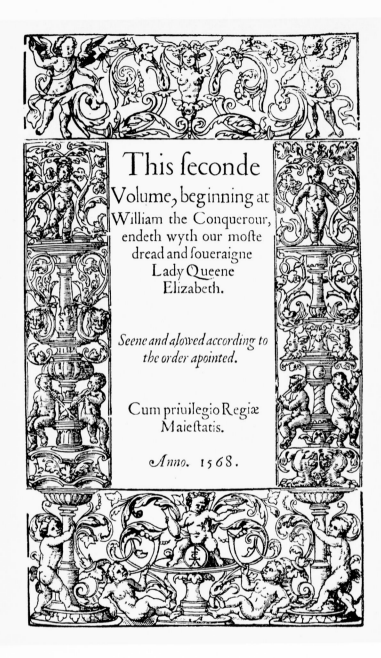

This seconde

Volume, beginning at William the Conquerour, endeth wyth our moſte dread and foueraigne Lady Queene Elizabeth.

Seene and aſowed according to the order apointed.

Cum priuilegio Regiæ Maieſtatis.

Anno. 1568.

Title-page of the second volume of Richard Grafton's *Chronicle at Large*, 1568–9

Numb.

The Daily Courant.

Wednesday, March 11, 1702.

From the Harlem Courant, Dated March 18. N. S.

Naples, Feb. 22.

ON Wednesday last, our New Viceroy, the Duke of Escalona, arriv'd here with a Squadron of the Galleys of Sicily. He made his Entrance dreft in a French habit; and to give us the greater Hopes of the King's coming hither, went to Lodge in one of the little Palaces, leaving the Royal one for his Majesty. The Marquis of Grigni is also arriv'd here with a Regiment of French.

Rome, Feb. 25. In a Military Congregation of State that was held here, it was Resolv'd to draw a Line from Ascoli to the Borders of the Ecclesiastical State, thereby to hinder the Incursions of the Transalpine Troops. Orders are sent to Civita Vecchia to fit out the Galleys, and to strengthen the Garrison of that Place. Signior Casali is made Governor of Perugia. The Marquis del Vasto, and the Prince de Caserta continue still in the Imperial Embassador's Palace; where his Excellency has a Guard of 50 Men every Night in Arms. The King of Portugal has defir'd the Arch-Bishoprick of Lisbon, vacant by the Death of Cardinal Sousa, for the Infante his second Son, who is about 11 Years old.

Vienna, Mar. 4. Orders are sent to the 4 Regiments of Foot, the 2 of Cuiraffiers, and to that of Dragoons, which are broke up from Hungary, and are on their way to Italy, and which confift of about 14 or 15000 Men, to haften their March thither with all Expedition. The 6 new Regiments of Huffars that are now raising, are in fo great a forwardness, that they will be compleat, and in a Condition to march by the middle of May. Prince Lewis of Baden has written to Court, to excuse himself from coming thither, his Presence being so very necessary, and fo much defir'd on the Upper-Rhine.

Francfort, Mar. 12. The Marquifs d' Uxelles is come to Strasburg, and is to draw together a Body of fome Regiments of Horse and Foot from the Garrisons of Alsace; but will not leffen those of Strasburg and Landau, which are already very weak. On the other hand, the Troops of His Imperial Majesty, and his Allies, are going to form a Body near Germefhein in the Palatinate, of which Place, as well as of the Lines at Spires, Prince Lewis of Baden is expected to take a View, in three or four days. The English and Dutch Minifters, the Count of Frife, and the Baron Vander Meer, and likewise the Imperial Envoy Count Lowenftein, are gone to Nordlingen, and it is hop'd that in a fhort time we fhall hear from thence of fome favourable Resolutions for the Security of the Empire.

Liege, Mar. 14. The French have taken the Cannon de Longie, who was Secretary to the Dean de Mean, out of our Caftle, where he has been for fome time a Prifoner, and have deliver'd him to the Provoft of Maubeuge, who has carry'd him from hence, but we do not know whither.

Paris, Mar. 13. Our Letters from Italy fay, That it of our Reinforcements were Landed there; that the Imperial and Ecclesiastical Troops feem to live very peaceably with one another in the Country of Parma, and that the Duke of Vendome, as he was vifiting feveral Pofts, was within 100 Paces of falling into the Hands of the Germans. The Duke of Chartres, the Prince of Conti, and feveral other Princes of the Blood, are to make the Campaign in

Flanders under the Duke of Burgundy; and the Duke of Maine is to Command upon the Rhine.

From the Amfterdam Courant, Dated Mar. 18.

Rome, Feb. 25. We are taking here all poffible Precautions for the Security of the Ecclesiastical State in this prefent Conjuncture, and have defir'd to raife 3000 Men in the Cantons of Switzerland. The Pope has appointed the Duke of Berwick to be his Lieutenant-General, and he is to Command 6000 Men on the Frontiers of Naples: He has alfo fettled upon him a Penfion of 6000 Crowns a year during Life.

From the Paris Gazette, Dated Mar. 18. 1702.

Naples, Febr. 17. 600 French Soldiers are arrived here, and are expected to be follow'd by 3400 more. A Courier that came hither on the 14th. has brought Letters by which we are affur'd that the King of Spain defigns to be here towards the end of March; and accordingly Orders are given to make the neceffary Preparations against his Arrival. The two Troops of Horse that were Commanded to the Abruzzo are pofted at Pefcara with a Body of Spanifh Foot, and others in the Fort of Montorio.

Paris, March. 18. We have Advice from Toulon of the 5th inftant, that the Wind having long ftood favourable, 22000 Men were already fail'd for Italy, that 2500 more were Embarking, and that by the 15th it was hoped they might all get thither. The Count d' Eftrees arriv'd there on the Third inftant, and fet all hands at work to fit out the Squadron of 9 Men of War and fome Fregats, that are appointed to carry the King of Spain to Naples. His Catholick Majefty will go on Board the *Thunderer*, of 110 Guns.

We have Advice by an Exprefs from Rome of the 18th of February, That notwithftanding the preffing Inftances of the Imperial Embaffador, the Pope had Condemn'd the Marquis del Vafto to lofe his Head and his Eftate to be confifcated, for not appearing to Anfwer the Charge against him of Publickly Scandalizing Cardinal Janfon.

ADVERTISEMENT.

IT will be found from the Foreign Prints, which from time to time, as Occasion offers, will be mention'd in this Paper, that the Author has taken Care to be duly furnifh'd with all that comes from Abroad in any Language. And for an Affurance that he will not, under Pretence of having Private Intelligence, impofe any Additions of feign'd Circumftances to an Action, but give his Extracts fairly and Impartially; at the beginning of each Article he will quote the Foreign Paper from whence 'tis taken, that the Publick, feeing from what Country a piece of News comes with the Allowance of that Government, may be better able to Judge of the Credibility and Fairnefs of the Relation: Nor will he take upon him to give any Comments or Conjectures of his own, but will relate only Matter of Fact; fuppofing other People to have Senfe enough to make Reflections for themfelves.

This Courant (as the Title fhews) will be Publifh'd Daily: being defign'd to give all the Material News as foon as every Poft arrives: and is confin'd to half the Compafs, to fave the Publick at leaft half the Impertinences, of ordinary News-Papers.

LONDON. Sold by E. Mallet, next Door to the King's-Arms Tavern at Fleet-Bridge.

The first daily newspaper published in England

SPECIMEN

By *JOHN BASKERVILLE* of BIRMINGHAM,

In the County of Warwick, *Letter-Founder and Printer.*

To CNEIUS PLANCIUS.

I Am indebted to you for two letters, dated from Corcyra. You congratulate me in one of them on the account you have received, that I ftill preferve my former authority in the commonwealth: and wifh me joy in the other of my late marriage. With refpect to the firft, if to mean well to the intereft of my country and to approve that meaning to every friend of its liberties, may be confidered as maintaining my authority; the account you have heard is certainly true. But if it confifts in rendering thofe fentiments effectual to the public welfare, or at leaft in daring freely to fupport

To *CAIUS CASSIUS*, proquæftor.

MY own inclinations have anticipated your recommendation: and I have long fince received Marcus Fabius into the number of my friends. He has extremely endeared himfelf to me indeed, by his great politenefs and elegance of manners: but particularly by the fingular affection I have obferved he bears towards you. Accordingly, tho' your letter in his behalf was not without effect, yet my own knowledge of the regard he entertains for you had fomewhat more: you may be affured therefore I fhall very faithfully confer upon him the good offices you requeft.

TO THE PUBLIC.

JOHN BASKERVILLE propofes, by the advice and affiftance of feveral learned men, to print, from the Cambridge edition corrected with all poffible care, an elegant edition of Virgil. The work will be printed in quarto, on a very fine writing royal paper, and with the above letter. The price of the Volume in fheets will be one guinea, no part of which will be required till the book is delivered. It will be put to prefs as foon as the number of Subfcribers fhall amount to five hundred, whofe names will be prefixt to the work. All perfons who are inclined to encourage the undertaking, are defired to fend their names to JOHN BASKERVILLE in Birmingham; who will give fpecimens of the work to all who are defirous of feeing them.

Subfcriptions are alfo taken in, and fpecimens delivered by Meffieurs R. and J. DODSLEY, Bookfellers in Pall Mall, London. MDCCLIV.

Baskerville specimen page, 1574

Opposite. Frontispiece to the Book of Common Prayer, published by William Pickering in 1853 and printed by Charles Whittingham. The illustrations are based on the so-called *Queen Elizabeth's Prayer Book*, printed by John Day in 1569, 1579 and 1581

2 PARALIPOM. 6.

*Domine Deus Iſrael, non eſt ſimilis tui Deus in cœlo & in terra, qui
cuſtodis paƈtum & miſericordiam cum ſeruis tuis, qui ambulant coram te
in toto corde ſuo.*

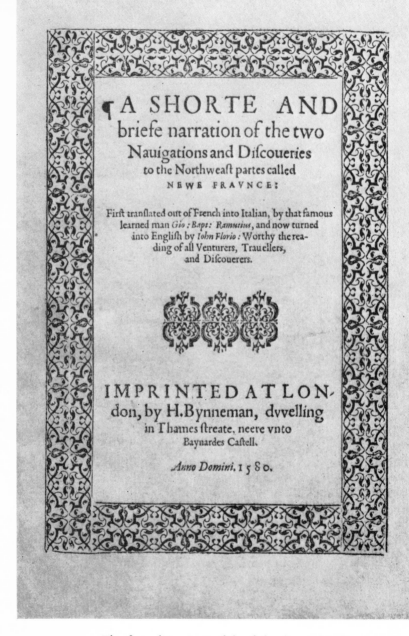

¶A SHORTE AND
briefe narration of the two
Nauigations and Difcoueries
to the Northweaft partes called
NEWE FRAVNCE:

Firft tranflated out of French into Italian, by that famous
learned man *Gio : Bapt: Ramufius*, and now turned
into Englifh by *Iohn Florio :* Worthy the reading of all Venturers, Trauellers,
and Difcouerers.

IMPRINTED AT LON-
don, by H.Bynneman, dvvelling
in Thames ftreate, neere vnto
Baynardes Caftell.

Anno Domini, 1 5 8 o.

The firft edition in English of the discoveries of
Jacques Cartier. The translator was John Florio

16 Jf any half voẃel, ꝺꝍ folow : r,
our ſpeḋ ſerueṫ ẃel,tꝍ ſpel ṫem tꝍgeṫer.

17 And ṫis ſtrṗk (,) iz erception general',
tꝍ ſpel woꝛḋ trulṗ, ẃen ṫæꝫ rulꝫ fail al'.

18 Ṅot ẃel, ṫér iz neuer tru ſillabl',
wiṫout voẃel, dipṫong, oꝛ half voẃel.

19 And ṫoẃ half voẃelꝫ be ſpelḋ beſt alón,
ṗet ṫe nert conſonant it depenḋeṫ on.

20 Bṗ eꝫ, oꝛ ꝫ, ṫe plural' ꝺꝍ ges,
ẃꝍꝫ ſimpl'ꝫ genitiuꝫ, end eꝫ, oꝛ ꝫ.

¶ The 12. Chapter,

ſheweth the vſe *of this amendment, by matter in*
proſe with the ſame ortography,conteining
arguments for the premiſſes.

An erer-
cṗꝫ foꝛ
erampl'.

Ꝝr-in iz ẃeẃed an erercṗꝫ of ṫe amended oꝛtogra-
pẖṗ befóꝛ ẃeẃed, and ṫe vc of ṫe pꝛikꝫ, ſtrṗkꝫ, and
nótꝫ, foꝛ deuṗding of ſillabl'ꝫ accoꝛding tꝍ ṫe rulꝫ
befóꝛ ẃeẃed.Ẃær-in iz tꝍ be noted,ṫat nó art,erer-
cṗꝫ, mirtur,ſciencc, oꝛ occupacion,ẃat-ſocuer, iz included in ón ṫing ónlṗ:but haṫ in it ſeueral' diſtinccionꝫ,elementꝫ,
pꝛincipl'ꝫ,oꝛ deuiꝫionꝫ, bṗ ṫe ẃiḋ ṫe ſám comeṫ tꝍ hiꝫ perfet vc.
And bicauꝫ ṫe ſingl' deuiꝫionꝫ foꝛ engliſẖ ſpeḋ) , ár at ṫis daṗ ſo ꝩn-
perfetlṗ pictured, bṗ ṫe elementꝫ(ẃiḋ we cal' letterꝫ)pꝛouṗded foꝛ
ṫe ſám,(aꝫ maṗ apper plainlṗ in ṫis fóꝛmer trætic) J haũ ſet furṫ
ṫis woꝛk foꝛ ṫe amendment of ṫe ſám : ẃiḋ J hóp wil be tákn
in gꝍd part accoꝛding tꝍ mṗ mæning : foꝛ ṫat,ṫat it hal' ſaũ char-
geꝫ in ṫe elder ſoꝛt, ꝫ ſaũ græt tṗm in ṫe ṗuṫ,tꝍ ṫe græt comodi-
tṗ of al' eſtátꝫ,ꝩntꝍ ẃꝍm it iz neceſſarṗ,ṫat ṫér be a knowledg of
ṫeir dutṗ, ꝩntꝍ God ḋeflṗ, and ṫen ṫeir dutṗ ón tꝍ an oṫer : in
knowing of ẃiḋ dutṗ , conſiſteṫ ṫe hapi eſtát of manꝫ lṗf : foꝛ ignoꝛanc cauꝫeṫ manṗ tꝍ go out-of ṫe waṗ, and ṫat of al' eſtátꝫ, in
ẃꝍm ignoꝛanc ꝺoṫ reſt : ṫær-bṗ God iz grætlṗ diſ-plæꝫed , ṫe
comon qietnes of men hindered : grat comon welḋꝫ deuṗded, ma-
giſtrátꝫ

Df pꝛo-
fit, ṫe
græteſt
iz tꝍ be
ḋóꝫn.

Jgno-
ranc cau-
ꝫeṫ ma-
nṗ tꝍ fal'
ꝫ offend.

Bullokars Booke at large, for the amendment of orthographie for English
speech. Henry Denham, London, 1580. William Bullokar was a
sixteenth-century phonetist who advocated a 40-letter alphabet

VENVS
AND ADONIS

Vilia miretur vulgus: mihi flauus Apollo
Pocula Castalia plena ministret aqua.

LONDON

Imprinted by Richard Field, and are to be sold at
the signe of the white Greyhound in
Paules Church-yard.
1593.

The title-page of the unique copy of the first edition of
Venus and Adonis (1593) now in the Bodleian Library,
Oxford

John de Beau Chesne and John Baildon's *A Booke containing
divers sortes of hands*. Page showing the text hand.
Thomas Vautrollier, London, 1571

features, for of the books supposedly printed at Ipswich by three different printers, all but one are attributed to the year 1548, and the remaining one was probably printed late in 1547 or early in 1548.

John Oswen printed nine books at Ipswich in the latter half of 1548, all of them works of the reformers; John Overton printed one book by a reformer at Ipswich in 1548 (according to the colophon); and Anthony Scoloker printed seven books at Ipswich—again all works of the reformers. Oswen stayed in Ipswich only for a few months, moving to Worcester before the end of the year; Scoloker only stayed in Ipswich for about six months; and John Overton we know only as the publisher of Bale's *Illustrium majoris Britanniae scriptorum summarium* (1548). His name is not found again. So we are confronted with the rather unlikely situation in which three printers suddenly decide to go to Ipswich for a few months, print a number of controversial books, and then go their separate ways, leaving Ipswich without a printer for the next century or so.

Oswen went to Worcester probably at the end of 1548, and on 6 January, 1549, received a privilege from Edward VI to print service books and books of instruction for his subjects 'of the principality of Wales, and the marches thereunto belonging' for the space of seven years. He had his press in the High Street, Worcester, and, from the colophons of some of his books he had an agent in Shrewsbury. At Worcester he printed some twenty books, the last ones being the *Statutes An. 7 Ed. VI.* (1553), and *An Homelye to read in the tyme of pestilence*, also 1553. In addition to various theological works he printed quarto and folio editions of the Book of Common Prayer, as well as the New Testament and the Psalter. He probably gave up printing on the accession of Queen Mary, and quite possibly went abroad.

Of Anthony Scoloker we know very little, save what we can gather from the imprint on his books, which shows that for a time he was associated with William Seres. His books are rarely dated and seem all to have been published between 1547 and 1548. A. W. Pollard, in his article on Scoloker in the D.N.B., says that he printed first in London and then went to Ipswich; E. Gordon Duff states that he printed first in Ipswich and then came to London. This seems more probable, since his name occurs (spelt Scolyca) in the Lay Subsidies, Middlesex, 1549, as dwelling in St Clement's in the Liberty of the Duchy of Lancaster. Despite the foreign-sounding name he is listed as an Englishman, with one servant, an alien named Hans Rycard.

According to the colophon of some of the books he printed at

Ipswich, Scoloker is said to have lived in St Nicholas Parish, but the early histories of Ipswich make no mention of him. B. P. Grimsey's monograph on the Parish of St Nicholas, Ipswich, quotes an extract from Stowe MS. 881 in the British Museum* concerning Scoloker, made by Christopher Le Neve, Norroy King of Arms, but this is merely compiled from the titles and colophons of one or two books by Scoloker in his possession.

All the books bearing Scoloker's name are poorly printed in types which are almost certainly of Antwerp origin, as are the woodcuts, one of which, from the *Ordinary for all faithful Christians* (c. 1548) shows the interior of a printing office, with a press being worked. This cut was first used by Josse Lambrecht at Gent, in a book by Cornelius van der Heyden, 1545.

Scoloker published several books in his own translation from French and German, including the one just mentioned; he also issued books by the reformers Luther, Ochino, and Zwingli, translated by Richard Argentyne. After issuing a few books in partnership with Seres 'without Aldersgate', he moved to Savoy Rents, where he printed several undated books. His device shows a hand rubbing a coin against a touchstone inscribed *Verbum Dei*, together with the motto 'Prove the spyrites whether they be of God'.

Was Scoloker a printer? And did he print at Ipswich? Overton did not; the Ipswich imprint on Bale's book is fictitious. I am inclined to think that Scoloker was merely a publisher and that the books he issued were printed in the Low Countries, and whilst there is nothing to disprove that he printed at Ipswich there remains the possibility that the Ipswich address may be fictitious in his case also.

Printing at Norwich began shortly after the arrival there of a master printer from Brabant named Anthony de Solen (Solempne, Solemne) about 1567. He was made a freeman of the city on 11 December, 1570, on condition that he exercised no profession other than 'his arte of prynting and selling of Renysh wine' (*Assembly Book*. Folio 180). The Psalms in Dutch came from his press in 1568, and in fact almost all his books were in Dutch, for he had set up his press for the benefit of the many Flemish refugees who had taken refuge in Norwich. The only known specimen of his printing in English is a broadside entitled *Certayne versis written by Thomas Brooke*, which has the colophon

---

* Manuscript notes on Ipswich collected by Thomas Martin of Palgrave.

'Imprinted at Norwiche in the Paryshe of Saynct Andrewe by Anthony de Solempne. 1570'. He continued printing until 1579, but as there is a large gap in his work between 1570 and 1578 it is probable that a number of works from his press are lost.

A second press functioned at St Albans from 1534 or earlier until the suppression of the abbey in 1539. The printer was John Herford (Hereford, Hertford). The first dated book known from this press is the *Lyfe and passion of Seint Albon* by John Lydgate (1534), which was printed at the request of Robert Catton, abbot of St Albans. In 1536 Herford printed a work by John Gwynneth, a monk of the abbey, entitled *The confutacyon of the fyrst parte of Frythes boke*, in which can be seen a curious device with the intertwined letters R.S., standing for Richard Stevenage, the last abbot.

Herford apparently got into trouble over printing a 'naughty book', for Stevenage wrote to Cromwell on 12 October, 1539, saying:

> Sent John Pryntare to London with Harry Pepwell, Bonere [Bonham] and Tabbe, of Powlles churchyard stationers, to order him at your pleasure. Never heard of the little book of detestable heresies till the stationers showed it me.★

Duff thinks this was a book called *A very declaration of the bond and free wyll of man*, which has no printer's name or date, but has the address of St Albans.[113] Whatever the result of the enquiry, the suppression of the abbey in 1539 precluded the printer from returning there, and he is later found working in London in Aldersgate Street, where in 1544 he printed Leland's *Assertio inclytissimi Arturii regis Britanniae*, a small quarto, which he followed in 1545 with the same author's *Cygnea cantio*. Herford was the printer of the folio *Compendiosa totius delineatio* with engraved plates by Thomas Gemini after anonymous woodcuts designed by Jan Stephan van Calcar for the 1543 Basle edition of Vesalius. Gemini's was only the second book to be published in England with copper-plate engraving.

Herford printed about twenty-four books in London, for Robert Toy and other stationers. No book of his is known later than 1548, which may have been the year of his death.

Not until 1521 was there any printing press in Cambridge, the

★ *Letters & Papers of Henry VIII*. Vol. XIV. Pt. 2. No. 315.

requirements of the University being met by licensed stationers. In 1517 Erasmus's old friend and pupil, Richard Croke, who had been teaching Greek at Leipzig, returned to Cambridge to become reader in Greek at the University. Finding no elementary text-book available for his pupils he commissioned a certain John Laer of Siegburg, commonly known as John Siberch, who acted as agent for Cologne and Antwerp printers and publishers, to have his *Rudimenta* printed. This was done by Eucharius Cervicornus at Cologne.

Croke and other members of the University, aware of the need for a press in Cambridge, obtained a loan of £20 from the University, to enable Siberch to come over and set up a press. Accordingly (though the loan it seems was never repaid) Siberch settled in Cambridge and printed in 1521 Henry Bullock's speech made when Cardinal Wolsey visited the University in 1520.

During his residence in Cambridge Siberch printed ten books, including an unauthorized edition of Erasmus's *Libellus de Conscribendis Epistolis*, which annoyed the author, who wrote in the preface to Froben's edition of this work (1522): 'Printers, with a brazen face, follow the satyrists' maxim: "Money smells good whatever it is made of".'

Another of Siberch's publications was the sermon delivered by Bishop Fisher when Luther's books were publicly burnt in London. Although a few Greek words, cut in wood, were introduced into De Worde's edition of Whittinton's *Syntaxis* in 1517, the first appearance of Greek type in England was in Lucan's *Dipsodes*, with Bullock's translation, printed by Siberch in 1521. By 1522 Siberch had left Cambridge, and after the closure of his press printing at Cambridge lapsed until 1584, when Thomas Thomas was elected University printer, by virtue of letters patent issued exactly fifty years previously, which gave the University licence

> to assign and elect from time to time . . . three stationers and printers, or sellers of books, residing within the University . . . empowered to print all manner of books approved of by the Chancellor or his viceregent and three doctors, and to sell and expose to sale in the University or elsewhere within the realm, as well such books as other books. . . .

This charter of Henry VIII was not favourably viewed by the Stationers' Company, which regarded it as an infringement of their monopoly, and when Thomas Thomas became University printer (despite the fact that, according to Lord Burghley, he was 'a man

utterlie ignoraunte in printing') the Company took drastic action and
seized both his press and the sheets of the book he was printing. The
University naturally prepared to defend its rights under the charter
against all attacks from outside, and the letters patent having been
found valid by the Master of the Rolls, Thomas resumed his printing.

He died in 1588, and was succeeded by John Legate, to whom falls
the honour of having printed the first Cambridge Bible—an octavo
edition of the Geneva Version; he had already printed a minute 48mo
edition of the Genevan New Testament in 1589.

The First Printing in Scotland

Printing was not introduced into Scotland before 1508, when
Andrew Myllar, with the financial assistance of a merchant named
Walter Chepman, established the first press. Myllar was an Edinburgh
bookseller with business connections among the printers of Rouen.
Among the books printed for him in that city were *Multorum vocabulorum equivocorum interpretatio* by John de Garlandia (1505) and *Expositio Hymnorum et Sequentiarum ad usum Sarum* (1506). Neither book
has the name of the printer, but from the woodcut on the title-page
of the John of Garlandia it is thought that he was probably Pierre
Violette of Rouen.

Chepman, as a prosperous merchant, alive to the advantages of a
press in Edinburgh, probably mentioned the fact to James IV of
Scotland, with whom he was on terms of personal friendship, and
suggested that Myllar was quite capable of undertaking the practical
work entailed by a printing office. At all events the king granted a
Letter of Privilege for the setting up of a printing press in 1507 and
the partners began to issue their first books at the latest in April, 1508,
from their printing house in the Southgait (now Cowgate) of Edinburgh. This was a series of ballads, the only known copies of which
are now in the National Library of Scotland. These small pamphlets
were first discovered, bound together in one volume, in 1785, a remarkable and valuable find. They are printed in a black-letter type
which Myllar probably got from Rouen, where he seems to have
learned his art. In some of these pieces is found Myllar's device—one
of the punning devices so popular with the early printers—showing
a windmill with a miller bearing a sack upon his shoulder climbing a
ladder into the mill. In each of the upper corners is a small shield
charged with three fleur-de-lis, with Myllar's name and merchant's
mark at the bottom.

In 1510 appeared the Aberdeen Breviary, produced at the instance of William Elphinstone, Bishop of Aberdeen. 'The patent granted to Chepman and Myllar', writes Robert Dickson, 'is so specific on the subject of the Aberdeen Breviary, while all the other material for the new press is left indefinite, that we are forced to the conclusion that the art was introduced chiefly to allow the Bishop facilities for personally superintending the production of his service-book.'[114]

Four copies of this Breviary are known, all of which are imperfect, and one of these copies contains, bound up with the *Pars Hyemalis*, eight extra leaves on which were printed *The Office of Our Lady of Pity* and *The Legend of the Advent of the Relics of St Andrew*. The colophon of these pieces informs us that they were printed at Edinburgh by John Story for Charles Stule. There is no date, and they are thought to have been printed about a decade later than the Breviary, but of the printer nothing is known.

The title-page of the Breviary tells us, in Latin, that it was printed in the town of Edinburgh at the charge of Walter Chepman, merchant, on the ides (13th) of February, in the year of our salvation and grace nine above the thousand and five hundredth (e.g. 1509–10). Neither in the first nor the second part is the name of Myllar mentioned, so the presumption is that he most probably died before the work was completed; no other book of his is known later than 1508.

Nothing is known of further printing in Scotland until 1541–2 when Thomas Davidson printed *The New Actis and Constitutionis of Parliament*. In the interim Scottish booksellers had been obliged to have their books printed overseas. Two copies of this work have survived, both printed on vellum. The most important book printed by Davidson was *The hystory and croniklis of Scotland*—a translation of Hector Boece's *Scotorum Historiae*. This appeared about the year 1542, and is described by Dickson and Edmonds (in perhaps an excess of national pride) as 'an almost unrivalled specimen of early British typography'.* Davidson's device of a shield hanging from a tree and bearing his arms and supported by wild men is not unlike that of the printer Peter Treveris of Southwark, some of whose material he seems to have possessed.

Between 1552 and 1571 the printer John Scot (Skot) was working first at St Andrews and then in Edinburgh, but although some have tried to identify him with a London printer of that name it seems

---

* Dickson and Edmonds. *Annals of Scottish Printing*. Cambridge, 1890.

unlikely that they were one and the same, for the Londoner was printing in 1521, if not earlier, and worked for Wynkyn de Worde as well as on his own account. The John Scot with whom we are here concerned printed books mainly of a theological character, some of which got him into trouble with the authorities, and in 1562 he was arrested and imprisoned by the Edinburgh magistrates for printing Ninian Winziet's *Last Blast of the Trompet*. He then seems to have had his materials confiscated by a creditor, and only reappears as a printer in 1567–8, when he printed for Henry Charteris *The warkis of the famous and vorthie Knicht Schir David Lyndesay*. This quarto he reprinted in 1571, and it is the last book known to have come from his press.

Contemporary with John Scot was Robert Lekpreuik, who, during the twenty years his press was in operation (1561–1581), issued a greater number of individual works than any native printer in Scotland in the sixteenth century. As a printer he was not in the same class as Davidson, but he printed many poems and ballads beloved of his countrymen, as well as theological works, such as the *Confessione of the fayth and doctrin beleved and professed by the Protestantes of the Realme of Scotland* (1561), his first dated book. He received considerable assistance from the leaders of the reformed church, and the General Assembly of December, 1562, awarded him, 'for printing of the psalms ... twa hundreth pounds, to help to buy irons, ink, and paper, and to fie craftsmen for printing'. In 1569–70 he received a further fifty pounds for 'the great zeale and love he beares to serve the Kirk at all tymes'.

In 1564 Lekpreuik obtained patents under the Privy Seal to print the Acts of Parliament of Queen Mary and the Psalms of David in Scottish metre. Two years later he was appointed King's Printer for twenty years with monopolies for the printing of several lucrative works, such as the *Donatus pro pueris* and the *Rudimenta Artis Grammaticae* (both important school text-books), the *Acts of Parliament*, the Psalms, the *Homelies* and the Geneva version of the Bible. One wonders, therefore, why he had to petition the Elders of the Kirk in 1570 for a loan in respect of his poverty.

In 1571 his premises were raided by order of Secretary Maitland, who suspected him of printing a satire on himself by George Buchanan, called the *Chamaeleon*. The printer had been forewarned and managed to escape to Stirling, taking his printing materials with him, for he printed one or two tracts in that town, where he was the first printer to exercise his art. From Stirling he went to St Andrews, where he printed some fifteen works, before returning to Edinburgh in January, 1573-4. Shortly afterwards he was arrested for unlicensed printing and his press and property were confiscated. How long he remained in prison is not known, but no other book of his is known before 1581, in which year he printed a few books, among them Patrick Adamson's *Catechismus Latino Carmine Redditus* and Fowler's *Answer to John Hamilton*. That is the last we hear of him.

Another Scottish printer of the latter half of the sixteenth century is Thomas Bassandyne, who is said to have learned to print in Paris and Leyden before he set up as a printer in Edinburgh. When we first hear of him, in 1568, he is in trouble with the General Assembly, who have ordered him to call in all copies of a book printed by him entitled *The Fall of the Roman Kirk*, in which the King was called 'supreme head of the primitive kirk', and not to sell any of the remainder until he had altered this title-page. The Church must have forgiven him for his offence, for when he offered, in partnership with Alexander Arbuthnot, to print the Bible in Scotland if the Church would assist him, the General Assembly fell in with the proposal. Until this time the Bible had never been printed in Scotland, for although Lekpreuik was granted a patent to do so, he never exercised it.

Letters of Privilege were accordingly granted to the partners in 1575, on condition that they delivered a certain number of copies before the last day of March, 1576, but a folio Bible is not a book that can be produced hurriedly, and in promising to complete it within eleven months the printers must have miscalculated badly, especially as an Edinburgh printing office at that time probably had a limited stock of material. Only the New Testament was completed by 1576, and the whole Bible was not completed and delivered until 1579. Bassandyne's name as printer appears only on the New Testament, for he died in October, 1577.

Arbuthnot carried on the business by himself and was made King's Printer in 1579, with an extensive privilege which enabled him to print, during his lifetime, 'all works in Latin, English, or Scots, tending to the glory of God, and commonweal of this realm'. Unfortunately he was slow and inefficient, and the first edition of Buchanan's *History*, which was published in 1582, was so incorrect that when Crawford published his Notes on Buchanan's History in 1708, the errata he found in Arbuthnot's edition filled twelve pages. So dilatory was Arbuthnot in producing the Bibles which he was licensed to print that the General Assembly, convened at Dundee in 1580, recommended that the London printer Thomas Vautrollier should be given licence to establish a press in Scotland 'because', as they said, 'ther is great necessitie of a printer within this countrey'.

Arbuthnot died in September, 1585. His device (McKerrow 228) was a copy of that used by Richard Jugge (McKerrow 125), and was the work of a Flemish woodcutter, Anton Van Leest (not 'Assuerus vol Londersel', as given in McKerrow). The surviving works of Arbuthnot are few; in addition to the Bible and Buchanan's *History* we know only *The Buik of Alexander the Great*; a Latin tract of six leaves by William Welwood; and the Acts of the Parliament held at Edinburgh in May, 1584.

John Ross, about whom little is known, printed in Edinburgh between 1574 and 1580, and worked mostly for Henry Charteris, who at the time of Ross's death acquired his printing material. Ross is best known for his quarto edition of *The Sevin Seages*, by John Rolland, which he printed for Charteris in 1578. Although 200 copies figured in the inventory made after Ross's death, only one imperfect copy has survived.

Henry Charteris was an Edinburgh bookseller and publisher who himself printed one or two books after he had acquired the stock of John Ross. Previously his books had been printed for him, chiefly by Ross, John Scot, Lekpreuik and Vautrollier. We know, too, that at least one book, Andrew Simson's *Rudimenta*, was printed for him by the famous Antwerp printer Christopher Plantin, who also supplied him with printing ink.[115] The most important book printed by Henry Charteris was the *Works* of Sir David Lindsay, which he first issued in 1582. The last work to bear his imprint was a book of sermons dated 1599, the year in which he died. His son Robert succeeded him in the business.

Thomas Vautrollier, having established a press in Edinburgh in 1584, was patronized by royalty and had the honour of printing in that year the first of King James's published works—*Essayes of a Prentise in the Divine Art of Poesie*—which was reprinted the following year with some slight variations. May it not have been as a reward for the printing of this book that Vautrollier received 'that peece of golde of the king of Skotlande weyinge about ten crownes' which he bequeathed to his son Simeon in his will?

In 1584 Vautrollier printed, as far as we know, eight books in Edinburgh, but in the following year only two. Even with royal patronage there seemed to be insufficient business in that city to warrant his staying there. Whether from lack of encouragement or for some other reason, Vautrollier returned to London in 1586, taking with him a manuscript copy of John Knox's *History of the Reformation*, which he put to press; but almost all the copies were seized by order of Archbishop Whitgift before the work was completed.

Towards the close of his career, Robert Waldegrave (see page 111) set up his press in Edinburgh and was King's Printer to James VI from 1590 until 1603. His Scottish productions were chiefly theological, but he also printed James VI's *Poeticall Exercises at vacant houres* (1591), which the royal poet confessed to having composed in his 'verie young and tender yeares'; and the same royal author's *Daemonologie* (1597) and his *Basilikon Doron*, or Instructions to his son Prince Henry (1599). This last-named book was privately printed and, Waldegrave having been sworn to secrecy, only seven copies were printed, and of these only one (in the British Museum) seems to have survived. The work gave offence to the Presbyterians, and in the second edition, published in London in 1603, the King made a number of alterations in the text.

In this account of early Scottish printing one printer remains to be mentioned, Robert Smyth, who married as his first wife the widow of Thomas Bassandyne. In 1599 he received an extensive licence enabling him to print a wide variety of books for a period of twenty years. In 1592 he followed the example of Ross in printing an edition of *The Sevin Seages*, of which the British Museum copy is the only one now extant. His last dated book is the *Catechisme* of 1602.

Little is known of the life of Robert Smyth; he may quite well have been that 'Roberte Smythe the sonne of John Smythe of Westbury' who was apprenticed to the London printer Hugh Singleton for twelve years from 2 February, 1564-5. Few books of his are known but many must be lost, since he was printing for a considerable time. In 1600 he brought out *Ane compendius Buik of Godly and Spirituall Sangis*, 'exactly correctit and newlye Prented at Edinburgh be Robert Smyth dwelling at the nether bow'. This was a reprint of the book known as the 'Dundee Psalms', of which the first known edition was printed by John Ross in 1578; though from the title of Ross's edition, which included 'sindrie gude and godlie Ballatis not contenit in the first editioun', there must have been at least one earlier edition, now lost. It was reprinted at Edinburgh in 1868.

The Introduction of Printing into Ireland

The first printer in Ireland was Humphrey Powell, who migrated to Dublin in 1550 after having worked for a time in London, where he had a business somewhere 'above Holborn Conduit', from which address he issued a few theological books between 1548 and 1549. In the *Acts of the Privy Council* (New Series. Vol. 3, p. 84) is the following note, under the date 18 July, 1550:

> A warrant to ———— to deliver xx^{li} unto Powell the printer, given him by the Kinges Majestie towardes his setting up in Ireland.

Whether he decided to try his fortune in Ireland because business was bad in London, or whether he was sent there at the instigation of the Government we have no means of knowing; the latter seems the more likely cause, seeing that Edward VI provided him with funds. Styling himself King's Printer, he set up his press in Dublin 'in the great toure by the Crane', and the first of his printings that we know is *The Boke of the common praier* which bears the date 1551. Since this was probably the date of publication he may have begun printing in 1550, soon after his arrival in Ireland. Only two complete copies of the work are known, one of which is in the library of Trinity College, Dublin, and the other in Emmanuel College, Cambridge.

After that, nothing more is known of Powell's work until ten years later. The probability is that most of it was in the form of proclamations and other broadsides which are now lost. His next surviving pieces of work in Dublin are *A Proclamacyon against Shan O'Neil*, an undated single sheet printed in 1561, and *Proclamation against the O'Connors*, dated 16 August, 1564. The last known book of Powell's is *A Brefe Declaration of certein Principall Articles of Religion*, a quarto tract of eight leaves, in which the printer's address is now given as St Nicholas Street. Humphrey Powell was an original member of the Stationers' Company, and most probably related to Thomas Powell, Berthelet's nephew. His name does not reappear after 1566.

The next extant pieces printed in Ireland belong to the year 1571. One is an Irish poem by Philip MacConn Crosach printed as a single sheet; the other an Irish Alphabet and Catechism by John O'Kearney, a small octavo of 56 pages containing the elements of the Irish language, the Catechism, a few prayers, and Archbishop Parker's articles of the Christian rule. These two pieces were issued at the cost of John Usher (Collector of Customs of the port of Dublin) and were probably printed by William Kearney, a relative of the translator of the Catechism.

Both pieces are printed from a fount of Irish type made to the order of Queen Elizabeth for the instruction of the native Irish in the Protestant religion, since, to quote from O'Kearney's preface, great benefits were anticipated for the Irish people as soon as 'their national tongue and its own dear alphabet' were put into print. This Irish fount was presented to John O'Kearney, then Treasurer of St Patrick's, Dublin, and his friend Nicholas Walsh, the Chancellor, who is reputedly the translator of the New Testament into Irish. Who is responsible for the type is not known: among the State Papers (Irish Series) is an entry made in December, 1567, from which we find that the Queen had disbursed £66.13s.4d. 'for the making of carecters for the testament in irishe'. It is not a genuine Irish fount, but a hybrid, only nine letters being specially cut, and for most of the upper case the ordinary roman forms were used. Both upper- and lower-case 'a' are italic, and some manuscript contractions and subscripts appear. According to Reed-Johnson the earliest appearance of this fount is in the broadside poem mentioned above, which was sent to England for Matthew Parker's inspection, presumably as a specimen of the type. The only copy known is in the library of Corpus Christi College, Cambridge, where it forms part of the Archbishop Parker collection, bequeathed to the College, of which he was Master, in 1575. It is quite likely, also, that the small Alphabet and Catechism was intended as a trial of the new fount, before it was used in the New Testament for which it was intended.

It was, however, some time before the Testament was ever printed in Irish, for although William Kearney is said to have had the manuscript of it around 1587, he only began the printing of it, as far as 2f2. It seems likely, as Dix has pointed out,* that this William Kearney is the same person as the William 'Carney' or 'Kerney' who worked as a printer in London, and who, by warrant dated 17 October, 1591 (*Acts of Privy Council, England. N.S.* Vol. XXII. p. 26), was authorized, together with his assigns, to take his presses and material into Ireland, where he was to 'printe the Iryshe Bibles in Ireland & soche other bookes as shuld be thought necessary by the Lord Deputie & Councell of that realme'. William Kearney seems to have been in Ireland on several separate occasions, but there is no record of his ever having printed an Irish Bible; the only extant specimen of his printing is a *Proclamation against the Earl of Tyrone and his adherents in Ulster*, printed in black-letter (differing from that used by Powell), which

---

* E. R. McC. Dix. *Printing in Dublin prior to 1601*. Dublin, 1932. Page 20.

bears the imprint 'In the Cathedrall Church of the Blessed Trinitie Dublin'.

The Irish fount of Queen Elizabeth was again used in 1602 by John Franke, or Franckton, who printed with it the first Irish New Testament, and again in 1608 for Daniel's Irish version of the Book of Common Prayer.* Nothing is known of the early history of Franckton, or where he came from, but he married an Irishwoman named Margery Laghlin, daughter of William Laghlin, a freeman of the city of Dublin.

The first dated work bearing Franckton's name is a proclamation dated 20 May, 1601. In the following year he was employed by Daniel together with William Usher as Clerk of the Council, to print the Irish New Testament mentioned above—a folio of some 215 leaves, beautifully printed and with an ornate title-page. Franckton was appointed King's Printer for Ireland in July, 1603, and thereafter printed a number of proclamations. In October, 1606, he was made a freeman of Dublin in the right of his wife, and later, according to an entry in the records of the Office of Arms, Dublin Castle, he became a sheriff of that city.

In 1608 Franckton printed the Book of Common Prayer in folio, in Irish type. It was subsidized in part by the Government, and probably also by the Archbishop of Tuam, for the printer was given £40 to enable him to buy paper and other necessaries. Although dated 1608, this Prayer Book has a dedication to Sir Arthur Chichester, Deputy-General in Ireland, dated 20 October, 1609.

The first law book known to have been printed in Ireland came from Franckton's press in 1615. It was drawn up by Sir John Davies, Attorney-General for Ireland, and the title, in the hybrid legal tongue of the time, reads: *Le primer Report des cases et matters en ley resolves et adjudges en les Courts del Roy en Ireland. Collect et digest per Sr John Davys, Chivaler Atturney Generall del Roy en cest Realme.* Sir John Davies was the author of *A Discoverie of the True Causes why Ireland was never entirely subdued, etc.*, printed in London for John Jaggard in 1612.

In 1617 Franckton printed John Mericke's *Briefe Abstract of all the Auncient English Statutes in force in the Realme of Ireland*, which was reissued with a new title-page in 1625 by the Stationers' Company. In the following year his patent as King's Printer ended, though whether it was cancelled or whether he sold it to the holders of the

---

* William Daniel, or O'Donnell, was consecrated Archbishop of Tuam in 1609.

new patent is not quite clear. A letter from the Privy Council to the Lord Deputy, Sir Oliver St John (*Sloane MS.* 4756, f. 153), says:

> Lastly you shall understand that whereas we are informed His Majesties Printer there is a person not fitt for that Office, both in respect of his weake estate, and of his Insuffitienty otherwise, we have been carefull to provide you another that shal be a man of skill and of abilitie to discharge that place; the Company of Stationers here in England haveing undertaken to send over such a person, and to settle a Factory of Booksellers and Bookbinders there at Dublin. . . .

From this we may assume that Franckton was by this time in a poor state of health and unable to carry on in his office any longer. A new grant was made to three nominees of the Stationers' Company —Felix Kingston, Matthew Lownes, and Bartholomew Downes— for a period of twenty-one years, giving them a monopoly of importing books for sale as well as of printing.

Possibly trade in Ireland did not measure up to the expectations of the Company, for when their grant expired they made no attempt to renew it, and the patent was taken over by William Bladen, who worked in Dublin from 1640. Franckton himself died in October, 1620. As to the fount of Irish type, after being used sporadically in books printed by the Company of Stationers, it disappeared from Ireland; nor is it to be found elsewhere.* Reed-Johnson says: 'There seems no reason for believing, as some state, that it was secured by the Jesuits and taken abroad.' The Irish seminary at Louvain had a fount of its own with which several books were printed between 1616 and 1663.[116]

---

* Bruce Dickins thinks it came to England; one word in this fount appears in Ware's *St Patrick's Opscula* (c. 1656).

CHAPTER SIX

Printing under the Stuarts

Among the 272 plates which illustrate Stanley Morison's *Four Centuries of Fine Printing* we find no example of English work before 1702. It would be unfair to deduce from this that there was no fine printing at all in England until the eighteenth century, but the fact remains that, when compared with the best seventeenth-century printing in France, that of the corresponding period in England is greatly inferior, and for the greater part of that century English printing sank to an extremely low level. The decline was especially marked in the period from 1550 to 1650, and was due to a variety of causes of which the chief was the increasingly severe restrictions placed on printing by the Crown. The system of monopolies deprived the trade of beneficial competition, and hatred of the foreigner deprived it of a needed technical stimulus. And as Reed has pointed out, whereas many of the first printers used types wholly cut and cast for them by expert foreign artists, their successors began first to cast for themselves from hired or purchased matrices, and finally to cut their own punches and justify their own matrices. By the end of the sixteenth century 'every printer became his own letter-founder, not because he would, but because he must, and the art suffered in consequence'.[117]

One of the outstanding characteristics of English printing during the seventeenth century was the severity of the restrictions placed on the printing of books, due largely to constant religious and political strife, for both Church and State feared the power of the printed word.

On his accession to the English throne in 1603 one of the first acts of James I was to recall the valuable patents which had been granted to John Day and his son Richard for Primers and Psalters and those of James Roberts and Richard Watkins for Almanacks and Prognostications. Instead, a royal grant was made of them 'to the whole Companie of Stacioners for the benefit of the poore of the same'. This formed the legal basis of what came to be known as the 'English Stock', and it differed from all previous grants in that it was not made to an individual or partnership of individuals, but to the Company as a whole.

Of course it was not granted for nothing—royal patents never were —and to provide for the working of the new patent as well as to buy up unexpired privileges with which it conflicted, the Company raised the sum of £9,000, roughly equivalent to some twelve times that sum today. This was divided into shares which consisted of 15 Assistants' shares of £200; 30 Livery shares valued at £100; and 60 yeomen's shares of £50. As there were only 15 Assistants, each one got a share, but only half the liverymen, and less than one-sixth of the yeomen could acquire a share, so that their portions were often divided between those eager to share in the investment in the ratio of equal parts between two suitors.

The Stationers' Company thus became itself a book-publishing organization, and since it now had in its own hands some of the most valuable privileges, it could look forward to a steady profit out of its English Stock. In this the Company was not disappointed, for sales of these 'bread and butter' lines brought a good financial return, and, encouraged by the sweet smell of success, the Company began to buy up and enter in the Register for its own account any profitable copy to come to the market. The drawbacks to a successful monopoly of this kind made themselves quickly felt. There was a marked disinclination to print anything other than those books which were certain to sell, and in the absence of competition the standard of workmanship tended to deteriorate. The Psalms with Music, which went through edition after edition, have been described by Miss Handover as 'among the most slovenly pieces of printing ever distributed from London. The paper was wretched stuff and the ink was spread as thickly as rationed butter'.[118]

The Stock was under the general control of the Master and Wardens and under the immediate supervision of six stock-keepers, elected annually, who represented the shareholders. The decisions as to what books should be printed by the Company, which member of the Company should be entrusted with the printing of them, and what he should be paid for his work were taken by the above-mentioned at regular meetings. Moreover, the Company saw to it that the printer did not print any extra copies for sale by himself by issuing him with just sufficient paper for the purpose. How much was paid to the shareholders in dividends is not known with any certainty. In 1606 the records of the Court show that Robert Barker received a dividend of £20 on an Assistant's share of £200, but whether this was a quarterly or half-yearly dividend is not clear. At all events those who benefited by the English Stock were no longer likely to protest against monopolies, seeing that they were profiting by the most lucrative monopoly of all except that enjoyed by the King's Printer. At that time this was a triumvirate consisting of Robert Barker; the son and successor of Christopher Barker, who enjoyed the privilege by reversion, but to whose patent were joined John Norton, with a privilege for printing all books in Latin, Greek and Hebrew; and John Bill, who seems to have obtained his share of the patent by purchase.

Although, theoretically, the poorer members of the trade should have benefited when patents were turned over to the Company, it did not always work out that way in practice, for the patents tended to be leased out by the Company to the more prominent and wealthy members as being the ones, owing to the capital and presses at their disposal, most likely to increase the dividends coming from the 'stocks' which, as more privileges were taken over, were divided into the English Stock, Bible Stock, Irish Stock, Latin Stock and Ballad Stock.

The English Stock consisted in 1620 of Law books—58 items; School-books—32; A.B.C.s and Primers—5; Psalms and Psalters in all volumes, almanacs, calendars, prayer books—13; and general works —8 (Arber III. 668–71). The Bible Stock alone at that time needed eight auditors to look after the accounts, which shows how profitable it must have been. The partners in the Bible Stock divided the right of issuing the Scriptures with the King's Printer.

By the end of the 1630s most of the printing offices in London were under the control of the Stationers' Company; many of the remainder were in the hands of a triumvirate—John Haviland, Miles Flesher and Robert Young—who had gone into partnership and bought up several old-established printing houses, such as those of William Stansby, Edward Griffin, and George Purslowe. Haviland published several of Bacon's works, including the *Essays* (1625) and his *Opera Moralia* (1638). Miles Flesher printed Francis Quarles's *Divine Poems* in 1633, and for John Marriot the same author's *Hieroglyphikes of the Life of Man*, with engravings by William Marshall. Another well-known publisher of the period was Bernard Alsop, who, in partnership with Thomas Fawcett, printed the plays of Beaumont and Fletcher and works by Dekker, Greene and Shirley.

Robert Barker's most important undertaking was the printing of the Bible of 1611, the so-called 'Authorized Version'. There is no extant authority for the phrase, or for the words 'Appointed to be read in Churches' which appear on the title-page, but it is hardly probable that the King's Printer would have made the assertion if it were not true. The text of the 1611 Bible is a great primer black-letter, with chapter headings and marginal references in roman and the alternative readings in italic. There are three issues assigned to the year 1611. The first quarto edition was printed in roman in 1612.

In a century of undistinguished printing it is well to recall the *Works of St John Chrysostom*, printed nominally by John Norton at Eton, but in reality by Melchisedec Bradwood of the Eliot's Court Press, which appeared in eight folio volumes between 1610 and 1613. The work was undertaken at the charge of Sir Henry Savile, and Reed called it 'one of the most splendid examples of Greek printing in this country.'[*] John Norton, whose name appears as printer, had been appointed King's Printer in Hebrew, Greek and Latin, in 1603. He was three times Master of the Stationers' Company, but it is doubtful if he was ever a working printer, any more than was Christopher Barker. They held their patents by purchase and were employers of labour to exercise that patent. The Greek type used in the *St John Chrysostom* eventually came into the possession of the Oxford University Press.

The Printers of Shakespeare

The first collected edition of Shakespeare's plays—the 'First Folio' of 1623—contains thirty-six plays. It omits *Pericles*, issued separately in 1609 but not included in any collected edition until the second issue of the third edition in 1664. Eighteen of the plays appeared for the first time in print in the First Folio; the others were issued in separate quarto editions before 1623. The poems were also published separately. The first separate editions of both poems and plays are given below, together with the names of their printers.

Venus and Adonis	1593	Richard Field
Lucrece	1594	Richard Field for John Harrison
The Passionate Pilgrim	1599	William Jaggard for W. Leake
The Phoenix and the Turtle		
(in Robert Chester's *Love's*		
Martyr)	1601	Edward Blount

[*] Reed-Johnson, page 128 and figure 25.

Sonnets	1609	G. Eld for Thomas Thorpe
Titus Andronicus	1594	John Danter for Edward White and Thomas Millington
Henry VI Part II	1594	Thomas Creed for Millington
Henry VI Part III	1595	Peter Short for Millington
Richard II	1597	Valentine Simms for Andrew Wise
Richard III	1597	Valentine Simms for Andrew Wise
Romeo and Juliet	1597	[John Danter]
Romeo and Juliet (corrected)	1599	Thomas Creed for Cuthbert Burbie
Love's Labour's Lost	1598	William White for Cuthbert Burbie
Henry IV Part I	1598	Peter Short for Andrew Wise
Henry IV Part II	1600	Valentine Simms for Andrew Wise and William Aspley
Henry V	1600	Thomas Creed for Thomas Millington and John Busby
The Merchant of Venice	1600	James Roberts
A Midsummer Night's Dream	1600	James Roberts for Thomas Fisher
Much Ado about Nothing	1600	Valentine Simms for Andrew Wise and William Aspley
Merrie Wives of Windsor	1602	Thomas Creed for Arthur Johnson
Hamlet	1603	James Roberts for Nicholas Ling and John Trundell
Hamlet (2)	1604	James Roberts for Nicholas Ling
King Lear (1st issue)	1608	N. Okes (?) for Nathaniel Butter
Troilus and Cressida (1st issue)	1609	G. Eld for Richard Bonian and Henry Walley
Pericles	1609	for Henry Gosson
Othello	1622	'N.O.' (Nicholas Okes) for Thomas Walkley

Shakespeare himself had no direct concern with the publication of his plays during his lifetime, for they were the property of the company of players for whom he had written them. Of the quartos published some were secured quite legitimately, others by more dubious means, as when Heywood complained in the Prologue to his play *Queen Elizabeth*, published surreptitiously in 1605:

> That some by stenography drew
> The plot: put it in print: (scarce one word trew).

Otherwise, copies may have been obtained from minor and generally impecunious actors.

In 1623, seven years after the author's death, the first collected edition of Shakespeare's plays, known today as the 'First Folio', was published. Its printers according to the title-page imprint were Isaac Jaggard and Edward Blount, and the volume ends: 'Printed at the Charges of W. Jaggard, Ed. Blount, I. Smithweeke, and W. Aspley, 1623.' One cannot help regretting that so famous a book should be so poorly printed. But, as Sir Francis Meynell remarked: 'It is a tragic fact that not one contemporary edition of Shakespeare, the Authorized Version, Donne, Herbert, Vaughan, Herrick, Marvell, was good to look upon as a piece of book-making.'[119]

The actual printer of the First Folio was Isaac Jaggard, son of the printer William Jaggard, for Blount was a bookseller-publisher who joined in the venture some time after the printing had begun. William Jaggard, who entered the copies in the Register, was undoubtedly the prime mover in the undertaking, but although still in control of the business, he had some years previously lost his sight, and it was doubtless owing to that affliction that his son Isaac was admitted a freeman of the Stationers' Company at the early age of eighteen. He had already printed several books, including an English translation of the *Decameron* (1620).

In the opinion of that excellent designer of books, Bruce Rogers, the *Nobilitas Politica vel Civilis* printed in 1608 by William Jaggard was one of the handsomest books of that period, and a 'compendious example for students of Elizabethan typography'. For it has

> large and small types, roman, italic, black-letter and Anglo-Saxon, both solid and leaded pages, tabular work with handsome braces, side-notes, woodcut initials, head-pieces and tail-pieces, and a series of costume plates engraved on copper and printed within the rules on folioed blank pages left for them in the form.*

With the accession of Charles I the book trade entered an era of further restriction and persecution, culminating in the famous Star Chamber *Decree concerning Printing* of July, 1637. This enactment, while repeating the earlier prohibitions against the printing, importation and selling of seditious and schismatical books, ordered that all books and pamphlets should be lawfully licensed and authorized before being entered in the Register of the Stationers' Company, and that every book, ballad, chart, portrait, etc. should bear the name of its printer, publisher and author, with severe penalties for non-

---

* Bruce Rogers: *Paragraphs on Printing*. New York, 1943.

compliance. Moreover, every printer had to enter into a bond in £300 (an enormous sum in those days) to print no books except those lawfully allowed to him.

A Star Chamber decree of 1615 had already limited to twenty the number of master printers allowed to have the use of one or more presses, and this decree was maintained in 1637 with the proviso that no printer was to keep more than two presses unless he had been Master or Upper Warden of the Company, who were allowed a maximum of three presses (unless for some great public occasion, when permission had to be obtained from the Archbishop of Canterbury or the Bishop of London). Four founders of letters for printing were allowed, and no more, and those nominated were John Grismand, Thomas Wright, Arthur Nichols and Alexander Fifield. Finally, no joiner, carpenter or any other person was allowed to make a printing press without notifying the Stationers' Company for whom it was intended.

In all, the decree, in addition to confirming previous ordinances, contained thirty-three additional clauses and was the most drastic of all the repressive acts concerning printing; but formidable as it was it lost much of its force a few years later when the Long Parliament, in 1641, abolished the Court of Star Chamber. For a brief period printers took advantage of the prevailing uncertainty engendered by the tense political situation and began to print and sell books without so much as a 'by your leave' to the Company, which was for the time being powerless to act when it found that not only were books being printed without licence or entry, but that existing patents were being openly infringed.

In 1643, in reply to a remonstrance from the Company, Parliament passed an Order of the Lords and Commons in 1643 which reinvested the Company with the powers of search and seizure conferred upon it by the decree of 1637. Further decrees, in 1647 and 1649, were passed 'to prevent and suppress the license of printing', and it was these various repressive measures which roused Milton to action. Disregarding the Acts completely, he published his treatise on the *Doctrine and Discipline of Divorce* without licence or entry, and when the Company took the matter up in Parliament, where, incidentally, nothing came of it, he wrote and published his famous advocacy of the freedom of the press, addressing directly to Parliament the *Areopagitica, A Speech for the Liberty of Unlicensed Printing* which came out in 1644, unlicensed, and without the name of either printer or publisher.

Milton was shrewd enough to perceive that the Remonstrance of the Stationers' Company was largely inspired by the fear that its shareholders were in danger of losing profitable privileges if their former control of the trade were not speedily restored, and found in the various enactments restricting the press 'the fraud of some old patentees and monopolizers in the trade of book-selling; who under pretence of the poor in their Company not to be defrauded, and the just retaining of each man his several copy (which God forbid should be gainsaid) brought divers glossing colours to the house'.

Meanwhile the Civil War had brought in its train a flood of vituperative pamphlets, for the most part ill-printed, and this pamphlet warfare assumed such dimensions that the Act of 1649, which was a virtual reimposition of the former Star Chamber decrees, imposed also a fine of 40s on anyone found carrying or sending by post seditious books or pamphlets. Yet, although the Act was renewed in 1652, it failed in its object and 'disorderly' printing flourished. The number of printers, which had previously been limited to twenty, had, after the disappearance of the Court of Star Chamber, grown to about sixty, due largely to an increasing demand for cheap books, the non-stop flow of political pamphlets, and the growth of periodical publishing.

Printing at Oxford

From 1520 until 1585 there was no printing at Oxford. In that latter year the University lent £100 to the Oxford bookseller Joseph Barnes to enable him to set up a press, and an ordinance of Star Chamber in 1586 made provision for one press, together with a chief printer and one apprentice to be set up at Oxford. Barnes was sole printer to the University until 1617, and although most of the products of his press were the inevitable sermons and theological treatises, he must be remembered as the printer of the first English edition of Richard de Bury's *Philobiblon* (1599),* edited by Thomas James, Bodley's first librarian.

First of the famous men associated with the Oxford Press was Archbishop Laud, who was Chancellor of the University 1630–41. Through his efforts Oxford obtained the royal Letters Patent for printing which Cambridge had enjoyed since 1534. A royal grant from Charles I came in 1632, which allowed the University three printers, each of whom were in the following year allowed two

* The *editio princeps* was published in Cologne in 1473.

presses and two apprentices. In 1636 Laud received confirmation of this Royal Charter giving the right to print 'all manner of books', but this privilege was curtailed in the following year when the Stationers' Company, in return for the meagre annual payment of £200, practically forced the University to curtail its privilege of printing Bibles, Almanacs and Grammars. It was not until 1672 that the restrictions on printing Bibles were removed.

Among the books published at Oxford between 1617 and 1642 were Burton's *Anatomy of Melancholy* (1621, and several times re-printed), the Laudian *Statutes* (1634) by which the University was governed until 1855, and Bacon's *Advancement of Learning* (1640). One clause from the Laudian *Statutes* relating to printing is worth quoting. It runs:

> And whereas it hath been found by experience in Printing that these Mechanick printers (being mostly on the look out for the acquisition of money by the output of their energy) do give far too little care to Fine Printing or decorative beauty in their workmanship, but issue to the light of day rough jobs badly corrected; THEREFORE be it enacted by the present Statute that there be appointed as scholar-printer for the printing of University publications in some House specially appointed for the purpose, a man of sound instruction in Greek and Latin and well versed in linguistic studies: whose duty shall be to superintend the compositors and other workers . . . and generally to take scrupulous care to secure the finish and elegance of every work.

Another great name in the history of Oxford printing during the seventeenth century is that of Dr John Fell, Dean of Christ Church, 1660–86. During the Civil War Charles I had made Oxford his head-quarters, but on 24 June, 1646, the city surrendered, and in the words of Falconer Madan, 'the press at Oxford perhaps never fell lower than when Sir Thomas Fairfax introduced his two careless and ill-equipped printers, John Harris and Henry Hills, in 1647'.[120] John Fell, who had borne arms for the King in the garrison of Oxford during the Civil War, was recompensed at the Restoration by being made a Canon of Christ Church in 1660, and six years later he was appointed Vice-Chancellor of the University. It was in that capacity, and as one of the Delegates of the Press, that by his munificence and personal exertions he set the 'Learned Press' once again on the road traced out by Laud. In 1671 he became the head of a partnership of four which rented the management of the University Press during the years 1672–90, and spent a great sum of money in equipping it with a foundry and a variety of matrices, some of which were obtained from abroad* and others made from punches cut by Peter Walpergen, who was chosen by the syndicate (after another punch-cutter, Herman Hermansen, had proved unsatisfactory) to work for them at Oxford. Fell's generosity in adding many typefaces to the equipment of the press, together with a presentation to the University by Franciscus Junius of type for Icelandic and other northern languages, put the press in possession of a greater variety of languages and type than could be found anywhere else in the country.† It was Dr Fell, also, who encouraged the setting up of a paper mill (which still exists) at Wolvercote. The Fell types are shown to advantage in the Clarendon Press edition of the *Poems of Richard Lovelace* (1925).

In 1699 the Oxford Press was installed in the Sheldonian Theatre; but about 1688 the 'Learned Press' was moved to 'Tom Pun's House' and the 'Bible Press' to St Aldate's. In 1713 the University Press took over the new Clarendon Building (see page 159).

Of the four great polyglot Bibles printed during the sixteenth and seventeenth centuries,[121] one was printed in England, the *Biblia Sacra Polyglotta* in six volumes, edited by Brian Walton and published between 1633 and 1657. This was the second book in England to be published by subscription, the first being John Minsheu's *Guide into Tongues*, a dictionary in eleven languages, printed in 1617. Walton's Bible was printed by Thomas Roycroft, and exemplifies seventeenth-century printing at its best. For a work of this nature it went through the press in the remarkably short space of four years, and as is pointed out in Reed-Johnson, 'the amount of labour and industry represented in its mere typographical execution is astonishing. Apart from this the arrangement of the different versions is a marked improvement on that of earlier polyglots.'[122] The exotic founts employed (Hebrew, Latin, Greek, Aramaic, Syriac, Samaritan, Ethiopic, Arabic and Persian) appear to have been furnished by the four English type-founders nominated under the Star Chamber decree, and the work is therefore a landmark in the history of letter-founding in England, since never before had a work of importance been printed in this country in any

---

* Many were the work of two famous Dutch punch-cutters—Dirck Voskens of Amsterdam and Christoffel van Dijck of Haarlem. In addition there were sixteenth-century founts of French origin, possibly by Granjon and Garamond.
† See further: *Notes towards a specimen of the ancient typographic materials, principally collected and bequeathed to the University of Oxford by Dr John Fell*.

of the learned characters except Latin and Greek. For his skill and pains Thomas Roycroft (Master of the Stationers' Company in 1675) was allowed to assume the title *Orientalium Typographus Regius*.

To a Yorkshireman named Joseph Moxon, born at Wakefield in 1627, we owe the first practical treatise in English on the mechanics of printing. A maker of mathematical instruments, Hydrographer to Charles II, master printer, and Fellow of the Royal Society, Moxon was interested in every kind of applied science. In 1677 he began to issue his series of *Mechanick Exercises, or the Doctrine of Handyworks*, giving practical instruction in various manual trades. In 1683 he brought out a second volume, devoted to the art of printing, in which are described in great detail the printing office and its equipment, the work of the punch-cutter and type-founder, composition and reading, press-work and warehousing.* An indispensable sourcebook on every aspect of printing as practised in the days of the hand press, the book itself is as atrociously printed as anything in a bad period of typography, though who the printer was is not at present known. The imprint reads: 'Printed for Joseph Moxon on the West-side of Fleet-ditch, at the Sign of Atlas.1683.' Moxon himself produced the rather curious fount of Irish type with which were printed an Irish *Church Catechism*, with the *Elements of the Irish Language* (1680) and William O'Donnell's Irish translation of the New Testament (1681). The printer was Robert Everingham, who later printed Dr William Bedell's Irish translation of the Old Testament (1685) with the same types.

About 1620 the Dutch cartographer and printer William Janszoon Blaeu (1571–1638) introduced an improved hand press embodying some minor alterations to an instrument which had remained virtually unchanged for nearly two centuries and was to remain so until Stanhope introduced his iron press. The main improvement in the Blaeu press was the replacement of the box-shaped 'hose' which enclosed the end of the screw used to raise and lower the platen by two bars of iron which passed through bearings in the 'till' (the wooden cross-piece), their lower end being attached to a plate furnished with hooks for cords connected with the platen. The improvement lay in the prevention of any slurring caused by the platen twisting at the moment of impression. Blaeu's press was not generally adopted in

---

* A modern edition of Moxon's *Mechanick Exercises on the Whole Art of Printing*, edited with notes by Herbert Davis and Harry Carter, was published by the O.U.P. in 1958.

England. Moxon considered that it was because 'many Press-men have scarce reason enough to distinguish between an excellently improved Invention and a makeshift slovenly contrivance'. But, as we have already seen, the various printing regulations of the first half of the seventeenth century not only limited the number of presses a printer might own, but also stipulated that no carpenter or joiner could make one without notifying the Stationers' Company.

During the reign of Charles I it was ecclesiastical rather than royal tyranny which the printing trade came to fear, and few printers and publishers managed to pass their lives without fine or imprisonment. Authors who happened to fall foul of the authorities were treated with unbelievable cruelty. The publication of William Prynne's *Histrio-Mastix*, 1633, although a scathing attack on plays and players, had nothing in it to justify the dreadful sentence passed upon its author, whose chief crime was opposition, as a Puritan, to Laud and his party.* Brought before the Court of Star Chamber in February, 1634, he was fined heavily, degraded from the Bar, placed in the pillory at Westminster and Cheapside, had one of his ears cropped at each place, and was sentenced to imprisonment for life. His publisher, Michael Sparke, had to pay a fine of £500 and stand in the pillory, but the printers of the book, 'W.J.' and 'E.A.' (William Jones and E. Allde) escaped with a short term of imprisonment. Three years later Prynne managed to publish, under a pseudonym, a tract called *News from Ipswich* (an attack on Wren, Bishop of Norwich), which cost him a second enormous fine and the branding of both his cheeks with the letters S.L., of which the official interpretation was that they stood for 'scurrilous libeller'. Prynne, with grim humour, remarked that they stood for *Stigmata Laudis*. The printer and publisher, John Lilburne, who had already published several seditious pamphlets, was condemned to be whipped at the cart's tail from the Fleet prison to Old Palace Yard, Westminster, where he was set in the pillory and afterwards carried back to prison. Prynne was a bigot, but brave and conscientious; Lilburne was a trouble-maker, and in the words of Judge Jenkins, 'if there was none living but he, John would be against Lilburne and Lilburne against John'. By his friends, however, he was known as Freeborn John.

Michael Sparke, the publisher of *Histrio-Mastix*, had already been in conflict with the church over the publication of various unlicensed

---

* A certain passage was construed as casting aspersions on the Queen.

books, which had been printed for him by William Jones. In 1629 he was charged with having published Henry Burton's *Babel no Bethel*, Spencer's *Musquil Unmasked*, and Prynne's *Antithesis of the Church of England*, and in defence declared that the Decree of 1586 was contrary to Magna Carta, and an infringement of the liberty of the subject. It was this same Michael Sparke who in 1641 wrote an exposure of the evils of monopoly, called *Scintilla or a Light Broken Into Dark Warehouses*, in which he attacked the holders of patents, such as Miles Flesher and Robert Young (John Haviland was no longer alive), whom he mentions by name, and the monopolists of the Stationers' Company by implication. Books are referred to by category and he shows, with prices to support him, how the monopolists had sent up the price of books and the immense profits they were making, together with their determination to admit no competition. Thus, of quarto Bibles, raised in price from 7s to 10s, sold in quires, he remarks:

> There hath been at least 12000 of these Bibles Quarto with Notes printed in Holland, and sold very reasonable: and many brought from thence hither, and they have been seised by the Kings Printers, and the parties that Imported them not only lost them, but were put in *Purgatory*, and there glad to lose their Bibles and all cost to get off; and then the Monopolists sold them again, and so kept al others in awe.[123]

These revelations were hardly to the liking of the Stationers, but like John Wolfe some sixty years before, Sparke managed to obtain support for certain changes in the working of the Company and his exposure of the huge profits made out of Bible printing induced Parliament, when it replaced the monarchy, to oppose this Bible monopoly.

Robert Young, although he never resided in Scotland, was appointed King's Printer for that country in 1633, largely through the influence of his patron Archbishop Laud and the powerful backing of Miles Flesher. He printed the first edition of the Authorized Version of the Bible to appear in Scotland (1633), but his most important work, for which no doubt he was given his patent, was Laud's Prayer Book, which that prelate was anxious to see adopted in Scotland.

On 19 September, 1635, Laud wrote to the Bishop of Ross to say that he had 'sent for Young, the printer, the better to prepare him to make ready a black letter, and to bethink himself to send to his servants at Edinborough, . . . that all things might be in the better readiness'. But when Young was ready Laud was not, for he made so many changes before the book was finally completed that it was not until

May, 1637, that it was finally published. This Scottish Prayer Book, the use of which was authorized by a Proclamation of Charles I dated 12 December, 1636, did full credit to the printer, for it is a handsome piece of work apart from the woodcut initials which are too disparate.

The King's Printers in the XVIIth Century

We have seen that on the death of Christopher Barker in 1599 his son Robert succeeded to the patent, becoming King's Printer under James I, and he soon came into prominence by printing the Authorized Version of the Bible in 1611. As his father had pointed out in his report of 1582, the printing of the whole Bible calls for the expenditure of a vast sum of money, and to finance the printing of the 1611 Bible Robert Barker received help from three other stationers—the cousins John and Bonham Norton, and John Bill—who put up the money in return for sharing in the profits of the patent. John Norton, a bookseller, died the year after the Bible was published. Bonham Norton was a wealthy bookseller and printer described by McKerrow as 'a hard, calculating and grasping man, who was continually in the law courts prosecuting his brother stationers'.[124] John Bill, who had been apprenticed to John Norton, was a well-known bookseller who had been Sir Thomas Bodley's agent in the buying of books for the Bodleian.

Robert Barker did not possess his father's business acumen, and in 1617 to raise money he assigned his interest in the patent to Bonham Norton and John Bill. This started litigation, for Barker claimed that the term was for one year, while Norton contended that no reservation had been made. In 1619 Barker's claim was upheld and for a while John Bill and Robert Barker were considered joint holders of the patent. The following year, however, the tenacious Norton managed to win his case, Barker's name disappeared, and Norton's name appeared together with that of Bill.

On the accession of Charles I Norton and Bill were confirmed in their appointment as joint King's Printers, and soon afterwards they moved the King's Printing House from Aldersgate to Hunsdon House, Blackfriars. Meanwhile Bonham Norton had been imprisoned on a charge of bribing the Lord Keeper and his share in the patent had once again been awarded to Robert Barker, who died in 1645 after having passed ten years in the King's Bench Prison for debt. John Bill had died in 1630, although his name remained for some time later on the imprint of Bibles, and Bonham Norton died in 1635. Robert Barker's son Christopher II had predeceased his father, and the Barker share in the patent passed to a grandson, Christopher Barker III, who followed the King around the country during the period of the Civil War, setting up his presses at York, Nottingham, Shrewsbury and Bristol (see page 151), an act of loyalty which cost him his patent when Cromwell came to power.

But at the Restoration Christopher Barker III was reinstated as King's Printer jointly with John Bill II, whose share in the patent had been left to him by his father. Although Bonham Norton's son Roger petitioned for his share of the privilege, inherited from his father, to be restored, asserting that the office is 'now held by gentlemen who do not understand printing', his claim was not granted; but as a recompense his son Roger II was granted a patent for forty years as printer and bookseller in Latin, Greek and Hebrew (which John Norton had been given in 1603), with the sole privilege of printing the Bible in Latin and all grammars in Greek and Latin.

In 1675 Thomas Newcombe and Henry Hills received the patent of King's Printers for thirty years, to date from the termination of the Bill and Barker patent in 1680. As the assign of John Bill II Newcombe had managed the printing house since the Restoration, whilst Hills had been one of the official printers during the Commonwealth. But although Hills was at one time a Puritan, he turned Catholic under James II, and at the Revolution of 1688 he fled to St Omer, where he died, his interest in the patent passing to his eldest son, also Henry. Thomas Newcombe died in 1682 and his son Thomas Newcombe II in 1691, and from then the imprint was Charles Bill and the Executrix of Thomas Newcombe, though Charles Bill seems never to have taken an active part in the business. After the expiration of the Barker patent in 1710 the name of Charles Bill disappeared and the imprint became the 'Assignes of Thomas Newcombe and Henry Hills deceased.'

In 1710 John Baskett, 'the greatest monopolist of the Bible who ever lived', succeeded to the patent, though at first in partnership with the assigns just mentioned, whose names remained on the imprint until 1723. Baskett also had a lease of the Oxford privilege for printing Bibles (see page 161) and in 1711 acquired a share in the patent of King's Printer in Scotland (see page 161).

The Origins of the Newspaper Press in England

The newspaper as we know it—a publication appearing at regular intervals, numbered and dated—did not make its appearance before the seventeenth century. During the Middle Ages the dissemination of news was carried on by news-letter writers, who supplied those by whom such reports were valued, particularly politicians, bankers and merchants, and this manuscript service (of which the Fugger news-letters is one of the best-known examples) continued after the news-paper had come into existence.

The first 'news-book', as we might term it, to appear in England came from the press of Richard Fawkes. Its full title reads *Hereafter ensue the trew encountre or Batayle lately don betwene England and Scot-lande. In whiche batayle the Scottsshe kynge was slayne*. This undated pamphlet of four leaves was probably published in September, 1513, shortly after the battle of Flodden, of which it gives an eyewitness account and a list of those Englishmen who had distinguished them-selves in the fighting. On the title-page is a woodcut of men-at-arms standing before a tent, with a group of soldiers fighting in the back-ground.

News pamphlets of this kind appeared occasionally in England during the sixteenth century, though not with any frequency until after 1590. During the next twenty years some 450 of these news-books were published, dealing mainly with foreign news. One of the first English printers to appreciate the commercial possibilities of news publishing was the anti-monopolist John Wolfe, who from 1589 on-wards published a series of news-books bearing titles such as *Credible Reportes from France and Flanders* (1590) and *Advertisements from Britany, And from the Low Countries* (1591). Contrary to the custom of the time, he made his titles as short as possible, and the title-page carried nothing more than this short title, Wolfe's device, and the imprint. Wolfe, however, on his appointment as Printer to the City, gave up news publishing; nevertheless, as Miss Handover rightly says:

> He made more progress in five years than his predecessors made in seventy. There is the standardization not only of layout but of title, the exploitation of many sources of news, the production of illustrations that really did illustrate the report, and the hint at regular, periodical publishing.[125]

Although dated news pamphlets were published in Germany in 1609, and in Holland from 1618 onwards, England lagged behind in producing a regular publication devoted to the dissemination of news. The earliest known extant 'coranto' (as the first newspapers were termed) in the English language was an English translation of a Dutch coranto published in Amsterdam by Pieter van den Keere on

2 December, 1620, though there may have been one or two published by him earlier in that year.

On 24 September, 1621, there was published in London a *Corante, or newes from Italy, Germany, Hungarie, Spaine and France, 1621*. This was a small sheet 'printed for N.B. . . . out of the Hie Dutch coppy printed at Franckford'. The initials, which might stand for either Nicholas Bourne or Nathaniel Butter, both well-known stationers, are considered by most authorities to stand for the latter.

Nathaniel Butter was the son of a stationer, Thomas Butter, who worked at St Austin's Gate, St Paul's churchyard, from 1576 to 1590. His widow afterwards married another stationer, John Newbery, who died in 1603. Nathaniel was admitted to the Stationers' Company on 20 February, 1603-4, by patrimony, and his first entry was registered on 4 December, 1604—an interlude entitled *The Life and Death of Cavaliero Dick Boyer*. In 1608 he brought out two editions of *King Lear*, one without an address, the other with the address of the Pied Bull. By 1620 he was well established as a stationer, and published a number of books in association with other booksellers.

It is thought that another stationer, Thomas Archer, began to issue news-sheets in London in 1621, but if such were the case none have survived. On 22 September, 1621, a certain Joseph Meade wrote to Sir Martin Stuteville: 'My Corrantoer Archer was layd by the heales for making or adding to Corrantoes etc. as they say.* But now there is another who hath got licence to print them honestly translated out of the Dutch.' (Harley MSS. 389. f° 122.)

This was the 'N.B.' whom we presume to be Nathaniel Butter, and the seven corantos he published in that year are the oldest surviving periodical news-books in England. In May, 1622, Archer came back into the picture once more, and in conjunction with Nicholas Bourne began a weekly series of quarto news-books. The first issue, of which no copy is known, was presumably dated 14 May; the following number (a copy of which is in the British Museum) bears the date 23 May. This *Weekeley Newes from Italy, Germanie . . . .* was printed for Archer and Bourne by John Dawson, later to become one of the printers allowed by the Star Chamber decree of 1615 filling the vacancy caused by the death of his uncle, Thomas Dawson.

Nicholas Bourne, who was soon to begin a long association with Butter, had been apprenticed to Cuthbert Burby (publisher of the first editions of *Romeo and Juliet* and *Love's Labour's Lost*) who had a

---

* He was imprisoned for a time.

shop in Cornhill, near the Royal Exchange. On Burby's death, Bourne was left the lease of the shop in recompense for his 'true and faithful service' to his late master. By 1622 he had already published nearly eighty books and pamphlets, a number of which were news-books, such as *A True Relation of strange accidents in the kingdom of the great Magor* (1622).

On 3 June, 1622, Nathaniel Butter and William Sheffard issued *More Newes from the Palatinate*, and from this time onwards news-books began to appear frequently. For a time most of the news-books published came from a syndicate of five stationers—Butter, Archer, Bourne, Sheffard, and Bartholomew Downes—for since the regulations prevented many of the printers from owning more than a single press, the participation of several stationers made it easier to maintain a regular series of periodical publications.

The driving force behind the publication of these news-books was undoubtedly Nathaniel Butter, who continued the publication of the *Weekeley Newes*, begun on 2 August, 1622, for many years. The title of the periodical should not, however, be taken too literally, for although Butter declared that he did 'purpose to continue weekly, by God's assistance, from the best and most certain intelligence', the arrival of news from abroad depended on wind and weather. It should be borne in mind that these early corantos dealt solely with foreign news, since the Crown did not permit the printing of any but the most trivial items of domestic news.

After the Star Chamber decree of 1632, when all printing of foreign news was likewise forbidden, more than six years passed before any further news-books were issued in England, though for a short period some news-books in English were printed in Amsterdam by Jan van Hilten and sent over to England. Publication had ceased with No. 1 of Butter and Bourne's ninth series of periodical news-books, on 16 October, 1632, after they had brought out more than 300 issues since 16 September, 1624, when they became sole publishers in place of the syndicate which had started the venture in 1622.[126]

What must have been galling for the partners was the fact that the period between 1632 and 1638 coincided with the campaigns of Gustavus Adolphus during the Thirty Years War. Finding themselves prevented by the Star Chamber decree from publishing the regular news-books, Butter and Bourne sought to supply the market for foreign news without falling foul of the authorities by the expedient of publishing *The Swedish Intelligencer*, which gave the news in the form of semi-annual compilations instead of weekly instalments. To a public deprived of news, no news is stale.

On 30 September, 1633, both stationers petitioned Charles I to be allowed to resume their news-books, promising that they would be 'careful in time to come that nothing dishonourable to princes in amity with his Majesty should pass the press'. But it was not until 20 December, 1638, that Butter and Bourne received letters patent from the King to publish news-books for a period of twenty-one years on payment of £10 a year towards the repair of St Paul's. Of this grant they had presumably been advised beforehand, for the first number of their new series bears that very date, 20 December, 1638. The series lasted until the following July, when a hundred numbers had been published; this was followed by a new series of a hundred numbers which ended in March, 1640, by which time Butter and Bourne had ceased their partnership. Butter continued to publish on his own, and brought out three further series, the final issue being published at the end of 1642. Foreign news was then at a discount, for the interest of the whole country was now centred upon the contest between King and Parliament. We find no news-books with which Butter's name can be associated after 1642, and in any case the royal patent became void when Parliament took over the government of the country.

After his partnership with Butter was dissolved, Bourne turned his attention to other branches of the trade, publishing such books as Richard Dafforne's *Merchant's Mirror* (1640), Lewes Roberts's *The Treasure of Traffike* (1641) and John Collins's *An Introduction to Merchants' Accounts* (1653). Bourne was twice appointed Master of the Stationers' Company, in 1643 and 1651, and was three times Warden, in 1637, 1639, and 1641. He died in 1660, a wealthy man. Butter, on the other hand, still clung to periodical journalism, producing news-books irregularly until the end of 1642. In January, 1643, he was imprisoned in the Fleet, where he seems to have remained until some time in 1644. He was by that time in sore straits financially, for in May, 1639, he had been obliged to make over to Miles Flesher twenty-five of his copyrights, including *King Lear*, the plays of Heywood and Dekker, and Chapman's translations of the *Odyssey* and the *Iliad*. He carried on, however, for the next twenty years, publishing occasional works of no great value, until, on 22 February 1663-4, 'Nath.Butter, an old stationer, died very poore', and had to be buried at the cost of the Company.[127]

The Civil War Period and the Growth of the Periodical Press

With the outbreak of the Civil War and the consequent momentous happenings at home, the number of news-sheets rapidly increased, and it has been estimated that nearly three hundred separate news publications appeared between 1640 and 1660. 'When hostilities commenced', writes Timperley, 'every event, during a most eventful period, had its own historian, who communicated *News from Hull*, *Truths from York*, *Warranted Tidings from Ireland*, and *Special Passages from several Places*. These were all occasional papers.'[128]

Each side had its own organs of propaganda advocating the party cause. With so much to record space became valuable, and the format of the old news-book gave place to something more nearly resembling the newspaper as we know it. Title-page and blank verso disappeared, and the news began on the first page, just below the title. 'At last', writes Miss Handover, 'these publications were newspapers in the full sense of that word. They were named, they appeared on regular days in regular series, numbered and dated, and they had a specific elastic format that distinguished them from books.'[129] Illustration began to play a part in the make-up, and the first newspaper to illustrate systematically was the *Mercurius Civicus*, which began to appear in 1643 and gave weekly on its title-page portraits of the statesmen and generals taking part in the civil strife.

It was the heyday of the 'Mercuries'. On the King's side was the *Mercurius Aulicus*, edited by Sir John Birkenhead, and issued as a counterblast to the Parliamentary newspapers such as *The Kingdoms Weekly Intelligencer*, published by Nathaniel Butter, and the *Mercurius Britannicus*, edited by Marchmont Needham. Other printed newssheets boasted such titles as *Mercurius Pragmaticus*, *Mercurius Elencticus*, *Mercurius Melancholicus* and *Mercurius Veridicus*.

The various news-sheets, usually of from four to eight quarto pages, contained news of the movements of the opposing armies, and reports of the proceedings either of Parliament or of the King's Council, at Oxford and elsewhere. At first published weekly, they were later distributed twice or three times a week.

Mercury as a title did not last more than three or four years, although it was revived after the Restoration. In its place came the *Intelligencers*, *Scouts*, *Spies*, and *Posts*, and the first number of *The Kingdomes weekly Post*, which appeared on 9 November, 1643, proved to be the forerunner of a number of periodicals with the name 'Post' in the title.

With the movement of the opposing forces presses were at work in a number of places during the Civil War. Even prior to the war itself, when Charles I marched north against the Scots in 1639, he established his headquarters at Newcastle and the Lord General of the Army, the Earl of Arundel, at once wrote off to the Secretary of State for a printer and press to be sent to that town to print the King's daily commands for his Court and Army. Proclamations printed by the King's Printer at Newcastle in 1639 are still extant.

Robert Davies, in a *Memoir of the York Press*,[130] gives the title of thirty-nine items from the Royal Press at York, the last of which is: *His Majesties Instructions to his Commissioners of Array. . . .* 'Dated at our Court at Nottingham, 29th August, 1642. Yorke: Printed by Robert Barker . . . 1642.' Another Royalist press was operated from York in 1642 by the printer Stephen Bulkley, and Davies lists twenty-seven productions of Bulkley's York press—a number which has since been added to. After the battle of Marston Moor, York fell into, the hands of the Puritans, and Thomas Broad printed for them in that city between 1644 and 1650. At Bristol, likewise, a Royalist press was functioning after the town had been captured for the King on 2 August, 1643, until its recapture by the Parliamentary troops.

Charles I was again in Newcastle in 1646, this time as the virtual prisoner of the Scots. However, Stephen Bulkley was permitted to set up a press there and printed *A message from his majestie to the Speaker of the House of Peeres, Pro Tempore*. It bore the imprint 'Newcastle. Printed by Stephen Bulkley, Printer to the King's most Excellent Majesty. 1646.'

In 1655 Cromwell, by then Lord Protector, suppressed all newspapers with the exception of two official publications, one published on Mondays and the other on Thursdays.

During all the first half of the seventeenth century a great part of the output of the press was made up of political and religious tracts disseminated by the opposing factions and denominations, for each party, whether political or religious, hoped to gain its object by printed propaganda, and soon the country was over-run with a flood of controversial tracts, vying with each other in the vehemence of their abuse. In workmanship slipshod, in typography vile, dressed up with ancient blocks and printed on the poorest of paper, these pamphlets show to what low levels the standards of the printing trade had fallen.

But repulsive as so many of them are to look at, these fugitive pieces are now of inestimable value to the historian, who has to thank the indefatigable George Thomason, a bookseller of that time, for having collected over the period between 3 November, 1640, and 23 April, 1661, every small book, pamphlet or newspaper he could acquire published in England—or even abroad, if in English. After an eventful history, the collection, at first known as the 'King's Pamphlets', but now better known as the 'Thomason Tracts', passed into the custody of the British Museum, a gift from George III in 1762. The collection contains 22,255 pieces, a figure which includes 7,216 numbers of newspapers and 97 manuscripts. Carlyle called this collection 'the most valuable set of documents connected with English history'.

Nevertheless, although much of seventeenth century printing is indisputably bad by any standard, there were one or two good printers, as Walton's *Polyglot* and Dugdale's *Monasticon Anglicanum* show. A printer of some note was William Dugard, a native of Bromsgrove, where he was born on 9 January, 1605. He was for many years a schoolmaster and in 1644 became headmaster of Merchant Taylors' School, where he set up a private printing press. On 10 February, 1647–8, he was admitted a freeman of the Stationers' Company on the grounds that 'It was thought fitt hee being a gentleman well deserving and may bee helpfull in the correction of the Companies School Bookes'.[131]

In January, 1649, Dugard printed the first edition of *Eikon Basilike*, which came out on the day after the King's execution. According to tradition Richard Royston, the royal bookseller, of the Angel, Ivy Lane, received the manuscript on 23 December, 1648, and every effort was made to issue it before the King's execution. It has been suggested that, had it been published a week earlier, it might have saved the King's life. It had such a sale that some fifty editions of it are said to have been issued in the same year.

Soon afterwards Dugard printed Salmasius's *Defensio Regia*, for which the Council of State imprisoned him at Newgate, seized all his printing plant, and wrote to the Governors of the school ordering them to elect a new master, 'Mr Dugard having shewn himself an enemy to the State by printing seditious and scandalous pamphlets, and therefore unfit to have charge of the education of youth'. Through the intercession of Sir James Harington, Dugard made his peace with Parliament. On condition that he abandoned the Royalist cause his printing plant was restored to him, and from that time he worked for the party in power, printing, among other things, Milton's reply to Salmasius, published by command of the Council of State.

Under the Commonwealth the annual output of books was far less than it had been during the seven years of the Civil War, when the number of printers, limited to twenty by the Star Chamber decree of 1615, was greatly increased following the abolition of Star Chamber and its decrees in 1641, and the temporary loss of its prerogatives by the Stationers' Company.

One book at least, printed during the Interregnum, has become an immortal and well-loved classic. In 1653, the year in which Cromwell was installed as Lord Protector, the following advertisement appeared:

> There is published a Booke of Eighteen-pence, called the Compleat Angler, or the Contemplative man's Recreation; being a discourse on Fish and Fishing. Not unworthy the perusal of most anglers. Sold by Richard Marriott in St Dunstan's Churchyard, Fleet Street.

A copy of the first edition of this eighteen-penny book was sold in New York in 1946 for 4,400 dollars. The Commonwealth period also saw the publication of Hobbes's *Leviathan* by Andrew Crooke in 1651, the first edition of which soon became scarce, and Pepys had to give three times the published price for a second-hand copy, because, as he puts it, 'the bishops will not let it be printed again'. The first volume of Sir William Dugdale's *Monasticon Anglicanum* was printed by Richard Hodgkinson in 1655, and Walton's *Polyglot* between 1653 and 1657.

The Restoration

The Long Parliament came to an end on 16 March, 1660, and after the landing of Charles II at Dover on 26 May, the Press once more came under the control of the royal prerogative. In May, 1662, an Act for preventing 'abuses in printing' was passed, by which the number of master printers was again limited to twenty, and the office of licencer of the press given to Roger L'Estrange, who was appointed Surveyor of the Imprimery and Printing Presses. In his view the prevalence of opinions dangerous to the Government was almost entirely due to the unlicensed printing of the period following the abolition of Star Chamber, and in his *Considerations and Proposals in order to the Regulation of the Press* (3 June, 1633) he recommended stringent enforcement of the Act of 1662 and the severest curbs upon the liberty of the Press. No longer was the Stationers' Company to be responsible for the search and seizure of unlicensed printing; that power was now vested in L'Estrange, who denounced the Stationers as having been deliberately ineffectual in the regulation of the Press for their own interests.

> Both printers and stationers [wrote L'Estrange] under colour of offering a service to the publique, do effectually but design one upon another. The printers would beat down the bookselling trade by managing the press as themselves please, and by working upon their own copies. The stationers, on the other side, they would subject the printers to be absolutely their slaves; which they have effected in a large measure already, by so encreasing the number, that the one half must either play the knave or starve.[132]

L'Estrange's contention that the booksellers were now in a position to enforce their own terms upon the printers is borne out by the petition made by eleven of the leading London printers, including Roycroft and Hodgkinson, for the incorporation of the printers into a body of their own distinct from the Company of Stationers. Their argument was that when the Charter was granted to the Company of Stationers in 1557 the number of booksellers was very few, but that

> now they are grown so bulkie and numerous, and so considerable withal (being much enriched by Printers impoverishment, and chiefly built upon their ruines) that there is hardly one Printer to ten others that have a share in the Government of the Company; and those that have, either dare not stand for the Interest of Printing, for fear of losing a Work-Master; or will not, because they have an interest among them; or if they do, it signifies nothing in such a disparity of number.[133]

The petition, however, was abortive, and no official reply is recorded.

Under L'Estrange the new act was rigorously enforced. He had not been in office for more than a few months before he caused the arrest of John Twynn, printer, who was indicted for high treason, having printed a 'seditious, poisonous, and scandalous book' entitled *A Treatise of the execution of Justice is as well the people's as the magistrates' duty*. It was alleged that several passages in this pamphlet were aimed at the King's life and the overthrow of the Government. It was proved that Twynn had two presses (in itself illegal) and that the printing had been done secretly, at night. Twynn was condemned to be hung, drawn and quartered. Two days later Simon Drover, printer, Thomas Brewster, bookseller, and Nathan Brooks, bookbinder, were indicted for printing and publishing a book called *The Speeches and Prayers of Harrison, Cook, Hugh Peters, and others condemned for the murder of the late King*, as well as another book called *The Phoenix*. Brewster was fined 100 marks, Drover and Brooks each 40 marks, and all three prisoners were condemned to stand in the pillory and afterwards to remain in prison during the King's pleasure.

L'Estrange was granted a monopoly of news publications and in January, 1664, began the publication of two newspapers, the *Intelligencer*, which appeared on Mondays, and the *Newes*, which came out on Thursdays. L'Estrange, however, later lost both the royal favour and his post, and in 1666 his publications were superseded by the *Oxford Gazette*, which had been authorized by the Lord Chamberlain (despite L'Estrange's privilege) during the residence of the Court at Oxford, whither the King had gone to escape the plague of 1665. On the King's return to London this newspaper became the *London Gazette*, and has continued its existence as an official organ ever since.

During the years 1665 and 1666 the book trade had to cope with disasters compared with which the repressions of L'Estrange were minor ills, for the plague of the former year carried off about eighty masters and men of the printing trade, while the Great Fire of 1666 not only destroyed the presses and material of the printers but consumed both premises and stock of the booksellers, whose main trading centre was in and around St Paul's churchyard. Here the stationers lost enormous stocks of books. All the great booksellers, Pepys was told, had been ruined; from Joseph Kirton, one of their number, he learned that above £150,000 worth of books had been burned, and 'not only these, but their warehouses at their Hall and under Christchurch, and elsewhere, being all burned'.[134] It took all the efforts of the Company to revive the stricken industry. Evelyn considered that the fire might not be without a salutary effect upon the Stationers, for, he declared, 'this sad calamity has mortified a Company which was exceedingly haughty and difficult to manage to any usefull reformation'.[135]

In the year following the Great Fire, Milton signed an agreement with the printer Samuel Symons for the publication of his poem *Paradise Lost*, by the terms of which he received £5 on signature of the contract, with the promise of a further £5 when the impression of 1,300 copies had been sold, and two similar sums at the end of the second and third impressions, if called for. He received £10 in all, and in 1680 his widow ceded the copyright to Symons for a further £8. After passing into the possession of Brabazon Aylmer, a publisher at the Three Pigeons in Cornhill, the copyright eventually fell into the hands of one of the most famous of London publishers, Jacob Tonson.

Music Publishing

The Playfords, father and son, were the great publishers of music in England in the second half of the seventeenth century. John Playford the elder (c. 1623–c. 1693–4) was a bookseller of the Inner Temple who dealt chiefly in music books, of which the most famous was *The English Dancing Master*. This compilation, first published in 1651, had run into 18 editions by 1728, and is an invaluable record of English popular melodies of the period. Playford was on intimate terms with Samuel Pepys, who in 1667 bought from him *The Musical Companion* and in April of that year records that he 'tried two or three grace parts in Playford's new book'. Playford's earliest publications were printed by Thomas Harper, and later William Godbid printed for him for many years. Although the bulk of Playford's work is printed from movable type, one or two of his music books were engraved on copper—*Musick's Handmaid*, 1678; *The Division Violin*, 1685. Playford's business was continued by his son Henry Playford (c. 1657–c. 1710). John Playford II, a nephew of John I, was a printer who was for some time in partnership with William Godbid, and was employed by his cousin Henry on almost all his musical publications.

The Chap-Book

Although the woodcut was more or less abandoned for the better class of book by the middle of the seventeenth century, it did not disappear completely, for it was just about this period that the chap-book made its appearance. With the Restoration the numerous obscure presses, which had made their living by pouring out a flood of partisan broadsides and pamphlets during the Civil War and the Commonwealth, now had to find some other way of keeping their presses employed. Popular stories, legendary tales, quips and jests, were collected and disseminated as a cheap folk-literature by the wandering chapmen. Many bore as their imprint: 'Printed for the Company of Flying Stationers', or 'Walking Stationers'.

Printed on a sheet of poor-quality paper folded to make a small

stitched book of eight pages, these chap-books had an enormous sale
both in the towns and at the country fairs all over the land, perhaps
more particularly in northern England, where many were printed in
Newcastle-on-Tyne. Later they were extended to twenty-four pages,
and became known in the trade as 'twenty-fours'. The ballads and
stories were illustrated by crude cuts which did not lack, at times, a
certain primitive vigour. Many of the blocks were well worn from
frequent use and the illustrations were often applied to the most
inappropriate subjects; at times they bore no apparent relationship
with anything in the chap-book. One of the biggest printers of chap-
books in the North was John White, a native of York, who in 1708
set up as a printer in Newcastle-on-Tyne. He had an immense stock
of quaint old cuts, inherited from his father, who had been a printer
in York, and some of these were undoubtedly the battered remnants
of blocks originally cut for early printers like Wynkyn de Worde and
Richard Pynson. Some cuts of the eighteenth century were made in
type metal instead of wood. Among the most popular of the chap-
books, which lingered on into the nineteenth century, were *The
Famous History of the Valiant London Apprentice*, and *The History of
Richard Whittington, thrice Lord Mayor of London.*

CHAPTER SEVEN

The Eighteenth Century

At the beginning of the eighteenth century English printing was still
at its ebb, the only exception to the poor work turned out by the
majority of printers being afforded by the Oxford Press, the flourishing
condition of which, as we have seen, was due almost entirely to Dr
Fell, who not only saw it well provided with good founts, but also gave
it his backing in the struggle with the Stationers' Company and the
King's Printers over the privilege for printing Bibles and Prayer Books.

Although fewer books were printed at Oxford during the eighteenth
century than during the second half of the previous century, numerical
deficiency was more than compensated for by the good workmanship
of the impressive folios, such as Clarendon's *History of the Rebellion*
(1702–4), and the intrinsic merit of the scholarly series edited by the
antiquary Thomas Hearne, among which were Leland's *Itinerary*
(1710–12) and the *Chronicles* of William of Newbridge, Alfred of
Beverley, William Camden, Peter Langtoft and many others.

Edward Hyde, Earl of Clarendon, gave his name to the Clarendon
Building in Broad Street to which the learned press moved in 1713,
and which was built largely from the profits accruing from the *History
of the Rebellion*, perpetual copyright in which was granted to the
University by Clarendon's son, Lord Cornbury. The press remained
there for a little more than a century before it had to transfer to larger
premises. An article in the *Quarterly Review* for December, 1839, gives
an account of the old Clarendon Press in the eighteenth century which
deserves to be reprinted as an illustration of the daily routine of a
large printing office in those days:

> As one enters it from the front, on the level of the top of the steps, the
> room on the right-hand side, with windows looking into Broad Street,
> was the Classical press-room—i.e. there men tugged at the handpresses of
> what Archbishop Laud called the 'Learned Press'; and over their heads,
> placed upon lines by means of a long-handled peel, were suspended some
> of the sheets to dry. The room on the same floor, with windows looking

to the South, was the council-chamber or board-room of the Delegates of the Press. Still keeping to the West side, it is said that the rooms above, both in front and at back, were allotted to the compositors and readers of the Learned Press; while still higher, in the 'set-off' or loft, were stored the printed sheets after they had been dried in the Music School, before they were gathered. The pressing and other warehouse work was done in the cellars of the Sheldonian Theatre hard by, and there the 'Classical books' were stacked.

On the opposite side was situated the 'Bible Press'. In the rooms on the ground floor, back and front, were carried on the slow and tedious processes of printing copies of Bibles and Prayer Books by hand. . . . Overhead were installed the Bible and Prayer Book compositors; and when, a few years later, the accommodation for these proved insufficient, some of them overflowed into a house on the other side of Cat Street. The printed sheets of Bibles and Prayer Books were dried over the heads of the pressmen, as in the case of the Learned Press books; and such as were required for immediate delivery were pressed and gathered and sent away. Those that remained were stocked in the large room adjoining the Tower of the Five Orders, called the Writing School. Subsequent orders for the binders involved still another move; for the sheets were carried up to the front of the Clarendon Building and packed in the passage; then two long planks having been put from the highest step to the top of a wagon drawn up outside, the bales were laboriously pushed and guided into the wagon, in which they securely jogged along the high road to London, where they were bound and supplied to the booksellers.

We have seen that the accommodation afforded at the Printing-house was insufficient for the printer; but what shall be said of his tools and other appliances of his craft? These had remained almost unchanged ever since the invention of the art of printing. The 'casting' or jerking of the hot metal into the mould, in making the types, was still always done by hand: the press upon which proofs were pulled, or final copies tediously worked off, was a crazy structure, built of wood, excepting that a stone slab made a bed upon which the forme of type was placed. The descriptions of old writers on printing appliances show how ramshackle the wooden presses were. . . . To ink the forme the workman dabbed the type with a round 'ball', or leather pad, stuffed with wool, and nailed to a wooden handle; and the means provided for cleansing these balls, when they became clogged with ink, were very unsavoury. They were soaked in urine, and the pelts, being stripped off, were placed near the feet of the pressman, to be trodden out as he worked. Again, the light by which the printer was expected to do his work on dark days was afforded by tallow candles stuck in tin candlesticks, which were loaded with lead at the bottom to prevent their being upset. The compositor placed his candles in the boxes of his case. He was allowed two 'fours' if he happened to be working, as he does now, with three pairs of cases; otherwise he had only one, and this he had to carry with him whenever he went to correct at the 'stone'. The pressman lodged his in the most convenient places he could find in or near his press. He had three: a 'four' for the bank; a 'six' for the tympan; and an 'eight' for the slab. The foreman printer gave out these candles, and a boy went round in the morning and collected the drippings and gutterings as his perquisite. How the Clarendon Building escaped being burned to the ground long before it was abandoned by the printers is a marvel.

Among the Bibles which came from the Oxford Press at the beginning of the eighteenth century was the magnificent large folio produced by John Baskett in 1716–17. Splendidly printed though it was, this Bible was marred by numerous misprints in the text, on account of which it came to be known as 'a Baskett-full of errors', and also as the 'Vinegar Bible' from a misprint for 'vineyard' in Luke XX. Baskett was a stationer for many years before he became a printer. A shrewd businessman, he purchased from the executors of Henry Hills and Thomas Newcombe a share in the patent of King's Printer about 1710 and eventually acquired the whole patent and its reversion. In 1711 he obtained a lease of the Oxford privilege and a third share of the Scottish patent. In 1716 he obtained a fresh privilege, which he shared with the widow of Andrew Anderson as King's Printer in Scotland. But he made no use of his share until 1725, when he set up a press in Edinburgh and produced several mediocre editions of the Bible.

Over the Bible patent in Scotland there was for long a feud between Baskett and the Edinburgh printer James Watson, who in 1720 accused the former of 'making the just privileges of his patent a scandalous cover for a notorious monopoly, thereby encroaching even upon trade itself, by engrossing the sole printing of Bibles, New Testaments, Common Prayer Books, etc., in England, putting what price he pleased upon the subject, raising the price fifty and sixty per cent upon them, by the mere power of his monopolizing press'.[136]

To appreciate Watson's attitude it is necessary to retrace the story from 1671, when the Glasgow printer Andrew Anderson obtained a monopoly as Printer of Bibles for Scotland, and was soon afterwards appointed King's Printer with right of supervision over all other printers in Scotland. He died in 1679 and his widow succeeded to the monopoly, which she exercised to the full; her husband's patent gave him an exclusive right to print all kinds of lawful books in Edinburgh, and Mrs Anderson did not hesitate to prosecute anyone who tried to set up as a printer in that city, saying that 'one press is sufficiently able to serve all Scotland'.

Unfortunately Mrs Anderson's press was not a good one. Its productions were, in the words of Lord Fountainhall, 'miserably wretched beyond all example. Her Bibles were shamefully set up and worse printed, and fewer of them to satisfy the requirements of the public —although she charged her own high prices for them.'[137] As a result Bibles were printed in the Low Countries and smuggled into Scotland. When the period of Mrs Anderson's patent had nearly expired Watson began to negotiate with Robert Freebairn, another Edinburgh printer, with a view to securing for themselves the patent of Queen's Printer for Scotland. They found it necessary to approach Baskett, then Queen's Printer for England, and the three of them made an application which was successful in August, 1711, when Freebairn obtained the warrant appointing him, his heirs, partners, assigns or substitutes Queen's Printer for Scotland for 41 years.

Mrs Anderson, having failed to have her patent renewed, sought to oust Watson, and intrigued with Freebairn to become his partner. He and Baskett then turned on Watson and together made application for the patent of 1711 to be declared void, and solicited a new warrant. This led to a lawsuit which was decided in Watson's favour. But Waton's troubles were not yet over, for during the 1715 rebellion, Freebairn threw in his lot with the Old Pretender and went to Perth as his official printer. This act cost him his patent, and a new one was granted in 1716 to John Baskett and the irrepressible Mrs Anderson. Probably the Watson family's connection with the Jacobites cost him his part in the patent. His father, James Watson, had been known as 'the Popish printer'.

James Watson the Younger set up as a printer in Edinburgh in 1695, and by 1700 more than thirty books are known to have come from his office. Much of his work was in connection with the periodical press. He was the first printer of Donaldson's *Edinburgh Gazette* (of which he printed forty-one numbers) and during his career he was the printer of the first *Edinburgh Courant* (1705), the *Paris Gazette* (1706), the *Scots Postman* (1708), and the *Scots Courant* (1710), which he published for ten years, the last known issue being that of April 20–22, 1720.

Like so many other printers of the time he had his skirmishes with the authorities, and in 1700 was arrested for printing and circulating certain pamphlets. Together with their author, Hugh Paterson, he was banished from Edinburgh and forbidden to come within ten miles of the city for a year and a day. However, he managed to carry on his business from a distance and in 1709 he opened a shop which became quite famous 'next door to the Red Lyon, opposite to the Luckenbooths'.

Two of the greatest names in Scottish printing of the eighteenth century were those of the brothers Robert and Andrew Foulis. Robert Foulis (1707–76) began his adult life as a barber, but meanwhile attended classes at Glasgow University. In 1738 he and his brother Andrew (1712–75) made a journey through England, France and the Low Countries, buying books on the way which they sold on their return to cover their expenses. This, and a similar trip in the following year, decided Robert to set up as a bookseller and publisher in 1741. His brother Andrew, although always closely associated with his brother's projects, did not become his partner officially until 1748.

The first books published by Robert Foulis, which were printed for him by others, were by no means good examples of printing, for at that time the state of printing in Glasgow was extremely poor. So poor, indeed, that the brothers, determined to improve the appearance of their books, 'attended a printing-house in town until they had gained a complete knowledge of the art'.[138] Both brothers were lovers of good literature, and editions of the classics formed a large proportion of their output, together with books on philosophy, such as Professor Hutcheson's 350-page treatise on Moral Philosophy—a subject always calculated to appeal to the Scot.

Early in 1743, Robert Foulis printed his first Greek text, *Demetrius Phalerus De Elocutione*, which he submitted with an application for the post of Printer to Glasgow University, a post to which he was nominated in that same year. In 1744 the foundry of Wilson and Baine was moved from St Andrews to Camlachie, a village bordering on Glasgow, and it was Wilson who thereafter not only supplied them with type, but cut special founts for them.[139] Alexander Wilson (1714–84), a native of St Andrews, was at first intended for the medical profession, but through the patronage of Lord Isla (later Duke of Argyle) he was able to devote himself to scientific research in which he was passionately interested. A chance visit to a letter-foundry led to an interest in typography and, in partnership with a friend named Baine, he started his own foundry in 1742.

The partnership between Robert and Andrew Foulis, dating from

1748, led to the production of a steady stream of books, most of which could stand comparison with anything being produced at the time either in England or on the Continent, while some of them were really outstanding. The one book which surpasses all their other work —'one of the finest monuments of Greek typography which our nation possesses'*—is the 4-volume folio *Homer* which appeared between 1756 and 1758. The double pica Greek was specially cut for it by Wilson, who was also responsible for many of the firm's roman founts, including a splendid double pica roman used in the quarto edition of Gray's *Poems*, published in 1768.

In the matter of title-page layout the Foulis brothers were not without influence; they eschewed the mixed types of their predecessors and dispensed with lower case and italics, achieving a classical simplicity which had seldom been seen in this country. Their classics were remarkable also for their accuracy, and the edition of *Horace* which they published in 1744 contained so few errors that it was dubbed the 'immaculate' Horace. The 20-volume *Cicero* of 1749 earned the commendation of Renouard, who preferred its type to that of the Elzevirs, and the small folio edition of *Callimachus* (1755) was awarded a silver medal for the finest book of not fewer than ten sheets.

Andrew Foulis died suddenly in 1775, and his brother Robert in the following year. The business was carried on for a time by Andrew Foulis, the son of Robert. He is the Andrew Foulis who was associated with Tilloch in his patent for stereotyping (see page 219). By 1795, when the younger Andrew Foulis finally closed down the business, the firm had issued around 700 titles.

The eighteenth century saw the introduction of a new kind of periodical literature, an innovation due largely to the initiative of the printer Edward Cave (1691–1754), who was quick to perceive that there was a public among the middle classes for miscellaneous information of a kind not obtainable from the daily or weekly news-sheets. For some time he earned a living as a writer of news-letters, and on one occasion was taken into custody for furnishing Robert Raikes, the proprietor of the *Gloucester Journal* and part owner of the *Northampton Mercury*, with minutes of the proceedings of the House of Commons (this was before the days of Hansard).

He saved enough money by furnishing news to various journals to

---

* Reed-Johnson. Page 260.

enable him to set up a small printing office at St John's Gate, Clerken-well, and there he began his career as a printer under the name of 'R. Newton'. He conceived the idea of forming a collection or 'maga-zine' as he termed it (he was the first to use the word in this sense) of essays and articles on a variety of subjects and in January, 1731, brought out the first number of a periodical miscellany called *The Gentleman's Magazine*. He had offered a half share in his project to half the booksellers in London, but all rejected the idea as absurd. So Cave produced it at his own risk and so great was its success that, in the following year, the very booksellers who had considered Cave's idea impracticable launched a rival periodical, the *London Magazine*. In a few years a number of such magazines were brought out, but the majority quickly perished. However, the success of *The Gentleman's Magazine* was assured, and in the course of a conversation at Sir Joshua Reynold's house, Dr Johnson told those present that

> Cave used to sell ten thousand of *The Gentleman's Magazine*; yet such was then his minute attention and anxiety that the sale should not suffer the smallest decrease, that he would name a particular person who he heard had talked of leaving off the Magazine, and would say, 'Let us have something good next month'.[140]

The Gentleman's Magazine was the first to introduce parliamentary reports, for despite Cave's earlier infringements of the orders of the House, he persisted in publishing the debates, the notes of which, taken *sub rosa*, were later edited for publication by the historian Guthrie, a writer for booksellers whom Cave retained for the purpose. In 1738, threatened with proceedings for breach of privilege, he prefaced the account of the debates with 'An Appendix to Captain Lemuel Gulli-ver's Account of the famous Empire of Lilliput' and the proceedings in parliament were reported under the title of 'Debates in the Senate of Great Lilliput', in which fictional guise they ran for many years, Guthries' post later passing to Dr Johnson (whose *Rambler** was later published by Cave). Cave had frequent brushes with the Government, and in 1747 was taken into custody for having printed in his magazine an account of the trial of Simon, Lord Lovat.

Cave died on 10 January, 1754, and was buried in the church of St James, Clerkenwell. In addition to his printing of periodical litera-ture his press turned out a number of learned books, such as Dr Halde's

---

* No. 1 appeared on 20 March, 1750. The printer was William Faden.

History of China (1736) and Dr Newton's *Compleat Herbal* (1752). Accounts of his life and work may be found in Timperley and Nichols.

Once the eighteenth century had got well under way, printing gradually spread to the provinces. In 1693 the so-called Press Restriction Act, which had put an end to all provincial printing in 1586, was allowed to lapse. But although it was now possible to carry on printing in any part of the country, there was no rush to set up presses in the provincial centres. Printing was started in Bristol in 1695, Plymouth in 1696, Shrewsbury in 1696, and Exeter in 1698; but it was not until the beginning of the new century that provincial printing began to flourish, and then only in the large centres of population, such as Birmingham; apart from 'job' printing, such as tradesmen's cards, funeral cards, and local notices, there was little yet for the printer to do in the smaller towns, which may account for a letter from William Brome to Richard Rawlinson dated 23 February, 1740 (in the Bodleian Library), which reads:

> In some of your letters you enquired after printing-presses in England: last spring I let an house I have in Hereford for that business: and since Christmas my tenant in one night removed all his effects and press, and put up, or somebody for him, over the door in capitals—
> 'Pray Landlord, Landlord, be content
> With the Key instead of your rent'
> and the key was under the door.

The market for books was, however, steadily extending, both in town and country and, to induce customers to buy, many stationers issued books in parts which came out a few sheets at a time, weekly or monthly, at prices ranging from a penny to a shilling for each number. This form of serial publication was quite common during the twenty years between 1730 and 1750, after which it gradually declined. Moxon's *Mechanick Exercises* was published in this manner, the first volume being made up of fourteen parts, each with its own title-page, published between 1677 and 1680. This was a very early example of the 'number trade'. The second volume is divided in parts numbered I–XXIV, intended probably for monthly issue although the original plan of publication was not adhered to. Ned Warde's *The London Spy* was also published as a part issue. One of the most industrious figures in the number trade was Robert Walker, who started the earliest local newspapers in Oxford and Cambridge. He published a weekly newspaper at Cambridge with the printer Thomas James.

Timperley says 'to establish the sale of it they printed, in octavo, Jacob Hooper's *History of the Rebellion*, and Harrison's *History of Queen Anne*, with neat cuts, &c. which they gave *gratis*, a sheet a week, till completed'.[141] In much the same manner Walker organized his part issue of *The History of the Holy Bible*. The inclusion of so many of these serialized publications in newspapers was an attempt to evade the stamp duty on periodical publications which came into force in 1712 (see page 182). An issue that contained six pages or more could rank as a pamphlet, liable to duty at the rate of 2s for each edition, which was far cheaper than the rate of ½d or 1d (according to whether half sheet or whole sheet) per copy payable by periodicals.

One of the most important printers of the first half of the eighteenth century was John Watts (1678–1763), whose output was both extensive and varied. An able coadjutor of the Tonsons, with the younger of whom he was for some time in partnership, Watts was celebrated for his good printing, the fame of which, declared John Nichols, 'will endure as long as any public library shall exist'.[142] It was in John Watts's printing house in Wild Court that some part of Benjamin Franklin's education as a printer was acquired—together with his nickname of the 'Water American'—as he so delightfully records in his autobiography.* Watts could produce large folios—like Matthew Prior's *Poems on several occasions* (1718), which he printed for Jacob Tonson and John Barber—or small 12mo classics with equal felicity, and the decoration of his books was always of a high standard. According to Nichols he lent William Caslon (see page 188) £100 to enable him to start up in business as a punch-cutter.

Engraving was an art much practised in the eighteenth century and among its ablest exponents in England was John Pine (1690–1756), said to have been a pupil of the famous French engraver, Bernard Picart. Between 1733 and 1737 Pine published the works of Horace in two volumes, in Latin, printed entirely from engraved copperplates, text as well as ornament. It is supposed that the text was first set in type and transferred to the plate before it was engraved. Plenty of 'white line' gave a brilliant and spacious air to the pages, and as Philip Gaskell points out, 'Pine approached the layout of the text as a typographer, not as a calligrapher, and achieved remarkable effects by way of simplicity, particularly in the title-pages and dedications'.[143]

---

* The press which Franklin worked at in Watts's shop in 1726 is now in the Smithsonian Institution, Washington D.C.

Samuel Richardson (1689–1761) is chiefly remembered as the author of *Pamela, Clarissa Harlowe* and *Sir Charles Grandison*. Few know that he was a printer by trade, and a very successful one. In 1706 he was apprenticed to John Wilde, a London printer, and, in his own words, 'served a diligent seven years to a master who grudged every hour to me that tended not to his profit'. In 1719, after a period as journeyman and corrector of the press, he set up in business on his own account in a small court off Fleet Street. Until he had established himself he eked out his living as a printer by compiling indexes for booksellers, writing prefaces, and composing what he called 'honest dedications'.

His business grew and he printed six numbers of the Duke of Wharton's *True Briton*, but severed his connection with it after the publisher had been prosecuted for libel. Then, through the interest of the Speaker, the Rt Hon. Arthur Onslow, he obtained the printing of the *Journals of the House of Commons*, of which he completed twenty-six volumes. In 1732 he printed for Andrew Millar a folio edition of Churchill's *Voyages*, and in 1733 part of De Thou's *History*, edited by Samuel Buckley. From 1736 to 1737 he printed the *Daily Journal* and in 1738 the *Daily Gazetteer*.

Of his own works, *Pamela* was published in 1741; *Clarissa Harlowe* in 1747; and *Sir Charles Grandison* in 1735. This last-named work was, much to the author's annoyance, pirated and printed before the English publication by certain Dublin booksellers, who took advantage of the fact that Ireland did not come under the jurisdiction of the Copyright Act of 1709 (see page 171). Richardson said the sheets were stolen from his warehouse, and three Irish booksellers each published cheap editions of nearly half the book before a volume appeared in England. Richardson added that he had heard an Irish bookseller boast that he could procure from any printing office in London sheets of any book that was being printed there.

In 1754 Richardson was appointed Master of the Stationers' Company, and in the following year he built new warehouses and a printing office in Salisbury Court. About the middle of 1760 he purchased a half-share in the patent of law-printer and carried on that part of his business in partnership with Miss Catherine Lintot, daughter of the publisher Henry Lintot. Richardson died on 4 July, 1761, and was buried in St Bride's Church. His business was carried on by his nephew, William Richardson, and for some time the law patent was held jointly by Miss Lintot and the widow of Samuel Richardson.

Employed for a time by Richardson was Thomas Gent, a rather

remarkable character, though a poor printer, who from being a run-away apprentice ended up as a master printer in York and historian of that town and others in the north of England. The three topographical works which he both wrote and printed are the *Famous History of the City of York*, the *History of the Loyal Town of Ripon* and *History of the Royal and Beautiful Town of Kingston-upon-Hull*. From 1710 to 1724 he worked as a 'smouter', or casual journeyman, for a number of printers, until he settled definitely in York after marrying the widow of Charles Bourne. In that city he died in his eighty-seventh year, having left in manuscript an amusing account of his life which was published in London by Thomas Thorpe in 1832, with an engraved portrait of the author by Valentine Green.[144] Of this volume Southey wrote: 'His autobiography is as characteristic as John Dunton's, and, like it, contains much information relating to the state of the press in his days, and the trade of literature.'

Another printer who has left us interesting information concerning the book trade of the day is Henry Woodfall, extracts from whose ledgers were published by an anonymous contributor to the first series of *Notes and Queries*. Woodfall, who died in 1769, had premises in Paternoster Row. A Master of the Stationers' Company in 1766, he printed for some of the best-known booksellers of his time, among them Bernard and Henry Lintot, Robert Dodsley and Andrew Millar. For Bernard Lintot he printed an edition of Pope's Works at the end of 1735, and his ledger contains the following entry:

> Decr. 15th, 1735—
>
> Printing the first volume of Mr Pope's Works,
> Cr., Long Primer, 8vo, 3000 (and 75 fine) @
> £2.2s. per sheet, 14 sheets and a half £30 9 0
> Title in red and black 1 1 0
> Paid for 2 reams and ¼ of writing demy 2 16 3

For Henry Lintot he printed Pope's translation of the *Iliad*, and Woodfall's entry on 15 May, 1736, runs:

> The *Iliad of Homer* by Mr Pope, demy,
> Long Primer and Brevier. No. 2000 in
> 6 vols, 68 sheets and ½ @ £2.2s. per sheet £143 17 0

For Andrew Millar, Woodfall printed several works by the poet James Thomson, and if Millar lost money on Thomson's *Liberty*, of which Woodfall printed 3,250 copies of the first part in 1735, he recouped himself handsomely over *The Seasons*, which was reprinted time and time again.

William Bowyer I and II

Thanks to the *Literary Anecdotes* of John Nichols,[145] we know a good deal about these two well-known printers, for Nichols had been with the firm since he was twelve years old. William Bowyer I (1663–1737) was apprenticed to Miles Flesher in 1679, made free of the Stationers' Company in 1686, and started business on his own account in 1699 at the sign of the White Horse in Little Britain. Before the close of that year he moved into Dogwell Court, White Friars, and on 6 May, 1700, was admitted to the livery of the Company.

On the night of 29 January, 1712–13, these premises were entirely destroyed by fire, together with almost all his stock. A subscription was at once raised by his colleagues and a royal brief★ was granted to indemnify Bowyer; altogether he received £2,540, with which he was able to resume business.

In 1715 he printed the *Anglo-Saxon Grammar* of Miss Elizabeth Elstob. This work had been begun in 1712, but the Anglo-Saxon type used was destroyed in the fire before the work could be completed. As a measure of practical sympathy with Bowyer Lord Chief Justice Parker (afterwards Lord Macclesfield) paid for the cutting of a new set of Anglo-Saxon types, made from the drawings of an eminent Saxonist, Humphrey Wanley. Unfortunately the cutting of the punches by the letter-founder Robert Andrews proved unsatisfactory. The type was nevertheless used for Miss Elstob's *Grammar*, and occasionally in other works printed by Bowyer and his son. Punches, matrices and type were eventually presented to the University of Oxford by William Bowyer II, though, owing to their long detention by his intermediary, Rowe Mores, they did not reach their destination until 1778. There is no record of any further use of these types during the eighteenth century, and the punches and matrices still remain with the Oxford University Press.[146]

In 1722 William Bowyer's only son, also William, joined him in the business, of which William Bowyer I still retained the management. The son, born in 1699, was a man of wide culture, and has been called 'the most learned printer of the eighteenth century' from his having been elected a Fellow of the Society of Antiquaries, to whose

---

★ Permission for special collections to be made in churches.

publications he contributed many papers and to which body he became printer in 1736. At first the younger Bowyer was mainly concerned with reading the proofs of the learned works which the firm of Bowyer and Son printed.

William Bowyer I was intimately connected with Caslon's first steps in the art of punch-cutting, but Nichols was mistaken when he asserted that Caslon's English roman was first used in printing the edition of Selden's works edited by Dr Wilkins and begun in 1722. The first volume of this work was printed by William Bowyer I, and it contains Hebrew types cut by Caslon, but according to Reed-Johnson the first of Caslon's roman types to appear was the pica roman in the Notes at the end of the *Anacreon*, issued in 1725.[147] Caslon's English roman seems to have made its first appearance in *A Discourse of the Judicial Authority belonging to the Office of Master of the Rolls* (1728).

A curious production from Bowyer's press was *A compleat and private List of all the Printing-houses in and about the Cities of London and Westminster* (1724), which was compiled by Samuel Negus, the 'malignant fellow-workman' who had tormented Thomas Gent when they were both employed by the Whig party printer, Wilkins. Negus arranged the printers under various classifications such as 'Well Affected to King George', 'Nonjurors' and 'Said to be High Flyers'.

William Bowyer I died on 27 December, 1737. His son carried on the business for many years. In 1738, when Hunsdon House was destroyed by fire and John Baskett and his family barely escaped with their lives, William Bowyer II, in remembrance of Baskett's gift to his father after he had suffered a similar disaster, presented him with a new press.

For more than half a century William Bowyer II stood almost unrivalled as a printer of learned books, of which the details are given in Nichols's *Anecdotes of William Bowyer* (1782) and *Literary Anecdotes*. From 1754 to 1757 William Bowyer II was associated with the printer James Emonson, and in 1766 took into partnership John Nichols, who had spent almost the whole of his life with the firm. William Bowyer II died on 18 November, 1777, and by his will left to the Stationers' Company £180 a year for specific charities, in addition to various trusts for the benefit of aged members of the printing trade.

The Copyright Act of 1709

'Copyright' in the sense in which we now use it, that is to say the exclusive property right of an author in his own work, was not recognized until the reign of Queen Anne. In the sixteenth century copyright had nothing at all to do with the author; it was the right of a printer or bookseller to the exclusive use of a 'copy' which he had either been the first to publish, or had acquired from some other stationer, for the rights in a 'copy' (i.e. title) could be sold, exchanged or assigned. That this was recognized by the Stationers' Company is shown by an entry in the Register for 1558/9 of a fine levied against Owen Rogers 'for printing another man's copy' (Arber I. 101). In fact Owen Rogers was frequently fined for that offence.

To establish ownership of a copy it became necessary to show prior publication and enter the copy in the Register of the Stationers' Company, though such entry was, after the decree of 1558 (see page 108), made conditional on the printer's obtaining a licecne for the work to be printed from the appointed authorities. The duration of such copyright was normally in perpetuity, but in 1557-8 it was stipulated that the rights in a title which was out of print should, if the owner failed to reprint it, become open for the benefit of the poorer members of the Company.

In 1709, however, an Act was made 'for the Encouragement of Learning, by vesting the Copies of printed Books in the Authors or Purchasers of such Copies, during the Times therein mentioned'. By this Act it was declared that the author or his assigns should possess an exclusive copyright for the term of fourteen years from the day of publication and no longer, and that after that term the sole right should return to the author, if he were living, for another fourteen years. (For books already in print the owners were to have the copyright for twenty-one years, dating from 1 April, 1710.) Thus, for the first time since the introduction of printing in England, an author had no need to sell his copy outright and thus lose control of it.

Since the copies which would thus fall into the public domain in 1731 included such very saleable authors as Shakespeare, Milton, Dryden and other famous writers, it was natural that London booksellers who had entered these titles as their copies were anxious not to lose them, and in their unsuccessful petitions to Parliament 'the trade', as it was termed, pleaded their Common Law rights to perpetual ownership of copyright. And when the Act came into force, although they were fully acquainted with its terms, they often ignored it. They complained, also, that there were no adequate provisions under the Act to prevent piracy by the importation of books from abroad, with the result that there was much price-cutting by editions printed in Ireland and Holland.

In 1734—three years after the expiration of copyright on old books —Jacob Tonson II and others who had been in the habit of printing the works of Shakespeare contested the right of Robert Walker to issue a pocket edition of Shakespeare's plays. The matter was brought to a head by Alexander Donaldson, who made a test case of his reprint of *The Seasons* by James Thomson. When legal action was taken, he lost the case and a perpetual injunction was granted against him. But with Scottish perseverance Donaldson took his case to the House of Lords where, in February, 1774, he obtained judgement by a majority of twenty-one votes to eleven, the House deciding that no Common Law right existed. A further unsuccessful attempt to render copyright perpetual was made in that same year, but although the Bill passed the Commons it was thrown out by the Lords. This put an end to the state of affairs concerning which Baskerville wrote to a friend on 4 January, 1757: 'Mr Basket has a patent for Bibles, Common prayer-books, and Law Books. The Booksellers claim an absolute right in Copy of Books, as old as even Milton and Shakespear; the former of which I did design to have printed, but am deterred by Mr Tonson & Co threatening me with a bill in Chancery if I attempt it . . . .'[148] This did not deter him, however, from printing his editions of Milton, for which we must be thankful.

When in 1777 John Bell announced his *Poets of Great Britain; complete from Chaucer to Churchill*, the London booksellers were alarmed. Since they could not prevent him they combined their various interests, and between them produced their own edition of *The English Poets* in sixty-eight volumes, for which Dr Johnson wrote the lives (for the very modest fee of two hundred guineas). This consortium sought to belittle Bell's edition, of which they spoke contemptuously. But they failed to include in their own collection, as Bell had done, either Chaucer, Spenser or Donne.

William Strahan

One of the most eminent and certainly one of the most successful printers of the eighteenth century, William Strahan was born at Edinburgh on 24 March, 1715. After serving his apprenticeship in that city he went to London, where he set up as a master printer with one or two journeymen in 1739. He was extremely methodical in his accounting all his life, and we can gain some idea of the growth of

his business by comparing the £234 which he paid out in journey-men's wages during his first year, with the £3,578.13s.0d. which he paid in 1783.[149] Admitted to the freedom of the Stationers' Company*
by redemption in 1737, Strahan was actively engaged in printing to the time of his death in 1785.

According to Boswell, Strahan, 'an old and constant friend', told Dr Johnson that the first book he published was 'the Duke of Berwick's Life, by which he had lost, and that he hated its name'. This was the *Life of James Fitzjames, Duke of Berwick*, published with Andrew Millar's name on the title-page. During his first years in business Strahan printed for many well-known booksellers and publishers—among them Millar, John Osborn, John Newbery, the Rivingtons and the first Thomas Longman. In 1749 he printed the *Monthly Review* for Ralph Griffiths.

In February, 1743, Strahan printed for Andrew Millar an edition of Fielding's *Joseph Andrews* (3,000 copies: 20 sheets @ £2.5s.0d. a sheet), and from Millar, who was Fielding's publisher, he later acquired shares in the copyright of that author's works. He had, like most of the big printers of his day, an interest in publishing, and by the exercise of sound literary judgment allied to industry and business acumen William Strahan built up one of the greatest printing houses in London. At his death his estate came to £95,000 and included, as well as much literary property, a share in the patent of King's Printer, in the Law Patent, in the *Public Advertiser* and the *London Chronicle*.

It was in 1766 that Strahan acquired a share in the patent of King's Printer. The patent had come to Charles Eyre, through his father, who had purchased it from John Baskett for £10,000. But Charles Eyre, not being himself a practical printer, sought the co-operation of Strahan, who paid him £5,000 for a third share of the patent, and received £300 a year for managing the printing office.† Four years before this Strahan had gone into partnership with Henry Woodfall in the law-printing business. (Their immediate predecessors in this patent had been the widow of Samuel Richardson and Catherine Lintot, daughter of the publisher Henry Lintot, who is said to have made £45,000 out of it.)

The extent of Strahan's business activities in 1771 may best be

---

* He was Master in 1774.
† Not Baskett's premises in Blackfriars, which had been the King's Printing House for more than a century, but new premises built on ground adjoining New Street (near Gough Square).

judged from the following extract from a letter written by the printer to David Hall on 15 June of that year:

> My eldest son William is now, you know, settled by himself, and will, I dare say, do very well; though the Printing Trade is by no means a very profitable one. It requires great Industry, Economy, Perseverance, and Address, to make any great figure in it . . . My second son, George, is now in Orders . . . My youngest, Andrew, is the only one now with me . . . but his time is almost totally taken up in the Printing House in looking after 7, 8 or 9 presses, which are constantly employed there: for besides the *Chronicle* and *Monthly Review* I have always a pretty large share of Book-work, in many Articles of which I am myself a Proprietor. I have also one half of the Law Printing-house, which is kept, separately, at some Distance from my own House; and as my Partner in that, Mr. Woodfall, died about two years ago, the whole Care of it lies upon me. As doth the Management of the King's Printing House, my Partner, Mr. Eyre, not being bred to the Business and being in the Country. . . .
>
> Add to all this the Multiplicity of Concerns I have in the Property of Books (about 200 in number) which require, every one of them, some Attention, and a separate and distinct Account, and a Variety of Avocations which cannot be particularly enumerated. . . .
>
> It is easy to manage one Branch of Business: but nobody in my Way ever before extended it so far as I have done. My Reason was this: I quickly saw that if I confined myself to mere *printing for Booksellers*, I might be able to live, but very little more than live; I therefore soon determined to launch out into other branches in Connection with my own, in which I have happily succeeded, to the Astonishment of the rest of the Trade here, who never dreamt of going out of the old beaten Track. Thus I have made the name of *Printer* more respectable than ever it was before, and taught them to emancipate themselves from the Slavery in which the Booksellers held them.[150]

One of the most famous works with which Strahan was connected was Dr Johnson's *Dictionary*, the printing of which was begun at the end of the 1740s, although it did not appear until 1755. The book was financed by a syndicate of booksellers, of which Dodsley was the principal, and Strahan was the printer. It was Strahan who, in conjunction with Thomas Cadell, undertook the publication of Gibbon's *Decline and Fall*, the first volume of which was published in 1776. On receiving a presentation copy of this volume, Hume wrote to Strahan: 'There will be no books of importance now printed in London but through your hands and Mr Cadell's', and certainly between them they published most of the notable books which appeared during the second half of the eighteenth century.

Thomas Cadell had been apprenticed to Andrew Millar, and later became his partner, succeeding to the business after Millar's death. Strahan was often associated with Cadell, as he had been with Millar, in the purchase of book properties. He was in fact a participant in the share-book system which had developed out of the Printing Conger of the early part of the century.

Even from the earliest times the printer did not always finance his own books. But the association of a number of booksellers for the publication of a work entailing a considerable outlay, although practised on the Continent in the sixteenth century, did not become common in England until the eighteenth. The Printing Conger (as it was termed) set up around 1719 consisted of seven booksellers, each of whom contributed a certain sum of money with which to buy copyrights, which were afterwards pooled, published and sold in collaboration, the production costs being shared among the members. There were several congers in operation during the first half of the eighteenth century, the largest of these organizations being known as The Chapter, from the Chapter Coffee House in Paternoster Row, where they met.

The conger system disappeared by the middle of the eighteenth century, but, says Miss Handover, 'though short-lived, it and the share-book system of which it was part were means of transition between the old copyright-owning bookseller or printer and the modern publisher who is neither a bookseller nor a printer, though he may have a separate printing works'.[151]

Among the authors in whose works Strahan had a share was Henry Fielding. In Strahan's notebook labelled 'List of Copies taken, 1739–1778',* is the following entry:

Date		Short title	Of whom bought	Price		
1769. June 13.	$\frac{1}{12}$	Fielding's Governess	Mr A. Millar	£ 6	16	4
	$\frac{1}{10}$	,, Jon. Wilde	,,	6	6	0
	$\frac{1}{12}$	,, Jos. Andrews	,,	18	0	6
	$\frac{1}{24}$	,, Tom Jones	,,	17	11	3
	$\frac{1}{12}$	,, Amelia	,,	8	18	7
	$\frac{1}{12}$	,, Phil. Trans. etc	,,	2	15	0

---

* British Museum. *Strahan Papers.* Add. Mss. 48805.

The first volume of Gibbon's *Decline and Fall* was originally planned as an edition of 500 copies, but, writes the author, 'the number was doubled by the prophetic taste of Mr Strahan'. Yet even his estimate fell short of the demand, for, as Gibbon adds, 'The first impression was exhausted in a few days; a second and third edition were scarcely adequate to the demand; and the bookseller's property was twice invaded by the pirates of Dublin.' The work was not finally completed until 1788, when the sixth volume was issued, by which time Strahan was dead. That Gibbon had no cause to be dissatisfied with his treatment by the publishers, the following statement of account shows:

State of the Account of Mr Gibbon's 'Roman Empire'. Third Edition.
1st Vol. No.—1,000. April 30th, 1777.

	£	s	d
Printing 90 sheets at £1. 6s., with notes at the bottom of the page	117	0	0
180 reams of paper @ 19s.	171	0	0
Paid the corrector, extra care	5	5	0
Advertisements and incidental expenses	16	15	0
	310	0	0

	£	s	d
1000 books @ 16s	800	0	0
Deduct as above	310	0	0
Profit on this edition when sold	490	0	0
Mr Gibbon's two-thirds is	326	13	4
Messrs Strahan and Cadell's	163	6	8
	490	0	0

William Strahan, who died on 9 July, 1785, had five sons and three daughters (two children died in infancy). William Strahan, the first-born, was a printer at Snow-hill, but died four years before his father. George, the second son, took Orders, and was Vicar of St Mary's, Islington, for some fifty years. Andrew, born in 1750, succeeded to his father's business. Among those who were apprenticed to William Strahan was John Bell, who was made free in 1762, and was destined to cause no small commotion in the trade.

John Bell (1745-1831)

John Bell was a remarkable man—bookseller and publisher, printer of books and newspapers, typographer and designer, editor and copywriter—the Proteus of the printing trade. He was a bookseller before he was twenty-four, and a newspaper proprietor three years later—one of the syndicate who founded *The Morning Post and Daily Advertiser* in November, 1772, and its chief proprietor for nearly fifteen years.

When in 1774 Alexander Donaldson, a pioneer of popular reprints (see page 172) had won his case against the supposed perpetuity of copyright, much to the annoyance of the London booksellers whom he was underselling, John Bell considered the time ripe to publish a *Shakespeare* in eleven volumes (1774) and to replace the cumbrous collections of the works of dramatic authors with his own neat *British Theatre* in twenty-one volumes (1776-8). (Although he discarded the long 's' in these publications he was not, as Nichols says, the first to set the fashion, for Ames had already done so in his *Typographical Antiquities* of 1749.) Bell also published, in association with the Martins of the Apollo Press, Edinburgh, the *Poets of Great Britain from Chaucer to Churchill*, which between 1777 and 1792 reached a total of 109 volumes. He chose his draughtsmen and engravers not for their cheapness but for their excellence, and in consequence these books were notable for an elegance not hitherto associated with cheap editions, though the London booksellers sought to decry them. Edward Dilly, writing to James Boswell in 1777, complains of Bell's books that 'the type was found so extremely small that many persons could not read them', and also states that 'the inaccuracy of the press was very conspicuous'. But this was prejudiced criticism; the books were well printed and enjoyed a merited success, encouraged by which Bell embarked on a second series of 12mo *Shakespeare* in 1785, which was edited by Samuel Johnson and George Steevens, and issued in weekly numbers. In 1788 he secured a patent as 'Bookseller to the Prince of Wales'.

The impact Bell made upon the book trade was echoed in the newspaper world. In 1779 he was associated with John Wheble in a thrice-weekly evening paper called *The English Chronicle*, but he greatly enhanced his reputation when after fourteen years with the *Morning Post* he sold his shares and in partnership with a rich officer of the Guards, Captain Edward Topham, founded the *World*, the first number of which appeared on 1 January, 1787. Topham was the editor; Bell was responsible for the typography, and for the first time the English reader was presented with a periodical that was neatly printed and leaded out to ease the eyes. In the number for 9 June of that year, Bell announced that he was setting up his own foundry, the British Letter Foundry, at his premises in the Strand (near Exeter Exchange), which, he declared, 'will produce an original cast of type from punches cut upon new, and I flatter myself very improved, principles'.[152] As punch-cutter Bell secured the services of Richard Austin, then at the beginning of his long and distinguished career. A specimen book of *Bell's New Printing Types* was issued in 1788, with the information that 'Printers in general may now be furnished with these original *Types*, at the Prices usually charged for common Types'.

John Bell had visited Paris in 1785, paying calls on printers and type-founders, and in the opinion of A. F. Johnson his type was probably inspired by the Didot letter of 1784, though it was no imitation. In 1790 Robert Merry's *The Laurel of Liberty* was published, set entirely in Bell type, well leaded. This was not the first use of Bell type in book-work however, for according to Anthoensen[154] it appears in the title of the *Dunciad* in Vol. III of the collected *Pope* issued in the Apollo 'Poets' series of 1787.[154] Stanley Morison calls the type cut for Bell by Richard Austin 'the first British modern face',[155] but A. F. Johnson seems to consider it transitional. It set a fashion in type design, but Reed-Johnson points out that 'unfortunately it was not the Bell type itself which was to be the model of the nineteenth century, but the exaggerated and inferior type introduced by Robert Thorne'. However, in 1931, Bell's type was cut for machine composition by the Monotype Corporation Ltd, from the original punches which eventually passed into the possession of the Stephenson, Blake foundry. In 1789 Bell had taken Simon Stephenson into partnership, but with so many other enterprises on his hands, Bell had to give up his interest in the foundry which, though carried on for a time by Simon and Charles Stephenson, ceased production in 1797.

In 1789 Bell and Topham parted and the former founded a new daily called the *Oracle: or Bell's New World*. Its success led him to start a Sunday newspaper in 1796 called *Bell's Weekly Messenger*. Another of his successful projects was a woman's monthly magazine called *La Belle Assemblée*, illustrated with fashion plates.

Walpole and the Strawberry Hill Press

Writing to Sir Horace Mann on 4 August, 1757, Horace Walpole says: 'I am turned printer, and have converted a little cottage here into a printing office. My abbey is a perfect college or academy; I kept a painter in the house and a printer.' Although doubtless begun as the whim of a rich dilettante, Walpole's private press lasted for thirty-two years, its productions were numerous, and among them are some interesting and now valuable works.

The first entry in the Journal of the printing-office runs:

> 1757—June 25th. The Press was erected. Wm. Robinson, printer.
> July 16th. Began to print. The first work was an edition of two new Odes by Mr Gray.[156]

Walpole was somewhat unlucky in his choice of printers, for five came and went in the first seven years. Robinson was, according to his employer, 'a foolish Irishman who took himself for a genius, and who grew angry when I thought him extremely the former and not the least the latter'. He was succeeded by Benjamin Williams, who was discharged after three weeks, to be replaced by James Lister, who only stayed a week. The next printer, Thomas Farmer, came to him in July, 1759, and printed Walpole's well-known *Anecdotes of Printing in England*. An entry in the Journal for 2 December, 1761, reads: 'Thomas Farmer ran away for debt. I thought he had finished the two volumes [of the *Anecdotes*] but he had left 19 sheets not printed off. Took one Pratt to finish the work.' To George Montagu, Walpole wrote: 'Just when I thought my book finished my printer ran away. . . . He had got into debt, and two girls with child.' Pratt was probably the printer of the *Memoirs* of Lord Cherbury, and he stayed with Walpole from 29 May, 1762, until the end of 1764. In March, 1765 Walpole engaged Thomas Kirgate, who proved to be the best and most reliable of his printers and who worked with him until the press came to an end in 1789 with the production of *Bishop Bonner's Ghost*, by Hannah More, to whom he wrote on 10 July, 1789: 'I beseech you not to fancy yourself vain on my being your printer. . . . My press has no rank but from its narrowness, that is, from the paucity of its editions, and from being a volunteer.' Two copies of this book were printed on brown paper, one of which he gave to the authoress. 'There is but one more such' he told her, 'so you may preserve it like a relic. I know these two are not so good as the white: but as rarities, a collector would give ten times more for them.'

The Development of the Periodical Press in the Eighteenth Century

The beginning of the reign of Queen Anne saw the periodical press firmly established, both in respect of newspapers and the periodicals of entertainment and instruction to which Cave had given the name of magazines. The *Tatler*, begun by Steele under the pen-name of Isaac Bickerstaff, ran from 12 April, 1709, until 13 January, 1711, and was essentially a newspaper, inasmuch as it gave considerable space to intelligence from abroad and contained advertisements; it differed from the newspaper proper in adding original articles on a variety of subjects. The *Spectator*, which succeeded it, and of which 638 numbers were published, printed in the same form and at the same price as the *Tatler*, namely one penny, was a periodical of far greater literary pretensions, news items being discarded in favour of essays and criticism. In the manner of La Bruyère, to quote the Doctor, these periodicals 'exhibited the characters and manners of the age'. The success of the *Spectator*, which appeared every weekday and the sale of which frequently amounted to 3,000 copies, encouraged the florescence of a host of imitators, most of which were short-lived. They included the *Guardian*, the *Lover*, the *Reader*, the *Tea-Table*, the *Trifler*, the *Plebian*, *Chit-Chat*, *Town Talk*, the *Englishman* and the *Crisis*. For assailing the conduct of the Tory administration in the two last-named papers Steele was expelled from the House of Commons.

The extension of the Post Office packet system at the end of the seventeenth century, together with the development of the by-Post and cross-Post systems for the carriage of mails to outlying localities, stimulated the development of the newspaper, which often acknowledged the debt by the inclusion of the word 'Post' or 'Packet' in its title. The word 'Coranto' had long since died out, but was remembered in the title of the *Daily Courant* and the *London Courant*.

The quicker dissemination of news by road and sea made it practicable to publish newspapers daily, instead of, as hitherto, twice or three times a week. London saw the appearance of its first daily morning newspaper on 11 March, 1702, when the *Daily Courant* was issued by a bookseller, E. Mallet, 'next door to the King's Arms Tavern at Fleet Bridge'; but on 22 April it began to bear the imprint of Samuel Buckley 'at the sign of the Dolphin, in Little Britain,'—'the worthy Mr Buckley, of Amen-corner' as Negus called him—who was also the printer of the *Monthly Register*. As a publisher he issued the edition

POLY-OLBION

GREAT · BRITTAINE

By
Michaell Drayton
Esqr.

London printed for ⎰ M·Lownes·I·Browne·Ongraue
⎱ I·Helme·I·Busbie

Michael Drayton, *Polyolbion*. M. Lownes and others, London, 1612. Engraved
title-page by William Hole

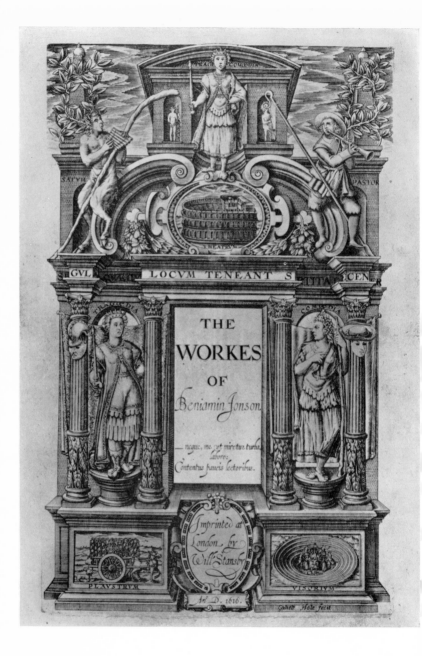

Ben Jonson, *Works*. William Stansby, London, 1616.
Engraved title-page by William Hole

John Donne, *LXXX Sermons*. Richard Royston and Richard Marriot, London, 1640.
Engraved title-page by Matthaeus Merian the Younger

Frontispiece to the edition of *The Pilgrim's Progress* by John Bunyan, printed for Nathaniel Ponder, 1678

Title-page of the first edition of *The Compleat Angler* by Izaak Walton, 1653

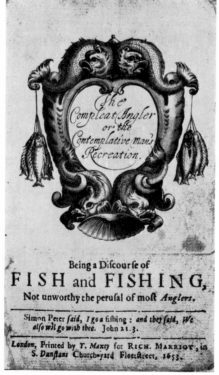

Title-page and frontispiece to John Pine's *Horace*, 1733

Virgil's *Bucolica, Georgica et Aeneis*, printed at Glasgow by Robert and Andrew Foulis in 1758. The type was supplied by Alexander Wilson. Their classics were renowned for the correctness of their text and the beauty of their typography

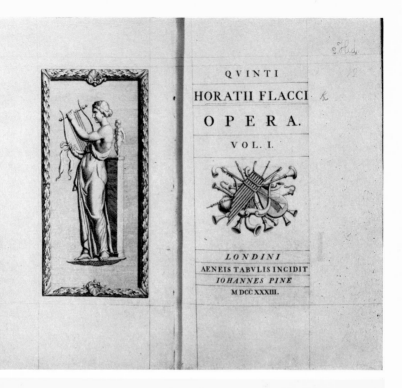

Ergo aegre rastris terram rimantur, et ipsis
Unguibus infodiunt fruges, montisque per altos
Contenta cervice trahunt stridentia plaustra.
Non lupus insidias explorat ovilia circum,
Nec gregibus nocturnus obambulat : acrior illum
Cura domat : timidi damae cervique fugaces
Nunc interque canes et circum tecta vagantur.
Jam maris inmensi prolem, et genus omne natantum
Litore in extremo, ceu naufraga corpora, fluctus
Proluit : insolitae fugiunt in flumina phocae.
Interit et curvis frustra defensa latebris
Vipera, et adtoniti squamis adstantibus hydri.
Ipsis est aër avibus non aequus, et illae
Praecipites alta vitam sub nube relinquunt.
Praeterea jam nec mutari pabula refert,
Quaesitaeque nocent artes : cessere magistri
Phillyrides Chiron, Amythaoniusque Melampus.
Saevit et in lucem Stygiis emissa tenebris
Pallida Tisiphone, morbos agit ante metumque,
Inque dies avidum surgens caput altius effert.
Balatu pecorum et crebris mugitibus amnes,
Arentesque sonant ripae, collesque supini.
Jamque catervatim dat stragem, atque aggerat ipsis
In stabulis turpi dilapsa cadavera tabo:
Donec humo tegere, ac foveis abscondere discunt.
Nam neque erat coriis usus: nec viscera quisquam
Aut undis abolere potest, aut vincere flamma:
Nec tondere quidem morbo illuvieque peresa
Vellera, nec telas possunt adtingere putris.
Verum etiam invisos si quis tentarat amictus;
Ardentes papulae, atque inmundus olentia sudor
Membra sequebatur. Nec longo deinde moranti
Tempore contactos artus sacer ignis edebat.

PVBLII
VIRGILII
MARONIS
GEORGICON
LIBER QUARTUS.

Protinus aërii mellis coelestia dona
Exsequar. Hanc etiam, Maecenas, adspice partem.
Admiranda tibi levium spectacula rerum,
Magnanimosque duces, totiusque ordine gentis
Mores, et studia, et populos, et proelia dicam.
In tenui labor : at tenuis non gloria ; si quem
Numina laeva sinunt, auditque vocatus Apollo.
Principio sedes apibus statioque petenda,
Quo neque sit ventis aditus, (nam pabula venti
Ferre domum prohibent) neque oves haedique petulci
Floribus insultent, aut errans bucula campo
Decutiat rorem, et surgentis adterat herbas.
Absint et picti squalentia terga lacerti
Pinguibus a stabulis, meropesque, aliaeque volucres;
Et manibus Procne pectus signata cruentis.
Omnia nam late vastant, ipsasque volantis
Ore ferunt dulcem nidis inmitibus escam.
At liquidi fontes et stagna virentia musco
Adsint, et tenuis, fugiens per gramina, rivus ;
Palmaque vestibulum et ingens oleaster inumbret.
Ut, quum prima novi ducent examina reges
Vere suo, ludetque favis emissa juventus,
Vicina invitet decedere ripa calori;

THE

LAUREL OF LIBERTY,

A POEM.

BY

ROBERT MERRY, A. M.

MEMBER OF THE ROYAL ACADEMY OF FLORENCE.

'Ήμισυ γάρ τ' ἀρετης ἀποαίνυται εὐρύοπα Ζεὺς
Ἀνερος, εὐτ' ἄν μιν κατὰ δούλιον ῆμαρ ἑλησιν.   Hom. Od.

Jove fix'd it certain, that whatever day
Makes man a slave, takes half his worth away.   Pope.

LONDON:

PRINTED BY JOHN BELL, BOOKSELLER TO HIS ROYAL HIGHNESS THE
PRINCE OF WALES,
AT THE BRITISH LIBRARY, STRAND.
M DCC XC.

[*Price Three Shillings and Sixpence.*]

The Bell type, cut by Richard Austin, is shown in this title-page, printed in 1790—three years after Bell had established a letter foundry in the Strand, near Exeter Exchange

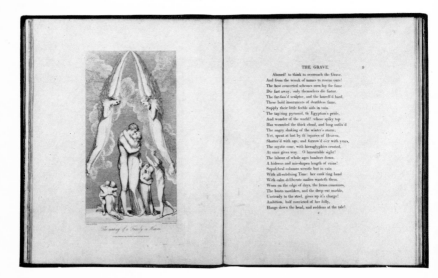

Opening from Robert Blair's poem *The Grave*, printed by Thomas Bensley for R. H. Cromek, quarto size, etchings by L. Schiavonetti from designs by William Blake, 1808

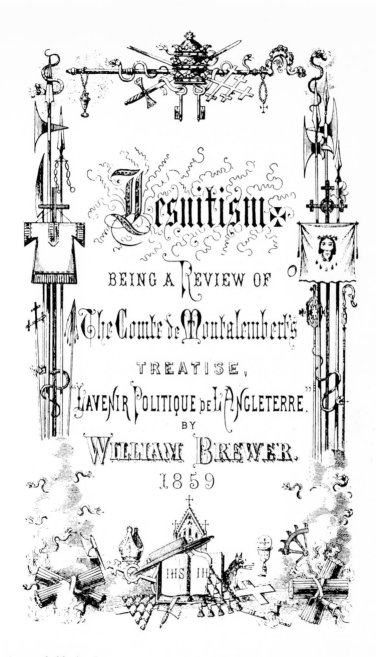

Jesuitism.

BEING A REVIEW OF

The Comte de Montalembert's

TREATISE,

"L'Avenir Politique de L'Angleterre."

BY

WILLIAM BREWER.

1859

A remarkable, but by no means isolated, example of how English printing had degenerated since the days of Caslon and Baskerville

Sunday after Chriſtmas-Day.

until the time appointed of the father. Even ſo we, when we were children, were in bondage under the elements of the world : but when the fulneſs of the time was come, God ſent forth his Son, made of a woman, made under the law, to redeem them that were under the law, that we might receive the adoption of ſons. And becauſe ye are ſons, God hath ſent forth the Spirit of his Son into your hearts, crying, Abba, Father. Wherefore thou art no more a ſervant, but a ſon ; and if a ſon, then an heir of God through Chriſt.

The Goſpel. St. Matth. i. 18.

THE birth of Jeſus Chriſt was on this wiſe : When as his mother Mary was eſpouſed to Joſeph, before they came together ſhe was found with child of the Holy Ghoſt. Then Joſeph her huſband, being a juſt man, and not willing to make her a publick example, was minded to put her away privily. But while he thought on theſe things, behold, the angel of the Lord appeared unto him in a dream, ſaying, Joſeph thou ſon of David, fear not to take unto thee Mary thy wife ; for that which is conceived in her is of the Holy Ghoſt : And ſhe ſhall bring forth a Son, and thou ſhalt call his name JESUS ; for he ſhall ſave his people from their ſins. (Now all this was done, that it might be fulfilled which was ſpoken of the Lord by

So after the Lord had spoken unto them, he was re-

ceived into heaven, and sat at the right hand, &c. Mar. xvi.

And Enoch walked with God, and was no more seen, for, &c. Gen. v.

There appeared a chariot of fire, and horses of fire, &c. ii Kings ii.

A page from Pickering's 1853 edition of the Book of Common Prayer. All the woodcuts were made by Mary Byfield and blend well with the Caslon type of the *History of Thuanus* in seven volumes, printed by subscription, each volume of which was the work of a different printer; Henry Woodfall, Samuel Richardson, James Bettenham, James Roberts, Thomas Wood, Edward Owen, and William Bowyer all participated in it.

The *Daily Courant* was a single sheet with a page size 13¼ by 7 inches. The first number was printed on one side of the sheet only; it gave notice that it would be published daily 'being designed to give all the Material News as soon as every Post arrives'. In Scotland James Watson brought out his twice-weekly *Edinburgh Courant* on 19 February, 1705, but later ceded it to Andrew Anderson, and in September of the same year he established the thrice-weekly *Scots Courant*.

Newspapers began to be published in the provinces, and by 1720 Norwich, Bristol, Stamford, Salisbury, Canterbury, York, Newcastle-upon-Tyne, Oxford, Exeter, Nottingham, Worcester, and Liverpool, all had their own newspapers.

The first evening thrice-weekly newspaper was the *Evening Post*, first issued on 6 September, 1709, and the first daily evening paper was the *Star* (1788), its regularity made possible 'in consequence of the increased facilities of communication by Palmer's mail-coach plan just started'.*

Advertising quickly became recognized as a medium of mass communication, not only for the convenience of trade but for a vast number of other purposes and the revenues from this source enabled the publishers of periodicals to produce them at a price the public was willing to pay; thus it was not long before every newspaper sought this economic support and some of them specialized in the insertion of advertisements. The *Daily Advertiser* was founded in February, 1730, and lasted until 1807. It was followed by the *General Advertiser*; the *Penny London Post, or the Morning Advertiser*; *Parker's General Advertiser* and others. The first advertisement block seems to have been used by the inventor of a chocolate-making machine, who inserted a cut of his contrivance in the *Daily Courant* in March, 1705. Advertising rates probably varied, but the *York Mercury* of 23 February, 1718 (the first issue), gives a list of booksellers where advertisements might be handed in at two shillings each.

For the greater part of the eighteenth century the text of newspapers

---

* John Palmer's mail coaches, first tried out in August, 1784, undertook the delivery of newspapers.

was set in varying sizes of type of one design, the sizes in general use around 1750 being small pica, great primer and bourgeois. Brevier came in about this time and was used increasingly until 1784, when minion (7-point) was introduced by the type-founders. The advertisements were usually printed one size smaller than the text and as yet there were no display types.

In August, 1712 the Government instituted the notorious Stamp Act which imposed a duty of a halfpenny on every paper contained in half a sheet or less, and a penny on every copy between half a sheet and a whole sheet (four pages). To show that the duty had been paid every issue printed had to bear a stamp, the design of which included the rose, thistle and shamrock surmounted by a crown, together with the motto (that of the Queen) *Semper Eadem*. Pamphlets paid duty at the rate of two shillings for each edition, and every advertisement was taxed at one shilling.

One result of this legislation was that publishers increased the size of periodicals to at least six pages, so that they might rank as pamphlets and thus pay two shillings on the whole edition instead of a halfpenny on each copy. To do this they introduced big mastheads, increased the size of the type and included features such as letters and essays, until they became more like magazines than newspapers. For some years the newspapers managed to exploit this loophole in the legislation, but the Act was revised in 1725 to circumvent this ingenious dodge. The Stamp Duty on newspapers was raised several times during the ensuing years, until by 1815 it stood at fourpence. Advertisement duty was also gradually increased until it stood at 3s. 6d. These taxes were not removed until the years 1855 and 1853 respectively.

On Saturday, 1 January, 1785, was issued the first number of *The Daily Universal Register*, which, its title being changed to *The Times* on 1 January, 1788, is the oldest surviving newspaper in England. Almost as remarkable is the fact that it has always been printed on the same site (at Printing House Square, Blackfriars), where once stood the King's Printing House.

The founder of *The Times* was John Walter I, who began his career as a bookprinter. His Logographic Press having proved a failure, he went ahead with his long-conceived plan to found his own paper, the first number of which was set in three sizes of roman, in four columns, and was sold at 2½d. The types used were Caslon old-face cut between 1720 and 1750, the largest size employed being a great primer (18-point), though the majority of the text was set in small pica (11-point). Subsidiary matter and advertising was in brevier (8-point). A new fount, advertised in advance, was used in May, 1793, which was again a Caslon face supplied by Fry's foundry; in November, 1799, *The Times* appeared 'printed in an entire new and beautiful type, from the family of Mrs Caslon'.

At the end of 1794 John Walter I appointed his eldest son, William, 'conductor' of the paper, but he was evidently not suited to the management of a large printing concern, and retired to start a new career, in 1802, being succeeded by the second son, John Walter II, then twenty-six years old. At the end of the eighteenth century, due largely to the Napoleonic wars, plus the weight of taxation and rising costs, all newspapers were badly hit. John Walter I was quite prepared to sell *The Times*; John Walter II saved it and made it prosperous. Its later history is related in another chapter.

Book Illustration in the Seventeenth and Eighteenth Centuries

By the middle of the sixteenth century the woodcut illustration had reached the limit of technical improvement, and although woodcuts continued to be used sporadically during the seventeenth and eighteenth centuries, the wood block dropped out of fashion until revived towards the end of the eighteenth century, when a completely different technique of 'white line' engraving was popularized by Thomas Bewick and others. Chap-books and popular ballads, it is true, continued to make use of woodcuts, but these were so crude as hardly to come under the heading of book illustration.

Even in Germany the art of wood-cutting had greatly declined by the end of the sixteenth century, and almost everywhere the more costly books were being illustrated by copper-plate engravings. In England some of the Emblem books which had such a vogue throughout the seventeenth century were illustrated with woodcuts—for example Thomas Combe's *Theatre of Fine Devices* (1614), printed by Richard Field, and Henry Peacham's *Minerva Britannia* (1612) with woodcuts by the author. But later ones, such as Francis Quarles's *Emblemes* (1635) and George Wither's *Collection of Emblemes*, had copper-plate engravings.

A common form of book decoration during the first two centuries of printing had been the woodcut initial, some of which, particularly the pictorial and heraldic initials, had a certain charm, though they were only too often used indiscriminately. Most of the woodcut initials with any claim to artistry found in English books of the sixteenth century came from abroad or were copied from foreign models, early Basle books being the begetters of a whole series of small pictorial initials. Of the larger initials some of the best are seen in the *Cosmographicall Glasse* printed by John Day in 1559, and the books of Cawood contain examples of the classical alphabet engraved by the Flemish wood-cutter Arnold Nicolai. Day also used a number of woodcut illustrations in his editions of Foxe's *Book of Martyrs*; the 1576 edition was the most plentifully illustrated which had up to then been produced in England. In the seventeenth century, however, initial letters were frequently dull factotums cut in metal. The one outstanding ornamental alphabet used in an English book before the end of the eighteenth century was that engraved on copper by Michael Burghers for the Oxford University Press and used in 1707 for Clarendon's *History of the Rebellion*.[157] By the middle of the eighteenth century the decorated initial had gone out of fashion; Baskerville never used them.

Intaglio printing is found in some books of the fifteenth century printed abroad,* but disappeared quite soon owing, no doubt, to the excessive cost in material, labour and the double printing involved. It was revived in the sixteenth century largely because of the tremendous vogue for single engravings—a market profitably exploited by the print-dealer Jerome Cock, whose shop in Antwerp, *De Vier Winden*, was the great entrepôt for this class of trade. Plantin bought enormous quantities of engravings from Cock, which he sent to his agents at Frankfurt and Paris.

The wealthy book-buyer, no longer able to indulge his taste in illuminated manuscripts, turned to books with copper engravings to enhance the value of his library. Copper engraving made its appearance in England later than in most other countries, and during the seventeenth century was used chiefly for ornamental title-pages. An early example of an English book with copper-plate engravings is the *Compendium Totius Anatomiae Delineato* printed in 1545 with a splendid engraved title-page and forty plates by the Flemish engraver Thomas Geminus, copied (very inaccurately according to the author) from the woodcuts of Hans Stefan van Calcar in the 1543 Basle edition of Vesalius's *De humani corporis fabrica*, a seminal book in the history of anatomy. But there was as yet no school of engravers in

---

* The French edition of Breydenbach, *Pérégrinations de Jérusalem* (Lyon, 1488), had copper-plate illustrations.

England to compare with those of Holland and Flanders, and the art only began to develop in Britain with the arrival of refugee craftsmen from the Netherlands.

From the beginning of the seventeenth century many quarto and folio volumes had an engraved title-page, usually of an architectural or monumental character. Often that was the sole illustration, but occasionally an engraved portrait of the author might serve as frontispiece. Nothing helped to spread the popularity of the engraved illustration more than the books of travellers, such as Sandys's *A Relation of a Journey begun A.D.1610* (1615), with its figures, maps, and diagrams, or Sir Thomas Herbert's *A Relation of Some Yeares Travaile* (1634, 1638, 1665, 1677), of which the first edition was printed by William Stansby. This work is illustrated with engravings printed together with the letterpress and depicting all kinds of remarkable objects seen by the author on his travels. The 1638 edition has a folding plate representing the ruins of Persepolis from a beautiful etching by Wenzel Hollar, signed and dated 1636, and presumably made by Hollar during his second visit to England. Among the few well-illustrated books produced in Britain during the seventeenth century mention may be made of two editions of Aesop's *Fables*. The first, paraphrased in verse by John Ogilby, the Master of the Revels, was a folio printed by Thomas Roycroft for the author in 1665, and 'adorn'd with sculpture' by Hollar, Stoop and Francis Barlow. A later edition of *Aesop's Fables, with his life: in English, French, and Latin*, was illustrated with charming etchings by Francis Barlow, for whom the book was printed in 1687 by H. Hills Junior, who succeeded to his father's share in the King's Printing House two years later. The French text is printed in roman, the Latin in italic, and the English verses, by Mrs Aphra Behn, are etched beneath the illustrations.

Intaglio printing, with its ability to reproduce fine line and delicate script, led to the spread of writing books, such as George Shelley's *Alphabets in All Hands* (c. 1715), which is said to have influenced Baskerville, and George Bickham's *The Universal Penman*, published in parts between 1733 and 1741. Copper-plate printers also found a source of profit in the elegant tradesmen's cards which, by the middle of the eighteenth century, had become highly ornate examples of the combined skills of the penman and printer.

The first half of the eighteenth century saw the appearance of a number of well printed and illustrated editions of the Greek and

Roman classics. One of the most ambitious efforts was the Latin edition of the works of Julius Caesar edited by Samuel Clarke and published by Jacob Tonson in 1712. This sumptuous folio is illustrated with full page copper-plate engravings, engraved head- and tail-pieces and initial letters. Foulis has already been mentioned as a printer who specialized in the classics, and John Watts printed for Jacob Tonson an excellent series of classics edited by Maittaire and illustrated throughout with charming engravings in the French manner of the period.

Although Herbals had retained their woodcut illustrations throughout the seventeenth century, the eighteenth saw the production of a number of botanical works with handsome engravings; Kirkall, in 1727, illustrated John Martyn's *Historia Plantarum Rariorum*, with etchings which were printed in colour and touched up by hand. One of the greatest British botanical works of the eighteenth century was undoubtedly the famous *Flora Londinensis of* William Curtis, of which the first part appeared in 1775, and parts appeared at intervals until 1798, in which year a two-volume edition was published. Three hundred copies of each part were printed, and the plates were hand-coloured by some thirty assistants. A second edition, edited by Hooker, and published in five volumes (1817–28), has 647 plates, as against 432 in the original edition.

Towards the end of the eighteenth century wood-engraving returned to fashion and had a vogue which lasted until the invention of photo-mechanical methods of illustration. The man responsible for this revival was Thomas Bewick, born in 1753 at Cherryburn, near Newcastle. Apprenticed to an engraver named Ralph Beilby, Bewick showed more aptitude for engraving in wood than for copper-plate work. After a year in London at the end of his apprenticeship he returned to Newcastle and went into partnership with his former master, and his younger brother John Bewick became their apprentice.

One reason for the previous neglect of the woodcut had been the difficulty, with the old technique of gouging out the whites with the knife on the side grain of a piece of soft wood, of securing good clean impressions once the woodcutter tried to reproduce the fine detail possible with copper engraving. Bewick, by using the graver on the end-grain of hard-wood, was able to produce lines as finely laid as those made by the engraver on metal. Moreover, by using a hard, smooth surface such as that provided by box-wood, it was possible to make a wood block capable of giving a large number of satisfactory impressions. Whether or not he invented either the use of the graver on wood or the practice of working on the end-grain of a hard-wood, he certainly made the process peculiarly his own, and the development of this technique by Bewick and his followers made possible the copious illustration of books in the nineteenth century.

Bewick's first major work was the *General History of Quadrupeds* (1790). The descriptions were written by Beilby and the illustrations were both drawn and engraved by Bewick. The first edition of 1,500 copies in demy octavo and 100 royal octavo sold quickly, and further editions were published in 1791 and 1792. A work of similar character, a *History of British Birds*, was published in two volumes (1797–1804). Beilby wrote the text for the first volume, but the partnership having been dissolved soon afterwards, Bewick himself wrote the text for the second. Both of these books owe much of their appeal to the way in which Bewick captured the spirit as well as the appearance of the animals and birds he drew. Much of Bewick's best work is to be found in the vignettes and tail-pieces with which he adorned many books of the period.

Bewick was the first to achieve almost continuous tone in wood engraving, and he achieved his grey tints in a manner he has thus described:

> The plain surface of the wood will print as black as ink and balls can make it, without any further labour at all; and it may easily be seen that the thinnest strokes cut upon the plain surface will throw some light upon the subject or design; and if these strokes again are made still wider or of equal thickness to the black lines, the colour these produce will be a grey; and the more the white strokes are thickened the nearer will they in their varied shadings approach to white; and if taken away then a perfect white is obtained.[158]

This effect was heightened by lowering the surface of the block slightly at certain points with a chisel, so that these parts took less ink and received less pressure from the platen than did the parts which were to print black.

Thomas Bewick died at Gateshead in 1828 and was buried at Ovingham. His younger brother John died in 1795.

CHAPTER EIGHT

Founders and Printers

Caslon & Baskerville

WILLIAM CASLON 1692–1766

William Caslon was born at Cradley, near Halesowen in Shrop-
shire, and in the baptismal register of the parish church at Halesowen
his father is inscribed as 'George Casselon'. Some writers affirm that
the father took his name from the Spanish town of Caslona, and that
he came over to England with William III in 1688. It seems much
more likely that the spelling was due to a mistake on the part of the
parish clerk.

Of the early life of William Caslon we know little, and what has
been recorded is based on no very reliable evidence. As a young man
he learned the trade of engraver of gun-locks and barrels, and when his
apprenticeship was over he set up in business in Vine Street, London,
near the Minories. William Bowyer I and John Watts, both well-
known printers, seem to have shared the credit for introducing William
Caslon to the art of punch-cutting after they had admired the neat
lettering produced by some punches he had made for bookbinders.

With the financial assistance of Watts and Bowyer, and of another
printer, James Bettenham, Caslon took a room in Helmet Row, Old
Street, and started on his career of letter-cutting for the printers.
Exactly when this was is the subject of controversy. Tradition in the
Caslon family places the year at 1716; other sources say 1720. It was
in 1720 that Caslon was commissioned by the Society for Promoting
Christian Knowledge to cut a fount of Arabic for a proposed printing
of the New Testament and Psalter for the benefit of poor Christians in
the Near-Eastern countries. It seems unlikely that they would have
chosen a complete beginner for this task. Caslon's fount was approved, and with it were printed first the Psalter, completed in 1725,
and then the Arabic New Testament, which followed in 1727.

Under the direction of his patron, Bowyer, Caslon then cut a fount of pica Coptic for the *Pentateuch*, edited by Dr David Wilkins, of which 200 copies only were printed and published in 1731. From that time onwards his business grew as his reputation became solidly established. But, as Hansard points out, in his *Typographia*, the obstacles he encountered at the outset of his career were considerable.

> He had not only to excel his competitors in his own particular branch of engraving the punches, which to him was probably the easiest part of the task, but to raise an establishment and cause his plans to be executed by ignorant and unpractised workmen. He had also to acquire for himself a knowledge of the practical and mechanical branches of the art, which require, indeed, little genius, but the most minute and painful attention to conduct successfully.

In 1727 Caslon removed to Ironmonger Row. By the time his first specimen sheet appeared in 1734 Caslon's roman was everywhere accepted as an outstanding book-type, but the statement that it first appeared in the *Opera* of John Selden, 1726, propagated by John Nichols, is incorrect. The roman in that book is, as pointed out in Reed-Johnson, of Dutch origin. From the same source we learn that Caslon's pica roman was first seen in the notes at the end of the *Anacreon*, published by Bower in 1725.[159] His English roman and italic were seen in 1728, but the great pica and double pica are not met with before 1732. The specimen sheet of 1734 contains samples of thirty-eight founts, including a pica black (a handsome specimen of traditional English black-letter), Greek, Saxon, Gothic, Coptic, Armenian, Samaritan, Hebrew, Syriac and Arabic. Caslon was by now at the head of his profession, and his roman became one of the most widely used book types for the next two centuries, with but a brief eclipse from about 1810 to 1840 (the era of Bodoni and Didot).

> By making his types himself, [write Carter and Ricks], or having them cut, struck and justified on the premises under his control, he was able to build up a stock united by a harmonious, if not quite uniform, design, and so he gave our books a harmony that French books had had since the time of Garamond nearly two centuries earlier.[160]

All but three of the founts shown on the 1734 specimen sheets were cut by Caslon himself—the fruits of some fifteen years of tireless work. In 1728 he had seriously thought of buying the Grover foundry which came on the market, but negotiations fell through, fortunately perhaps for English printing, for he was able to concentrate exclusively on his own types. He did, however, join with John James in 1739 to purchase Robert Mitchell's foundry, the matrices including music type and some old black-letter. By then he had cut the best of his own types.

From then until the end of the century almost all important books were printed with Caslon's types, or imitations of them. The dominance of the Dutch foundries in the matter of English printing was ended. Nevertheless Caslon was no innovator in the matter of letter-forms; he took the Dutch models and improved upon them by giving them more character, for even the best of Dutch types were apt to be monotonous. In some indescribable way he transformed what was typically Dutch into something essentially English—a type which Bernard has described as 'easy on the eye', and which, though lacking in elegance, has a humanity lacking in the founts of Baskerville and Bodoni.

Baskerville himself paid tribute to his predecessor, saying of him that 'his ingenuity has left a fairer copy for my emulation than any other master'.[161] John Smith, in his *Printer's Grammar* (1755), praised the punch-cutter, due to whose skill 'letter is now in England of such a beautiful cut and shape as it never was before'. But to most pros there are cons, and so eminent a designer of type as Bruce Rogers finds it 'at most a *safe* type for general use, and moderately picturesque'.[162]

In one respect Caslon performed a great service to the printing trade in England. For the first time a printer could procure from one foundry a sound and well-cut letter in matching founts in a full range of sizes. In 1737 Caslon moved his foundry to Chiswell Street, where it continued in business on the same site until 1911, when it was transferred to the opposite side of the street; there it remained until 1936, when the stock was purchased by Stephenson, Blake and Company. The sites of both Chiswell Street premises were destroyed by enemy action in 1940 and 1941.

An interesting engraving of the interior of the first Chiswell Street foundry was published in the *Universal Magazine* for June, 1750, and is reproduced as the frontispiece of A. F. Johnson's revision of Reed's *History of the Old English Letter Foundries* (1952). It shows four of the casters at work, each in his separate booth, and, working in front of the large windows, a rubber and a dresser. These two men were, respectively, Joseph Jackson and Thomas Cottrell, both of whom later set up in business as letter-founders on their own account.

William Caslon died on 23 January, 1766, and was buried in the churchyard of St Luke's, Old Street, the parish in which all three of his foundries had been situated. He seems to have been universally liked and respected, and his home was the meeting place of both literary men and music lovers, for Caslon was very fond of music, and often gave concerts at his house.

Caslon was married three times, and by his first wife, Sarah Pearman, he had a daughter, Mary, and two sons: William, who joined his father's business about 1740 and succeeded to it on his father's death, and Thomas, who was a bookseller of repute and became Master of the Stationers' Company in 1782.

JOHN BASKERVILLE 1706–1775

Like William Morris, Baskerville was an amateur who came to printing fairly late in his career. Like Morris, he was a man of means, who could afford to experiment and produce the books he wanted to in his own way. Unlike Morris, he was a self-made man, who (if the Rev. Mark Noble is to be trusted) had started life as a footman in a country rectory.[163] Even as a lad 'he was ever to be found with a pen in his hands' and letter forms were his abiding interest. At the age of nineteen, in 1725, he went to Birmingham, where he taught writing and book-keeping and also developed an interest in stone-cutting. Still preserved in the chief Public Library of Birmingham is a slab of slate which he used as an advertisement; in five different kinds of letter it announced 'Gravestones cut in any of the hands by John Baskerville, Writing Master'.

For some ten years he worked at these trades and gained a reputation—though little money—as a writing master. He was, however, determined to make money, and, noting that a Birmingham man named John Taylor was developing a large and prosperous business in japanned ware, determined to follow his example and do even better by turning out superlative goods. With his persistence, energy and a certain inventiveness, he quickly succeeded. In 1742 he was granted a patent for 'a new method of making and flat grinding thin metal plates, and of working and fashioning the same by the help of iron rolls and swages'. By 1745 he was rich enough to buy land just outside the town and build for himself a large house, and startle the staid burgesses of Birmingham with his gorgeous carriage and startling eccentricities of dress. He was now independent financially—he was always independent of spirit—and for the rest of his life the income from his japan business enabled him to live in comfort and indulge his whims. He had money to spend on a hobby, and that this should be printing was only natural in view of his early training as a calligrapher and his japanner's interest in metals and varnishes. 'Having been an early admirer of the beauty of Letters,' he tells us, 'I became sensibly desirous of contributing to the perfection of them.'[163]

In 1750, at the age of forty-four, Baskerville began his new career as a printer, with everything to learn; especially as he was not satisfied with becoming an ordinary commercial printer, buying his types from the foundry, and executing whatever commissions came his way. He already had a paying business; printing was to be his relaxation. 'It is not my desire,' he wrote, 'to print many books, but such only as are books of consequence, of intrinsic merit or established reputation . . . at such a price as will repay the extraordinary care and experience that must necessarily be bestowed upon them.'

Just as in his japan business he prided himself on the superior quality and excellent design of his wares, equally was he determined that whatever he printed should show similar craftsmanship, and he set about building his own presses, making his own ink and designing his own type. His presses were no different in design from those used by other printers, but they were built with greater precision. His experience in flat-grinding and fashioning metal plates enabled him to provide brass platens ground with extreme accuracy so as to present a perfectly flat surface. His ink, the formula for which probably owed much to his experience in mixing varnishes for his japanned wares, was blacker and more velvety than that used by the printers of his time. Baskerville also had paper specially made for him by James Whatman, though not primarily for books, but writing paper which he marketed through Dodsley in London; some of it he may have used for his *Virgil*, the prospectus for which announces that it will be printed 'on this writing royal paper'.

This *Virgil* was the first book from the new press, and its publication was undertaken by Dodsley, to whom Baskerville had been introduced by his friend, the poet William Shenstone. But first came the lengthy and laborious process of designing and cutting the type. From Baskerville's designs the punches were cut by John Handy, who was later employed by Myles Swinney, who set up a letter foundry in Birmingham after Baskerville had dispersed his.

Six years elapsed before any work came from Baskerville's press, during which time he is said to have spent between £600 and £800 in an effort to produce a type with which he was satisfied. Although in order to relieve Dodsley's impatience he sent him an impression of fourteen punches of the two-line great primer on 2 October, 1752, it was not until 1757 that the *Virgil* was issued to subscribers. It is a squarish quarto set in great primer leaded, with italic capitals for the running heads, and though it has been described as the first book wholly to be printed on the new wove* paper, it would seem that all known copies are printed partly on wove and partly on laid paper. The *Paradise Regain'd* of 1759 seems to have been the first book Baskerville printed throughout on a wove paper, and there is still a doubt as to whether this book, or Edward Capell's *Prolusions*, also published in 1759, was the first wholly printed on wove.

The *Virgil*, published at a guinea, at once established Baskerville's reputation as a printer, although there was considerable divergence of opinion as to the book's merits as a specimen of fine printing. Realizing that his new type, with its refinement of outline, needed above all careful press-work, and a very smooth printing surface, Baskerville had his paper specially made so that it would take an even impression from his meticulously smooth platens with less than the force normally employed. To give his work a high finish he calendered, or 'hot-pressed', the sheets, giving a gloss that many objected to, declaring that it was dazzling and hurtful to the eye—what Mores alluded to as 'trim glossy paper to dim the sight'.[165] But whereas Mores went so far as to deny the claims of Baskerville to a place among letter-cutters, Dibdin thought this *Virgil* a beautiful production and 'one of the most finished specimens of typography'.[166]

It is, as Updike says, very easy to read, yet can we call it a beautiful book? The copy in the British Museum does not seem to have been unduly trimmed in the binding, but the page appears overloaded. Three lines less to the page and a little more space between the running head and the text would, one ventures to think, have improved the appearance. As to the title-page, its widely spaced capitals give it a monumental quality with a slightly repellent flavour, and then one remembers that Baskerville was at one period a cutter of inscriptions on tombstones.

To belittle Baskerville became something of a fashion among those who lacked all knowledge of typography, and Benjamin Franklin (a friend and admirer of the printer) wrote to Baskerville of the practical joke he had played on one of these ignorant critics. Showing him a

---

* Whereas 'laid' paper, when looked through, shows a series of translucent lines running across the sheet, crossed at intervals by others running at right angles, 'wove' paper shows an even texture in the look-through.

specimen sheet of Caslon's types, from which he had torn off the top, and pretending it was Baskerville's, he asked this self-styled connoisseur to point out the disproportion he had alleged in the form and cut of Baskerville's letters. Franklin was given a long discourse on the faults so clearly obvious to the tutored eye, and the critic further complained that the strokes of the letters, too thin and narrow, hurt his eyes. 'I spared him that time', wrote Franklin, 'the confusion of being told that these were the types he had been reading all his life, with so much ease to his eyes.'[167]

No man was less likely to be deterred by criticism than Baskerville, who brought out the works of Milton in two quarto volumes in 1758, a fine piece of printing which was at once successful; the work was also published as an imperial octavo in the same year, and again in quarto in 1759. The publishers were J. and R. Tonson.

It was indeed fortunate that Baskerville had his thriving japan business to live on, for his printing venture must have cost him a small fortune. Two books in eight years, with a printing office staff of at least a dozen to be paid regularly throughout the year, would have spelt bankruptcy for a man without other means of livelihood.

Like all the great printers, Baskerville wanted to produce a folio Bible and a Book of Common Prayer. With this end in view he entered into negotiations with the Cambridge University Press, who granted him permission on somewhat onerous terms, or as he himself expressed it, 'under such Shackles as greatly hurt me'. He tells Horace Walpole that he is obliged to pay the Syndics of the Cambridge Press £20 for every 1,000 copies of the octavo Prayer Book and £12.10s.0d. the 1,000 for the 12mo edition. In addition the Stationers' Company wanted £32 for their permission to print one edition of the Psalms in Metre. Furthermore, in order to obtain the privilege he had to carry out the printing at Cambridge. He himself did not go to live there, but he sent two presses and all the necessary material to that city in charge of his assistant and representative, Thomas Warren, though he must have made numerous journeys to and from Cambridge to supervise the work.

The first work to appear was the Book of Common Prayer, the first edition of which appeared in 1760. The type, he wrote, 'is calculated for people who begin to want Spectacles but are ashamed to use them at Church'. Four editions of the octavo Prayer Book came off the press between 1760 and 1762—three in long lines and one in double columns. A 12mo edition was printed in 1762.

The Holy Bible was first issued in 1763 (with the date 1762), and was undoubtedly Baskerville's crowning achievement. This magnificent folio Bible, in a handsome great primer type, is one of the most beautiful ever printed in this country; but alas! it was a financial failure. The price was four guineas in sheets, and subscribers for six copies were allowed another gratis. Even so, only half the edition of 1,250 copies was sold, and within two years the rest were remaindered to a London bookseller.

This experience made Baskerville weary of the profession of printer, and in 1762 he made an offer of his foundry to the Court of France for £8,000 through the intermediary of the French ambassador, the Duc de Nivernais; but the offer was politely refused. To his friend Benjamin Franklin he wrote a few years later 'suppose we reduce the price to £6,000. Louis XIV would have given three times that sum, or Czar Peter.' But the French treasury at that time had no money to spare for luxuries. Baskerville more or less retired from business, leaving his printing house in the care of his former journeyman, Robert Martin, who produced five books, including Somerville's *The Chase* (1767) and the works of Shakespeare in nine 12mo volumes (1768).

However, Baskerville's interest revived in 1769, when he found that Nicholas Boden, another Birmingham printer, was beginning work on a folio Bible to be issued in weekly parts with a type very similar to his own. The two printers carried on a wordy warfare in the pages of the *Birmingham Gazette* concerning the respective merits of their rival editions, which were completed simultaneously in 1772.

In 1772 the brothers Pietro and Giovanni Molini, a large firm of booksellers with branches in London, Paris, and Florence, commissioned Baskerville to print Ariosto's *Orlando Furioso*, which was issued in 1773 in a small and large paper edition. One or two copies of this work bear the date 1771, an error which was soon noticed and rectified.

Between 1770 and the time of his death in January, 1775, Baskerville printed a series of quarto editions of classical authors—Horace; Lucretius; Catullus, Tibullus and Propertius; Terence; Sallust and Florus. The Horace alone was adorned with plates, but all are distinguished by their excellent typography.

Although the typographical merit of Baskerville's roman and italic types was immediately recognized by competent authorities, no one had a good word to say for the Greek fount which he cut and cast in 1758 for the Delegates of the Oxford University Press. The quarto and octavo editions of the New Testament which were published in 1763 added nothing to the printer's reputation, and criticisms of the type ranged from 'stiff and cramped' to 'execrable'. A proposed edition of Euripides in this fount was cancelled, and it was never used again, but the punches, matrices and some of the type are still preserved at Oxford.

After the printer's death his widow carried on the letter foundry for a time, but eventually, since nobody in England was interested, she sold it for £3,700 to the Duc de Nivernais, acting for Beaumarchais and the Société Littéraire-Typographique of France. As is well known, Beaumarchais used Baskerville's types for printing the famous 'Kehl' edition of the works of Voltaire.

After passing through various hands the Baskerville punches and matrices were eventually acquired by the firm of Deberny and Peignot, who with notable generosity presented the punches to the Cambridge University Press in 1953, and there they are now preserved in the Press's collection of historic material.

Baskerville's influence was widespread, particularly in Europe, where both Pierre Didot and Bodoni praised his designs, Bodoni going so far as to say that he considered the finest printing houses then were at Birmingham and in Madrid (where Joaquin Ibarra was bringing out some magnificent editions). Baskerville himself declared 'my labours have always been treated with more honour abroad than in my native country.' The prejudice against Baskerville's types in certain quarters in England was perhaps due partly to the inherent English mistrust of the 'gifted amateur', and partly to his methods of printing. Nevertheless his influence did make itself felt later in England, when imitations were cut by Fry and Wilson, among others. In 1827 William Pickering published an edition of the *Treatyse of Fysshynge wyth an Angle* printed in Fry's small pica roman No. 1, which was an imitation of Baskerville.[168] In the present century Baskerville type has gained considerable popularity as a book-face since its recutting by the Monotype Corporation in 1924.

Baskerville's roman holds a position midway between the old-face of Caslon and the modern-face which was being introduced by the French at about the same time. But, as Stanley Morison points out, 'it appeared more "modern" than indeed it was from the sharpness of contrast conferred upon it by his printing methods'. Few type designs have given rise to greater divergence of opinion respecting their merits, and whereas Reed considered it 'one of the most beautiful we have had', William Morris and Emery Walker both considered it poor and uninteresting. H. V. Marrot considers Baskerville's founts to be 'a definite advance on those of Caslon in finish, grace, and general suave attractiveness'. There are probably many who would dispute this and, while acknowledging the refinement of Baskerville's design, find his type completely lacking in charm. One great disadvantage of his method of using hot-pressed paper is that with the passage of time the pages of his books have in many instances acquired a yellowish tinge, and the ink now fails to present that pleasant contrast with a white paper which looks so well.

To his credit he eliminated superfluous ornament in his books and relied on pure typography, and his sober title-pages, clean and un-cluttered, with their spaced capitals, gave an air of distinction to the books he printed, though possibly the general effect is a little chilling in the larger formats.

Bulmer and Bensley: Printers of Fine Books

WILLIAM BULMER 1757–1830

Bulmer was a native of Newcastle-upon-Tyne and served his apprenticeship with a local printer. After serving his time he came to London and entered the printing office of John Bell (see page 177). By chance he made the acquaintance of the bookseller George Nicol who was looking for a printer good enough to be entrusted with the printing of his projected magnificent edition of Shakespeare, illustrated with plates in the possession of the art publishers, Messrs Boydell.* For this work type was cut by William Martin of Birmingham, brother of the Robert Martin who had been Baskerville's foreman.

In 1790 premises were taken in Cleveland Row, St James's, and there the Shakespeare Printing Office was established under the firm of 'W. Bulmer and Co.'. In January, 1791, the first part of the Shake-speare (containing *Richard III* and *Much Ado about Nothing*) was issued and at once gained for Bulmer an enviable reputation. Dibdin praised the work highly; it was the kind of ornate publication in which he delighted. Plomer terms it 'one of the most pretentious books that had ever come from the English press', but it was certainly well printed and set Bulmer among the ranks of the country's finest printers.[169]

Following the Shakespeare came the works of Milton in three folio

---

* Nicol married a niece of Alderman Boydell.

volumes (1793-97), and in 1795 Bulmer produced a very beautiful specimen of the printer's art in the *Poems* of Oliver Goldsmith and Thomas Parnell, a quarto volume illustrated with wood-engravings by Thomas and John Bewick. In the 'advertisement' to this volume Bulmer stresses the fact that the productions of the Shakespeare Printing Office were 'particularly meant to combine the various beauties of Printing, Type-founding, Engraving and Paper-making'. The paper was made for Bulmer by the firm of Whatman, and the ink was made by Bulmer from a recipe of Robert Martin, to whom Baskerville had imparted the secret of preparing a rich black ink. A companion volume, William Somerville's poem *The Chase*, appeared in 1796, also with vignettes by the Bewicks. Of William Martin, who cut the types for the Shakespeare Printing Office, Reed claims that 'the productions of the Shakespeare Press justify his reputation as a worthy disciple of his great master Baskerville'. His foundry, which belonged to the press, was in Duke Street, not far from Cleveland Row, and although it was in this respect a private foundry, Martin seems occasionally to have supplied his types to other printers. A poem called *The Press*, 'published as a specimen of typography' and printed at Liverpool in 1803 by the author, John McCreery, was printed from Martin's types.[170]

So highly did Dibdin think of Bulmer that he chose him to print three of his own works at the Shakespeare Printing Office—the *Typographical Antiquities*,* (4 vols. 1810-19); the *Bibliotheca Spenceriana* (4 vols. 1814-15); and the *Bibliographical Decameron* (3 vols. 1817). In these volumes Martin's roman, a type much favoured by Bulmer, is shown to great advantage. Although Martin seems not to have issued a specimen, his types were displayed in one issued in 1807 by the Liverpool printer G. F. Harris, successor to McCreery. Martin's typefaces, as might be expected, were largely influenced at first by Baskerville, but his later types, following the fashion imposed by Bodoni, became increasingly 'modern' in face.

Much of Bulmer's work was done for learned bodies. He printed for the Royal Society, the Africa Society, the Society of Antiquaries, the East India Company, the British Museum and the Board of Agriculture. He became almost automatically the first choice of publishers seeking a well-printed text to accompany fine illustrated books.

---

* Dibdin's enlarged edition of the Ames-Herbert work. The first volume was not printed by the Shakespeare Press, but by William Savage.

That he and Bensley were recognized as being the best printers of their time for book-work is clear from the fact that they were chosen to print many of the publications of the Roxburghe Club,* though Bulmer printed more of them than Bensley.

Bulmer printed one or two enormous folio volumes, among which one stands out for its remarkable series of coloured portraits. This is *A Series of Portraits of the Emperors of Turkey, from the foundation of the Monarchy to the year 1815*, by John Young, published in 1816. The page size of this volume is 22 by 16 inches and the portraits, in chromolithograph, measure $14\frac{3}{4}$ by $10\frac{1}{4}$ inches. This work was printed at the expense of the sultan Selim, and Timperley states that the whole impression was sent to the Ottoman Court.

Some of the books printed by Bulmer were financed by the author, a case in point being the two folio volumes of the *Museum Worsleyanum* (1798–1803) upon which, according to Dibdin, Sir Richard Worsley spent some £27,000. It was never published commercially; some copies were presented to English and Scottish universities, others were given to Worsley's friends.

Although Bensley's career as an independent printer was considerably longer than that of Bulmer—thirty-nine years as against Bulmer's twenty-eight—it was Bulmer who was the more successful of the two financially, and in 1819 he retired to Clapham Rise with a considerable fortune. There he died on 9 September, 1830.

That both printers were recognized during their lifetime is borne out by lines in McCreery's poem *The Press*, a panegyric on printers and literature, in which the following lines occur:

> Pleased as we now the grateful strain pursue,
> Two sons of science pass before our view,
> Who to their works perfection can impart,
> And snatch from barb'rous hands our sinking art;
> Their skill the sharp fine outline still supplies;
> From vellum leaves their graceful types arise;
> And whilst our breasts the rival hopes expand,
> BULMER and BENSLEY well-earn'd praise demand.

Yet strangely enough they were both forgotten men for nearly a century after their deaths, until H. V. Marrot's article in *The Fleuron* (Vol. 5, 1926) rescued them from near-oblivion. Since that time Peter

---

* Roxburghe Club—the oldest existing society of bibliophiles in Great Britain, founded in 1812, and named after John Ker, 3rd Duke of Roxburghe (1740–1804), a great book collector.

C. G. Isaac has made the life of William Bulmer a subject very much his own.[170]

THOMAS BENSLEY ?–1835

This eminent printer, himself the son of a printer, was first established in the Strand, but afterwards removed to Bolt Court, Fleet Street, where he specialized in the production of fine books, a field in which he rivalled his contemporary, William Bulmer. One of his earliest works is a quarto edition of Lavater's *Physiognomy* (1789), which was followed by Allan Ramsay's *Gentle Shepherd* (1790).

In 1797 Bensley printed a handsome edition of James Thomson's *The Seasons* with engravings by F. Bartolozzi and P. W. Tomkins from originals by W. Hamilton, R.A. This has a beautiful title-page, on which the name of Vincent Figgins features as designer of the type. This folio volume, wrote Reed, 'still remains one of the finest achievements of English typography'.

Figgins, who had been apprenticed to Joseph Jackson[171] and was later manager of his foundry, started his own foundry after the death of his master in 1792, largely owing to the encouragement of John Nichols, whose generosity he never forgot. At the beginning of his career he was fortunate enough to obtain a commission from Bensley to cut a fount for Macklin's Bible, for which Jackson had cut a two-line English roman fount just before his death. Figgins was required to match this, which he did with uncommon dexterity; in a similar manner he completed the double pica fount for Hume's *History of England* upon which Jackson had been engaged at the time of his death.

Macklin's Bible and Hume's *History* made the reputations both of Bensley and of Figgins. The Bible, in seven volumes, was completed in 1800; Hume's History did not appear until 1806.

Between the years 1804 and 1807 Bensley was engaged upon J. T. Smith's *Antiquities of Westminster*, which he printed for the author. This was the first book published in Britain with a lithographic illustration, and contains Smith's own description of the new process, from which we learn that after 300 impressions had been taken off, owing to an oversight on the part of the pressmen, who failed to keep the lithographic stone sufficiently moist, pieces of the drawing were torn in attempting to remove them from the stone. In consequence only the first 300 copies of the book contained the lithograph. The remainder of the plates are aquatints and mezzotints, together with one or two wood-engravings.

An early book of Bensley's which has all the charm of a period piece is the folio edition of Bürger's poem *Leonora* in W. R. Spencer's translation, published in 1796 with designs by Lady Diana Beauclerc. In the same year Bensley issued Townshend's *Poems* in an edition which Marrot terms 'a marvel of fragile delicacy'. Marrot stresses Bensley's tendency to extreme lightness, almost to tenuity of texture. 'He turned out the most adorable little books, employing a frail, light type, heavily leaded. Indeed, the only heavy thing about Bensley was his leading!'[172]

In 1808 Bensley printed for R. H. Cromek Blair's poem *The Grave* —a publication which included several of William Blake's best-known drawings etched by Louis Schiavonetti, together with an engraved portrait of Blake from the painting by T. Phillips, R.A. and a frontispiece by Schiavonetti to which the title-page, beautifully composed and printed, is preferable by far.

In 1822 Bensley printed the *Posthumous Papers of William Huntingdon*, which he edited in part. He was, it appears, one of the acting trustees of Providence Chapel, opened in Gray's Inn Road in 1811, after the previous chapel of the 'coal-heaver saint' in Tichfield Street had been burned down. Huntingdon (whose real name was Hunt) died in 1813.

Like William Bowyer I, Bensley had his premises destroyed by fire. On 5 November, 1807, they were badly damaged as a result of boys letting off fireworks; on 26 June, 1819, they were almost totally destroyed—printing offices, warehouse and part of the dwelling house in Bolt Court, formerly the residence of Dr Johnson.

John Johnson, best-known today for his manual of printing called *Typographia, or the Printers' Instructor* (1824), worked for a time with Thomas Bensley, before moving to premises of his own in Brook Street, Holborn, where he set up in business as the Apollo Press. He printed a number of books illustrated with wood-engravings, among them James Northcote's *One Hundred Fables* (1828).

Bensley was one of those associated with Frederick Koenig in the production of the first practical steam-powered press (see page 212). When his premises were destroyed in 1819 his machinery for power printing was not badly damaged, but he decided to retire soon afterwards, although he still retained the management of a smaller business in Crane Court. Like his rival, Bulmer, Thomas Bensley lived at Clapham Rise, where he died on 11 September, 1835.

The beginning of the eighteenth century had found English printing bogged down in a morass of mediocrity; by the end of the century the situation had undergone a remarkable change. Thanks to such punch-cutters and letter-founders as Caslon, Baskerville, Wilson, Martin, Austin, and Figgins, England could at last hold her own typographically with the Continent, and the monopoly held by the Dutch as suppliers of type was broken. Thanks to James Whatman and William Balston, fine printing, writing and plate papers, all of which were used for letterpress printing, could be obtained on the home market; there was no longer any need to send to Genoa. Moreover, the eighteenth century saw a great increase in customs duty on imported paper in order to protect the home industry. Finally, thanks to printers like Bowyer, Bell, Bulmer and Bensley, book production at last reached a very high standard. The half century from 1780 to 1830 may indeed be looked upon as the high watermark of British book production.

James Catnach—Printer for the Poor

While Bulmer and Bensley were turning out their handsome quartos for the moneyed few, another printer was making a fortune by providing the vast semi-literate population with the only sort of printed matter they could either appreciate or afford. Newspapers, then selling at sevenpence or eightpence a copy, were far beyond the means of the working classes, nor could they have been read by the majority.

But there was one class of literature which their modest intellectual attainments could appreciate, and that was the 'Halfpenny Ballad', the demand for which was supplied by the jobbing printer James Catnach (1792–1841), whose father John Catnach had been a printer at Alnwick and Newcastle before removing to London in 1813, where he died soon after opening a shop in Wardour Street.* His son, who had been working in Newcastle, came to London after his father's death and set up in business at 2, Monmouth Court, Seven Dials. Using old wooden presses and odd lots of type and woodcuts, some of which had formed part of his father's stock, he specialized in the printing of cheap literature for sale by street vendors. There were large coloured penny books, halfpenny coloured books, farthing books, penny and halfpenny panoramas, valentines, scripture sheets,

---

* John Catnach published at Alnwich (about 1795) selections from Buffon, entitled *The Beauties of Natural History*, with 67 wood-engravings by Bewick.

book and sheet almanacs, penny and halfpenny song books, and above all ballads, of which he had several thousand. The ballads were of various kinds, but those from which he amassed a fortune were the 'Gallows Ballads'.

According to a writer in the *Quarterly Review*,[173] the 'dying speech and confession ballad' was not known in the trade until 1820, when a change in the law prolonged the interval between trial and execution. 'Before that', said a street vendor to Mayhew, 'there wasn't no time for lamentation; sentence today, scragging tomorrow, or leastways, Friday to Monday.' Catnach's broadsides usually bore titles like *The Life, Trial, Execution, and Dying Behaviour of Joseph Hunton* (1828), and exploited to the full that popular interest in crime which flourishes to this day.

The sales of these 'Execution Ballads' were enormous. With his passion for statistics Mayhew gives the following figures:

Of Rush's murder	..	..	..	..	..	2,500,000 copies
Of the Mannings	..	..	..	..	..	2,500,000 copies
Of Courvoisier	..	..	..	..	..	1,666,000 copies
Of Greenacre	..	..	..	..	..	1,666,000 copies
Of Corder	..	..	..	..	..	166,000 copies

and these were sold to the street vendors at 3d. a dozen. These figures must be treated with some suspicion, for in the case of the account of the murder of Weare by Thurtell and his accomplices in 1824, which brought Catnach a profit of over £500, it was only by working day and night for a week with four 'two-pull squeezers' that he managed to print off some 250,000 copies. During the Peninsular War, and more especially during the trial of Queen Caroline, Catnach was so overwhelmed with orders that he kept his presses going twenty-four hours a day.

The authorship of the verse which emanated from Seven Dials may safely be attributed to some consortium of hack writers who haunted the neighbouring taverns. 'Jemmy' Catnach himself is said to have been the author of some of the ballads he printed, but not, one hopes, of the following stanzas, published on the occasion of the death in childbirth of the Princess Charlotte, which ran:

> She is gone! sweet Charlotte's gone!
>   Gone to the silent bourne;
> She is gone, she's gone, for evermore—
>   She never can return.

> She is gone with her joy—her darling Boy,
> The son of Leopold blythe and keen;
> She Died the sixth of November,
> Eighteen hundred and seventeen.

Doggerel, yes; but as one writer has pointed out, compared with a volume of the famous *Roxburghe Ballads*, ranging from 1560 to 1700, those issued from Seven Dials are models of purity and cleanliness. And they netted for James Catnach a fortune of several thousand pounds. Catnach retired from business in 1839 and died two years later. His business was for a time taken over by his sister, Mrs Ryle, in partnership with a Mr Paul, trading as Paul and Ryle, and later as A. Ryle and Co. It afterwards passed to W. S. Fortey, who had at one time worked for James Catnach; but he was less successful.

CHAPTER NINE

Dawn of the Machine Age

The first twenty years of the century followed more or less the same pattern in printing as the last twenty years of the preceding century. The established printers of fine books, the Bulmers and Bensleys, continued to produce sound examples of the classical manner in printing, but on their retirement the impetus was lost and it was not until the happy association of William Pickering and the printer Charles Whittingham twenty years later that a new standard in book production was reached.

Perhaps the greatest change which came over printing during the first two decades of the nineteenth century was the gradual transition from old-face to modern-face in the founts used by the leading printers. In the *Specimen of Modern Printing Types cast at the Letter-Foundry of Alex. Wilson & Son, at Glasgow* (1833) every roman and italic type shown is modern-face. But not all modern-faces were as good as those supplied by Wilson, and as Hansard remarked in 1825: 'Caslon's founts rarely occur in modern use, but they have too frequently been superseded by others which can claim no excellence over them. In fact the book printing of the present day is disgraced by a mixture of fat, lean, and heterogeneous types, which to the eye of taste is truly disgusting.' But the worst had yet to come.

However, the greatest and most revolutionary change in the whole history of printing had been heralded, though too faintly to be appreciated, as early as 1790, when the engineer William Nicholson took out a patent for a printing machine embodying the cylinder principle. The hand press was doomed.

That necessity is the mother of invention was never more clearly stressed than in the replacement of the slow and cumbersome hand press by the power-driven printing machine. In 1700 the population of England was around five and a half million; in 1801 it was nine million. The population of London alone had risen from 674,000 in 1700 to 1,274,000 in 1820, and thereafter increased at an incredible rate. Great towns sprang up in the country as England changed from an agricultural nation to an industrial one, with such speed that by 1850 half the population was urban. The great spread of education led to an increased demand for knowledge, to satisfy which was impossible with printing presses which were still limited to turning out a daily quantity of printed sheets not much greater than in the days of Caxton. Andrew Corrigan has worked out that to print a 24-page issue of a daily newspaper such as the *Daily Express* on hand presses, no fewer than 30,000 of them would be needed on an 8-hour run.

But to speed up the rate of impression was of no use in itself unless accompanied by progress in the ancillary arts of typecasting and paper making. While paper was still being formed by hand, sheet by sheet, in a wire mould; while type was still being cast by hand and set up letter by letter, just as in the fifteenth century, there was little point in inventing a machine which would greatly increase the rate of impression.

The first essential, therefore, was to have sufficient paper to print on; this was particularly important in the case of newspapers, with their rapidly increasing circulation.

Progress in Paper Making

Until the end of the eighteenth century all paper was made by hand, inevitably a slow process. From C. Leadbetter's *The Royal Gauger* we find that the daily output from a paper mill in 1739 varied from five to eight reams a day, according to size. The figure must clearly have been dependent upon the number of vats employed. Moreover, for fine paper the printer in Britain had to import supplies from the Continent. John Tate's mill near Stevenage, mentioned by Wynkyn de Worde, did not function for long, and his mark soon disappeared, the latest date known for it occurring in a Canterbury document of 1512. About the middle of the sixteenth century the Bishop of Ely brought back with him from the Court of Charles V a certain Remigius, with whose help he started a paper mill at Fen Ditton, near Cambridge. Some time between 1565 and 1575 Sir Thomas Gresham is said to have built a paper mill near his country residence at Osterley in Middlesex, but it had fallen into decay before the end of the century.

Although Tottel's petition in 1585 for a grant of land on which to establish a mill, and for the sole privilege of making paper for thirty-one years, was refused, four years later Queen Elizabeth granted a concession for paper making to John Spilman, a German (later knighted), who had acquired Bicknor Manor, near Dartford, with its wheat and malt mills. He established a paper mill there after having been granted leave 'for the gathering of all maner of linen ragges, skrolles, or scrappes of parchement, peaces of Lyme, Leather, Shreddes and Slippinges of Cardes and oulde fishinge Nettes, fitte and necessarie for the makinge of anie sorte of white wrightinge paper'. Thomas Churchyard wrote some doggerel rhymes on the subject, which paint a vivid word-picture of the paper mill in action:

> The hammers thump and make as lowde a noyse
> As fuller doth, that beates his wollen cloth,
> In open shewe; then sundry secret toyes
> Make rotten ragges to yeelde a thickened froth:
> Then it is stampt, and washed as white as snowe;
> Then flong on frame, and hang'd to dry I trow;
> Thus paper streight it is, to write upon,
> As it were rubde and smoothde with slicking-stone.[174]

According to Churchyard, Spilman gave employment to six hundred people. After a century or so the Spilman business declined when others entered the field, and in 1732 the decayed mill became a gunpowder factory. But the Spilmans had established paper making as a Kent industry, which it remains to this day.

By 1635 paper makers were at work in Hounslow and High Wycombe, and the paper mill at Bemerton, Wiltshire, established towards the end of the sixteenth century, was still in use at the beginning of the nineteenth. By the end of the seventeenth century, if we are to believe a document of 1696 called the *Case of the Paper Traders*, there were not a hundred paper mills in all England, and these made little except the coarser sorts of paper. Most of the paper for fine printing came from Holland, Italy and France.

Richard Garnett has told the story of how the printing of Conyers Middleton's *Life of Cicero* was held up in 1740 because the war with Spain had delayed the ships coming from Genoa with the necessary paper, not a sheet of which could be had in London. In 1759, however, the first step was taken to make England more independent in this matter when James Whatman the Younger succeeded to the Turkey Mill at Hollingbourne, near Maidstone, after his father's death in 1759. In that year he made paper on wove moulds for Edward Capell's

Prolusions, published by Tonson in 1760, about two years after the publication of Baskerville's *Virgil*, said to have been the first book printed on wove paper. It seems likely that Baskerville obtained his paper for that work from the Turkey Mill. Whatman's paper rapidly became noted for its consistently good quality and gained a universal reputation.

But with an ever-increasing demand for more and cheaper paper it was natural that attempts should be made to invent a machine to replace the slow hand process. The first one was invented around 1799 by a Frenchman, Nicolas Louis Robert, and a model of it may be seen in the Science Museum at South Kensington. This machine made little headway in France, which had not yet recovered from the effects of the Revolution, and the patent was soon afterwards taken up in England by the brothers Henry and Sealey Fourdrinier, stationers and paper makers. They built the first practical machine in 1803 at Frogmore, and although they lost almost all their private fortune in perfecting the machine, and ultimately became bankrupt, their name is immortalized in the paper industry, for the paper making machine used today, based on the same essential principles, is still known as a 'Fourdrinier', though the vast size of the present-day machines would undoubtedly astonish the original inventors. Some of the mammoth machines run by the Bowater Corporation have a wire width of 320 inches and can make a continuous sheet of paper at the rate of 1,500 feet per minute. In paying tribute to the Fourdriniers one should not forget Bryan Donkin, the English engineer, who also played a great part in the development of mechanized paper making and built the first working machine from the patents of the original inventor. He built a press based on Nicholson's ideas with a Norwich printer named Bacon, but it never became a practical proposition.

Whereas with the hand mould paper is made sheet by sheet, the paper making machine makes one continuous sheet or 'web', and is really several machines linked together which reproduce mechanically the various operations employed in making paper by hand, though on a vast scale.

With the coming of this machine the output of paper increased ten-fold, and the price fell considerably. In 1740 the percentage allowed for paper in the cost of book production was as high as 20·5 per cent. By 1910 it amounted to only 7·1 per cent. A problem encountered soon after the introduction of the machine was shortage of traditional material, namely the linen rags which had always been used for the best-quality paper. These could no longer be obtained in sufficient quantity or at an economic price for the cheaper grades of paper. Experiments were made with an enormous number of fibrous materials, as various patents between 1801 and 1862 show. Straw was one of the first to be suggested, and other substances included the bark of various trees and shrubs, pine-needles, reeds, artichoke stalks and hop bine. Although the use of wood pulp for the manufacture of paper had been suggested by Réaumur as early as 1719, the idea did not take practical shape until 1840, when mechanical or ground wood pulp was introduced, to be followed a decade later by first the soda, and then the sulphite process of treating wood until it is reduced to a pulp of cellulose fibres. In 1856 Thomas Routledge introduced esparto grass as a suitable fibre for paper making. Owing to the relative shortness of its fibres esparto grass produces a paper lacking the strength of that made from rags, but as it readily absorbs dyes and pigments it is extensively used for tinted papers. In England Edward Lloyd* did much to develop the paper trade during the latter part of the nine-teenth century. In 1877 he built his own large mill at Sittingbourne which in its day had the largest output of any paper mill in the world. He also leased over 100,000 acres of land in Algeria for the growing of esparto grass.

For a long period paper was subject to excise duty. The Stamp Act of 1712 made English and Scottish paper subject to an excise. In 1794 this method of assessing the duty was replaced by a tax on weight, with home-made paper paying a duty of 2½d per lb. Taxation of imported paper was very heavy, in order to protect the home industry. The Act of 1794 meant that paper was no longer taxed according to quality, with the result that the increased duty on ordinary printing papers was more in proportion than that paid on fine papers, thus placing a heavy burden on most printers. The excise taxes on paper were doubled in 1801, reduced somewhat in 1803, and in 1838 further reduced from 3d to 1½d per lb. The tax was not totally abolished until 1861.

The Advent of Mechanical Power

The hand press had a long reign. For three hundred and fifty years the wooden press had existed without much modification. Willem

---

* Edward Lloyd (1815–1890) was the founder of *Lloyd's Weekly London Newspaper* (1843), and in 1876 purchased the *Daily Chronicle*.

Janszoon Blaeu, at the beginning of the seventeenth century, substituted for the earlier box-shaped hose two iron pillars passing through bearings in the till to guide the downward movement of the platen, but from that time the hand press remained unchanged in essentials until the end of the eighteenth century. Its production was limited, but so was the demand for print. The era of general literacy did not arrive until the middle of the eighteenth century.

Theodore de Vinne considered the Blaeu press little better than the makeshift presses that had preceded it.

> Let any intelligent mechanic [he writes in a paper on *Medieval Printing*] examine this 'improved' press of van Blaeu's, and he must see in the shrinking nature of the wood framework; the sparsity of iron in the running movements; the fragility of the stone bed; and the general ramshackliness of its construction, abundant evidences of feebleness and unreliability. How then, it may be asked, could such a faulty press do even ordinary good work? It did it only by doing it very slowly.

How could production be other than limited when it took nine separate operations to print a sheet on the old hand press? First the dabbers or pelt balls had to be evenly covered with printing ink placed on the 'slab' attached to the side of the press. Then the forme had to be inked by the balls—always used in pairs—and considerable skill was required to apply the ink uniformly over the surface of the type. During this operation the ink balls had to be constantly rubbed together to keep the ink evenly distributed over their surface. The third step was to place the dampened sheet of paper upon the tympan. Next, the frisket had to be folded down to keep the paper in position, and with the same movement tympan, frisket and paper were folded down on to the type surface. The fifth step was to run the carriage under the platen, and the sixth was to pull the impression. The three final operations were to slide the carriage back again, to raise the tympan and frisket and, finally, to deliver the printed sheet.

The first significant improvement took place in 1800, when the wooden press was superseded by Earl Stanhope's iron press, which, by an ingenious combination of lever and screw motion, made possible a considerable increase of pressure at the moment of impression. The new press also needed less effort to operate. The result was greater speed of production, and a whole battery of Stanhope presses was used to print *The Times* for the first fourteen years of the nineteenth century. Previously that newspaper had been printed on a wooden press similar to that now in the St Bride Institute. The first Stanhope press (made by his engineer Robert Walker) was used in 1800 by William Bulmer. It is worthy of note that Earl Stanhope refrained from patenting his design so that the printing industry could make free use of it.

Other iron presses followed, of which the best-known were the Columbian press, invented about 1816 by George Clymer of Philadelphia, and the Albion press of R. W. Cope, which was introduced around 1822. Both these presses and others working on similar principles were being used well into the twentieth century, and the Albion press was employed by many well-known private presses in England, notably the Kelmscott and Doves. Whereas the early wooden press could not be relied upon to produce more than about thirty sheets an hour, the number of impressions produced on the Stanhope or other improved iron presses was about 200 an hour. (A maximum of 250 sheets an hour was possible with a crew of experienced pressmen. This was the rate at which *The Times* was printed on the lever press.) The *Manchester Guardian* of 6 May, 1871, recorded that 'the little sheet which first bore our name was laboriously printed by hand, the old-fashioned Stanhope press then employed turning out 200 impressions of a single side in an hour'. Twice that time was needed for perfected copies.

Although mechanical power had been applied to many branches of industry by the late eighteenth century, it was slow in being adopted by the printers, possibly because the printing industry had so far been able to satisfy demand with the equipment it possessed. But with the rapid growth of literacy and the increasing demand for printed matter change became inevitable.

It was the newspaper offices, and *The Times* in particular, which initiated mechanization in the printing trade through their need for ever increasing operational speeds to satisfy a steadily growing demand for newspapers, which had, of necessity, to be produced during the early morning hours.

The first step towards faster printing was the substitution of cylindrical pressure for the flat weight of the platen. The idea of printing by means of an impression cylinder was not a new one, for it was used in the sixteenth century by printers of copper-plate engravings. But these early cylinder presses were built of wood and were rudimentary in design.

In 1790 William Nicholson took out a patent for several inventions relating to printing on textiles as well as on paper. His patent was never carried out in practice, and since the inventor died in a debtors' prison the reason was probably that he was unable to secure financial backing. Nevertheless, his name deserves a mention in the history of printing, since his specifications embodied many of the essential features of the later printing machines, such as the reciprocating table with geared impression cylinder; the inking of the forme by rollers instead of ink balls; the distribution of ink upon the rollers by means of subsidiary rollers; an ink duct for supplying ink in pre-determined quantity at each revolution; and grippers for carrying round the sheet. Another part of his invention foreshadowed rotary printing, in that he suggested the use of curved stereotype plates to fit the cylinders.

In 1807 John Brown took out a patent for improvements in the construction of the printing press, and just as Nicholson's ideas were later to be realized in the development of the flat-bed and cylinder machine, so Brown's suggestions, though crude, foreshadowed the later forms of mechanical platen machines.

The first practical power-driven printing machine was the invention of a native of Thuringia named Frederick Koenig, who after spending some years in trying to adapt power-drive to a conventional hand press, turned his attention to the cylinder type of machine suggested by Nicholson's patent. He came to England in 1806, being at first employed as a journeyman printer, but managed to become acquainted with the eminent printer Thomas Bensley, to whom he described his ideas for a powered printing machine. Bensley was a shrewd man who grasped the significance of Koenig's proposals and saw that their practical realization would give him a great advantage over his competitors. An agreement was drawn up between Bensley and Koenig to the effect that if the 'entire new method of printing by machinery' fulfilled the claims of its inventor, Bensley would purchase the secret. More money being needed to develop the machine than Bensley cared to risk, two other printers, George Woodfall and Richard Taylor, joined in the partnership.

Koenig's first English patent for a power-driven printing machine was taken out in 1810. This machine, built with the help of Koenig's fellow-countryman Andreas Bauer, a skilled engineer, was nothing more than a platen screw-press driven by steam-power, and although it was used in Bensley's establishment in April, 1810, for printing part of the *Annual Register* for that year, there is no record of any other work being done by it, and it was eventually abandoned.

So far, both in his own country and in England, Koenig had been working on the wrong lines, trying, as Jacobi says, 'to make an improvement on what was hardly capable of improvement'.[175] Now he realized that the retention of the screw and platen was a mistake, and for his next design he adopted Nicholson's idea of the impression cylinder, although his machine differed considerably from that suggested by Nicholson, who proposed having the type imposed upon the surface of another cylinder, a method not feasible at that time. In Koenig's machine the forme was fixed to the flat bed of the press, consisting of a cast-iron plate, which had a reciprocating motion, moving in and out to bring the type alternately under the action of the inking roller and the cylinder which pressed the paper into contact with the type. Since the inking was carried out automatically as the table was being run in and out, the nine operations which had been necessary in hand printing were reduced to three: the placing of the paper, the impression and the taking off of the printed sheet. The output of Koenig's first cylinder printing machine, built in 1812, was 800 impressions an hour.

One of those who inspected the machine when it was displayed for the first time in Koenig and Bauer's workshop in White Cross Street was John Walter of *The Times*, who found in it the very machine he had been looking for, except that this single-cylinder machine was only intended for book-work. Koenig having explained how a double machine on the same principle could be built for the printing of newspapers, Walter ordered two of them. On 29 November, 1814, *The Times* was printed on the new machine, which increased the rate of production to 1,100 impressions an hour as compared with the maximum 250 of the Stanhope.

The machine was erected at Printing House Square in secret, for the pressmen, who had heard rumours of what was intended, were afraid of losing their jobs. Aware that some of the men had threatened to smash the machine, Walter assembled them in the pressroom and informed them that if they attempted violence there was a force ready to suppress it; but that if they took the news calmly every man would be paid his full wages until he could obtain employment elsewhere. There was no demonstration, but not unnaturally the advent of the printing machine was viewed with mistrust by the majority of those in the printing industry.

By 1816 Koenig and Bauer had built their first perfecting machine, which printed both sides of the paper in one operation at a rate of

900–1,000 sheets an hour. In 1817 Koenig left England, in despair at the many infringements of his patent and disgusted with the attitude of Bensley, who refused to take proceedings against the infringers. Richard Taylor, the other partner in the patent, subsequently wrote that

> Mr Koenig left England suddenly, in disgust at the treacherous conduct of Bensley, always shabby and overreaching, and whom he found to be laying a scheme for defrauding his partners in the patents of all the advantages to arise from them. Bensley, however, while he destroyed the prospects of his partners, outwitted himself, and grasping at all, lost all, becoming bankrupt in fortune as well as in character.[176]

After Koenig's departure *The Times* appointed Augustus Applegath and Edward Cowper as their engineers. Cowper, who was Applegath's brother-in-law, was one of the first to apply himself to developing Nicholson's idea of a curved printing surface. In 1816 he patented a process for curving stereotype plates made by the plaster process, and a machine employing them was used for printing £1 notes at the Bank of England. But the rotary machine proper did not come into being until the middle of the century.

In 1827 Applegath and Cowper built a new machine for *The Times* —a four-feeder which printed four sheets at a time, though on one side only, and increased the speed to 4,200 sheets an hour. The forme travelled the whole length of the machine, the cylinders rising and falling alternately, so that one pair printed as the carriage moved one way, and the other pair on its return.

Between 1828 and 1832 the search continued for higher speed and greater production capacity. Although the four-feeder used by *The Times* was capable, with the steam-power increased, of giving an output of 6,000 an hour, that newspaper's constantly increasing circulation now demanded an output of 10,000 an hour, and development of the newspaper press was stimulated by the competition between *The Times* and the American firm of Robert Hoe.

Meanwhile the platen principle had been revived by David Napier for book-work, and his double-feeder power platen of 1830 was largely used for quality printing before the introduction of the Wharfedale in 1858.

Between 1842 and 1852 the circulation of *The Times* doubled, and when Applegath learned that the demand for the paper could only be met by the building of an even faster machine, he designed and constructed a vertical cylinder eight-feeder press which came into use in 1848. It was very similar to the Hoe four-cylinder rotary which had been erected in the printing house of the Philadelphia *Ledger* in 1846, the most important difference being that the Hoe type cylinder was horizontal and that of the Applegath vertical. The type cylinder (or rather 'polygon', for it was not a true cylinder) was of cast iron, 5 feet 6 inches in diameter, and there were eight impression cylinders. The eight feeding stations were approached from a raised circular gallery six feet from the ground.

Ordinary type was used, held in position by column rules of wedge shape, a development of the Bacon and Donkin rotary of 1813, which had type arranged on the four sides of a revolving prismatic forme. The Applegath press gave a normal 8,000 impressions an hour (printed on one side only), but could achieve a maximum output of 10,000 sheets an hour. In introducing the machine to the public *The Times*, in its issue of 29 December, 1848, noted that

> The printing cylinders surrounding the central drum and in occasional contact with it bear about the same visible proportion to it as the pillars of the temple of Tivoli to the circular wall within.

Two more machines of this specification were used at Printing House Square, the third having nine instead of eight impression cylinders.

Applegath's machine, after doing useful service for many years, was eventually superseded by the Hoe horizontal cylinder machine, one of which was ordered in 1856 by *Lloyd's Weekly Newspaper* and installed in the Salisbury Square printing house of that paper, whereupon the advantages of the horizontal over the vertical cylinder became at once apparent to John Walter III. Since *Lloyd's* had a six-cylinder machine, *The Times* went four better and, turning out the Applegath nine-feeder, installed two Hoe ten-cylinder presses in 1857-8.

Meanwhile, in 1850, a London printer named Main had patented a cylinder machine embodying new principles. In this machine the cylinder did not rotate, but oscillated, making about three-quarters of a revolution. Instead of the paper being fed at the top, as hitherto, in the Main machine it was fed to the underside of the cylinder, where it was seized by grippers. This made possible the use of a smaller cylinder for a given sheet size. By the employment of eccentric bearings the cylinder was lifted clear of the forme on the reverse stroke.

Two years later a Frenchman named Dutartre patented a machine in which the cylinder made one complete revolution as the carriage moved forward and then stopped while the carriage returned. This was the origin of the so-called stop-cylinder machine, the principle of which was embodied in one of the most successful flat-bed cylinder machines for book printing and general commercial work, known as the Wharfedale, from its place of origin, the first model having been built around 1858 at a factory in Otley, Yorkshire, by William Dawson and his foreman, David Payne. This machine was both efficient and economical, simple in construction, and among its most practical features were the accessibility of all parts of the machine and the convenience of laying-on and taking-off. The Dawson-Payne machine was never patented and became so popular that all machines of that type, wherever made, became known as Wharfedales. One of the earliest improvements was the provision of flyer sticks which delivered the printed sheets, thus doing away with the need for a taker-off.

During the years since the original Wharfedale was introduced many improvements have been made, including automatic feed and delivery, and Wharfedale machines can now be had for two-colour work, with two type beds and a separate inking arrangement at each end. In this case the cylinder makes two revolutions, the paper receiving an impression from each printing forme in turn.

For many years experiments had been going on with a view to making curved stereotype plates for use on rotary machines. Cowper, as we have seen, patented a method of curving cast stereotype plates by heating them, but there was always a tendency for the plate to crack or break in the process, and it was quite inapplicable to newspaper printing. The problem was eventually solved when John Walter III invited an Italian founder, James Dellagana, to experiment at Printing House Square. He found that by using papier mâché moulds (see page 220) separate columns could be cast in them quite rapidly with stereotype metal, type-high, and these were first adapted for use with the polygonal chases of the Applegath vertical rotary. When the Hoe machines were installed, instead of casting separate columns, a papier mâché matrix was taken from the whole page at one operation by means of specially constructed roller-presses.

Thus after 1857 it became possible to fasten as many stereotype plates as necessary on to a cylinder, so making possible increased speeds; the speed could be doubled by printing both sides of the sheet at one operation (known as 'perfecting'), which was accomplished by passing the paper under and over two cylinders carrying plates. Still further increase in speed was obtained when the solution of the feeding problem was reached in the William Bullock rotary of 1865 and the famous 'Walter' press of 1866. In these machines single sheets were no longer used, and instead a continuous roll of paper, four miles long and mounted on a reel, travelled through the machine, being printed on both sides from curved stereos during its passage. In the Bullock press the roll was cut into sheets before printing, but in the 'Walter' press the cutting into sheets took place after printing. This press, the wonder of its day, was, in short, a fully automatic web-fed perfector, capable of turning out 12,000 perfected eight-page papers an hour. At first the printed sheets were folded by hand, but in 1870 the problem of folding papers automatically was solved by George Ashley Wilson, whose 'Victory' machine of 1870 combined a folder with the printing machine used to produce the *Glasgow Weekly Mail*.

During the 1870s the reel-fed rotary press displaced the sheet-fed machine in all the London newspaper offices and many were introduced into the provinces. For the first time the mechanical advantage which had been enjoyed for so long by *The Times* alone was challenged by other newspapers as new rotary machines came on the market. One of the biggest competitors of the Walter press was the web-fed rotary produced by the American firm of Hoe, first installed in London in 1871 for printing *Lloyd's Weekly News*, with its circulation, phenomenal for those days, of 600,000. In 1874 eight of these Hoe machines were ordered for the *Daily Telegraph*.

By 1880 the rotary web press had established itself firmly as the accepted machine for the printing of newspapers, and although as the years passed various developments took place with a view to increased productive capacity, the fundamentals remained unchanged; but, whereas the Walter press had only one printing unit, the enormous newspaper presses of today may comprise as many as sixty units. The Hoe machines in use by *The Times* at the present time can impress the reels of paper at a speed of 20,000 revolutions an hour, and each unit will print two sections of eight pages each at every revolution. The only factor forbidding even higher speeds is the tensile strength of the paper itself.

The platen press, in which the forme is held in a vertical position, was first introduced into England in the form of the Minerva Press of the American, G. P. Gordon, in 1866. Being a comparatively simple machine, which could be worked by one man, it was used mainly for jobbing, and was known in England as the Franklin Press.

The Invention of Stereotyping

One of the most useful inventions in the history of printing, from the point of view of the economics of the trade, was that of stereotyping, a method of reproducing a relief printing surface so that the type can be released for use elsewhere. The impression from the stereotype plate corresponds in every respect to that obtained from the original, and since the duplicate is only about one-sixth of the thickness of type, it is easier to store than a page of standing type.

The problem of preserving pages of type for an eventual reprint so as to avoid resetting the copy was exercising the minds of many printers in the early years of the eighteenth century, and the history of the solution to the problem is somewhat obscure. Briefly the process of stereotyping, shorn of its technical details, is as follows: from the forme of 'matter' to be duplicated is taken a matrix or mould, which is naturally in intaglio; from this can be cast a plate in relief corresponding to the original. The oldest method of preparing stereotypes was by making the mould from gypsum (plaster of Paris), which was baked before a cast could be made. The plaster mould was broken in the process, and so only one plate could be made at a time, each additional duplicate calling for a new mould. Later, a papier mâché mould (called a flong) was used, which could be used to make more than one plate, and had, moreover, the advantage of being flexible, so that from it could be cast curved plates ready for fixing to the cylinder of a rotary press. It was the development of the papier mâché flong which enabled the newspaper press to reap the full advantage of the rotary method of printing.

The earliest stereotype plates are thought to have been the invention of a Lutheran minister named Johann Müller in conjunction with the Leyden firm of Van der Mey, and the first book printed from stereotype plates made by his process is said to have been a small prayer book printed in 1701.* Müller then went into partnership with the Dutch bookseller Samuel Luchtmans and several books bearing their joint imprint were printed from stereotypes. The British Museum possesses a stereotype plate used for printing a Dutch Bible issued by Müller's sons and Luchtmans & Co. in 1718, the inventor having died in 1710.

---

* French historians of printing say that a Parisian named Valleyre printed almanacs from stereotype plates about the year 1700.

In Great Britain the first successful stereotype plates were made about 1727 by William Ged of Edinburgh, though we have no authentic proof of his manner of working. By profession a goldsmith, he began experimenting about 1725 and within two years had produced, at the cost of all his available capital, a plate of a page of type sufficiently serviceable to induce a London stationer named William Fenner to offer to finance him if he came to London and to go into partnership with him. The partnership was later extended to include the letter-founder Thomas James and his brother John James. In 1730 John James and Fenner managed to secure from the University of Cambridge a licence under their privilege for printing Bibles and prayer books. Unfortunately disagreements frequently bedevilled the partnership, and Ged had constant trouble with his workmen. In 1733 he returned to Scotland and no book completely printed by his process at Cambridge is known to survive. The only volume known which is thought by John Carter to have been partly printed at Cambridge from Ged's stereotype plates is an octavo Common Prayer of 1733, which bears the imprint of William Fenner, Printer to the University.*

In 1739 Ged published an edition of Sallust in Edinburgh which bears on the title-page an announcement in Latin to the effect that it was printed 'by William Ged, Goldsmith of Edinburgh, not with movable type, as is commonly done, but with cast plates'. This, and the reissue of 1744, were printed entirely from Ged's own plates.

About 1779 another Scotsman, Alexander Tilloch, without being acquainted with Ged's work, perfected, in conjunction with the printer Andrew Foulis, his own method of producing stereotype plates, and in 1784 the two men took out patents for 'a method of making plates and for the purpose of printing by or with plates, instead of the movable types commonly used', though the specification gives very little in the way of details of the method used. Tilloch himself said that he used plaster of Paris for preference to make his moulds. Later the 3rd Earl Stanhope purchased the invention from Tilloch and Foulis and further developed it in association with the printer Andrew Wilson, who set up the Stereotype Office in Duke Street,

---

* Carter, John. 'William Ged and the invention of Stereotype.' *The Library*. Vol. XV, No. 3, September, 1960. Fenner died insolvent about 1735. Ged was implicated in the 1745 rebellion and narrowly escaped execution. He later went to Jamaica.

Lincoln's Inn Fields. In a circular letter of August, 1803, Wilson states that

> This valuable art will enable me to afford, at any time or times, an equal Number of copies of any Work which has a very extensive Sale (such, for example, as the Bible, or the Book of Common Prayer) TWENTY-FIVE *per cent.* cheaper than I could do if the same book were to be printed by me in the usual manner.[177]

For almost half a century the 'plaster' process was the only method employed, but in 1844 J. M. Kronheim patented a method of making moulds for the casting of curved stereo plates in which he made use of alternate layers of paste and thin paper. Some authorities consider this method to have been first invented by Jean Baptiste Genoux of Lyons around 1829.

However that may be, in 1846 an Italian named Vanoni introduced into England this method of making moulds in papier mâché, at that time in common use in France. About the same time another Italian, James Dellagana,* came to England and set up a factory for making stereotype plates, becoming the most successful stereotyper of his time. In 1855 he perfected a system for casting stereo plates type-high, but hollow inside, by making use of a core in the casting box. By 1863 he and his brother had successfully used a curved casting box which enabled them to produce convex plates which could be fitted directly to the cylinder of a rotary press, thus enabling the full potentialities of this form of printing to be used for newspapers, where increased machine speed was of primary importance.

Later the Autoplate, invented by Henry Wise Wood of New York, brought about economy of both time and labour by eliminating the hot-press and by forming from forty to fifty plates simultaneously.

The Composing Machine

Setting by hand is a slow process, however skilful the compositor. The most the nimblest fingers can accomplish is just over 1,000 letters and spaces an hour. A Victorian novel often ran to 200,000 words—that is to say between a million and a million and a half characters. The Authorized Version of the Bible contains 774,746 words.

Speed in setting is not inevitably vital for book and jobbing printing,

---

* The Dellagana brothers had worked in Paris at the printing office of *Le Constitutionnel* before emigrating to England for political reasons.

though it often may be, but for a newspaper it is of the utmost importance. Between 1816 and 1874 improvements to the newspaper printing press increased the speed of printing by something like 60,000 times. But as long as composing was done by hand these advantages could not be fully utilized. Mechanization of the printing press, to be fully effective, had to be accompanied by mechanical composition, and the search for a practical solution to the problem of speeding type-setting occupied the minds of inventors and produced a variety of devices during a large part of the nineteenth century.

The first known inventor of a type-composing machine was Dr William Church of Vermont, U.S.A., who in 1822 took out a British patent for an improved printing press, a casting machine and a composing machine. The last-named was a machine in which the type was stored in inclined grooves, each character being released by the operation of a keyboard and assembled in a continuous line. No provision was made for the justification of successive lines, which was performed by a second operator. There is no evidence that a machine to Church's patent was ever built.

The first practical composing machine was the joint effort of James Young and Adrien Delcambre, aided by the engineer Henry Bessemer. It was on the lines of Church's design and was used to set the weekly magazine *The Family Herald*, raising the speed of composition to over 6,000 letters and spaces an hour. The machine dates from 1840.

About 1857 came the machine invented by Robert Hattersley, which was more successful than the Young-Delcambre—although it was constructed along similar lines—possibly because its keyboard was more compact, and it was used in a number of provincial newspaper offices. It could set 7,500 letters an hour in the hands of a skilled operator.

In the U.S.A. one Timothy Alden invented the Alden type-composing and distributing machine. He died at the end of 1858 after spending twenty years of his life and a small fortune in bringing his machine into operation. A company was formed in 1862 by his cousin, Henry W. Alden, to exploit the machine, for which a patent was taken out in England. But after a trial in the offices of the *New York Herald Tribune* the machine was abandoned as a failure. It does not seem ever to have been made in England. An engraving of it was published in *The Printer's Journal* in 1867.

One great disadvantage of all these machines in which the type was stacked in grooves, each containing supplies of one kind of character, was that after the used type was distributed it had to be once again set up in rows ready for insertion into the proper channels. This was a time-wasting process which tended to minimize the advantage of having a composing machine.

Next came the Kastenbein typesetter of 1869, invented by Charles Kastenbein, which, although it made no radical departure from the principles embodied in its predecessors, had one advantage in that later models were provided with a distributing machine. *The Times* employed a battery of Kastenbein machines, which after 1880 were used in conjunction with the Wicks typecasting machine. Invented by Frederick Wicks about 1878, this machine was said to be capable of casting 60,000 finished sorts each day.

Up till 1880 the composing machine had no means of justifying the lines, an operation which had to be done separately. Many ingenious suggestions failed the practical test. One machine, the American Paige typesetting machine, was built about this time with the financial assistance of Mark Twain, who lost money on the venture, for although the machine could set, justify and distribute type at the same time, its colossal size and weight, coupled with the fact that it could set only one size of type, made it commercially impracticable.

The Thorne composing machine, patented in the U.S.A. in 1880, had two vertical grooved cylinders, placed one above the other, the lower one being the magazine, and the upper one a receptacle for used type ready for distribution. Each character and space was distinguished by a particular combination of nicks on the rear edge, and the grooves in the lower cylinder were provided with various wards corresponding with the nicks on the type allotted to that particular groove. When in use, the upper cylinder revolved step by step, and as each type reached the groove with wards corresponding to the nicks, it was automatically dropped into its proper place in the magazine. The *Manchester Guardian* was one of the newspapers which used the Thorne machine.

The Linotype

Mechanization of type-setting was not satisfactorily solved until 1886, by which time Ottmar Mergenthaler had developed the Linotype, which composed lines of type in the form of slugs. It was a very ingenious invention, for all the operations of casting, composing, justifying, and eventually distributing, were combined in one machine. When a key on the keyboard is depressed it releases, from a magazine above, a brass matrix corresponding to the character selected, which is carried by a travelling belt to an assembler box. After each word a spaceband, consisting of two opposing wedges, is released. When there are sufficient matrices in the box to make a line they are conveyed to the face of the mould, where the wedge-shaped spacebands are forced upwards until the spacing is increased sufficiently to fill out the line to the required measure. Once justified, the line of matrices moves along until it forms the front of a horizontal mould, and there molten metal is pumped against and into the matrices, forming as it cools a solid line of 'slug' or metal with the letters in relief along one edge. The slug is automatically trimmed to the correct size and ejected from the mould on to a receiving galley, while the matrices are conveyed to the top of the magazine and distributed, to be used again.

One essential element in the success of Mergenthaler's invention was not his own, for the double-wedge spaceband used for justification had been patented by J. W. Schuckers of Philadelphia some time previously, and it cost nearly half a million dollars to secure the rights of this invention. Moreover, without an extremely accurate mechanical engraver to renew the punches for the matrices, the type-composing machine would have been gravely handicapped; but fortunately for Mergenthaler, Linn Benton's pantographic engraver was available.

The advantages both of the Hattersley and the Kastenbein machines were to a large extent discounted by the problem of distribution, for the distributing machines supplied by the manufacturers were not altogether satisfactory and could only be worked economically by cheap juvenile labour, which the London Society of Compositors would not countenance. *The Times*, being a non-union house, was at that time among the few newspaper offices making use of mechanical composition.

Much of the success of the Linotype lay in the solving of the problem of distribution, for this was completely avoided by the remelting of the slugs after the forme had been printed. The first London newspaper to adopt the Linotype (first used by the *New York Tribune* in 1886) was the *Globe*, in 1892, to be followed shortly afterwards by the *Financial News*. By 1895 at least 250 machines were in use by provincial papers, as against 32 Hattersleys and 14 Thornes.

'There had been two major typographic inventions since Gutenberg' writes Stanley Morison. 'The first, relating to the multiplication of sheets, was the steam press of König and Bauer—the second, relating to the multiplication of punches, was the mechanical engraver made by Linn Boyd Benton of Milwaukee in 1885.'[178] The Linotype needed matrices on a scale hitherto unprecedented, and this in turn called for the mass production of punches. Neither the Linotype nor the later Monotype could have functioned properly in the absence of some method of mechanical punch-cutting.

The modern punch-cutting machine (based on Benton's, with certain later modifications) is a vertical pantograph with a pendulum-like arm pivoted above a specially prepared copper pattern of the character for which a punch is required. Using this copper pattern as a master, the lower end of the pendulum follows the outline of the pattern while the other end carries the steel to be engraved. This piece of soft steel is revolved around a small cutting tool which, guided by the pantograph, makes a reduced replica of the pattern—reducing the size from the $2\frac{1}{2}$ inches of the character on the pattern to the required point size of the matrix to be formed. The steel punch is then checked for accuracy and hardened, justified and trimmed. Punch-cutting machines in use today have a dimensional accuracy of within one twenty-five thousandth of an inch.

Mechanical Typecasting

Just as all early punches were cut by hand, so were types cast by hand, the manual process lasting until well into the middle of the nineteenth century. In 1851 the hand mould was still being employed by founders, and the *Jury Reports* on the Universal Exhibition of that year declared that 'since the invention of casting types by Peter Schoeffer . . . this art has made little progress'. Another decade passed before the majority of founders were using typecasting machines.

The only improvement in the construction of the hand mould had been made in 1811 by a Scotsman named Archibald Binny, who patented in America a device consisting of a spring lever attached to the mould which gave a quicker release of the casting and increased the output of each workman from four to five hundred medium-sized castings an hour to around eight hundred.

One of the first typecasting machines was that invented by Dr William Church as part of his combined British patent of 1822 for a printing press, casting machine and composing machine. But the first effective machine was that of David Bruce of New York, who patented his invention in the U.S.A. in 1838. This was the forerunner of what are known as 'pivotal' casters, in which the mould is on the end of an arm which, by the action of a cam, is brought in the proper position to receive the molten type-metal, which is forced into the matrix by means of a pump.* With the early forms of pivotal caster it was still necessary, as with the hand mould, to remove the jets and dress the types by hand after casting.

For many years England lagged behind the U.S.A. and a number of continental countries in making use of machinery for casting, due, it is said, to the reluctance of many founders, who feared trouble with their workmen if they introduced it. The jurors at the 1851 Exhibition reported how M. Louis Pouchée, who had bought the patent rights for Henri Didot's machine known as the 'Polymatype', could not market it in England on account of the opposition of the type-founders, who bought one of the machines and destroyed it; a piece of vandalism reminiscent of the Luddites. One of the first firms in England to cast by machinery was that of William Clowes, which had its own foundry (see page 227).

In 1878 came Frederick Wicks's rotary typecasting machine, patented in 1881, which in its later versions could cast and deliver 60,000 finished types per hour. This was of great importance to *The Times*, by whom Wicks was employed, for it meant that when used in conjunction with the Kastenbein composing machine fresh type could be employed for the newspaper every day, and the labour of distribution was saved. It was, however, superseded by the Linotype, in which casting and composing were combined in a single machine.

Electrotype

Another nineteenth century invention of significance to the printer was that of electrotyping, a process invented in 1839 by H. von Jacobi of St Petersburg and Thomas Spencer of Liverpool, independently of one another. Having noticed that a metallic deposit was formed in a Daniel cell, Jacobi tried the effect of immersing in it a copper plate incised with a graver, and he obtained a reproduction in relief. In 1841 E. Palmer took out the first British patent for producing metallic plates with raised printing surfaces.

When an original is to be duplicated by the electrotyping process it is prepared, first of all in the same way as for stereotyping. The surface is then brushed over with graphite, which acts as a lubricant and facilitates the removal of the mould. Melted wax is allowed to

---

* The first English patents for a pump for this purpose were taken out by A. F. Berte in 1806 and 1807.

set and when still warm is placed on the surface of the original, and together they are placed in a hydraulic press, where great pressure is applied.

The mould is then separated from the original and built up by running melted wax on those parts where there are large areas with no type. A small piece of copper is sunk into the wax side of the mould, which, after it has been coated with black lead to increase its electrical conductivity and sprinkled with iron filings, is placed in a depositing vat. In this is a solution of copper sulphate and the chemical reaction which ensues deposits a copper shell on the mould. This shell is allowed to grow until it has reached the desired thickness, after which it is removed from the mould and 'backed up', namely, made type-high by the addition of a metal backing. It then undergoes the necessary finishing processes to make it perfectly level. Where greater durability is required the shell can be nickel-faced electrolytically, and these are now customary for colour work since coloured inks have a tendency to set up a chemical action with copper. The average number of good impressions that can be obtained in one run is about 100,000 from an electro of type as against 50,000 from stereos. Nickel-faced electros will give about a third more again.

Tolbert Lanston and the 'Monotype'

Tolbert Lanston of Ohio was a man with no mechanical training but possessed of an enquiring and inventive mind. The punched card system used in the Hollerith tabulator interested him, and he thought it possible that the principle might be embodied in a composing machine (the Linotype was not yet on the market). The idea had certainly been foreshadowed by a machine invented in 1867 by a Warrington journalist named Alexander Mackie. A paper ribbon, perforated on a keyboard, was then fed into Mackie's composing machine, releasing type contained in containers at the periphery of a rotating horizontal wheel. Justification was by hand. This machine was used in the office of the *Warrington Guardian*.

Lanston began his experiments around 1885, and a prototype was built in 1887 which proved a failure. Although it embodied many of the features found in later versions of the 'Monotype' the justification was not successful, and cold type was hammered out by dies. A second machine, this time casting type from molten metal, was built, but was both slow and unreliable. It was not until 1897 that the first successful 'Monotype' machine was built. In that same year a syndicate headed by Lord Dunraven bought the British rights for £220,000 and from then on the development of the 'Monotype' keyboard and caster was in the hands of two independent companies—the Lanston Monotype Machine Company in the U.S.A., and in England the Monotype Corporation Limited. The further development of this machine is described later (see page 286).

Among the factors which aided the expansion of the British printing industry during the Victorian era were the rapid growth of literacy among the working classes, the reduction in 1838 of the excise duty on paper, the repeal of the newspaper stamp tax in 1855, and—outside London—the introduction of the penny post and the spread of the railways. Productivity was now capable of keeping pace with demand; but it was attainable only at the cost of a general lowering of standards.

William Clowes—Multiplier of Books

William Clowes, the founder of the vast printing establishment of William Clowes & Sons Ltd, was born on 1 January, 1779, at Chichester, where he was apprenticed to a printer of that town named Joseph Seagrave—he who printed William Hayley's *Life of Cowper*, with engravings by Blake. His apprenticeship over, Clowes came to London in 1802 and worked as a compositor with Henry Teape, a printer in George Street, Tower Hill. There he remained for two years. About the end of 1803, with the help of friends and what money he had been able to save, he started his own printing office in Villiers Street, Strand. He began with one assistant, a man named Pardoe, and his stock of type was so small that at first he was compelled to work well into the night to print off what he had set so that the type could be distributed ready for the next day's work.

His old master, Joseph Seagrave, gave him his first important job in Villiers Street. This was *A Full and Genuine History of the Inhuman and Unparalleled Murders of Mr William Galley and Mr Daniel Chater* (1813?), a joint publishing venture of Seagrave in association with Longman & Rees. Clowes's business gradually increased, and through his wife, whom he married when he was twenty-four, he managed to secure some useful orders from her cousin, William Winchester, a stationer in the Strand, who supplied the government offices with official forms. Within a few years William Clowes became a printer on quite a large scale and moved to larger premises in Northumberland Court.

Clowes was an industrious man; he had come into the printing trade at a time when it was expanding rapidly, and his main concern was with printing large quantities of work of varying kinds with both accuracy and speed. This latter requirement he found almost impossible to effect with the hand press, and since power-printing had recently become available Clowes installed the newly patented perfecting machine of Applegath and Cowper, becoming, by so doing, the first book printer to make regular use of steam presses.

Unfortunately Clowes's printing office was almost adjoining Northumberland House,★ and the Duke of Northumberland objected violently to the noise and smoke coming from the steam presses. When Clowes failed to abate the nuisance, which he was quite powerless to do if he wanted to continue his business, the Duke began an action against him, and the case was tried in the Court of Common Pleas in June, 1824. The printer won his case, but consented to remove his presses to another neighbourhood on payment of a sum to be determined by arbitration. In the following year he moved to Duke Street, Blackfriars, into the premises which had been previously occupied by Applegath.

There his business prospered, for the move into more extensive premises coincided with the remarkable growth in the demand for works of popular information. In the course of a few years Clowes had installed no fewer than twenty Applegath and Cowper machines, and was busy printing the numerous publications of the Society for the Diffusion of Useful Knowledge, the *Penny Magazine*, edited by Charles Knight (which reached a circulation of 200,000) and the *Penny Cyclopaedia*.

By 1839 Clowes was casting his own types, at a time when typefounding was still considered to be a trade in itself; and, according to a writer in the *Quarterly Review*, he was supplying his compositors with new type at the rate of 50,000 sorts a day;[179] to this he added stereotyping on a large scale. In that year (1839) we are told that

> the number of sheets now standing in type in Messrs Clowes's establishment, each weighing on an average about 100 lbs, are above 1,600. The weight of type not in formes amounts to about 100 tons—the weight of the stereotype plates in their possession to about 2,000 tons: the cost to the proprietors (without including the original composition of the types from which they were cast) about £200,000. The number of wood-cuts is about 50,000, of which stereotype casts are taken and sent to Germany, France, etc.

★ Demolished around 1873.

The statistically minded were likewise informed that 'in the course of a year Messrs Clowes consume white paper enough to make petticoats of the usual dimensions (ten demys per petticoat) for three hundred and fifty thousand ladies!' For that time the establishment of William Clowes was indeed gigantic, and its growth had been exceptionally rapid. Its founder died in 1847, and in the words of Samuel Smiles 'it will probably be admitted that, as the greatest multiplier of books in his day, and as one of the most effective practical labourers for the diffusion of useful knowledge, his name is entitled to be permanently associated, not only with the industrial, but also with the intellectual development of our time'.[180]

CHAPTER TEN

Book Illustration in the Nineteenth Century

During the nineteenth century the use of illustrations in books of every kind greatly increased. The new process of lithography was widely used in the outsize topographical books which were a feature of the first twenty years of the new century. A victim of the increasing demand for books, and particularly inexpensive books, was the copper-plate engraving, which was too costly for a cheap series and too soon gave signs of wear. About 1823 it was replaced by steel engraving, which stood up to a far greater number of impressions; but, despite the fact that artists of the calibre of Turner and Constable tried their hand at it successfully, the fact remains that compared with copper engravings those on steel appeared somewhat hard and cold. Moreover the medium was largely used by second-rate artists employed as hacks by the print-sellers. Volumes of poetry in particular were illustrated with small steel engravings, as were the keepsakes and annuals that became such a feature of the early part of the century. These latter were indeed produced more for their illustrations than for their text. Steel engravings were also used in the many popular volumes of 'picturesque tours', as exemplified in Tombleson's *Views of the Rhine*.

The principal process employed, however, throughout the century, was wood-engraving, but with a change of technique from the white-line employed by Bewick and his followers. This was replaced by a thin black-line illustration, drawn by the artist, but more often than not cut by trade engravers. One of the first periodicals to make use of woodcuts on a large scale was Charles Knight's *Penny Magazine*, founded in 1832, one of the several excellent educational ventures started by that enterprising publisher. The woodcuts for the 305 numbers published cost him £12,000—a very large sum of money in those days. Then came the welcome discovery that woodcuts could be stereotyped, with the result that copies of the same illustration could be printed on more than one machine at a time. Furthermore, if a wood block were irreparably damaged, there was an identical copy to take its place. In 1843 the firm of William Clowes had no fewer than 80,000 woodcuts in stock.

From about 1840 onwards the periodical press used woodcuts on a steadily increasing scale, and in 1842 the first issue of the weekly *Illustrated London News* came out with sixteen pages of letterpress and thirty-two woodcuts. By the middle of the century wood had almost entirely supplanted metal for engravings; most of the early work of Cruikshank was etched, but for the greater part of his life he worked on wood. Other notable illustrators who worked in this medium were 'Phiz' (Hablot K. Browne), who, like Cruikshank, worked for Dickens; John Leech, of *Punch* fame; the amusing Dickie Doyle; and, as the century drew on, we find among the artists drawing on the block such famous names as Rossetti, Millais, Houghton, Du Maurier, Walker, Sandys and Charles Keene. It did not follow that because an artist was a good painter that he was successful in other mediums, and an artist's reputation as an illustrator of books on occasions owed much to his engraver. The Dalziel brothers, who were both publishers and engravers, wrote that Rossetti was an outstanding example of a complete lack of acquaintance with the requirements necessary for drawing on the block. Many artists indulged in a vast amount of often unnecessary cross-hatching, all the whites of which had to be meticulously dug out by the engraver.

The 1860s saw a great vogue for gift books illustrated with wood-engravings, among which were such items as Tennyson's *Poems*, published by Moxon and illustrated by the Pre-Raphaelites Rossetti, Millais, and Holman Hunt, and *The Parables of Our Lord*, illustrated by Millais and published by Routledge in their series known as 'Dalziels Fine Art Gift Books'. For landscape work in this medium Birket Foster was much admired, and his *Pictures of English Landscape* was published in the same series.

Sir J. Tenniel, closely associated with *Punch*, although he contributed to many gift books, is most readily remembered for his delightful illustrations to *Alice in Wonderland* (1865), while Sir John Gilbert, a prolific general illustrator, did some of his best work in the robust drawings (engraved by the Dalziels) for the *Shakespeare* edited by Howard Staunton and published 1858-60.

Another *Punch* artist, Charles Keene, although most of his work was done for that periodical, illustrated a number of books, including Douglas Jerrold's *Mrs Caudle's Curtain Lectures* (1866) and some of the novels (such as Meredith's *Evan Harrington*) which first appeared in the pages of *Once a Week*.

So great was the demand for woodcuts in the 'fifties and 'sixties that the number of skilled wood-engravers increased rapidly. To save time very large cuts, such as those employed in many of the pictorial journals of the period, were made by dividing up the wood block, with the drawing on its surface, among several engravers, after which the separate portions were assembled, bolted together and the joins carefully eliminated. They were then electrotyped and the mounted electros sent to the printer. No longer was it necessary, as in the early days of the news-book, to rely upon the imagination of the artist for scenes of battle, since artists were specially commissioned to send back sketches from the theatres of war, and these were quickly reproduced on wood by staff engravers.

The introduction of photography was at first, until the half-tone process was developed, of considerable assistance to the wood-engraver, after W. L. Thomas of the *Graphic* had managed to transfer a photograph on to the surface of the wood block. The engraver, with his experience in converting wash drawings into line, had little difficulty in coping with the continuous tone of the photograph, and was thus enabled to introduce more life-like effects into the illustration of topical subjects.

In the 'seventies and 'eighties attempts were made to etch a photograph on metal to provide a relief surface for printing with type. One such was the Pretsch process, in which a relief block was obtained by electrotyping from a grained gelatine image, the basic principle of which has been retained in the collotype. But the greatest innovation from the point of view of the periodical press was the introduction of the half-tone process. Fox Talbot seems to have been the first (in his patent of 1852) to suggest the breaking up of the tones of a photograph by means of a screen. Berchtold, in 1857, specified the use of a glass plate 'covered with a multitude of very fine parallel lines close together'. But it was a Leamington firm of photographers, E. and J. Bullock, who first put forward the idea (in 1865) of placing the screen in front of the sensitive plate in the camera, and thus laid the foundation of the present-day half-tone process. It was left to Meissenbach of Munich to popularize the process and make it commercially practical. In England, the half-tone process was first used by the *Graphic*, and by the end of the century the process camera was in general use. Only the jobbing printer continued to use the wood-engraving for advertisements and catalogues. Sadly one of the brothers Dalziel wrote, at the turn of the century: 'By the introduction of the various processes by which artists' drawings are nowadays made applicable for reproduction the days of the wood engraver are practically over, and we have to bow to the new light which we had long felt would come . . . we feel that our occupation is gone.'

The Development of Colour Printing in England

'From the time when the *Boke of St Albans* was published, down to the issue of Le Blon's *Colorito*, a period of nearly 240 years, the voice of the colour printer was scarcely heard in the land.' So writes Burch.[181] In Germany and Italy early printed books were frequently embellished by the hand of the illuminator; an excellent example is the copy in the British Museum of the 42-line Bible printed at Mainz about 1453–5. In England, however, the use of colour in early printed books is almost unknown, except for the red and black printing in service books, the occasional two-colour title and the red printing for rubrics, colophons and inititals. But even the service books were mainly printed abroad for the English market; in fact two-colour printing in England was mainly confined to almanacs. The first specimen of colour work in English printing occurs in the treatise on coat armour in the *Book of St Albans*, 1486, the heraldic shields being coloured in red, blue and brown, in addition to the normal black by press-work, although it is thought that the yellow on some of the shields was added by hand.

Apart from a few roughly coloured woodcuts, illustrations in colour were unknown in England until the time of Le Blon. Johannes Teyler of Nijmegen had produced line engravings in colour around 1670, but nothing similar had been done in England. Jacques Christophe Le Blon (1667–1741), a native of Frankfurt, invented a colour process which consisted of printing successively, and in register, from three mezzotint plates inked in red, blue and yellow. His first prints by this method were produced about 1704, and, having tried without success to exploit his invention commercially in France and Holland, he came to England in 1719, and with the financial help of Colonel Sir John Guise took out English patents and formed a company called the Picture Office. This proved a commercial failure and Le Blon left England in 1732. His theory of colour mezzotint, based on the three primary colours, was set out in *Colorito*, a book published in 1722 with text in English and French and nine full-page mezzotints in colour. However, the proper exploitation of the trichromate process had to wait until the invention of photography and the subsequent half-tone process. Later producers of mezzotints reverted to Teyler's method of laying tints on the single plate.

Edward Kirkall became one of the pioneers of printing in colour by using a sequence of wood blocks appropriately tinted, in what Walpole described as a 'new method of printing, composed of etching, mezzotinto and wooden stamps'. Between 1722 and 1724 Kirkall published a series of chiaroscuros, engraved by himself, in which the outlines and dark parts of the figures were printed from copper plates, and sepia-coloured tints were afterwards superimposed from wood blocks.

In 1754 an English wood-engraver, John Baptist Jackson, brought out his *Essay on the Invention of Engraving and Printing in Chiaro Oscuro* which contained eight prints, four of which were printed in what Jackson called 'proper colours', and which Chatto described rather unfairly as 'egregious failures'.

The predominant methods for book illustration in colour during the early part of the nineteenth century were aquatint in conjunction with hand-colouring. This became very popular as a result of the vogue for illustrated topographical books during the latter part of the eighteenth and the beginning of the nineteenth centuries. The man who did more than any other to popularize this process was Rudolph Ackermann (1764–1834), from whose 'Repository of Arts' in the Strand, London, came a constant flow of colour books. Strangely enough Ackermann, a native of Schneeberg, in Saxony, had been for ten years a saddler and coachbuilder in Germany, France and London, before he established his print shop in the Strand in 1795.

A tremendous amount of work was involved in the hand-tinting (largely done by children) of these illustrations, and one of the most famous of Ackermann's publications, *The Microcosm of London* (1808–11), necessitated the hand-colouring of 104,000 aquatint plates. Rowlandson and other famous artists were contributors to the publications of Ackermann, who also introduced the fashion of the popular English Annuals, the first of which was *Forget-me-not*, published in 1825.

From 1754, when Jackson had published his treatise on chiaroscuro, until 1819, when the first part of William Savage's *Practical Hints on*

Decorative Printing appeared, the only chiaroscuro wood-engravings published in England appear to have been those made about 1783 by an amateur named John Skippe.* Savage (1770–1843) seems to have been the first engraver to realize fully the possibilities of the wood block for colour printing. He set up as a printer and bookseller at Howden, Yorkshire, in 1790, but by 1797 he was in London, and in 1799 was appointed printer to the Royal Institution. He started business on his own account in 1803 and first came to the attention of the public with his printing of Forster's *British Gallery of Engravings* (1807). His *Practical Hints on Decorative Printing*, completed in 1823, contains many chiaroscuro prints as well as prints produced from a large number of wooden blocks. The print of 'Mercy' facing page 116 (painted by W. H. Brooke and engraved by G. W. Bonner) was printed from a suite of 29 blocks, in one of which two colours were introduced, making 30 tints in one working.

Savage wrote also *A Dictionary of the Art of Printing* (1841), and in 1832, after many years spent in experimenting with printing inks, he published his *Preparations in Printing Ink in Various Colours*. Savage's work had no immediate influence, and no further attempts to develop the process were made until George Baxter (1804–1867) turned his attention to it. Basically his method did not differ greatly from that of Savage, except for the use of metal key plates in addition to wood blocks, and the use of oil-colours. Baxter called his process 'Polychromatic Printing', and Robert Mudie, in the preface to his *The Feathered Tribes of the British Islands* (2 vols. 1834), of which the plates were by Baxter, says:

By this method every shade of colour, every breadth of tint, every delicacy of hatching, and every degree of evanescence in the outline can be obtained; and 50,000 facsimiles of a painting may be produced with perfect uniformity and at a moderate expense . . . In carrying this very beautiful branch of the typographic art successfully into effect, Baxter has, I believe, completed what was the last project of the great Bewick, but which that truly original and admirable genius did not live to accomplish.

One of the most successful works (aesthetically, though not commercially) with Baxter colour plates was the *Pictorial Album, or Cabinet of*

---

* Skippe (*c*. 1742–*c*. 1796) was noted chiefly for his series of wood-engravings in chiaroscuro done in imitation of the works of Ugo de Carpi and other early Italian artists. (D. N. B.).

Paintings, published in 1837 by Chapman and Hall, containing eleven colour reproductions of paintings. In 1842 appeared Sir Harris Nicolas's *History of the Orders of Knighthood of the British Empire*, four quarto volumes published by William Pickering and printed by Charles Whittingham, with 21 plates by Baxter in addition to a double-spread title-page in colour, which Ruari McLean claims to be 'one of the finest title-page openings of the century'.[182] Most of the Baxter prints in books were frontispieces only, which were often sold separately as individual prints.

Charles Knight (1791–1873) patented in 1838 a colour-printing process which he called 'Patent Illuminated Printing', by which a picture could be printed from wood or metal blocks in any number of colours from four to sixteen by means of a press fitted with a revolving polygonal frame to which blocks were fitted, each one being brought into position as required. The process was used in two popular educational works, *Old England*, published in 96 parts, 1844–5, and *Old England's Worthies*, 1847. These were the first books with colour plates intended to cater for the popular market, and the result was highly successful from the point of view of the colour plates; but for some reason (possibly expense) Knight made no further use of colour in his succeeding publications.

The appearance in 1836 of J. D. Harding's *Sketches at Home and Abroad* was a landmark in the history of lithography, for it ushered in a series of large books with tinted lithographic views which had a vogue lasting for many years. Tinted lithographs were not new, of course, for Senefelder himself had made them, but Harding's book, thanks to the collaboration of the printer, Hullmandel, showed considerable development. Charles Joseph Hullmandel (1789–1850), whose mastery of the technical details of lithography was joined to a high standard of artistic integrity, did much to bring the art into repute in England. Harding and Hullmandel worked in close collaboration from 1820 onwards and it is almost impossible to tell how much of the developments shown during this period is due to each.

Harding's book used only one tint in addition to black, but that very beautiful book of Thomas Shotter Boys's, *Picturesque Architecture in Paris, Ghent, Antwerp, Rouen* (1839), made use of four tints. Boys, in his dedication to the printer, Hullmandel, pays tribute to his 'many great improvements and highly important discoveries in lithography'. The publishers termed the process 'the new style of Chroma-lithography', but we now use the term chromolithography to denote full colour-printing by lithography.

During the early period, until about 1836, lithographs were occasionally, like aquatints, coloured mainly by hand, but gradually the growing demand for coloured illustration led to the perfecting of chromolithography. An important work historically was the two-volume *Plans, Elevations, Sections and Details of the Alhambra* by Owen Jones and Jules Goury, which Jones produced at his own expense, Goury having died in Spain in 1834. A Welsh architect, Jones approached colour lithography with aims quite different from those which actuated Harding and Boys; he was less interested in providing artistic views than in putting on record in their correct colours the decorations which interested him for professional reasons. Finding that no printer could produce exactly what he wanted he set up his own press, with help from the firm of Day and Haghe in John Street, Adelphi, where he trained his own workmen. Among the 104 plates included in his work on the Alhambra were 69 chromolithographs, the first of their kind to be produced in England. Jones produced several other works, in one of which, *Illuminated Books of the Middle Ages* (1844), he collaborated with another famous illustrator and author, Henry Noel Humphreys.

Humphreys's first successful book was *The Coins of England*, which, published in 1846 by William Smith, reached its sixth edition by 1849. It contained, besides coloured woodcut initials, 24 chromolithograph plates of coins, in copper, silver, and gold, against a background of royal blue. It was the forerunner of many books from the same illustrator, whose work has been sympathetically described in some detail by Ruari McLean in his *Victorian Book Design*, a book indispensable to all students of book illustration in the nineteenth century.[182]

Humphreys was a man of wide interests, with a particular penchant for medieval illumination, to which his own work owes much. *The Miracles of Our Lord*, and *Maxims and Precepts of the Saviour*, both published in 1848, are striking examples of chromolithographed illumination, in which some twelve colours were employed. Many of the large books containing chromolitho plates published during this period were issued in parts to subscribers, and were, understandably, expensive. Lewis Gruner's *Specimens of Oriental Art* (1850), for instance, was published at twelve guineas, a sum which would have to be multiplied five-fold at least to bring it up to present-day values.

Day and Son, the firm which produced several of the illuminated books of Owen Jones, also published in 1861 *The Sermon on the Mount*, with designs by the Liverpool architects W. and G. Audsley, chromolithographed by W. R. Tymms. It was a large book, containing twenty-seven leaves, 22 by 17 inches, printed on one side only, the style of ornament deriving from that of ancient manuscripts. It cost eight guineas. The Audsleys also designed an illuminated edition of Byron's *Prisoner of Chillon* (1865), as well as several books on design and ornament. An attempt to introduce colour gravure was made in the 1850s, after Paul Pretsch of Vienna had come to England and formed the Photo-galvanographic Company to exploit his process of intaglio printing, which was somewhat akin to collotype. In 1857 a way was found to colour Pretsch's photogravures, but the business failed and Pretsch returned to Vienna. Another Austrian, Karl Klic (1841–1926), was largely responsible for the present half-tone method of photogravure (see page 262), but machine-coloured photogravure did not become a practical proposition until well into the twentieth century. In 1903 the firm of George Newnes brought out what was to have been a quarterly publication called *The Ideal Magazine* with colour photogravure executed by the Art Photogravure Company, but the high price deterred the general public and only one number was issued.

Towards the end of the nineteenth century there was a general revival of printing in colours from wood blocks, for the success of which Edmund Evans was largely responsible. Born in Southwark, London, in 1826, Evans was, like Birket Foster, his senior by one year, apprenticed to Ebenezer Landells (one of the founders of *Punch*) and in 1847 he went into business on his own account as printer and wood-engraver. His first colour printing of importance was an edition of the *Poems by Oliver Goldsmith* (1858) with drawings by Birket Foster and ornaments by H. N. Humphreys. From 1858 onwards he published the very popular 'Common Objects' series, among which was Thomas Miller's *Common Wayside Flowers* with drawings by Foster. Evans's chief claim to fame may well be his introduction to a delighted public of a number of children's books with coloured illustrations by Walter Crane, Randolph Caldecott and Kate Greenaway. All three were artists who not only entered into the spirit of the books they illustrated but were adepts at the application of flat tones of pure colour, applied so simply that they facilitated the work of engraver and colour printer.

CHAPTER ELEVEN

Two Famous Presses

The Chiswick Press

For a century and a half the name of the Chiswick Press stood for good printing and book design. The imprint was first used in 1811 by its founder, Charles Whittingham the Elder (1767–1840), who after serving his apprenticeship with a Coventry printer came to London in 1789 and set up a press in Fetter Lane, beginning in a very humble way as a jobbing printer. In 1807 he had premises in Goswell Street, and three years later, after taking into partnership his foreman, Robert Rowland, he left the city business in the latter's hands and himself went to live at Chiswick, where in 1809 he had started a paper pulp manufactory. He leased High House, Chiswick, and there set up a press, where he continued to work until his death in 1840.

The elder Whittingham owed his success largely to his small editions of the classics of English literature, which were well printed for their modest price; his books were notable for the excellence of their wood-engravings, in the machining of which he was unsurpassed. He was one of the first in England to use a steam engine for making paper pulp, though he never used steam power for printing.

In 1803 John Sharpe of Piccadilly began to issue the 'British Classics' series, all of which were printed by the elder Whittingham. *The Spectator*, in eight octavo volumes, was the first work in this series which was illustrated, or 'embellished' as Whittingham would have said, with engravings by the best artists of the time. For Thomas Tegg of Cheapside he printed a series of duodecimo volumes, also illustrated with small woodcuts, known as 'Whittingham's Cabinet Library'.

About the time that the elder Whittingham was founding the Chiswick Press, his nephew, who bore the same name, was apprenticed to his uncle. The younger Whittingham was made a freeman of the Stationers' Company in 1817, and in the following year went to Paris with an introduction to the Didots. In 1824 his uncle took him into partnership, and the following year saw their joint production of Singer's *Shakespeare* in ten volumes. However, the partnership was dissolved in 1828 and Charles Whittingham the Younger started his own printing office at 21, Took's Court, off Chancery Lane. There he began his fruitful association with the publisher William Pickering (1796–1854).

Pickering had started off as a second-hand bookseller in 1820, but soon went into the publishing business and first made his name with the 'Diamond Classics', described as 'the smallest edition of the Classics ever published'. The books were set in diamond type, which is so small (equivalent to 4½-point) that it cannot easily be read without a magnifying glass, a fact which did not, however, interfere with their success. The first titles in the series were printed by C. Corrall, of Charing Cross, and the remainder by Thomas White, D. Sidney and the younger Whittingham. One of this series is thought to have been the first book to be bound in cloth instead of the paper-covered boards in use at the time.

Pickering then turned his attention to books in a larger format, and Thomas White printed for him a number of his early books, including an edition of *The Canterbury Tales* in 5 volumes (1822), a publishing venture Pickering shared with Richard and Septimus Prowitt. In 1825 Pickering published, in association with Talboys and Wheeler of Oxford, a series of 'Oxford English Classics' in forty-four volumes. In 1827 White printed for him an edition of *The Treatyse of Fysshinge wyth an Angle* from the *Book of St Albans*, though not, as has been stated, with a fount of Baskerville's types, but in Fry's No. 1 pica, based on Baskerville.

Pickering was one of the first to do away with the crowded and cumbersome title-page so prevalent in books of the early nineteenth century, and in 1828 he found in Charles Whittingham of Took's Court a printer whose ideas on the subject of book design were in harmony with his own. Simplicity was the keynote of the Pickering style, and can be seen at its best in the 'Aldine' edition of the British poets which he began with Whittingham in 1830, and which ran to fifty-three volumes published between that date and 1853. The title-page of each volume bore Aldus Manutius's device of the dolphin and anchor with the words ALDI DISCIP. ANGLUS. Not that he servilely imitated the style of the printer whose work he so much admired, but, like that of Aldus, his work was mainly devoid of ornament.

Nevertheless Pickering did not neglect ornament entirely, but 'he made it keep its place'. If he used a border or an ornament it was never allowed to subdue the lettering. In some of his reprints of early classics Pickering made use of woodcuts, nearly all of which were done by Mary Byfield, who worked for the Chiswick Press nearly all her life. Her masterpiece was the Book of Common Prayer, printed at Took's Court in 1853. This was based on the so-called 'Queen Elizabeth's Prayer Book' printed by John Day in 1569, and for it Mary Byfield cut more than a hundred blocks, which harmonize perfectly with the Caslon old-face type in which the book is set.

From 1840 onwards Whittingham and Pickering had been experimenting with Caslon's types, at that time outmoded, and using Caslon capitals on some of the title-pages of books published by Pickering. In 1844 Whittingham printed two books set in Caslon's old-face: one was *The Temple* by George Herbert, for Pickering; the other *The Diary of Lady Willoughby* for Longman, though which was the earlier is still a matter of conjecture. The *Diary* met with considerable success, and led to the gradual reintroduction of old-faces into English printing, though for many years they were used only for devotional or gift books.

Here is the Chiswick Press account for the printing of the *Diary*:

1844.	£	s	d
April 1. Printing 750 'Diary' Lady Willoughby.			
Twenty-two sheets and a half fcap. 4to.			
rules, cuts, side-notes, etc. @ 45s.	50	12	6
Corrections £6.8.0; pressing £1.2.6	7	10	6
Woodcut arms	4	0	0
Printing 750 labels and slips, and white paper (2 qrs.)	0	11	0
Printing 750 labels, straw-coloured paper	0	7	6
	63	1	6

A further 1,000 copies were printed towards the end of December and this was followed by a small edition (500) of *Some further portions of the Diary of Lady Willoughby* in November, 1847, with a further 1,500 in March, 1848.

About 1840 the Chiswick Press acquired a very fine collection of head- and tail-pieces, borders and other typographical ornaments.

No other printer in Europe, [writes John Southward], could boast of a similar collection, either in regard to number or excellence. The best books of the great printers were searched for designs, and these, if approved of, were copied. Many of them afforded suggestions for better designs and these suggestions were carried out.[183]

One curious work printed by the Chiswick Press for Pickering was Oliver Byrne's *The First Six Books of the Elements of Euclid*, 'in which coloured diagrams and symbols are used instead of letters for the greater ease of learners'. This was one of the few books printed in colour by the Chiswick Press. Each proposition of Euclid was set in Caslon italic, with a four-line initial engraved on wood, and the pages were enlivened by diagrams and symbols in brilliant colours, 'attaining a verve not seen again on book pages till the days of Dufy, Matisse and Derain' says Ruari McLean.[184]

On the death of his uncle in 1840 the entire business had passed into the hands of the nephew, and he carried on both businesses until 1848, in which year he was made a liveryman of the Stationers' Company. Although the lease of Took's Court expired in 1849, he returned there in 1852.

During the 1840s Whittingham printed for Pickering a series of reprints of the Prayer Book, comprising the six Books of Common Prayer from that of Edward VI, 1549, to Charles II's of 1662. These were printed on hand-made paper, in red and black Old English type, with title-pages and ornaments similar to those used in the original editions. A seventh volume was a Prayer Book for contemporary use, known as the 'Victoria' Prayer Book (1844), also set in black-letter, rubricated, with a magnificent but somewhat overpowering wood-engraved border to the title-page made up of the arms of all the sees.

Pickering died in 1854 and, though Charles Whittingham the Younger lived until 1876, he retired from business in 1860, and in 1880 the Chiswick Press was acquired by George Bell.★ 'The world of printing, after the Whittingham-Pickering period', write the authors of *A Survey of Printing*, 'passed into something worse than the meanness and squalor of the late seventeenth and eighteenth centuries;'[185] but that stricture never applied to the Chiswick Press even in its later days. In 1885 Charles Jacobi, who had been an apprentice with the firm, became manager of the Chiswick Press, and later on a partner. Although no innovator, Jacobi successfully maintained the high reputation of the firm, which continued to produce many excellent books. When the Roxburghe Club brought out its magnificent *Epistole et*

★ John Wilkins, Whittingham's partner, was in charge from 1860 to 1880.

Evangelii et Lectioni Volgari in Lingua Toscana (1910) with facsimile reproductions by Emery Walker of the woodcuts of the Florentine edition of 1495, the Chiswick Press printed it.

Just as, in the days of Whittingham, the Press had been highly regarded for the excellence of its engravings and fitting use of ornaments, so, after its amalgamation in 1919 with the firm of William Griggs,★ it gained a deserved reputation for its work in collotype. The founder of the firm of Griggs, who died in 1911, had been for many years the most skilful reproducer of works of art in Britain.

After a century and a half of notable work the Chiswick Press ceased to exist in 1962. The Press's historic collection of blocks, punches, and matrices is now on permanent loan to the St Bride's Foundation Printing Library, and the firm's ledgers can be consulted in the Manuscript Department of the British Museum.

Among the periodicals printed by the Chiswick Press was *The Hobby Horse* (1886–92), a magazine devoted to the crafts and edited by Herbert Horne and Selwyn Image. It was an example of 'antiquarian' printing, set in Caslon Old Style, and contributed in a small measure to the revival of interest in fine printing which culminated in the work of William Morris and the private presses which came after him. Most of the initials and tail-pieces used in *The Hobby Horse* were designed by Herbert Horne, and were inspired by those of the incunabula period.

William Morris and the Kelmscott Press

Like Baskerville, William Morris took up printing late in life, and although his interest in fine books was life-long, his practical participation in the craft was determined by a lantern lecture given by Emery Walker to the Arts and Crafts Exhibition Society on 15 November, 1888. Miss May Morris writes that 'during the time when he was writing *The House of the Wolfings* (published 1888), his taste of younger days for early printed books had been developing into a practical interest in all the details of fine printing'.[186]

Walker, of whom Sir Sydney Cockerell wrote 'It is scarcely too much to say that his influence direct or indirect can be discerned in nearly every well-designed page of type that now appears', was the man directly responsible for Morris's active interest in the production of printed books, and in November, 1889, we find Morris writing to

---

★ The name of the firm was changed to Charles Whittingham and Griggs.

F. S. Ellis: 'I really am thinking of turning printer myself in a small way; the first step to that would be getting a new fount cut. Walker and I both think Jenson's the best model, taking all things into consideration.'[187] In the following month Morris asked Walker to go into partnership with him as a printer, and although Walker was unable to accept the offer, the founding of a press was decided upon.

In December, 1889, Morris began to design his first type, which he based on Jenson's roman as used in Pliny's *Natural History*. At first he called the type, the punches of which were cut by Edward Prince of Islington,* the Jenson-Morris, but later the 'Golden Type', because it was to be used (and wasn't) in an edition of *The Golden Legend* which Morris had set his heart on printing, and which was eventually printed in a black-letter to which he gave the name of Troy.† The Golden type, which was cast at the Fann Street Foundry of Sir Charles Reed & Son, was the first fount to be used at Morris's press, to which he gave the name of the Kelmscott Press, and which was situated in a cottage near his house on the Upper Mall, Hammersmith. The first book issued by the Kelmscott Press was Morris's own *The Story of the Glittering Plain*, completed in April, 1891. Morris was fifty-eight when what he called his 'little typographical adventure' began.

Morris's crowning achievement was beyond doubt his production of the *Works of Geoffrey Chaucer*, on which he laboured for nearly four years. It was printed in black and red, in double column, in Morris's Chaucer type, with headings to the longer poems in Troy type. These two founts were black-letter, based on early German models, the Chaucer being a smaller version of the Troy, which was found to be too large for the body-text of the Chaucer. (Incidentally this type was pirated by a Leipzig firm and advertised as *Die amerikanische Triumph-Gothisch*.)

The book, of which 425 copies were printed on hand-made paper supplied by Joseph Batchelor of Little Chart, Kent, and 13 on vellum, by Henry Band of Brentford, contained 87 illustrations designed by Sir Edward Burne-Jones and engraved on wood by W. H. Hooper, as well as 14 large borders, 18 frames and 26 initials designed by Morris. The book was completed on 8 May, 1896; Morris died on 3 October of that year.

The Kelmscott Press was at first installed, on 12 January, 1891, in a

---

* Prince died in 1923. He cut the punches for the types of many private presses.
† This book was so long in the press that it was nicknamed 'The Interminable'.

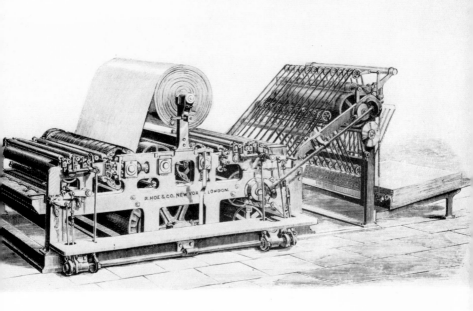

The first Hoe Web Press used in England was installed in the printing office of *Lloyd's Weekly Newspaper* in 1871

Hoe ten-cylinder rotary-type revolving press, as used by *The Times* in 1857–8

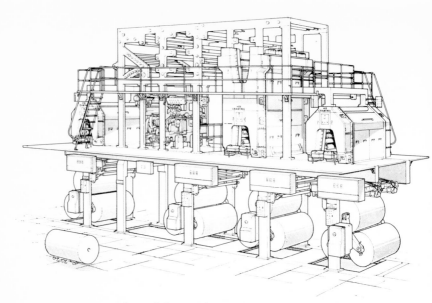

A 3-unit 'Viceroy' press. 2-colour half decks

The machine room, Southern Newspapers Ltd, Southampton

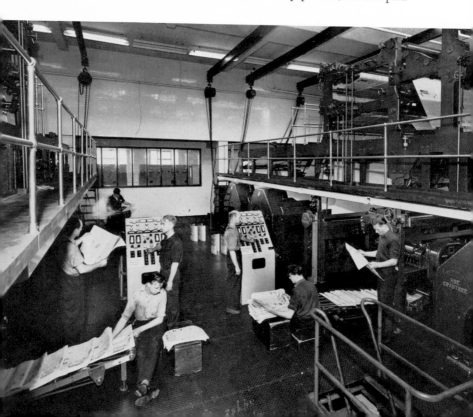

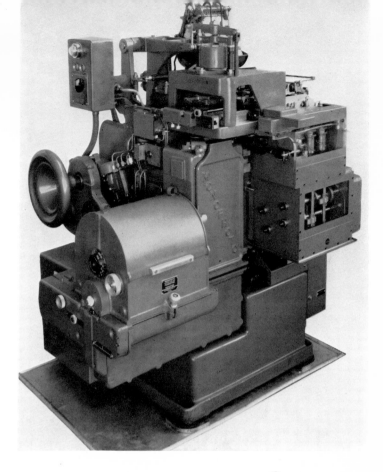

A 'Monophoto' Filmsetter

A diagram of the optical system of a 'Monophoto' Filmsetter

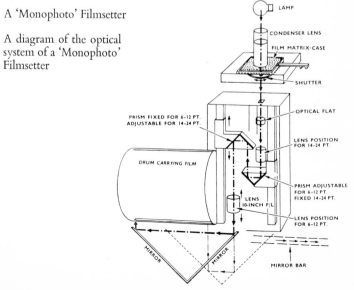

LAMP

CONDENSER LENS

FILM MATRIX-CASE

SHUTTER

PRISM FIXED FOR 6-12 PT.
ADJUSTABLE FOR 14-24 PT.

OPTICAL FLAT

LENS POSITION
FOR 14-24 PT.

DRUM CARRYING FILM

PRISM ADJUSTABLE
FOR 6-12 PT.
FIXED 14-24 PT.

LENS POSITION
FOR 6-12 PT.

LENS
10-INCH F/L

MIRROR

MIRROR

MIRROR BAR

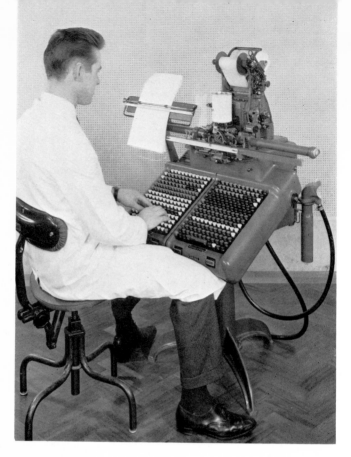

A Standard English 'Monotype' keyboard machine,
fitted with '14 × 12' hot-metal keybutton banks

Operator at illuminated make-up table

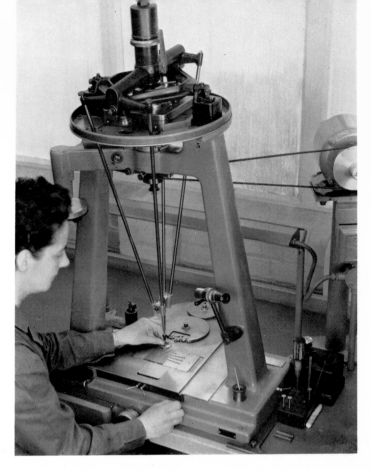

Punch-cutting machine without cover, with
operator cutting Gill Sans Cap. V. Pattern

A '16 × 17' hot-metal matrix case

Intertype 'Fotosetter' machine

Harrison automatic vertical press

D.P.E. 20″ × 30″ letterpress jobber

A 'Monotype' composition caster

L & M high-speed Miehle

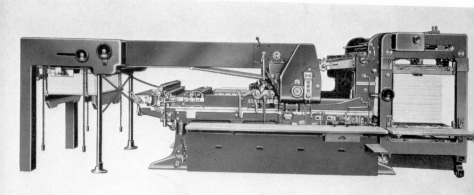

cottage at 16, Upper Mall, Hammersmith, but was later moved to larger premises in Sussex House, next door to its original home. On 26 November, 1891, Morris bought from Hopkinson and Cope, of 103, Farringdon Road, 'one Super Royal genuine Albion Press complete' for £42.10s.0d. During the printing of the Chaucer another press was added and the two were almost continuously at work.

After the death of Morris, the Kelmscott Press was continued for a while by Sydney Cockerell and F. S. Ellis, ceasing publication in 1898 with the founder's *Note on his aims in founding the Kelmscott Press*. The total number of books issued by the Press was 52, in 66 volumes. In addition to the *Chaucer*, outstanding books from the Kelmscott Press included a reprint of Caxton's translation, *The Recuyell of the Historyes of Troye* (1892), in which the Troy and Chaucer types were used for the first time; the *Poetical Works of Percy Bysshe Shelley* (3 vols. 1894–5); Morris's *News from Nowhere* (1892), probably the author's most widely read work; and his *Earthly Paradise* (8 vols. 1896–7).

Even during the last years of his life Morris's energy was unflagging. He himself, in addition to supervising the press, drew 644 of the initials, borders and decorative designs used in the Kelmscott Press books. Of the seven years during which the Kelmscott Press was in existence, Morris was in sole charge for five—the last five years of his life. In that short space of time he exerted an influence on printing that was widespread and lasting, though on the nature of that influence opinions vary.

The Kelmscott books were beautiful, of their kind. 'It was the essence of my undertaking,' wrote Morris, 'to produce books which it would be a pleasure to look upon as pieces of printing and arrangement of type'. But their kind is alien to our modern preference for simplicity. They are heavy in appearance and over-ornate. The archaic type is difficult to read for those unused to seeing early printed books, and the flowery decoration, so typical of the period, often has the appearance of a garden run riot. Moreover the throwback to medievalism in the printing of books savours too much of the retrograde passion for 'mock Tudor' in architecture. The supreme virtue of Morris's 'typographical adventure' was his insistence on good workmanship, fine materials and careful press-work. Nothing was too much trouble for Morris, and in his striving for perfection as he saw it he studied carefully all the contributory crafts which go to the making of a book. One can dispute the beauty of his books, but one cannot belittle his ideals, and his attempt to give the world 'books whose only ornament is the necessary and essential beauty which arises out of the fitness of a piece of craftsmanship for the use which it is made for'.

The conditions under which Morris worked made it inevitable that his books should be costly; his own predilections in art and literature made it likewise inevitable that his books should have a limited appeal. For these reasons he was sometimes attacked by those who, knowing Morris to be a Socialist, considered that he should have produced books for the masses. A certain Arthur Pendenys took a whole page in *The Books of Tomorrow* for the publication of an open letter to the author-printer, in which he said:

> Dear William Morris,
>
> I presume that the Kelmscott Books are published for your own amusement, because I have enquired extensively and find that they do not amuse anyone else. They are very dull books . . . You ignore the masters of printing—Bodoni, Foulis, Baskerville and Whittingham—all these men printed books in readable type and of a convenient size at a moderate price.
>
> If you were consistent your Printing Press would exist for the sake of spreading knowledge. As it is your publications appeal to capitalists and others of the wealthy classes. . . . Your books are *bric-a-brac* and they appeal only to a class which I am told you are continually condemning.[188]

As books the productions of the Kelmscott Press lie off the main stream of printing in a backwater of their own. But the ideas behind them fecundated the work of a series of private presses which sprang up under the example of William Morris and through them exerted in turn a considerable influence on the more enlightened printers of commercial books. There had been private presses in England long before William Morris, but none of them had in any way influenced the general trend of book printing.

Among the private presses which sprang up at the turn of the century the best-known were the Ashendene Press, the Vale Press, the Eragny Press, the Essex House Press, and the Doves Press. The last-named was run by Emery Walker, the former colleague of Morris at the Kelmscott Press, in conjunction with T. J. Cobden-Sanderson, a well-known bookbinder. The most famous work produced by the Doves Press was the folio Bible issued in 1905, which in quality of press-work and typography may justly be compared with that of

Baskerville. The lovely initial letters were drawn by one of the finest of modern calligraphers, Edward Johnston.

The Doves Press had its own typeface, based on Jenson, but whereas Morris had sought to thicken it, so that, in his own words, it tended rather more to the Gothic than Jenson's, the Doves Press face was Jenson fined down. As in the case of the Kelmscott Press, the punches were cut by Edward Prince and the hand-made paper (rather thinner than that used by Morris) was supplied by Joseph Batchelor. The Doves Press issued fewer books than the Kelmscott and, unlike Morris, Cobden-Sanderson eschewed decoration entirely. Unfortunately, although his books achieved great beauty in their simplicity, and the utmost care was bestowed upon composition and press-work, no attempt was made to vary the style of successive books.

Founded by Lucien Pissarro in 1894, the Eragny Press was named after the Norman village where Lucien had worked with his father, Camille Pissarro. A friend of Charles Ricketts, whose Vale Press was founded in 1896, Pissarro obtained permission to print with the Vale Type (a roman fount derived from Jenson) on condition that the books printed with this new type were issued through the Vale Press, and the first sixteen Eragny Press books were issued to Vale Press subscribers. The Vale Press closed down in 1903 and in the following year Pissarro designed the Brook Type (his press having been removed to The Brook, Hammersmith, in 1900). Thirty-two books were printed at the Eragny Press, mostly small volumes, many of which contained coloured wood-engravings drawn by Pissarro and engraved either by himself or by his English wife, Esther.

CHAPTER TWELVE

Further Nineteenth Century Developments

North of the Border

The early years of the nineteenth century saw the emergence of Edinburgh as a great centre of literary production and the seat of some important printing and publishing enterprises. Eminent among the publishers of the Scottish capital was Archibald Constable, the first publisher, as Sir Walter Scott remarked, to break in upon 'the monopoly of the London trade'. To him more than anyone was due the rise of Edinburgh as a centre of scholarship once he had established the *Edinburgh Review* in 1802 and attracted to it a distinguished body of contributors. A man of great enterprise, he was judged extremely rash when in 1807 he paid 1,000 guineas for Scott's poem *Marmion*; but by 1825 he had sold 36,000 copies. His career belongs more to the history of bookselling and publishing than to that of printing; the disastrous end to that career has been recounted in Lockhart's *Life of Sir Walter Scott* and elsewhere. Having gone 'too far when money was plentiful', as Scott wrote later, he was involved in the financial crisis which in 1827 ruined several printing and publishing firms, and the collapse of his business also involved the printing firm of James Ballantyne and Co., who had printed Scott's *Minstrelsy of the Scottish Border* in 1802, and who had been largely financed by the author of the Waverley novels.

Constable's great rival in Edinburgh was William Blackwood, who began business as a bookseller in 1804, and founded the magazine which still bears his name, the first number of which appeared in April, 1817. One of Blackwood's outstanding publications was the *Edinburgh Encyclopaedia* in eighteen quarto volumes. Another famous Edinburgh firm was that of Adam Black, which came to the fore when Black, after the fall of Constable and Ballantyne, acquired the copyright of the *Encyclopaedia Britannica*, which had been Constable's property since 1812. Later he purchased the copyright of Scott's Waverley novels and other works. The firm became known as Adam and Charles Black after the former had taken his nephew into partnership.

Robert and William Chambers, the sons of a muslin weaver of Peebles, started in a small way of business. At the age of sixteen Robert opened a small bookstall in Leith Street, Edinburgh, and when he undertook the editorship of a small weekly periodical called the *Kaleidoscope*, William taught himself to print, and with an old fount of type and a clumsy wooden press which he had bought for three pounds, set up and worked off all the impressions.

In 1823 Robert Chambers, while still only twenty years old, produced the *Traditions of Edinburgh*, printed by his brother. The first edition makes a curious contrast with the handsome edition of the same book published in 1869. In 1832 appeared the first number of *Chambers' Edinburgh Journal*, which was an immediate success. It was William who started it, but almost at once Robert was called in as editor, and the two brothers finally entered into partnership as publishers.

The House of Nelson, still one of the largest printing and publishing firms in Britain, was founded by Thomas Nelson, a native of Throsk, near Stirling, who after acquiring some experience of the publishing business in London, started as a bookseller in a small way of business at the corner of West Bow, Edinburgh, about 1798. His eldest son, William Nelson, built up the business considerably, and was later joined by his younger brother, Thomas, who was the originator of the extensive series of school books for which the firm soon gained a reputation. A printing office was added to the firm within thirty years of its inception, and one of the periodicals printed by the firm, the *Family Treasury*, had a large circulation during the latter half of the century.

During this period Edinburgh was responsible for a great deal of printing for the London market, for excellence of machining was the hallmark of a number of printers in the Scottish capital, notably T. and A. Constable, J. and J. Gray, Ballantyne and Hanson, and R. and R. Clark.

Printing the Bible

In the nineteenth century the market for Bibles was greatly increased by the spread of Sunday Schools, the efforts of the missionary societies, and in general by what is known as the 'Bible Movement', which began in 1804, fostered by the British and Foreign Bible Society founded in that year. Within ten years of the formation of this society one 'auxiliary' or more in each county brought the whole of England into touch with the Bible House in London. Two years later, 236 'auxiliaries' and 305 'branches' were spread over the United Kingdom.*

The exclusive copyright in Bibles was then, as now, in the hands of the University Presses of Oxford and Cambridge and the Royal Printers, who, at the beginning of the century, were George Eyre and Andrew Strahan. At this time nearly half the Bibles, Prayer Books, and Church service books produced in England were printed at Oxford, where this field of printing had become so important that in 1688 a 'Bible Press' had been set up as a special department, separated from the 'Learned' or Classical Press.

In 1820 the output of the 'Bible Press' at Oxford was some three-quarters of a million books, and in 1822 there were on sale nineteen editions of the Bible, nine of the New Testament, and twenty-one Prayer Books, ranging in price from £5.10s.0d. for a Royal Folio Bible to eightpence for a nonpareil 24mo Prayer Book. In 1895 seventy-eight editions of the Bible were available at Oxford.

In a work like the Bible, which contains nearly 800,000 words, and of which every page in an average octavo edition is printed from some 5,000 pieces of metal, the possibility of errors due to displacement of letters is very great, despite the vigilance of proof readers. When in 1806 George Woodfall set about printing a new quarto edition of the Bible for the King's Printers, basing the copy on the Cambridge edition, numerous errors were detected in the Cambridge copy; a comparison with the contemporary Oxford edition showed that it also abounded in errors. Today we may safely say that no edition of the Bible can be termed, as were John Field's in the seventeenth century, 'egregiously erroneous', for once stereotyping had become general practice an accurate text could be reproduced without trouble.

A complete Bible is a book of more than a thousand pages in the normal format, and therefore the introduction of the paper which came to be termed 'Oxford India' met with an immediate welcome. This extremely thin, yet tough and opaque, paper, was first tried at the Oxford Press about 1842 and, according to Henry Frowde, a former publisher to the University, it was brought to England from

---

* See William Canton: *The Bible and the Anglo-Saxon People.* 1914.

the Far East and with it were printed 'twenty-four copies of the smallest Bible then in existence', a 24mo one of which was exhibited at the Paris Exhibition of 1900. This was apparently a hand-made paper, but the India paper developed later was machine-made. The India Paper Bible of 1875, the paper for which was made at Wolvercote paper mill, which the Clarendon Press had bought in 1870, sold a quarter of a million copies in the space of a few weeks. According to Harry Carter the monopoly for this paper was shared by the Oxford University Press and the firm of Brittains, makers of thin copying and other papers.*

In 1829 the King's Printers, in England alone, sold 51,500 Bibles and 75,691 Testaments, and throughout the century there was keen competition between them and the two University Presses to capture the growing market for cheap editions of the Bible. Unfortunately for the printers the demand was more and more for those published at lowest cost.

Between 1804 and 1819 the British and Foreign Bible Society had printed cheap Bibles for the poor in the five languages spoken in Great Britain and Ireland; namely English, Welsh, Irish, Gaelic and Manx—as well as in French for the inhabitants of the Channel Islands. The first 'Highland' New Testament had been printed in Edinburgh in 1767; the Bible Society published its first Gaelic Bible in 1807. The first printed book in the Manx tongue seems to have been a Gospel of St Matthew issued in 1748. A Manx version of the Old Testament was published in two octavo volumes in 1773, and in 1775 a small number of copies of the complete Manx Bible were issued. The British and Foreign Bible Society produced its Manx New Testament in 1810 and the Bible in Manx in 1819. 'But,' remarks William Canton, 'apparently there was in the Isle little or none of that pathetic clinging to the mother-tongue which is associated with the Keltic races. In 1825 an intimation was received from the Bishop that the Manx people preferred now to have the English Authorized Version.'

In 1877 Cambridge began to issue their Cambridge Bible for Schools and in 1881 and 1884 the New and Old Testaments in the Revised Version were published jointly with the Oxford University Press. From 1653 to 1871 demands had been made from time to time both by clergy and scholars for a revision of the King James version

---

* Carter, H. *Wolvercote Mill*. Oxford Bibliographical Society, N.S., extra publication, 1957.

of the Bible, but it was not until 1870 that a committee was appointed by the Convocation of Canterbury to prepare a thorough revision of the whole Bible.

The New Testament was completed in November, 1880, and published on 17 May, 1881, when a copy was presented to Queen Victoria. This proved to be one of the most sensational events in the publishing history of the nineteenth century. The Oxford Press alone sold a million copies on the first day of publication, and it is said that all day the streets around Paternoster Row were blocked by the succession of wagons carrying parcels of them to the railways for distribution.

A curiosity of Bible printing was the Caxton Memorial Bible, printed for the opening of the great Caxton Exhibition on 30 June, 1877, of which one hundred copies were printed and bound within the space of twelve hours. Printing began at Oxford at two o'clock on the morning of the opening day, and one hundred copies, each of 1,052 pages, were printed, artificially dried, and despatched to London by the 9 a.m. express. There they were bound at the O.U.P. bindery in turkey morocco, with gold lettering and the arms of the University on the side, and ten copies were delivered to the Exhibition by two o'clock in the afternoon.

Another curiosity of Bible printing was the New Testament printed in gold on porcelain paper by Thomas De La Rue in 1831 and presented to William IV in the same year. According to Timperley two years had been spent in perfecting the work, the gold in which was valued at five guineas. De La Rue's firm were specialists in gold printing and it was on 29 June, 1838, that the *Sun* newspaper was at his suggestion and with his aid printed in gold in honour of Queen Victoria's coronation, though the actual printers of the newspaper were William Clowes and Sons Ltd. According to Burch 'the text was rubbed over with a mixture of varnish and gold size whilst the sheets were still wet from the press, and bronze powder was then applied'.[189] One hundred thousand copies of the gold *Sun* were published.

Display Faces and Ornamented Types

The first attempts at display in book printing were made by employing a type much larger than the body-text for those portions of the book which called for relief or emphasis, for by the end of the fifteenth century the illuminator and professional rubricator had practically disappeared and the printer himself had to devise some means of enlivening a monotonous page or calling attention to a title or chapter heading. In fact the grouping of the words of a title in a short line in a contrasting fount or larger body-size over the text of the page was the first stage in what we have come to call display.

The use of ornamental initials was one way of relieving the austerity of a printed page and this method was employed from an early date, although certain of the finest printers abjured them. But it was not until the end of the seventeenth century that to the standard roman, italic, and black-letter types was added the decorated type, which flourished in France throughout the eighteenth century thanks to the vogue established by Fournier le Jeune, the real originator of the *lettre de fantaisie* in typography.

Strangely enough the first complete decorated fount known to the typography of Western Europe is an English design called Union Pearl, and described by Mores as 'a letter of fancy'.[190] It is an open script type, the interstices bearing circular nodules which gave rise to the name 'pearl'. Its earliest known use is in 1708, and it came from Grover's foundry. Matrices were later acquired by Messrs Stephenson, Blake and Co. Ltd, who were selling founts of this type as late as 1939. Earlier than this a French decorated type was used on the title-page of a play *La Devineresse* published in 1680, but capitals only are shown. Some of the early French decorated types may have been suggested by the woodcut titling of the first French periodical news-paper, the *Gazette* (1632), reproduced in Thibaudeau's *La Lettre d'Imprimerie*.

At all events, Union Pearl did not make much headway in England, and remains a typographical curiosity, with no immediate successors. Ornamented and display types were in the main a product of the nineteenth century; used chiefly by the jobbing printer, whose market had expanded with the growth of commercial advertising, and al-though sometimes used on the title-pages of books, the display types of the nineteenth century were first and foremost advertising types.

The development of display type in the early part of the nineteenth century began with the so-called 'fat faces', for the exaggeration of the thick strokes of a letter was a fairly obvious way of securing emphasis. According to Mores, Thomas Cottrell, one-time apprentice of Caslon, cut a '*Prescription* or *Posting letter* of great bulk and dimen-sion as high as to the measure of 12 l. of *pica*'.[191] But the real inventor of the fat face is thought, on the evidence of Hansard and Savage, to have been Robert Thorne, Cottrell's apprentice, who in 1819 was commissioned by the Imprimerie Royale to cut for them a fat face. Hansard disliked them, writing of the 'folly of fat-faced preposterous disproportions'.[192]

Although fat faces, as distinct from bold faces, were intended for posters, playbills and broadsides rather than for book-work, nevertheless we often come across them on the title-pages of popular chapbooks. Soon, in the words of Seán Jennett, 'an invasion of fat faces laid waste the typographical landscape of this country; and through this country, that of other countries also'. France, Germany and Holland accepted them with enthusiasm, and the Paris jobber was able to acquire a *Didot extra-gras* in both roman and italic, to which was given the name of *normande* in type-specimens.

In the later years of the nineteenth century fat faces gradually dropped out of the founders' specimen books, but they were occasionally used and one or two have been revived in recent times. The American Typefounders showed their Ultra Bodoni in 1928. It was well named, says A. F. Johnson, 'for that is exactly what a fat face is —an exaggerated design after the true classical modern face or Bodoni'.[193] In 1934 the Kynoch Press showed a 30-point, 48-point, and 60-point Elephant.

Two other innovations followed hard on the success of the fat face —the first, originally given the name of Antique, but later given the alternative name of Egyptian, was characterized by slab serifs and uniform thickness throughout. It was first shown in an 1815 specimen book of Vincent Figgins, but whether he or Thorne was responsible for the design is not certain. The second face, in this case originally called Egyptian, was likewise of uniform thickness, but had no serifs, and was apparently the first unserifed lettering to be used in print. It was first cut in 1816 by William Caslon IV, but failed to attain any measure of popularity until it was revived in the 1830s under various names, among them Grotesque and Sans Serif. 'All these letters', writes Stanley Morison, 'ministered to the need for black, bold types and were predominantly used in job printing.'[194]

The first shadowed letters were fat faces in white outline with strong black shadow. Later, similar treatment was accorded to the Egyptians, though with less success, for as Nicolette Gray points out, 'slab serifs do not lend themselves to opening and the designer has never got it quite clear whether his letter is to be open or shadowed'.[195] Nevertheless the Egyptian family proved both prolific and long-lived, for the present century has seen several Egyptians of improved design, among which we may pick out Rockwell, Memphis, and Karnak, the first-named in particular having proved extremely popular.

One reason for the popularity of Egyptians was that they were soon found to be more suitable for commercial printing than the fat faces, the hairlines of which were easily damaged. A very good example of the use of heavy bold Egyptians and fat faces is shown in a travel notice printed in black on yellow paper by Nichols of Cranbourne Street about 1830, a copy of which is among the Oxford University Press collection of ephemera.

If Thorne's innovations were looked upon with disfavour by the purists, they made money for William Thorowgood, who bought Thorne's factory in 1820 and that of Dr Edmund Fry eight years later. Fry, retiring from business after forty-six years, looked back with regret at the abandonment of the Old Style faces of Caslon and viewed with dismay the new 'fancy letters, of various anomalous forms, with names as appropriate'.[196]

Tuscan, a fat face capital with bifurcated serifs, was brought out by Figgins in 1815, and Thorowgood, in 1825, showed a four-line pica Italian Tuscan, which Nicolette Gray alludes to as a 'characteristic Regency letter . . . large, jovial and curly'.[197] The face does not appear to have been revived. The opulence of some of the ornamented Tuscans is perhaps more than we can stomach in these less uninhibited times.

One of the most hideous types ever to appear in a specimen book was the curious variation on the Egyptian face called Italian, shown by the Caslon foundry in 1821, although several versions had appeared in France during the First Empire. In this face the vertical stress of the Egyptian is replaced by a horizontal stress and triangular serifs are reversed and joined to the thick horizontals at the point. A lower case version was produced by Figgins as late as 1846.

The decade from 1840 to 1850 was the heyday of the ornamented type. In 1835 Figgins showed fewer than ten designs; ten years later the firm had more than fifty varieties of decorated types. Some of the early ornamented types, where the decoration was not excessive, are pleasing; one such, that has lasted up to the present day, is that of Fry and Steele shown in Stowers's *Printers' Grammar* of 1808. It is a small series of flowered titling-letters.

But in the 1840s the letter foundries went all out to supply the sudden craze for decorated types, some of which were so heavily ornamented that the letters could scarcely be discerned beneath their load of decoration. Typical of this extravagance are the 7-line pica Ornamented No. 1 of Wood and Sharwood (specialists in jobbing and ornamental types) cut about 1842, or the Extra-Ornamented of Figgins in 1845. Of the former foundry's English Union, Reed-Johnson notes that it 'was as fanciful as anything of that generation'.

Many of the larger sizes of ornamental letters found in posters and advertisements of the nineteenth century were printed not from metal type but from wood blocks. 'The universal use of this article among printers', we read in the *Printers' Journal* of 26 September, 1868, 'and the splendid effect produced by the almost endless variety and great beauty of our large show-bills, is one of the most striking improvements connected with the art of printing.'

One of the pioneers in the cutting of founts of wood type for advertising purposes was the New York printer Darius Wells, who after having made several founts for his own use, gave up his printing business in 1827 to concentrate on the manufacture of wood type. Brass patterns with raised outline were used to draw the outline of the letters on the wood block, and it was Wells who first used the term 'routing out' to the cutting away of the surplus wood.

In the 1880s two movements sprang up, known respectively as Artistic Printing and Antique Printing, the former being the more influential and likewise the more detrimental to good typography. The true begetters of Artistic Printing were the Americans William J. Kelly (editor of the *American Model Printer*), John Earhart and Andreas Haight. Their work was propagated in England through the intermediary of *The Printers' International Specimen Exchange*, first published in 1880 under the editorship of Andrew Tuer (see page 257). This work had considerable influence on British jobbing printing, and examination of the various specimens which were contributed by printers from the United States and all over Britain shows great technical skill allied to a complete absence of taste in the majority of the examples.

In the introduction to the first volume, Tuer included an 'interesting and characteristic communication' from Ruskin, who wrote:

> It seems to me that a lovely field of design is open in treatment of decorative type—not in mere big initials in which one cannot find the letters —but in delicate and variably fantastic ornamentation of capitals and filling of blank spaces or musically-divided periods and breadths of a margin.

Ruskin's advice on the filling of blank spaces was supererogatory, for the Victorian printer abhorred a vacuum, just as he ignored one of the basic principles of typography, which is to use together only such faces as harmonize.

In Artistic Printing, writes John Lewis,

> the compositor attempted the task of producing a formula for jobbing printing that owed nothing either to book-work or to the vigorous displays of the earlier years of the century. This formula consisted of an asymmetrical arrangement... of panels of colour, patterns of printers' ornament, and brass rules bent and twisted in all kinds of unlikely ways.*

In fact John Earhart went so far as to bring out a machine which he called the 'Wrinkler', designed expressly for twisting printers' rules into weird contorted shapes.

The father of Antique Printing was Andrew Tuer (1838–1900), a printer-publisher with decided antiquarian tastes, who in 1863 went into partnership with Robert Field. About 1868 the partners moved to Leadenhall Street, where they printed and published *The Paper and Printing Trades Journal*, which was printed in Old Style, a type which attempted to combine the advantages of old-face and modern. Tuer was a great admirer of English printing of the late eighteenth century and in his work was rather too affectedly 'olde-worlde'. Much of his jobbing work, often excellently designed and printed, was marred by such affectations as calling his press 'Ye Leadenhalle Presse', and alluding to his employees as his 'merrie menne'. He published a number of books which showed his antiquarian leanings, among them his own *History of the Horn Book* and *Old London Street Cries*, and reprints of early chap-books with illustrations by Joseph Crawhall.

> Alone in his generation [writes Stanley Morison], he possessed and used a set of open outline capitals of old-face design, like those to be found in the specimen books of Wilson (1780) and Caslon (1795). This letter—and Tuer possessed but one size of it—seems to have been the only fount obtaining regular use in English books between Thorne's generation and our own.[198]

Tuer had taken over the editorship of *The Printers' International Specimen Exchange* at the request of his friend Thomas Hailing, proprietor of the Oxford Printing Works, Cheltenham, who was agent

* John Lewis: *Printed Ephemera*. Ipswich, 1962.

for certain American firms. But Tuer could never reconcile his own tastes for what he called 'the modern "medieval" style' with the brash transatlantic typography of men like Andreas Haight, and after a while the *Exchange* was taken over by *The British Printer*. It continued until 1898, but the last years of the publication were beset with dullness. The verve and sparkle of 1880 had disappeared. One of the poorest specimens in the 1895 volume is the title-page of *The British Printer* itself.

By the 'nineties commercial printing was strongly permeated by American influence, largely diffused through the agency of Thomas Hailing of Cheltenham, agent for ' "All-alive" American Ads'. 'It was the first article of the botchers' creed', writes Andrew Corrigan, 'to set every possible line out to the full width of the measure, and crowd out the full depth of the job with everything that covered the whole of the space . . . A blank which had no utile purpose to serve was the only possible indecency in design.' Variety for variety's sake was the order of the day, a twenty-line advertisement might include fifteen or more different founts, and lack of harmony in typefaces was often accompanied by an atrocious incongruity of decoration.

Most of the frivolous typefaces of the latter half of the nineteenth century—Rustic, Telegraph, Helvetian, Enchorial, Aesthetic (far from!), Japanese, Milanese, Mikado, and so on—were what Seán Jennett calls 'mania types',[199] produced merely to satisfy a demand for novelty. Some of the least obnoxious are still with us.

In the field of book printing there was less scope for a complete departure from traditional methods, except for title-pages and borders. It is true that the quality of ordinary book printing deteriorated between the 'sixties and 'eighties, and this was due largely to the mass production of cheap books on poor paper with type so battered from long use as to be almost unreadable. But the actual typefaces, though for the most part undistinguished modern, made no radical departure from tradition.

The majority of the title-pages produced during the second half of the nineteenth century were completely lacking in any kind of distinction when not downright bad. This was largely because hardly anyone (there were exceptions, like Pickering) considered typography and type design worthy of study. In the ordinary commercial house the evolution of a title-page was the result of a continual struggle between the compositor charged with setting it and the printer's reader. Throughout the trade there was a 'house style' for title-pages just as for punctuation and orthography, but however cognizant the compositor might be with the style of the house his views seldom, if ever, coincided with that of the reader.

The surfeit of ornamentation which characterized much of the book production of the latter half of the nineteenth century inevitably led to a certain austerity in the following century. But love of ornament is inherent in man's nature, and ornaments and decorated type will always be with us, to attract the eye in jobbing work and in book-work to prevent the printed page from becoming too monotonous. But the ornamented letter of today is better-mannered than most of the Victorian specimens, showing more restraint and less exuberance. Having passed through the ordeal of two great wars in thirty years we no longer have the verve and gusto, the full-blooded delight in somewhat vulgar ostentation, enjoyed by the Victorians.

CHAPTER THIRTEEN

Progress in Printing Machinery

John Walter and the Logographic Press

Strangely enough the man who brought into existence a newspaper destined to have a tremendous influence both on modern journalism and the means of adapting printing to its ends was a complete stranger to the trade when he entered it as a middle-aged man. John Walter I, born in 1739, was partner in one of the largest coal businesses in London and was for some time chairman of the committee of the London Coal Exchange, which he helped to found. He was also an underwriter at Lloyd's, but the capture of homeward bound West Indian fleets by American privateers involved him in bankruptcy.

After twenty-six years in business he found his fortune gone and, with a large family to support, he had to look for a new job. Disappointed in his hopes of a Government post he purchased from one Henry Johnson, a compositor formerly an employee of Caslon, an invention (which Johnson had patented) for printing by means of 'logotypes', or slugs of metal forming commonly occurring words or syllables, thus expediting composition—or so its inventor claimed. It might have suited Johnson's original plan—the limited one of filling in the blanks on lottery tickets—but for general printing the process proved far too cumbersome, since the fount necessitated four enormous cases.

In 1784 Walter took over the King's Printing House, Blackfriars, which had been vacated by Andrew Strahan, and established there his Logographic Press. In that same year he started to print a series of reprints of English classics, the first being Dr Watts's *Improvement of the Human Mind*. To advertise his press he was advised to start a newspaper, and on 1 January, 1785, appeared the first number of *The Daily Universal Register*, 'printed logographically'. It was not until three years later that the title was changed to *The Times*, and it was not until 1792 that the words 'printed logographically' were dropped. At what precise date the logographic process was abandoned is not known for certain, but it was in use in 1789. Difficulties arose with his competitors in the book trade and his compositors insisted on being paid by the amount of type set up and not by the time occupied in setting it, which of course deprived the system of its economic *raison d'être*. Since no economic advantage could satisfactorily offset the mechanical difficulties involved the logographic process was reluctantly abandoned. In 1853 a Polish refugee named Major Beniowski made an unsuccessful attempt to reintroduce logotypes, and partial use was made of them in some of the early composing machines, notably the Wicks machine of 1880.

Platen Machines

The old hand press was a platen press; it had a heavy platen which came down on the forme and gave the impression. But the term platen machine as used today denotes a machine in which the forme is attached to a flat bed and contact is made between platen and forme in a vertical position. The early powered platen machines were in many ways similar to the old hand press, except that the operations of inking, raising and lowering the tympan, sliding the type-bed in and out and pulling the impression were all performed mechanically. The laying-on and taking-off of the paper was still done by hand.* To speed up production a double-ended platen was built so that two operators could be employed, but for speed they could not compare with the cylinder machine, which soon rendered them obsolete.

In 1856 the American George P. Gordon brought out a treadle platen which was the forerunner of the modern platen machine. About 1867 it was introduced into Britain by Messrs Cropper and proved so popular that nearly all treadle platens became known to jobbing printers as 'Croppers', irrespective of the maker.

Today platen machines are of two kinds: light, or jobbing platens, and heavy, or art platens. The former are used mainly for the printing of ephemera such as hand-bills, bill-heads, leaflets, visiting cards and office sundries, where the type area is not very large. The inking arrangement consists of an inking slab in the form of a rotating disk with inking rollers which act also as distributors, moving over the face of the forme as it rises. In general design the various platen machines resemble one another, the type bed being held in a more or less vertical position as the platen closes like a hinge to meet the type bed.

---

* This type of machine was known as the Scandinavian, or 'Scan'.

Light jobbing platens are often worked by hand lever or treadle, but the heavy commercial platens are motor-driven and are capable of a wide variety of high-class work, including the heaviest forme of half-tone blocks. One of the best-known makes of fully automatic platen machines is the German Heidelberg, which for many years remained unchallenged in this field; but it has a rival which can compare favourably with it in the Thompson British automatic platen, a machine particularly easy to operate since all settings are made from the front and are clearly indicated. Although many old-type platens are still doing useful service in small printing works, today the most widely used are platens of the Heidelberg type, mostly with fully automatic feed and delivery devices forming an integral part of the machine.

Photogravure

This is an intaglio process, a marriage between photography and mezzotint, and was invented by one Karl Klic (Klietsch) who, in association with a firm of calico printers in Lancaster, made successful prints by this method around 1895. An employee of the firm named Samuel Fawcett had himself been working on an intaglio photo-engraving process at about the same time, and Fawcett assisted Klic in perfecting the process, which was developed by the Rembrandt Intaglio Printing Company and kept secret for some years. About 1910 a German, Dr Mertens, applied Klic's method, hitherto used for the reproduction of prints, to newspaper printing and brought out the *Frankfurter Zeitung* printed by photogravure. In Britain the *Illustrated London News* was pioneering photogravure about the same year.

Many of our cheap illustrated periodicals are now printed in photogravure, but it was used for a time during the early part of the century for book illustration. In those days impressions were made from a flat plate, but nowadays the process is carried out almost exclusively on rotary presses,* and though, on account of the heavy initial cost of preparing the printing surface, it is unsuited for printing small editions, for illustrated periodicals with long runs it remains the most economical of the three main printing processes for good quality work, although recent progress in web-offset is changing the position for very long runs. Type in photogravure is not as sharp and clear as in

---

* Mainly reel-fed, although a few sheet-fed presses are in use for shorter run high quality work.

letterpress or lithographic printing, since a screen has to be used over the type. But where illustrations are more important than text, quality or economy may still recommend gravure. Nowadays gravure is less used for cheap books, for it cannot compete with web-offset if illustrated, or rubber plate rotaries for type only.

By and large, sheet-fed gravure has almost disappeared in Britain although it survives to some extent on the Continent. For monochrome work, since when used on a matt paper gravure gives a richer result than is easily possible in lithography, sheet gravure is still used for certain art, topographic and museum publications, but its high cost, compared with that of other processes (and the increasing use of colour), has diminished its use.

Colour gravure was attempted in the early days of the Rembrandt Company, but the expense was too great and before long the firm confined itself to monochrome. The idea was later revived by F. Thevoz and J. Frey in Geneva, just before the outbreak of the 1914–18 War, which temporarily ended their researches; but in 1923 the work was resumed and good results were obtained. In England the chief exponents of colour gravure were the Sun Engraving Company of Watford. For long colour gravure was confined to sheet-fed presses, but nowadays colour work is printed on multiple-unit rotaries. The technical difficulties of registration have been largely overcome by the use of electronic signals set in action by colour strips printed along the edge of the paper as it comes from the different colour cylinders.

In addition to its widespread use in recent years for mass-produced colour magazines, the process is widely employed for the printing of postage stamps and packaging; in fact for any work where identical copies of a design are required in very large numbers. The improvement in the standard of colour-printing by gravure is now incomparably higher than it was before the last war.

In view of the universal use now made of both offset and photogravure, it is interesting to recall that in an article in the special number of *The Times* published on 29 October, 1929, the writer said:

Another method [besides photogravure] which is surely commending itself to the progressive printer is the litho-offset process. Although neither of these processes has succeeded in making a definite appeal to either the reading or advertising public, the time will come when their attractiveness and advantages will be recognized, and great strides will of necessity take place in the printing industry generally.

Lithographic and Offset Printing: The Beginnings

The invention of the planographic method of printing known as lithography was due to a Bavarian named Aloys Senefelder who, having failed as actor and author, experimented with printing and lettering. Thinking that the smooth Kelheim stone could be used as a printing surface for lettering in place of copper, he began by a process of trial and error to find a satisfactory way of transferring lettering to the stone. In 1798 he hit upon the solution, based on the power of certain kinds of minerals to absorb fatty organic substances and the antipathy of grease and water.

One face of a piece of porous carboniferous limestone is polished smooth, and upon this the lettering or design is drawn with a greasy pigment. It is then fixed in the pores of the stone by means of a slight acid bath. The stone is then damped and a roller charged with a greasy printing ink is passed over it, whereupon the ink adheres to the design but is repelled by the remainder of the damp stone. If a sheet of paper is placed upon the stone and sufficient pressure is exerted on it, a faithful reproduction of the design in reverse is secured.

Senefelder obtained the patent rights for his invention in Bavaria for fifteen years, and later went into partnership with a music-seller from Offenbach named André. After a lithographic press had been established in that town, André sent his brother Philip and Senefelder to London to negotiate an English patent, and in 1803 Philip André published a collection of prints by T. Stothard and others under the title *Specimens of Polyautography*, this being the first book lithographed in England. One of the first major works to be produced wholly by lithography was a collection of drawings by Dürer, redrawn on the stone by Strixner, and produced by Senefelder and Baron Aretin at Munich in 1808. Senefelder wrote a manual of lithography in German, giving an account of how he discovered its principles and describing its technique—a book which was translated into English and published here in 1819.

The lithographic process was patented by Senefelder in London in 1800 and in Paris in the following year, and before he died in 1834 Aloys Senefelder saw his invention develop into a flourishing branch of the printing industry in many European countries. The best lithographic stone comes from the quarries of Senefelder's homeland, Bavaria, but stone is heavy, inconvenient to handle and liable to fracture. Senefelder himself realized this fact and experimented with various substances, but it was not until some time later that zinc was employed in place of the cumbersome and fragile stone, by using dilute phosphoric acid and gum as an etch after first graining the metal so that minute hollows are formed which will retain the necessary moisture. For many years after its introduction lithography was confined to hand presses and used chiefly as an artistic medium, especially in France, where Delacroix, Daumier, Degas and Toulouse-Lautrec used lithography with great effect.

The use of lithographic stone or zinc plate depends on the type of work to be done. Although the stone is now rarely used, nevertheless, since the surface is found by many artists to be more sympathetic for drawing, designs for book jackets and illustrations are sometimes drawn on the stone and transferred to offset plates for printing.

In England lithography, though less popular than in France during the nineteenth century, was well practised by Blake, Cotman, Prout, Whistler and others. Autolithography, as the process is sometimes termed, to distinguish it from photolithography, made a special appeal to certain artists because there was nothing to come between the artist's work and its printed impression. One of the latest developments in the use of autolithography is the use of grained transparent sheets of plastic—a process perfected and patented by W. S. Cowell Ltd, under the name of Plastocowell.

The chromolithograph, which came into being about the middle of the nineteenth century, was an attempt to apply colours to the lithographic principle. A different stone was required for every colour employed, and usually between ten and thirty were needed. The time necessary to prepare these stones for an elaborate piece of work was often many months, and owing to the oily nature of the coloured inks employed, most of the mid-Victorian chromolithographs were rather garish in appearance. Great care and skill was required to ensure perfect register when so many stones were used. The results seldom justified the amount of labour and time involved in drawing the different parts of the design upon so many stones. There were, of course, notable exceptions, such as the books of Owen Jones (see page 237).

Among the firms which specialized in lithographic printing in the nineteenth century was Day and Son, which employed some two hundred artists, draughtsmen and printers. There were often some 800 tons of stone stored on the premises, where they were kept in a room termed by the workmen 'The Quarry', arranged in niches, all carefully numbered and catalogued.

Photolithography was already in an experimental stage by the middle of the nineteenth century, and the first book in which photographs were transferred to the lithographic stone seems to have been, according to Gernsheim's *History of Photography* (1955), a compilation by J. Pouncy called *Dorsetshire Photographically Illustrated*, published in 1857, and containing eighty plates. But, says Ruari McLean, 'despite the author's claims of fidelity and truthfulness, he has improved on the camera's eye by drawing in human figures where he thought they were lacking, with ludicrous results'.[200]

In 1875 Robert Barclay patented his 'offset' printing process for printing design on tin plate for commercial use, such as biscuit tins, tea caddies, and the like. The name 'offset' was given to it because the impression was not made directly from the printing surface onto the tin, but was made first on an intermediate surface from which it was then transferred to the metal. The first offset machine for printing on thin metal sheet had the normal reciprocating bed found on a letterpress machine, and this carried the lithographic stone to and fro. But instead of one cylinder there were two, one above the other. The lower cylinder was covered with specially prepared card which received the design from the stone. The tin sheet then passed between the two cylinders and the design was transferred to it from the card. Later the card was replaced by rubber sheeting and eventually by a rubber-covered blanket.

For some thirty years the offset process was exclusively the province of the tin-printer, and it was not until the beginning of the twentieth century that offset began to assume any importance in book production, especially after the introduction in America of the first rotary offset paper-printing machines.

The Development of Offset

From about the year 1906 onwards 'offset' printing became an increasingly important method of planographic, or surface, printing. As we have already said, the offset principle had been in use since 1875, but for some thirty years had been the exclusive province of the tin-printer. The first British offset machine for printing on paper, constructed by George Mann, was a modification of the one used for transferring designs to tin plate.

During the latter part of the nineteenth century, autolithography and photolithography, although the heavy stone had been replaced by zinc plates, were still carried out on a flat-bed machine. Later the employment of thin metal plates which could be bent to a cylindrical form led to the adoption of the rotary principle for certain branches of lithographic printing.

The rotary used for ordinary letterpress needed a paper with the smoothest possible surface to reproduce with clarity the minute dots of half-tone reproductions. On the other hand, for lithography a grained or toothed paper of the kind used by artists was far more suitable. The solution of how to use such a paper with a rotary press lay in the interposing of a transfer medium between the plate and the paper. About the year 1906 Ira W. Rubel, an American lithographer, developed a rotary offset machine for paper printing, and in 1910 the French engineer Voirin brought out a similar machine, which he called the Rotocalco, the name being derived from the French word *décalque*, meaning a transfer or tracing.

A rotary offset press consists basically of three cylinders: the plate cylinder, with its inking rollers; a rubber-blanketed cylinder on to which the design is transferred, or 'offset'; and the impression cylinder carrying the paper. At first rotary direct litho machines were used for printing posters and the like material, which would normally only be viewed from a distance. The grained zinc plate then in use only transferred good detail in the design when it was allied to the offset principle. Then the rubber blanket was sufficiently yielding to accept ink from the rough surface of the plate and could also be used to print on a rough surfaced paper. This made it particularly suitable for the reproduction of pencil drawings or brush work, and the initial rather grey effects of limited ink films did not greatly matter. Later, better inks, multi-colour machines, the use of coated papers, technical developments in the field of photography, and better printing plates, produced results which began to compete with letterpress.

Progress in the development of offset litho has been particularly rapid since 1950, and a wide range of paper can be used to suit the desired effect. Photolithography is often used for reprints of books, each sheet of the printed book being photographed and printed on to litho plates. This is a useful method when small runs only are required, but for straightforward book printing it is still more economical to print by letterpress. Moreover, the reproduction of letterpress by offset lacks the bite and crispness resulting from the pressure of metal type on paper, and any excess of pressure from the rubber blanket tends to blur the characteristics of the typeface. But as soon as illustrations have to be taken into account letterpress loses on quality.

Although not primarily book printers, the Baynard Press became well-known in the 'thirties for the high quality of its colour lithography, under the guidance of Thomas Griffits, one of the great masters of lithographic printing, who drew the plates for *The Bayeux Tapestry* in the excellent little King Penguin series, a series which has used photolithography consistently for reproduction, the plates generally being made and printed by John Swain and Sons Ltd, of Barnet. The firm of Batsford has long been noted for its delightful book jackets reproduced by six-colour photolithography. Indeed, book jackets, posters and show-cards are among the subjects particularly suited to printing by offset-litho.

Colour offset-litho is at its best when reproducing water-colours and soft-toned subjects, and when well executed they can present the appearance of original drawings. A case in point is the reproduction of a page from Kate Greenaway's *Marigold Garden* of 1885 in Sir Francis Meynell's *English Printed Books* (Collins, 1948).

An important development in the history of newspaper printing in Britain was the installation in 1964 of the first British-built web-fed offset newspaper press at Q. B. Newspapers, Colchester. The installation in question was a 5-unit balcony type Hoe-Crabtree press, similar in shape and build to the conventional rotary newspaper press.

Although web-offset has only recently been adopted in this country for the printing of newspapers, the process had been used both on the Continent and in America for many years, the main reason for its later arrival in England being that ordinary newspapers produce much better quality illustration in this country and also usually have longer runs.

The use of offset for newspaper printing removes many of the limitations imposed by the use of metal, though obviously the day is still distant when rotary letterpress will be superseded by offset, particularly in view of the immense amount of capital represented by, say, a ten-unit rotary newspaper press of conventional design. But with the advent of filmsetting the whole trend of the printing industry is towards greater use of litho at the expense of letterpress. Progress in this respect has been facilitated by the introduction of new forms of litho plate, in which field many changes have taken place in recent years, such as the increasing use of presensitized plates.

Since the discarding of the litho stone on account of its size and weight, various other materials have been tried. Zinc and aluminium are still used, and since 1933 much use has been made of anodized aluminium, with its improved resistance to corrosion. Bi-metallic and tri-metallic plates have been tried out and many experiments in this field are still taking place. At first concerned mainly with pictorial reproduction, offset litho is nearing the point where it will be just as capable of satisfactorily reproducing text matter, a factor not without its influence on the development of filmsetting.

In the first issue of *The Fleuron* (1923), Bernard Newdigate remarked: 'Of late years no printing method has made such strides as that of the photo-litho-offset. The three principles which give it its name—photography, lithography, and offset printing—achieve in combination results which are likely to make the method one of the most important of all ways of printing.' Those words have been amply justified during the ensuing forty years.

The Development of Typographical Standards

For many years after the invention of printing from movable type there were no standards of measurement for body size, height to paper, or depth of strike in matrices, nor was there any definite relationship between sizes. Hansard, in his *Typographia*, points out the inconvenience caused by deviations in body size, which he attributes to the original lack of some generally understood standard and persisted in by some printers who, 'to avoid the inconvenience of lending sorts . . . still order their founts to be cast on an irregular body.' Some founders even went so far as to make type to arbitrary sizes so that their customers would be obliged to re-order from the same firm.

These complications led to such material difficulties that France attempted to regulate body size and height to paper by means of a royal decree in 1723, the results of which were completely negative. The Paris type-founder Pierre Simon Fournier was the first to attempt to standardize body sizes, and by the use of a definite scale to fix a relationship between them. The sizes approximated to those in common use, but all were multiples of a unit which he termed a *point typographique*, which was based on a scale of 144 points (equivalent to 12 times the size of the type known in France as 'Cicero') and this he divided into two *pouces*, the *pouce* into twelve *lignes*, and the *ligne* into six *points*. This point system was published by Fournier in 1737 and the point size of a particular type could be referred to by means of a metal gauge which could be obtained from his foundry.

About 1775 François-Ambroise Didot, the founder of the famous printing works of that name, revised Fournier's point system by relating it to the legal standard of measurement then in force, the *pied de roi*. This resulted in an augmentation of Fournier's point by a twelfth, 12 points Didot being the equivalent of 13 points Fournier. There was naturally some opposition from those founders who had already adopted the Fournier system, but in the end the Didot point prevailed. In 1801 the metric system replaced the *pied de roi*, but although Firmin Didot wanted to revise his father's system this had by then become generally adopted in France and was soon after adopted also by German type-founders.

In England, however, the point system aroused little interest and it was not until half-way through the nineteenth century that some thought was given to the standardization of English type-bodies. In 1841 the firm of Bower Brothers, type-founders of Sheffield, published their *Proposals for establishing a graduated scale of sizes for the bodies of Printing Types, and fixing their height-to-paper, based upon Pica as the common standard*. A similar proposal had been made about 1824 by the London printer James Fergusson, but with nonpareil as the standard, made to exactly one-twelfth of an inch. Neither scheme came to anything.

In 1855 the firm of J. H. King and Co. attempted to introduce a system of point measurement for types, adopting a system of 10 points to 1 nonpareil. Similar attempts to achieve some sort of uniformity were made in 1868 by the Patent Typefounding Co., and by the Caslon foundry in 1886, but the schemes received little support and failed in their purpose.

The greatest incentive towards standardization came from the United States, where the number of foundries was rapidly increasing during the second half of the nineteenth century, and where De Vinne[*] had long been advocating the introduction of the point system for type measurement. In 1886 the United States Type Founders' Association set up a committee to consider the matter, and it was decided to make the standard a pica body of 12 points based on the metric system, 83 picas being equal to 35 centimetres. In other words a typographic point measured 0·0138 inches. By 1890 most American type-founders had adopted the American point system, but in Britain standardization was delayed by disagreement among the founders. James Figgins put forward all the disadvantages (from his point of

---

[*] Theodore de Vinne, the famous American printer.

view) and as late as 1900 described the American system as 'entirely out of harmony with existing facts' and pointed out the 'disastrous and costly effect of attempting to carry out a system so thoroughly unnecessary, and possessing no merit whatever, except perhaps that which is generally conceded to an aspiration or a theory'.[201]

Nevertheless, although Figgins considered the general adoption of such a system as 'highly improbable' in Britain, the American point system had by 1905 become general in England as well as in the United States. But it has not yet become international. The Didot system is still used on the Continent. Possibly the increasing use of photo-composition will eventually lead to a new and international system of type measurement.

CHAPTER FOURTEEN

Printing in the Twentieth Century

The situation of the printing industry at the beginning of the present century was far from satisfactory. If the idea of factory planning was at last being studied by the big printing firms the average plant was still inadequately housed in old premises, badly lit, and almost always overcrowded. In all but the largest printing offices composition was still entirely by hand, often leading, as Andrew Corrigan has so amusingly shown, to constant shortage of type.[202] Prejudice against the machine was still strong and, owing to the general lack of type-casting equipment, coupled with the cost of replacing type from the founders, the founts in many cases were worn and battered. Moreover many offices hesitated to incur the expense of renewing their stocks of type until they had seen whether the new machines were likely to make foundry type uneconomical. Added to this was the further complication that the old body founts were now being discarded in favour of point-bodies.

In the average office at the beginning of the century the flat-bed press was usually a comparatively inexpensive Wharfedale, but the two-revolution machine invented by Robert Miehle around 1887 was becoming increasingly popular, though at first opinions varied as to its merits and demerits. The chief defect in the early models was the difficulty, when printing a heavy forme, of keeping the cylinder on its bearings whilst the impression was taking place. But the Miehle had come to stay, for it was speedier and more efficient than the stop-cylinder machine, and it held the field almost unchallenged for half a century.

At the beginning of the twentieth century the majority of the two-revolution machines employed in British printing works were of American make, such as the Miehle, Babcock, Cottrell, and others; but later a Miehle two-revolution machine was built in Britain by the Linotype & Machinery Co. Ltd, at Altrincham. After the First World

War machine design, both rotary and flat-bed, concentrated on ways of obtaining greater speed and output without sacrificing quality, and by the middle of the century a quad crown high-speed Miehle could produce 3,000 impressions an hour.

In 1901 machines were almost all hand-fed, and the inking rollers were not yet driven by gears, as nowadays, but by friction, which often resulted in an unsightly succession of 'monks' and 'friars'.★ Later, both automatic feed and delivery were incorporated.

In the middle of the nineteenth century the description 'Steam Printing Works' was synonymous with an up-to-date plant; and although by 1875 the gas engine was beginning to supplant steam, right up to the end of the century most machines were still driven by steam power. One of the first big printing offices to employ gas was Nelson of Edinburgh, which in 1880 changed over to gas engines for all their machinery.

The first newspaper printed by electricity was the *Somerset County Gazette* in June, 1884; it was printed on a Wharfedale flat-bed press driven by electric power from the Corporation mains. But this experiment was not entirely successful, and the firm went back to steam power. Seven years later the *Birmingham Daily Gazette* made use of electric power, employing a 24-hp Crompton engine to drive a single roll press. At first the energy was transmitted to the machine by means of intermediate shafting, pulley, and belts, and the first newspaper to run its presses by means of an electric motor attached directly to the machine was the *Liverpool Post* in 1898. The year before, the firm of Hazell, Watson and Viney had begun to use electric power for their flat-bed machines, but it was not until about 1920 that practically all printing machines were run by electricity.

Of great importance to the newspaper industry was the introduction in 1915 of the automatic ink-pumping mechanism patented by Hoe & Company for use on their high-speed presses, which did away with the dirty and difficult work of filling and cleaning ink ducts by hand. Under the old-fashioned method the ink was poured into the ducts from drums or cans, picking up a good deal of dust on the way. By the pump-feed method the ink, stored in a central tank, is pumped by compressed air to a pump box located on the side of the machine, passing through several strainers on its journey. Adjusting screws control the flow of ink.

★ 'Monk'—a black patch on the printed sheet; 'Friar'—a light or broken patch.

The years 1915 to 1919 saw no important developments in printing presses, but with the end of the 1914–18 war newspapers began to increase in size and the need for printing mass-circulation newspapers at high speed led to the introduction of new ideas in the field of rotary presses. The 1920s saw the abandonment of the deck system for web-rotary presses, in which the units were placed one above another, in favour of the floor-level installation. In 1920 the Goss Printing Company of England (which had in 1905 introduced into England the American Goss Rotary Presses) brought out the first of the 'Line' type of press—a collection of low-construction press and folder units placed in a long row, the number of units in line being dependent on the available length of space in the machine room.

In 1921 the Leeds firm of Crabtree installed the first of their rotary presses in the Dublin office of the *Irish Independent*, in which the main innovations were the worm-drive applied to cylinders and ink drums and a waving cam device designed to give a better distribution of ink. The worm-drive, although it gave smoother acceleration to the presses, proved too expensive to manufacture and was later abandoned. Messrs Crabtree were also responsible for the introduction of an ingenious device for checking any tendency of the web to wander.

To avoid loss of time in changing an empty reel spool for a full reel an automatic pasting system, the 'flying paster', was patented by Hoe and Company in 1924. This device enabled the end of a new reel to be joined to the almost finished web without stopping the press.

A Typographical Revival

During the first two decades of the twentieth century there were sporadic efforts to raise the standard of commercial printing in Britain, and designers, remembering perhaps some of the typographical atrocities of the latter part of the nineteenth century, kept closer to the traditional faces of the past, while the type-founders' specimen books were purged of their worst eccentricities. But it was not until after the First World War that there was any noticeable improvement in the national standards of typography and book design as a whole.

In Britain the influence of the Bauhaus,* with its emphasis on 'fitness for the purpose', was not immediate, and most of the credit for the improvement in commercial printing was due to the private

---

* Bauhaus was the name given by the architect Walter Gropius to the school of design which he founded at Weimar in 1919.

press movement and the influence exerted by a number of individuals who by their example did much to create public interest in good book design. Francis Meynell, first with his Pelican Press (founded during the First World War), and more especially with his Nonesuch Press, founded in 1923, set an example to the commercial printer by showing how mechanical methods of production could be fashioned to the needs of fine book printing.

William Morris, in spite of his revivalist outlook and medieval mannerisms, and despite the fact that his typographical ideas were retrograde rather than progressive, showed such honesty of purpose in pursuing his conception of a book as an organic whole, in which press-work, paper, type and binding should be nothing less than the best, that he provided the impetus to others who, equally imbued with the spirit of fine craftsmanship, nevertheless felt that a handsome book (as opposed to the 'Book Beautiful') could depend solely on its typographical treatment, without the need for excessive decoration or ornament.

Much greater was the effect on the course of English printing of the Doves Press, which eschewed the ornate in favour of austere simplicity. But after the production of the magnificent Doves Bible (set entirely by hand and printed on one hand press)* the Press seemed unable to show any further development.

The various private presses which came into being at the beginning of the present century showed how beautiful a book could be when good taste and fine craftsmanship were bestowed upon it. But their productions were limited in number (in itself a refutation of the very nature of printing), costly, and laboriously printed by methods of the past.

It remained for the more enlightened commercial printers to show that good design and typographical distinction could be applied to the machine-produced book. Even before 1914 some of the cheap reprint series, such as Dent's 'Everyman's Library' (begun in 1906) which sold at a shilling a volume; the 'World's Classics', founded by Grant Richards and later taken over by the Oxford University Press; the 'King's Classics'; and the 'Temple Classics', showed that cheap and nasty were not necessarily synonymous terms.

But it was from 1920 onwards that the level of design in book

---

* The compositor was J. H. Mason, who later became Head of the London School of Printing.

production began to rise in Britain. The first practical book to concern itself with design in commercial printing was *Printing for Business*, published in 1919 by Joseph Thorp, and this, together with the writings of Gerard Meynell in a magazine called *The Imprint*, made some printing firms realize how much could be done in raising the general standard of printing.

Harold Curwen, grandson of the founder of the Curwen Press, and a pupil of Edward Johnston,* added book printing to the activities of a firm which had hitherto been mainly concerned with music printing, and, with the help of Oliver Simon, showed that general printing could be distinguished by good taste both in design and materials. Francis Meynell (cousin of Gerard Meynell of the Westminster Press), who had founded the Pelican Press, which planned and set commercial advertisements (an innovation at that time), started the Nonesuch Press and successfully demonstrated his contention that 'to produce desirable editions at a reasonable cost, one must exploit the best mechanical equipment and the highest technical skill available'. The Nonesuch Press differed from the generally accepted notion of a press in that it did no printing; the design and planning of the books produced were Meynell's—the execution was entrusted to whatever printer it was considered could make the best job of it.

In the provinces Herbert Simon and Harry Carter were upholding the standard of good typography at the Kynoch Press in Birmingham in the days before the latter polymath became Head of the Typographic Design section at the Stationery Office. In Oxford and Cambridge the University Presses decided to move with the typographical times under the enlightened surveillance of John Johnson and Walter Lewis respectively. The Cambridge University Press had the added advantage of a typographical designer second to none in the person of Stanley Morison.

Another factor which contributed to the revival of good printing was the benefit conferred on the industry by the wise policy of the Monotype Corporation in placing at the service of their customers not only a range of outstanding classical typefaces, but also a series of founts by the best contemporary designers, such as Eric Gill, whose sans serif, in the first of its many variants, was originally cut by the Monotype Corporation in 1927. That and his Perpetua, designed at

---

* If the importance of Johnston's work lies mainly in his influence as a teacher of writing and lettering, he was also a designer, and his sans serif typeface, designed for the London Underground in 1916, is still in use.

the instigation of Stanley Morison, typographical adviser to the Monotype Corporation, have already become classics. Perpetua was begun in 1925 but the finished version was not completed until about 1930. Concerning the production of this type, Morison writes in *A Tally of Types*:

> It was intended to preserve absolutely the chiselled quality of Gill's capitals and lower-case, and for this reason it was decided not to make a direct photographic and pantographic reproduction of the drawings. Instead they were given to Charles Malin of Paris. A set of punches in upper- and lower-case twelve-point Didot* was cut in May, 1926, and a set of titling capitals in the same year. Matrices were struck and type cast by Ribadeau Dumas, the Paris typefounder.

Among other types designed by Eric Gill is Joanna, which he created for the printing firm of Hague and Gill which he had founded with his son-in-law, René Hague, and named after his daughter, Joanna.† From 1924 onwards Gill was associated with Robert Gibbings, then in charge of the Golden Cockerel Press, for whom he designed some decorative initials and a typeface, the Golden Cockerel (1929) which was a more rounded version of Perpetua. Gill, writes Robert Harling (editor of the quarterly *Typography* for some years), 'was nearer the manner of Caslon or Baskerville than any of his contemporaries, perhaps because he had spent a major portion of his working life cutting letter-forms without thought of type-foundries, advertising and commercial printing'. Gill, too, was a pupil of Edward Johnston, of whom he said 'I owe everything to the foundations that he laid'.

Oliver Simon, an amateur who took to printing with all the enthusiasm of a religious convert, showing a particular aptitude for book design, was responsible for the production of a magazine devoted to typography which played an important part in stimulating the interest of professional and layman alike in the revival of good printing. *The Fleuron* first appeared in 1923 and between that date and 1930 seven beautifully produced volumes were issued, the first four of which were edited by Oliver Simon and printed by the Curwen Press; the remaining three volumes, printed by the Cambridge University Press, were edited by Stanley Morison, whose

---

* 12-point Didot is the equivalent of 13-point on the Anglo-American system.
† Joanna was used in Eric Gill's book *An Essay on Typography*. 1931.

classic essay on *The First Principles of Typography* appeared in the final issue. Among the many distinguished contributors to *The Fleuron*, apart from its two successive editors, were Sir Francis Meynell, Holbrook Jackson, Bernard Newdigate, A. F. Johnson, Frank Sidgwick, Frederic Warde, H. V. Marrot and Paul Beaujon (Mrs Beatrice Warde).

During the period between the two great wars a number of private presses were in operation. The Golden Cockerel Press, founded in 1920 by Harold Midgely Taylor, was taken over in 1924 by Robert Gibbings, who remained its director until 1933. It made little experiment with type, but provided a medium for the wood-engravings of Robert Gibbings, Eric Gill, John Nash and Eric Ravilious. After 1933 Christopher Sandford and Owen Rutter took over the Press, and its publications were printed by the Chiswick Press.

The Gregynog Press was founded in 1922 by the Misses G. E. and M. S. Davies, at Gregynog Hall, near Newtown, Montgomeryshire, for the purpose of introducing fine printing in Wales and to print literature relating to Wales and the Welsh. During its eighteen years of existence the Press turned out some handsome volumes, including the Psalms of David in Welsh (1929) set in Poliphilus with decorated initials designed and engraved by Horace Bray, and Joinville's *History of St Louis*, translated by Joan Evans (1937), also set in Poliphilus with initials and headings designed by Alfred Fairbank and cut in wood by R. John Beedham. During the period 1934-6, when Lloyd Haberly controlled the Gregynog Press, he brought out Robert Bridges's *Eros and Psyche* in a typeface called Paradiso designed by himself and the calligrapher Graily Hewitt, another famous pupil of Edward Johnston. The Ashendene Press had a longer life than most of the private presses. Founded in 1894 by C. H. St John Hornby (later to become senior partner of the famous firm of stationers and booksellers, W. H. Smith & Son), the Press functioned until 1935. The first book from the Press, *The Journal of Joseph Hornby*, issued in the spring of 1895, was a small octavo printed in Caslon old-face pica, and all the books printed up to and including 1901 were either in Caslon or in Fell types supplied by the Oxford University Press. In 1902 appeared an octavo edition of Dante's *Inferno*, set in the Subiaco type modelled on the transitional roman of Sweynheym and Pannartz and designed by Emery Walker and T. J. Cobden-Sanderson. The punches were cut by E. P. Prince, who as we have seen had cut the punches for William Morris's types, and the type itself, on great primer body, was cast by the firm of Miller and Richard. Five large folio volumes were printed with the Subiaco type between 1909 and 1925 whilst another type, based on that used in Holle's edition of Ptolemy, was used for folio editions of *Don Quixote* and Thucydides's *History of the Peloponnesian War*, which was printed in red and black, with initials in red.

In 1920 the Shakespeare Head Press, which had been started in 1904 by the Elizabethan scholar and publisher A. H. Bullen, was taken over by a group of people interested both in scholarship and fine printing, with the active participation of the printer Bernard Newdigate and the publisher Basil Blackwell. Newdigate had at one time been with the Arden Press, which had in 1908 been purchased by W. H. Smith & Son. The Shakespeare Head Press, which was a printing firm rather than a private press, turned out handsome reprints of the great authors, as well as some attractive editions of Jane Austen and Anthony Trollope, until Newdigate's death in 1944. Originally established in Stratford on Avon, the Press was moved to Oxford in 1929.

The revival of good printing in the twentieth century was not confined to book-work. In 1908 *The Times* began to replace its Kastenbein and Wicks composing machines with the 'Monotype', and the fount chosen was based on one originally cut by William Miller & Co. of Edinburgh about 1813. This was a readable type and probably as good as any for newsprint at a time when the range of suitable faces for newspaper printing was limited.

Many factors not inherent in book printing have to be taken into account in the make-up and printing of newspapers. The narrow measure (less than 12 ems per column) makes a small-size text letter imperative, 7-point being the average nowadays. Yet it must be easily read by people of all ages.

From 1925 onwards several London newspapers adopted Ionic, an American reintroduction of an English jobbing type first cut in 1821. This was extensively used for newspaper composition in the United States, but although better adapted to the requirements of high-speed rotaries than light-faced modern faces, it is too monotonous in character to be entirely satisfactory, and to be legible has to be set on a body at least 1-point larger, thus involving loss of space in depth, whilst its relative fatness also means loss of space in width.

In an attempt to find a type that should be both distinguished, as befitting a newspaper with the international reputation of *The Times*, and easy to read, even on a train journey, many experiments were made with existing founts at Printing House Square. A 9-point Perpetua was specially cut, and trial pages were set up in a number of existing founts. As an outcome of these investigations Stanley Morison prepared his famous *Memorandum on a Proposal to Revise the Typography of* The Times. This technical report led to the preparation of drawings for an entirely new face, and the first size of 'The Times New Roman' was cut in 9-point at the Monotype Works, Redhill, in April, 1931. The punches were made on a Pierpoint punch-cutting machine accurate to within one 25,000th of an inch. Before the task of providing the new face was completed over 7,000 punches were cut for the 38 founts needed, of which 1,075 were rejected.

Although designed primarily as a type for a quality newspaper the Times roman proved so versatile that it is now procurable in an extensive range of sizes, with matching bold and italic, suitable for book, periodical and general printing. For newspaper work its space-economy was a factor of importance, and unlike Ionic it did not need leading. At first cut only in 5½-point, 7-point and 9-point for the needs of *The Times*, Times roman now ranges from the remarkable 4¾-point—known as Claritas and specially designed for the classified advertisements referred to as 'smalls'—to 14-point for line composition as well as a display range up to 72-point.

In 1954 the Linotype Company brought out a new text face called Jubilee, a compromise between the thick-thin contrasts of Times roman and the lack of contrast in the monotonous Ionic. It was soon adopted by a number of newspapers. The *Daily Telegraph* and the *Sunday Times* adopted it in 1959, and the *Daily Mail* abandoned Ionic in favour of Jubilee in November, 1964.

Among the contemporary types cut for machine composition by the Monotype Corporation Limited, mention must be made of Bruce Rogers's Centaur (1929), originally cut for its designer by Robert Wiebking and first used in 1915 for the book after which it was named—Maurice de Guérin's *The Centaur*. The Monotype version was used for the beautiful Oxford Lectern Bible, designed by Bruce Rogers and composed and printed at the Oxford University Press. Three of the finest designs of Jan van Krimpen—Lutetia, Romulus, and Spectrum—originally cut by the master punch-cutter of the Enschedé printing works, P. H. Raedisch, have been made available for machine composition by the Monotype Corporation.

In 1930 appeared the first of seventeen numbers of *The Book-Collector's Quarterly*, edited by Dr Desmond Flower and A. J. A.

Symons, and printed by the Curwen Press for Cassell & Co. Ltd and the First Edition Club. 'Both editors', wrote Oliver Simon, 'were lovers of "fine printing" and encouraged the use of good paper, care and ingenuity in the setting of the advertisements, and variety in the vignettes appearing on the title-pages.'

When this periodical ceased publication in 1935, Oliver Simon, his enthusiasm undiminished, brought out a 'quadrimestrial of Typography and the Graphic Arts' entitled *Signature*, the first number of which appeared in November of that year. It continued until December, 1940, when the war brought it to an untimely end; but in July, 1946, a new series was begun, still under the editorship of Oliver Simon, and lasted until 1954. In addition to most of those who had been responsible for the success (in artistic terms) of *The Fleuron*, the contributors on typographical subjects included Dr Desmond Flower, John Carter, James Wardrop, Ellic Howe, Harry Carter, John Dreyfus, Ruari McLean, and S. H. Steinberg; while the graphic arts were well represented by Graham Sutherland, John Piper, Barnett Freedman and Paul Nash. The editor himself was responsible for a noteworthy article on 'English Typography and the Industrial Age'.

To show the printing industry what a commercial printing firm could offer in the way of typography in the 'twenties, Oliver Simon compiled and edited for the Curwen Press a type-specimen book which was issued in 1928 in an edition of 135 copies. It cost over £1,000 to produce, for as its compiler remarked, 'the actual printing of the specimen book was taken as a challenge to show our standard for presswork'. Indeed, it set a high standard, being, in the words of Charles Prentice, then a director of Chatto & Windus, 'a model of design, discrimination and knowledge'. This was indeed 'praise from Sir Hubert', for Charles Prentice, who died in 1949, was himself no mean designer of books, and had done much to establish the reputation of his firm for the unobtrusive excellence of their editions. Oliver Simon, whose own *Introduction to Typography* first appeared in 1945, died in 1956 at the age of sixty-one, and by his death the printing world suffered a heavy loss, for he was an exceptionally gifted designer both of books and periodicals.

When we turn to the illustration of books the only work which in the early years of the twentieth century showed any standard above the mediocre was that commissioned by the private presses, and the chief medium employed was the traditional wood-engraving. Fiction, so often lavishly illustrated in Victorian days, was seldom treated to more than a frontispiece in book printing; but for the fiction in popular magazines there was frequently employed a hybrid form of illustration known as half-tone engraving, in which drawings were given a quasi-photographic effect.

Compared with the enormous quantity of illustrated books turned out in France, where Vollard was engaging the finest artists of the day to illustrate books in a variety of processes, in England the illustrated book appeared to have gone out of fashion. Nevertheless in England illustration was still subordinated to the text of the book, whereas in France the book was hardly more than a pretext for the illustrations, which might well have been, and often were, sold separately. As examples of the artists' work they were usually excellent, but the medium in which they were executed did not always marry happily with the letterpress.

With the revival of interest in book design in the 'twenties illustration came into its own once more, and although most of the private presses had by this time disappeared, the more adventurous among the commercial publishers were now making use of the skill of a number of gifted illustrator-designers such as Paul Nash, Eric Ravilious, Albert Rutherston, Thomas Lowinsky, Edward Bawden, Barnett Freedman and others. The art of wood-engraving, which had suffered during the latter part of the nineteenth century from the divorce between artist and engraver, revived when the artist once again cut his own blocks, and among the finest exponents in this medium were Eric Gill, Clare Leighton, and John Farleigh; Bernard Shaw's *Adventures of the Black Girl in her Search for God*, with wood-engravings by the last-named artist, caused a minor sensation in the publishing world when issued in 1932 at the remarkably low price of half a crown.

The most usual method of reproduction for illustrated books was the line block and the half-tone, the latter being used mainly for informative books, such as technical, travel, and biography. Although adult fiction ceased to be illustrated after the First World War, children's books, on the other hand, and rightly so, were better illustrated than ever, even though few of the books themselves have been outstanding.

A new approach to advertising during the years following the First World War was not without its effect in the realm of book production. The 'fancy printing' of the jobbing firms, with their deplorable stereotyped woodcut blocks, had given way towards the close of the nineteenth century to better-designed display advertisements, and capable artists were engaged to boost the wares of the large commercial firms on gigantic posters. Advertising gradually became, after the birth of the advertising agency, a highly specialized profession, offering considerable scope to outstanding graphic designers. Public companies became patrons of artistic printing and the late 'twenties saw the appearance, on London's Underground railways, of the striking posters of E. McKnight Kauffer.

Many of the most skilled advertising artists were equally well-known as illustrators of books, and McKnight Kauffer showed his versatility in the line drawings of the illustrations to *The Anatomy of Melancholy* and the combination of lithography and gouache stencilling* used in Cassell's edition of Arnold Bennett's *Elsie and the Child*, printed incidentally by the Curwen Press, responsible for so much fine printing in the inter-war period. Advertising and book production met in the designing of book jackets, which were promoted from their original function of mere protective wrappers to become both an adjunct to sales and a special field for the commercial artist. Apart from those used to stimulate the jaded appetites of sensation-seekers, the artists' jackets used by front-rank publishers are often so delightful that one regrets their inevitable impermanence. One thinks instinctively, in this connection, of the jacket designs of Edward Bawden and Barnett Freedman for Faber and Faber, and those of Lynton Lamb for Collins. A good jacket need not necessarily be a picture jacket, and the typographical may be just as effective if the lettering and layout is good. Victor Gollancz is an example of a firm which has always relied on purely typographical jackets, with black lettering on a yellow ground; one result is that Gollancz books are immediately recognizable on the booksellers' shelves without any need to look for the imprint.

One commercial printing firm which established a reputation for fine printing in the 'twenties was the Bradford firm of Lund, Humphries & Co., printers and publishers. This firm has for some time past been responsible for the designing, printing and publishing of a very old-established organ of the printing industry called *Penrose's Annual*, which contains a yearly account of the progress of the industry as a whole, dealing mainly with technical innovations.

No account of printing in the twentieth century can pass over the

---

* The stencil process is a hand process, known in France as *pochoir*. The Curwen Press had a special stencil department operated by girls.

appearance in July, 1935, of the first Penguin books, on the success of which it would be superfluous to dwell. They were not by any means the first cheap paper-backed books on the English market. Only a year or so previously Ernest Benn, to mention but one publisher, had brought out a series of paper-back novels at ninepence a volume. But Penguin Books, the brain-child of Allen Lane, nephew of the founder of the Bodley Head, was the first series to succeed, despite the head-shakings of the majority of booksellers.

Electronic Photo-Engraving

Rapid technological progress in the field of electronics, speeded up by the exigencies of war, has made possible the production of illustrations by completely new methods. The two chief machines for producing engraved plates without the need of camera or chemicals are the American Fairchild Scan-a-Graver and the German Klischograph. The first-named cuts a block in plastic foil; the latter can be used with plastic foil or metal. In these machines a photo-electric scanner follows the picture as it revolves on a cylinder, transmitting impulses, which vary according to the tonal densities of the picture, to the engraving tool, which, by means of a heated stylus, burns out parts of the block mounted on another cylinder revolving on a common shaft. Although originally limited to making same-size reproductions, both machines now have enlarging and reducing models, named respectively the Scan-a-Sizer and the Vario-Klischograph, and both machines have models adapted for the production of colour blocks. The Klischograph, the invention of Dr Rudolf Hell, was first placed on the market in 1954, and from this machine was developed a further range which includes the Vario-Klischograph, the Colorgraph, and the Chromograph—the last-named being a drum-type electronic colour scanner used in the production of colour-corrected separations from transparencies.

The plastic foil blocks are used mainly for short runs on flat-bed or rotary presses, but metal blocks cut by the Klischograph are used for newspaper work, notably by *The Times*. At the time of writing the Klischograph is extensively used in the preparation of lithographic reproductions; but developments in this field are rapid and a number of other electronic machines seem likely to bring a rapid improvement in quality as well as economy.

At the moment it seems unlikely that the new technique will replace conventional photo-engraving, with its control of etching, for quality book-work; but the light plastic blocks, which can easily be trimmed, may be well suited to a variety of jobs where quality of reproduction is not a primary consideration.

Mechanical Type-setting

THE LUDLOW

This machine may be termed semi-mechanical, in that it has a casting unit but no keyboard. It is used chiefly for setting large display type, such as the banner headlines of newspapers. The matrices are hand-set and justified in a Ludlow composing stick, the type is cast in the form of a slug and the matrices are then returned to case. The Ludlow casts a line of one standard measure—24 ems—but the slug can be cut for narrower measures while for wider measures slugs can be pieced together. A companion machine is the Elrod, which casts blank spacing material, rules and borders from 1 to 36 point in thickness, and of any required length.

LINOTYPE AND INTERTYPE

The introduction of the Linotype towards the end of the nineteenth century has already been mentioned. Now used in almost every newspaper office as well as in many general printing offices, it remains basically unchanged, though with added refinements such as automatic quadding and centering. The scope of the Linotype has been widened by the use of duplex matrices, having two different faces on one matrix.

The Intertype, first introduced in 1912, is similar in appearance and function to the Linotype, and like the latter is made with either single or double distributor, or mixer. The single-distributor model is for ordinary straight composition, while the mixer is used for display and mixed composition.

AUTOSETTING

Both Linotype and Intertype machines can nowadays be operated from a distance by means of a teletypesetter unit—a system often alluded to by the initials TTS. It was first introduced into Britain in 1934 by *The Scotsman* to link their London and Edinburgh offices. Later, *The Times* adopted the system for setting Parliamentary reports, which are transmitted by keyboard from the Houses of Parliament to the composing room at Printing House Square. For TTS operation specially fast slug machines are employed, such as the High Speed Intertype and the Model 79 Linotype, which can set and cast twelve lines a minute. The TTS system of remote operation is carried out by means of a perforator worked by a typewriter keyboard. The perforated tape is fed through a 'sender' which transmits electrical impulses over the telephone wire to a reperforator, which in turn reproduces the original perforations on another tape; this is fed into the special mechanism of the Linotype and automatically operates the keys which select the required matrices for slug-casting.

Type composition by remote control is apparently no modern idea, for *The Printers' Journal* for 26 September, 1868, quotes an extract from the *American Artisan*, in which the writer, referring to a machine for setting and distributing type (make not stated) adds:

> This is truly wonderful, but I want to say the wonder does not stop here. By means of one of these machines, located in the large newspaper offices in the principal cities, and connected by telegraph with the capital, the reporter or operator can set type himself, the machine standing in New York or New Orleans, and he being in the capital.

THE TYPOGRAPH

This machine was invented about the year 1888 by John R. Rogers, and was later bought up, as far as the United States was concerned, by the Linotype Company, in order that they might acquire the rights of the wedge-space of J. W. Schukers (see page 226). The machine was later manufactured in Canada and Germany, and was first seen in Britain in 1908. It has two main portions: a base containing the spacing and casting mechanism; and an upper portion which is the magazine unit, with its keyboard. Depression of the keys releases matrices which slide down a guide wire into the assembling channel. In its original form it cast one face only, but later a two-letter matrix became available.

THE 'MONOTYPE'

Since its first appearance on the British market in 1897 the 'Monotype' machine has become an indispensable adjunct to every important letterpress printing firm. For book-work, especially, it is unrivalled both for its versatility in setting complicated matter and its large repertory of both traditional and modern book-faces. The machine is divided into two main components: a keyboard and a caster, the former punching a ribbon with perforations which control the caster by passing over air vents. Stop-pins rise by the action of compressed air as the perforations of a particular letter pass over the vents, and stops the matrix case at the required position over the mould for just that fraction of time necessary for the selected character to be cast and ejected.

The matrix case in general use has for some time provided fifteen rows of seventeen matrices, giving a total of 255 matrix-case positions but in 1963 the latest machines were fitted with a new type of matrix case with 16 by 17 rows, giving a total of 272 matrix positions. The matrix-case slides forward until checked by the stop-pin corresponding to the row selected and then moves at right angles, until another stop-pin checks it at the correct position in that row for the required character. The matrix is then clamped to the mould, which is provided with a movable mould blade that determines the set width of every character and space. When each type is cast it is ejected and carried to the galley. The caster is normally used for all sizes up to 14-point, but a composition attachment can be used to extend the size range up to 24-point. The 'Monotype' Super Caster is designed principally for casting type for case—display type up to 72-point, as well as leads, rules, borders and spacing material.

Filmsetting

Photographic type composition, usually termed filmsetting or photosetting, which probably foreshadows the eventual end of printing from metal type, is an application of photography to composition which dates experimentally from the end of the nineteenth century, for W. Friese-Greene, that early pioneer of the cinema, patented a device for reproducing text by photographic means in 1895, but apparently no prototype was ever built, the inventor's interests having shifted to other fields. Although many experiments in photographic composing were made during the early part of the present century, and a number of systems were hailed as providing a solution to the problem, most of them fell by the wayside.

One of the first machines for leadless composition, though not purely photographic, was the Orotype—a development of the Typary machine first seen in 1925. This is similar in principle to the Linotype, but uses raised letters called patrices instead of matrices, and a printing unit replaces the caster. The letters are set from a keyboard, and the justified lines of patrices are printed on to cellophane film or Baryta paper. Proofs are obtained on sensitized photographic paper for transferring to lithographic plates.

In 1929 the American Luminotype claimed to be able to set photo-graphically 7,000 letters an hour, and in England the August-Hunter photo-composing machine was introduced about 1933. But the most promising fully automatic machine of the pre-war period was the Uhertype, invented and constructed by the Hungarian engineer Edmond Uher, and developed from 1931 onwards in Augsburg. In this machine the keyboard operator set in motion mechanism which printed the characters and automatically photographed each line, the image being received on a spool of film developed in the machine. Different founts were obtained from hollow glass cylinders bearing the master alphabets. The film band was developed either as a negative or positive for either photogravure or offset-litho.

The editor of *Penrose's Annual* for 1933 remarked:

> It must not be expected that the practice of photo-composing will come quickly. . . . Just as it was difficult at first to introduce type-composing machines, so it will be no easier to persuade the trade to accept photo-composing; in fact it will be harder, because it will be necessary to bring about changes in printing methods.

As if to justify his words, at the last International Printing Exhibition to be held before the war, in 1936, there was not a single photo-composing machine to be seen on any of the stands.

The war came and halted further progress in this field for some years. After the war the scene had changed. Nothing more was heard of the Uhertype, and the patents for another photo-setting machine, taken out by Scheffer in Switzerland in 1937, had been acquired by the Intertype Corporation of America, and used in their Fotosetter. In England Arthur Dutton's promised Flickertype had apparently given its final flicker, and interest was centered upon two main sys-tems—Rotofoto and 'Monophoto'—the former the invention of George Westover (one of the pioneers of filmsetting in Britain) and the latter developed by the Monotype Corporation. In America, in addition to the 'Fotosetter', the immediate post-war years saw the introduction of the Linofilm, a product of the Mergenthaler Linotype Corporation, and the Photon, invented by the French engineers René Higgonet and Louis Moyroud. This was originally called Lumitype, the name still retained by the French model. The Photon has been developed in the United States by the Graphic Arts Research Foun-dation.

Perhaps the first really effective photo-composing machine was the

Intertype 'Fotosetter', which was installed in the Government Printing Office in Washington as long ago as 1946. In appearance the 'Fotosetter' resembles the normal slug-casting machine, and in fact its basic mechanical operation is similar, save that the hot-metal casting unit is replaced by a camera, and the metal matrix by type-transparency matrices. The 'Fotosetter' makes use of the circulating matrix system, which the keyboard operator releases from the magazines and which are returned to it by the distributor after they have passed the photographic point where light is reflected on them. According to James Moran the first complete filmset book—*Handbook of Basic Microtechnique*—was set on the 'Fotosetter' and published in the United States in 1952.[203]

The Monotype Corporation's 'Monophoto' filmsetter is in effect a Monotype machine with a photographic unit substituted for the caster. With one or two minor modifications the keyboard is the same as that used for the 'Monotype' and the perforated paper ribbon controls the positioning of the film matrix-case of the 'Monophoto' filmsetter. Each character selected from the transparency matrices is projected onto the film by means of an optical system and projection lamp, the positions of the lens and prisms in this system being adjustable to give whatever degree of magnification is required, from 6-point to 24-point, and—as in the case of the 'Monotype'—to a measure of up to 60 ems. Correction is manual. Matter filmset in this way can then be made up into page by assembly on a transfer sheet, preparatory to being used to prepare a printing surface for gravure or photo-offset. Here it should be remarked that at the time of writing filmsetting is mainly used for lithographic and photogravure workings, providing a photographic original to print down direct on the gravure or offset plates, thus doing away with the necessity of making a proof from lead composition. The film can, however, be chemically reversed from positive to negative and used for making wrap-around letter-press printing plates by the powderless etching process; but for the time being, as far as letterpress printing is concerned, the advantages of filmsetting is to a large extent offset by the cost of making the plates. But there is little doubt that in time filmsetting will invade the field of letterpress printing.

Whereas both the 'Fotosetter' and the 'Monophoto' are based on the existing mechanisms of the Intertype and 'Monotype', the Photon-Lumitype works on a completely different system. Its keyboard, which resembles an ordinary electric typewriter, operates electronic memory devices which convey to an electronic computer in the photographic unit the character selected and its width, and at the same time the spacing between words is recorded for automatic justification. The codified information is turned into electrical impulses which control the photographic unit, in which is a constantly revolving glass disk bearing the characters for sixteen founts, arranged in concentric rings. The selected character is photographed by a powerful light source at the precise fraction of a second when it passes the photographic unit. Sizes from 5- to 48-point can be set up to 42 ems measure, and there are facilities for correction and deletion.

The first machine for filmsetting introduced by the Mergenthaler Linotype Company in the U.S.A. was an adaption of their hot-metal Linotype machine and was called the Linofilm. Later, while still retaining that name, the company produced a completely new machine on different principles. This machine consists of four units—the keyboard and photographic system, together with a corrector and a composer. The keyboard, in the form of an electric typewriter, punches a tape conveying information to the photographic unit. This unit contains electronic coding and scanning devices which control the transparent negative plates, and according to the code received via the punched tape presents the selected character from a chosen fount to the projector for photographing. The composer unit is an additional photographic system used for enlargement and make-up purposes, and can make up a page to standard newspaper size in the form of a film positive to be used in plate-making.

The Hadego Photocompositor, a Dutch invention, was designed primarily for display work, and is in fact not unlike the Ludlow in that the machine operates from matrices hand-set and justified in a special composing stick. The matrices, which are of plastic, bearing the letter in white on a black background, are clamped to the machine, enlarged or reduced to the desired size and photographed on film. Special effects in the way of shading or outline are made possible by the use of special screens.

Filmsetting is, at the time of writing, still very much in its infancy, but its advantages are so numerous that developments are bound to come quickly in this field, and hot-metal setting, though it may be necessary for some time to come for certain kinds of technical work, will eventually become a thing of the past. One thing in favour of filmsetting is its versatility, for by changing the adjustments of the machine the size of type becomes instantly variable over a wide range.

The film for a whole book, packed for storage, takes up very little space, and its weight, compared with the tons of metal needed for conventional letterpress printing, is negligible. New types of photo-setting machines allied to computer techniques are on their way and the coming years hold a promise of rapid changes.

The post-war years have witnessed the phenomenal growth of 'paperbacks' which pour from the presses in what appears to be an ever increasing deluge. The vast majority of these are printed on reel-fed machines using rubber or similar plates. It is interesting to recall that when in July, 1935, Allen Lane brought out the first batch of Penguin Books, paper-bound at sixpence apiece, most people connected with the book trade looked upon the venture as ill-starred, arguing that the British public did not like paper-bound books and were unlikely to buy them. In 1946 Penguin Books Ltd brought out the first of their 'million' books—the simultaneous issue in one day of a million copies of books by a single author. The first author to be launched in this spectacular way was Bernard Shaw, and others have since followed. Today most publishers issue 'paperbacks', but all honour is due to the brothers Lane—Allen, Richard, and John—who, with a modest capital of £100, backed their convictions against the incredulity of the book publishing world and won.

Another dominant feature of post-war printing and publishing is the great increase in illustrated books made possible by improved techniques, particularly in photography and lithography. As late as 1939 colour photography was hardly used at all in books. Today it is a commonplace and is rapidly superseding all other forms of colour illustration, due to the constant improvement both in colour films themselves and in the means of reproducing them in the form of book illustrations. Art books and travel books are the categories in which this development is especially evident.

I can think of no better way of ending this book than by quoting the words of George D. Painter in his introduction to the magnificent collotype facsimile of Aldus Manutius's *Hypnerotomachia Poliphili*, published by the Eugrammia Press in 1963. 'The future hope of printing', he writes, 'lies in the new miracles of film and electronic setting by which the whole art will be revolutionized, for good or for bad. If these techniques only replace the craftsmen by inhuman mechanism, they will fail. They will succeed if, by immeasurably increasing his resources, they reinstate the conscious and unconscious powers of the human artist.'

Notes

1. Mores, E. Rowe. *A Dissertation upon English Typographical Founders and Foundries (1778).* Edited by Harry Carter and Christopher Ricks. 1961.

2. Stevenson, Allan. *Observations on Paper as Evidence.* Lawrence. Kansas, 1961.

3. Le Clert, Louis. *Le Papier.* 2 volumes. Paris, 1926.

4. Bennett, H. S. *English Books and Readers 1475–1557.* 1952.

5. Plomer, H. R. 'The Importation of Books into England in the 15th and 16th centuries.' *The Library.* Ser. 4. No. 4. 1924; and 'The Importation of Low Country and French Books into England, 1480 and 1502–3'. *The Library.* Ser. 4. No. 9. 1929.

6. McKerrow, R. B. *Introduction to Bibliography.* 1927.

7. *Catalogue of Books . . . Collected by Rush C. Hawkins.* 1910.

8. *Archaeologia Cantiana.* Vol. 5. 1863. Page 324.

9. Ibid. Vol. 2. 1860. Page 232.

10. Wheeler, John. *A Treatise of Commerce.* 1601.

11. Blades, William. *The Life & Typography of William Caxton.* Vol. 1. 1861. Page 56.

12. Birch, Lieutenant-Colonel J. C. 'William Caxton's Stay in Cologne.' *The Library.* Ser. 4. No. 4. 1924. Pages 50–2.

13. Sheppard, L. A. 'A New Light on Caxton and Colard Mansion.' *Signature.* New Ser. No. 15. 1952. Pages 28–9.

14. *The Cely Papers.* R. Hist. Soc. Camden. Ser. 3. Vol. 1. 1900.

15. Crotch, W. J. B. *The Prologues and Epilogues of William Caxton.* 1928. Page xxxii.

16. Tanner, L. E. 'William Caxton's House at Westminster.' *The Library.* Ser. 5. Vol. XII. No. 3. 1957. Pages 153–66.

17. Hansard, T. C. *Typographia.* (n.d.) Page 89.

18. Duff, E. Gordon. *The Printers . . . of Westminster and London from 1476 to 1535.* 1906. Page 12.

19. Hodnett, E. *English Woodcuts 1480–1535.* 1935. Page 4.

20. Morgan, P. and Painter, G. D. 'The Caxton Legenda.' *The Library.* Ser. 5. Vol. XII. No. 4. 1957. Page 233, footnote.

21. Crotch. *The Prologues.* Op. cit. Additional notes, page cxxxviii.

22. Hind, Arthur M. *An Introduction to a History of Woodcut*. Vol. 2. 1963 edition. Page 716.

23. Updike, D. B. *Printing Types*. Vol. 1. 1937 edition. Page 119.

24. Bühler, Curt. *William Caxton and his Critics*. Syracuse University Press, 1960. Page 11.

25. Winship, G. P. *William Caxton and the First English Press*. New York, 1938.

26. Mores. *A Dissertation*. Op. cit.

27. Stevenson. *Observations*. Op. cit. Plate 3.

28. *The Seven Sorrowes that women have when theyr husbandes be deade, Compyled by Robert Copland*. Printed by William Copland. (n.d.)

29. Palmer, Samuel. *The General History of Printing*. 1732.

30. Plomer, H. R. *History of English Printing*. 1899.

31. See further: Nixon, H. M. 'The Book of XX Songs.' *British Museum Quarterly*. Vol. XVI. No. 2. 1951.

32. Letts, Malcolm. *Sir John Mandeville*. 1949. Page 91.

33. Bennett. *English Books*. Op. cit. Appendix I.

34. Marshall, Harold. *The First Press in the City of London*. Privately printed. 1929.

35. Haebler, Conrad. *The Study of Incunabula*. New York. 1933.

36. Duff. *The Printers*. Op. cit.

37. Smith, George. *William de Machlinia—The Primer on Vellum printed by him in London* about 1484. 1929.

38. Plomer, H. R. 'Richard Pynson, Glover and Printer.' *The Library*. Ser. 5. Vol. XV. No. 1. 1960. Page 53.

39. Johnson, A. F. *Type Designs*. 1934. Page 58.

40. Holdsworth, Sir W. *A History of English Law*. 1924.

41. Rhodes, D. E. 'Some documents printed by Pynson for St Botolph's, Boston, Lincs.' *The Library*. Ser. 5. Vol. XV. No. 1. 1960. Page 53.

42. Duff. *The Printers*. Op. cit.

43. Reed, Talbot Baines. *A History of the Old English Letter Foundries*. New edition, revised and enlarged by A. F. Johnson. 1952. Page 87. This work will henceforward be referred to as 'Reed-Johnson'.

44. Furnivall, F. J. *Pynson's Contracts and his Letters of Denization*.

45. See Duff, E. Gordon. *English Provincial Printers . . . to 1557*. 1912. Page 124.

46. Welch, C. E. 'Julian Notary and Andrew Rowe.' *The Library*. Ser. 5. Vol. XI. No. 4. 1956. Page 278.

47. Plomer. *History of Printing*. Op. cit.

48. Butterworth, Charles. *The English Primers (1529–1545)*. 1953. Page 87.

49. King, A. Hyatt. *Four Hundred Years of Music Printing*. 1964. Plate XI.

50. Reed, Arthur. *Early Tudor Drama*. 1926. Page 79.

51. Johnson. *Type Designs*. Op. cit. Page 144.

52. Bennett. *English Books*. Op. cit. Page 197.

53. Pollard, A. W. *Fine Books.* 1912.

54. Duff, E. Gordon. *A Century of the English Book Trade.* 1905. Page 108.

55. Frère, Edouard. *Des Livres de Liturgie des Eglises d'Angleterre imprimés à Rouen dans les XVe et XVIe siècles.* Rouen, 1867.

56. Gibson, Strickland. 'The Protocollum of Thomas Berthelet.' *The Library.* Ser. 5. Vol. 1. No. 1. 1946. Page 47.

57. Greg, Sir W. W. 'Notes on the types, borders, etc., used by Thomas Berthelet.' *Transactions of the Bibliographical Society.* Vol. 8. 1907. Pages 187–220.

58. Reed-Johnson. Op. cit. Pages 87, 88.

59. *Diary of H. Machyn.* Camden Society Publications XLII. 1848.

60. Sheppard. 'A New Light on Caxton.' Op cit.

61. In *The English Bible under the Tudor Sovereigns* (n.d.) the author, the Rev. W. T. Whitley, attempts to prove, on rather flimsy evidence, that the Thomas Matthew of the 'Matthew' Bible, was a fishmonger and burgess of Colchester of that name.

62. Mozley, J. F. *Coverdale and his Bibles.* 1953. Page 218.

63. Herbert's revision of Ames's *Typographical Antiquities,* ed. T. F. Dibdin. Vol. 4. 1819. Page 396, footnote.

64. Sayle, C. E. 'Initial Letters in Early English Printed Books.' *Transactions of the Bibliographical Society.* Vol. 7. 1904.

65. Clair, Colin. 'On the Printing of Certain Reformation Books.' *The Library.* Ser. 5. Vol. XVIII. No. 4. December, 1963.

66. Pollard, A. W. *Records of the English Bible.* 1911.

67. *Domestic State Papers. Elizabeth.* Vol. XLVIII, 6.

68. Garrett, C. H. *Marian Exiles.* 1938. Pages 142–3.

69. Astle, Thomas. *The Origin and Progress of Writing.* 1784.

70. Mores. *A Dissertation.* Op. cit. Page lxvi–lxviii.

71. Updike. *Printing Types.* Op. cit. Page 92.

72. Ibid. Page 126.

73. Delen, A. J. J. *Oude Vlaamsche Graphiek.* 1943. Page 110.

74. *The Autobiography of Thomas Wythorne.* Edited by James M. Osborn. 1961. Page xlvi.

75. *Calendar of the Patent Rolls. Edward VI.* iii. Page 314.

76. Wijnman, H. F. 'Nederlandse Emigrantendrukkerijen te Emden.' *Het Boek.* Ser. 3. Vol. XXXVI. 1964.

77. Van Ortroy. *Les Imprimeurs Belges à l'Etranger.* 1922. Page 35.

78. Duff. *English Book Trade.* Op. cit. Page xxiv.

79. Pollard, A. W. *Old Picture Books.* 1902. Page 137.

80. Plomer, H. R. *Abstracts from the Wills of English Printers.* 1903.

81. Hansard. *Typographia.* Op. cit. Page 119, footnote.

82. Eccles, Mark. 'Bynneman's Books.' *The Library.* Ser. 5. Vol. XII. No. 2. 1957.

83. Johnson. *Type Designs.* Op. cit. Page 186.

84. De Vinne, T. L. *A Treatise on Title-Pages.* 1902. Page 76.
85. Sayle. 'Initial Letters.' Op. cit.
86. Arber, E. *Transcript of the Registers of the Stationers' Company.* 1554–1640. 1875–1894. Vol. II. Page 856.
87. Plomer, H. R. 'The Eliot's Court Press.' *The Library.* Ser. 4. Vol. III. 1923. Pages 194–209.
88. Arber. *Transcript.* Op. cit.
89. Greg and Boswell. *Records of the Court of the Stationers' Company, 1576–1602.* Pages 7, 8.
90. Updike. *Printing Types.* Op. cit.
91. Pollard. *Fine Books.* Op. cit. Page 221.
92. *Edinburgh Council Records.* Vol. 6. Footnote 32.
93. Plomer, H. R. 'Thomas East, Printer.' *The Library.* Ser. 2. Vol. 2. 1901. Pages 298–310.
94. Fuller-Maitland, J. A. Article on Thomas East in D.N.B.
95. Arber. *Transcript.* Op. cit. Vol. I. 111 (from Lansdowne MS. 48).
96. Hulme, E. Wyndham. 'History of the Patent System under the Prerogative and at Common Law.' *Law Quarterly Review.* Vol. 12.
97. Siebert, E. S. *Freedom of the Press in England, 1476–1776.* Urbana, Illinois. 1952. Page 74.
98. Lansdowne MS. 48.
99. Arber. *Transcript.* Op. cit.
100. Ibid.
101. *Acts of the Privy Council, 1623–1625.* Page 274.
102. Bühler, Curt. *William Caxton and his Critics.* Op. cit. Page 13.
103. *Anno Primo Richardi Tertii.* Act regarding printers.
104. Duff. *The Printers.* Op. cit.
105. Ibid.
106. Blagden, C. *The Stationers' Company.* 1960.
107. Siebert. *Freedom of Press.* Op. cit.
108. Arber. *Transcript.* Op. cit.
109. Hansard. *Typographia.* Op. cit. Page 66.
110. Madan, Falconer. *A Brief Account of the University Press at Oxford.* 1908. Page 3.
111. Burch, R. M. *Colour Printing and Colour Printers.* 1910.
112. Pollard. *Fine Books.* Op. cit. Page 208.
113. Duff. *The Printers.* Op. cit. Page 149.
114. Dickson, R. *Introduction of Printing into Scotland.* 1885.
115. Clair, Colin. 'Christopher Plantin's Trade-Connexions with England and Scotland.' *The Library.* Ser. 5. Vol. 14. 1959.
116. Reed-Johnson. Op. cit. Page 68.
117. Ibid.
118. Handover, P. M. *Printing in London.* 1960.
119. Meynell, Francis. *English Printed Books.* 1948. Page 20.

120. Madan. *Oxford Press*. Op. cit. Page 8.
121. The first great *Polyglot* Bible was the Complutensian Bible of Cardinal Francisco Ximénez de Cisneros, printed at Alcalá de Henares 1514–17.
122. Reed-Johnson. Op. cit. Page 159.
123. Sparke, Michael. *Scintilla*. 1641.
124. McKerrow, R. B. *Dictionary of Printers and Booksellers 1557–1640*. 1910. Page 202.
125. Handover. *Printing in London*. Op. cit. Page 109.
126. Dahl, Folke. *A Bibliography of English Corantos and Periodical Newsbooks, 1620–1642*. 1952.
127. Smyth, R. *The Obituary of Richard Smyth*. Camden Society. 1849.
128. Timperley, C. H. *Encyclopaedia of Literary and Typographical Anecdote*. 1842. Page 506.
129. Handover. *Printing in London*. Op. cit. Page 116.
130. Davies, Robert. *A Memoir of the York Press*. 1868.
131. Plomer, H. R. *Dictionary of Booksellers and Printers 1641–1667*. 1907. Page 67.
132. L'Estrange, Roger. *Considerations and Proposals in order to the Regulation of the Press*. 1663.
133. *A Brief Discourse concerning Printing and Printers*. 1663. Published for 'A Society of Printers'.
134. Pepys, Samuel. *Diary*. Entry for 6 October, 1666.
135. Evelyn, John. *Diary*. In a letter to Sir Samuel Tuke he estimated the loss to the booksellers at near £200,000, a truly vast sum in those days.
136. Watson, James. *History of the Art of Printing*. 1713.
137. Gibb, J. S. 'James Watson, Printer.' *Publications of the Edinburgh Bibliographical Society*. Vol. 1. 1896.
138. Murray, David. *Robert & Andrew Foulis and the Glasgow Press*. 1913.
139. Reed-Johnson. Op. cit. Page 260.
140. Boswell, J. *Life of Dr Johnson*.
141. Timperley. *Encyclopaedia*. Op. cit.
142. Nichols, John. *Literary Anecdotes*. 1812. Vol. 1. Page 292.
143. Gaskell, Philip. 'Printing the Classics in the 18th Century.' *The Book Collector*. Vol. 1. No. 2. 1952. Page 102.
144. *The Life of T. Gent, printer, of York, written by himself*. 1832.
145. Nichols, John. *Literary Anecdotes of the 18th Century*. 9 volumes. 1812–14.
146. Reed-Johnson. Op. cit. Pages 148–9.
147. Ibid. Page 256.
148. *Letters of John Baskerville*. Compiled by Leonard Jay. 1932.
149. *Strahan Papers*. B.M. Add. Mss. 48801.
150. Leigh, R. Austen. *The Story of a Printing House*. 1912.
151. Handover. *Printing in London*. Op. cit.
152. See also: Morison, Stanley—*John Bell*. 1930; *The English Newspaper*. 1932; *Edward Topham*. 1933.

153. Johnson. *Type Designs.* Op. cit. Page 96.
154. Anthoesen, F. *John Bell Type.* 1939.
155. Morison. *John Bell.* Op. cit.
156. *Journal of the Printing Office at Strawberry Hill.* First printed, with notes by Paget Toynbee, in 1923.
157. *Printing and the Mind of Man.* Catalogue of the Exhibition in the British Museum. 1963. No. 102. Plate 10.
158. Bewick, T. *A Memoir of Thomas Bewick, written by Himself.* 1862.
159. Reed-Johnson. Op. cit. Page 256.
160. Mores. *A Dissertation.* Op. cit. Page 86.
161. Straus, R. and Dent, R. K. *John Baskerville: A Memoir.* 1907.
162. Rogers, Bruce. *The Monotype Recorder.* Vol. XXII. No. 199. 1924.
163. Straus and Dent. *Baskerville.* Op. cit. Page 15.
164. Bennett, William. *John Baskerville.* Birmingham, 1937.
165. Mores. *A Dissertation.* Op. cit. Page 81.
166. Benton, J. H. *John Baskerville.* New York, 1944. Page 40.
167. *Letters of John Baskerville.* Op. cit. Page 17.
168. Dreyfus, John. 'The Baskerville Punches.' *The Library.* Ser. 5. Vol. 5. 1951.
169. Plomer, H. R. *A Short History of English Printing from 1476 to 1898.* 1900. Page 274.
170. Isaac, Peter. 'William Bulmer.' *The Library.* Ser. 5. Vol. 3. A handlist of the books printed by Bulmer and Bensley was published by Sir William Croft in *Signature,* New Series, Nos. 16, 17 and 18. 1952.
171. Reed-Johnson. Op. cit.
172. Marrot, H. V. *The Fleuron.* Vol. 5. 1926.
173. *Quarterly Review.* 'The Poetry of the Seven Dials.' Vol. 122, January and April, 1867.
174. Churchyard, Thomas. *A Discription and playne discourse of paper.* 1588.
175. Jacobi, C. T. *Printing.* Sixth edition. 1919.
176. Jennett, Seán. *Pioneers in Printing.* Pages 136–7. 1958.
177. Circular letter headed 'Stereotype Office, Duke Street, Lincoln's Inn Fields, August, 1803'.
178. Morison, S. *The Typographic Arts.* 1949.
179. 'The Printer's Devil.' *Quarterly Review.* December, 1839.
180. Smiles, Samuel. *Men of Invention and Industry.* 1884.
181. Burch. *Colour Printing.* Op. cit.
182. McLean, Ruari. *Victorian Book Design.* 1963.
183. Southward, John. *Progress in Printing and the Graphic Arts during the Victorian Era.* 1897.
184. McLean. *Victorian Book Design.* Op. cit.
185. Morison, Stanley and Jackson, Holbrook. *A Brief Survey of Printing History and Practice.* 1923. Page 17.
186. Quoted by Sparling, H. H. in *The Kelmscott Press.* 1924.

187. Mackail, J. W. *The Life of William Morris.* 1899.
188. Pendenys, Arthur. 'Letters to London Publishers' in *The Books of Today and The Books of Tomorrow.* March, 1895.
189. Burch. *Colour Printing.* Op. cit.
190. Mores. *A Dissertation.* Op. cit.
191. Ibid.
192. Hansard. *Typographia.* Op. cit.
193. Johnson. *Type Designs.* Op. cit.
194. Morison, Stanley. *On Type Designs Past and Present.* New edition. 1962.
195. Gray, Nicolette. *Nineteenth Century Ornamented Types and Title Pages.* 1938.
196. Reed-Johnson. Op. cit. Page 308.
197. Gray. *Types and Title Pages.* Op. cit.
198. Morison. *The Fleuron.* No. VI. Pages 119–120.
199. Jennett, Seán. *The Making of Books.* 1951.
200. McLean. *Victorian Book Design.* Op. cit.
201. Figgins, James. *Type Founding and Printing during the Nineteenth Century.* 1901.
202. Corrigan, A. J. *A Printer and his World.* 1944.
203. Moran, J. 'Filmsetting—Bibliographical Implications.' *The Library.* Ser. 5. Vol. XV. No. 4. December, 1960.

Index

(Main references are distinguished by **bold type**)